Douglas + (Puryear)

TURNING POINTS

Treating Families in
Transition and Crisis

A NORTON PROFESSIONAL BOOK

TURNING POINTS

Treating Families in

Transition and Crisis

Frank S. Pittman III, MD

W·W·NORTON & COMPANY

NEW YORK·LONDON

Published simultaneously in Canada by Penguin Books Canada Ltd., 2801 John Street, Markham, Ontario L3R 1B4.

Printed in the United States of America.

First edition.

Library of Congress Cataloging-in-Publication Data

Pittman, Frank S., 1935–
  Turning points.

  "A Norton professional book."
  Bibliography: p.
  Includes index.
  1. Family psychotherapy.   2. Life change events —
Psychological aspects.   I. Title.
RC488.5.P58   1987   616.89′156   86-33151

ISBN   0-393-70040-2

W. W. Norton & Company, Inc. 500 Fifth Avenue, New York, NY 10110

W. W. Norton & Company Ltd., 37 Great Russell Street, London WC1B 3NU

1 2 3 4 5 6 7 8 9 0

To Elizabeth Buckley Brawner Pittman
and our kids
Justina Buckley Pittman
Frank Smith Pittman IV
Virginia Blount Pittman
and also
Anne Booth Brawner and James Daniel Namnoum
Jennifer Buckley Brawner
James Newton Brawner IV
John Paul Rutter III
Harrison Rogers Rutter
Virginia Elisabeth Rutter
Shannon White Rutter
and the memory of
Lt. Frank Pittman Rutter, USN, 1959–1985.

CONTENTS

Preface   xi
Introduction   xv

SECTION I

Family Crisis Theory and Therapy

1. A Theory of Family Crisis: Ideas About Stress and Snag Points   3
2. A Treatment Model: Ordering Chaos   27
3. Techniques of the Desperately Resourceful Therapist: Wet Cocker
   Spaniel Therapy   39

SECTION II

Crises of Marriage

4. The Nature and Transitions of Marriage: All or Nothing   49
5. The Range of Marital Crises: From Incidents to Disasters   65
6. Treating Marriages: The Delicate Balance   83

vii

SECTION III

Disruption of the Family

7. Infidelity: The Secret Insanity   *97*
8. Divorce and Remarriage: Fragments and Emulsions   *129*

SECTION IV

Crises of Development

9. Parenting: The Flip Side of Childhood   *155*
10. Adolescence: The Time of Normal Psychosis   *175*
11. Emancipation: Emptying the Nest   *205*
12. Aging: The Brighter Alternative   *216*

SECTION V

Families in Perpetual Crisis

13. Crisis Prone Families: The Struggle to Stay the Same   *233*
14. Phobic Families: Hiding Together   *237*
15. Psychosomatic Families: Making One Another Sick   *246*
16. Substance Abuse: A Sport the Whole Family Gets to Play   *261*
17. Violent Families: The Pain of Love   *283*
18. Incest: Family Affairs   *302*

SECTION VI

Caretaking Families

19. Caretakers and Chemistry: When People Aren't Quite Right   *317*
20. Mania: So Much Fun It Hurts   *322*
21. Depression: Wringing the Hankie   *330*
22. Schizophrenia: Life in the Shallow End   *342*

Coda   *356*
References   *358*
Index   *363*

LIST OF CASES

1. The Black Sheep of the Family (Shep) — 8
2. Chastity Belt (Twink) — 11
3. Friday Night at Home (Ursula, Uppingham and Uppy) — 14
4. Housekeeping (Winston and Winona) — 17
5. The Pleasure of His Company (Abner, Alexandra and Leroy) — 67
6. A Real, Live, Growing Doll (Barbi and Bartram) — 70
7. Going Out Together (Carl and Carrie) — 75
8. Greetings (David and Sheba) — 80
9. Tennis, Anyone? (Eve and Egbert) — 107
10. Puppy Dog Tails (Fritz and Felicia) — 111
11. Sex Manuals (Gilda and Grover) — 114
12. The Nurses Station (Hubert, Helena and Boots) — 117
13. No Bed of Roses (Bud, Rose, Aphid, Thorn, and extended family) — 150
14. The Baby's Bottle (Ida) — 171
15. The Belly of the Whale (Jonah) — 172
16. Mother in Distress (Knight) — 173
17. Playing the Palace — 226
18. When the Opportunity Arises (Tom and Gerri) — 227

ix

19. The Eternal Dinner Party (Pearl)   228
20. A Pain in the Back (Lumbago and Leona)   252
21. Perfectly Beautiful (Moonbeam)   256
22. A Drinking Man   276
23. Closeted (Nona, Nipper and Neissler)   276
24. Under the Tent (Omar and Ophelia)   293
25. In the Dark   293
26. Poetic License (Petunia and Penrod)   294
27. Begetting Violence (Viola and Vic)   299
28. In Orbit Around the Globe (Quentin)   319
29. Canned (Roy and Rebecca)   340
30. Nailed Down (Xavier)   353
31. All That Jazz (Yolanda and Yaz)   354

PREFACE

I AM A FAMILY THERAPIST. That has been my professional and perhaps even personal identity since the early '60s. When I look back, I see that I was raised to be a family therapist, as perhaps we all are. I grew up in a series of Faulkneresque southern towns where the chief parlor game was the exploration of people's effects on one another. We lived in the gone-to-seed antebellum mansion on the hill overlooking the town. The place looked so impressive that passersby didn't realize the primitive state of the plumbing or the lack of central heat — presumably eight fireplaces, a pond and plenty of trees were sufficient. We were the impoverished gentility, and while we had respectability and even security, we had no money. We had something better, as I was told daily — we had FAMILY. The live members were not always impressive but there were rumors of grandeur in the graveyard.

My mother's hobby was recollecting the old family furniture that Great-great-aunt Lavonia had sold to finance her trips to California to visit her nephew, Charles, who was trying unsuccessfully to play Ashley in *Gone With the Wind*. Charles had been marked for success; he had been a Rhodes scholar, won the Metropolitan Opera auditions, and run the pentathlon in the 1920 Olympics. He didn't make it in life though. He did work for the telephone company for a while, and there were some nice actors who took care of him from time to time. And when Aunt Lavonia died he sold the Old Family Home where Grandma Lewis had raised her daughter and all her grandchildren and even her great-grandchildren, although it hadn't been easy what with the Yankees coming and with William Whitlock's drinking.

With each recovered piece of furniture came at least one new story about people's effect on one another. I slept in the bed to which William Whitlock retired after the War Between the States "to let his mother-in-law, Grandma Lewis, support him by taking in paying guests. His wife died of shame, so your poor little great-grandmother had to bring him his beer every day from the time she was six and her brother Fred got shot in the saloon. So that's why she made your great-grandfather, the Judge, so miserable about his drinking, and that's why we're not rich today."

The family hero was usually Grandma Lewis, who hid the silver from the Yankees, and who rocked the baby Alexander Stephens (later vice-president of the Confederacy) in that rocking chair in the living room. My special hero was Great-great-uncle Willie, who lived with a black woman named Agnes and had quite a few children whom he sent to college up north to become the best educated members of the family.

The family villain was clearly Great-uncle Jos. He had married my Great-aunt Ora and was treasurer of the family cotton mills in Griffin, Georgia. He got himself into an affair with his secretary, a woman I'll call Cat Cole, and wore the office walls thin with her. He embezzled money to cover his presents to her, and then gambled on cotton futures to make it back, and lost, and faked the books, and finally ended up in prison. The mills failed, and my grandfather lost everything except the newspaper he'd bought to publish his poetry in. He was still a judge and a state senator but he was broke and sick and he drank himself to death within a year, leaving my grandmother with two small daughters, debts, and the newspaper. Grandmother edited it, and my aunt, when she was old enough, studied journalism at Georgetown and became this country's first female sports editor for a daily newspaper. Aunt Ora took Uncle Jos back when he got out of prison, but we never knew what happened to Cat Cole. She'd be over 100 now but I like to think she's still out there, threatening to do to other foolish families what she did to mine.

Mother, the glamorous belle, went to finishing school in Washington, learned to pour tea, met Mrs. Wilson and Mrs. Coolidge, and, her education then complete, ran off and married my father, the handsome athlete next door. His father, a hot tempered farmer, had married a musician who played the organ for the church and for the movies. When sound movies came in, she talked him into becoming an undertaker so she could play for the funerals. And when he died, she took over the funeral home and wrote a book on genealogy.

My sturdy, reliable father ran the cotton mills in Prattville, Alabama and

Mother drank and hoped for letters from poor Cousin Charles, still destitute in Hollywood, and we lived in seedy grandeur holding on to the only thing anyone considered important—FAMILY. While mother drank and Dad worked and adored her, I learned to cook and my sister (younger, tougher, and my closest friend growing up) learned to manage things, and we operated what I now recognize as a kind of adolescent crisis unit, to which we welcomed our troubled friends. The problematic rule of the establishment was that no mention could be made of Mother's drinking, or her behavior while doing so—even when incoherent, it was always flamboyant, usually charming. We were immunized to embarrassment, but dedicated to reality.

My parents tried for a decade to have me, and I was born with a heart murmur, so Mother protected me from physical activity. Being unathletic at that time in rural Alabama was a social disaster—I've never been able to play at being macho, an advantage subsequently. I went through medical school with the professional opinion that I would not live past 30. Strangely, the murmur disappeared at about that age and I can now climb the highest mountains. In a way, I owe my jaunty optimism to this experience—most of my adult life has seemed like a freebie, an unanticipated favor. Anything that happens is better than I expected.

My talents, while hardly spectacular, have fitted me well for a life as a family therapist. I have a great sense for the absurd, I have little dignity of my own to protect, and I don't like privacy. I particularly don't like secrets, mine or anyone else's. I can't treat anyone delicately and protectively—I tried that with Mother, and it didn't work. I'm basically optimistic about the human condition. I see life as short and I have no patience with people who are wasting it. I don't have much feeling for gender stereotypes, they always confused me so I dismissed them as inapplicable. At one time that made me weird, but it prepared me for a world in which those old gender stereotypes no longer apply.

It seems to me that mine was the perfect training for a family therapist. Yet there have been successful family therapists from quite different backgrounds. The source of the power of family therapy has been sought in the styles of the "first generation" therapists: Ackerman, Bowen, Jackson, Satir, Whitaker, among others, who more or less independently discovered the power of family therapy and attempted to explain it. If styles as disparate as those of Minuchin and Satir, or Whitaker and MacGregor, have been successful, then surely the power of family therapy does not lie in the style of the therapist. It seems to me unfortunate that family therapy has been taught by demonstration of charismatic therapists or by writers who focus on being family therapists rather than doing family therapy. The "style" of family therapy is idiosyncratic and has received too much attention, yet the power of family therapy may derive in part from the "posture" of the therapist, some inexplicable openness or comfort or personal security that permits people to expose not just their secrets, but their living family conflict. Much of the training of family therapists centers on developing this posture in people who did not luck into it through their own family misfortunes.

My optimism about marriage and family has been bolstered for 27 years by the outrageously sane Betsy, my beloved and respected partner in life and work, and a continuous source of impatient practicality and good humor. We have produced three marvelously human children, who do have the sort of talents Cousin Charles had; they've been state champions at running and acting and singing, and triathlons, and one is now a family therapist. Our seven nieces and nephews have, quite generously, permitted us to take a hand in the gratifying process of raising them. Not even family therapy can compare with child-raising, and particularly adolescent-raising, as a way of developing a connection with oneself and one's world. They finally permitted me to detach myself sufficiently to write this book. During the writing two of them married and one of them died. I dedicate the book to them, my family.

I'm also indebted to several other people for getting this book put together. Among them are Al Gurman for enthusiastically encouraging it, and Carol Anderson, Maxine Berzok, Mary Coffey, Randy Gerson, Tina Pittman, and Seymour Weingarten for their hours of reading it and reacting to it. Kitty LaPerriere, Monica McGoldrick, and Rich Simon are among the friends who have tried to help me clarify my thinking as I went along. Susan Barrows understood the book, edited it, and pampered it firmly but gently into its final form. Susan has been a joy to write with; every writer should be so lucky.

*****

All of the stories in the case illustrations here are totally real. The names and identifying data have been disguised, of course. To further protect anonymity, many of the cases are composites of two or more stories with similar dynamics but different circumstances and details. I feel great gratitude toward the families who served as the models for these stories. I am honored that they have let me go through their transitions and crises with them. I know that they will be pleased with the lessons their experiences have taught them, and me, and now you.

INTRODUCTION

THIS BOOK IS the culmination of over 25 years as a family therapist and over 40,000 hours of treating families in various stages of transition and crisis. My professional life as a family therapist began in my training at Emory Medical School in 1960. Unsupervised, I did what seemed natural to me—I saw patients with their families, and then just couldn't stop. In 1962, Al Messer, trained by Nathan Ackerman, came to Emory and both supervised and encouraged me in a life as a family therapist.

The story of this book really begins in 1964 in Denver, where I went after my psychiatric training. Don Langsley and Dave Kaplan were putting together a team to provide family therapy as an alternative to psychiatric hospitalization. It was part of a NIMH funded demonstration project concerned with collecting the data and developing the techniques for the community mental health centers that were soon to develop.

The project clinical team consisted of me, social worker Kal Flomenhaft, and nurse Carol DeYoung. Psychologist Pavel Machotka joined us a year later and oversaw the research. We took a random sample of patients who had been evaluated by the emergency room psychiatrist and were determined to require immediate psychiatric hospitalization. Our job was to keep them out of the hospital and get them back to normal, or better, as quickly as possible. These were not easy patients. One-third were suffering from acute psychoses, another third were suicidally depressed or had made suicide attempts, and the rest included manic states, organic brain conditions, alcohol withdrawal, adolescent runaways, school phobias, etc. We made home visits, used medication when indicated (I had the reputation as the "fastest syringe in the West"), brought in whatever collateral people we could, and resorted to whatever desperation we could dream up. We were called "Psychiatric Cowboys." We were winging it. There was no guidebook. In fact, the only books on family therapy at all, as far as we knew then, were Ackerman's book (1958) and *Multiple Impact Therapy With Families* (1964), written by MacGregor and his colleagues from Galveston.

In 1964, frightened by our early successes, I made a pilgrimage to the holy shrine of family therapy—Palo Alto. I spent time with Jay Haley, Don Jackson, John Weakland, Paul Watzlawick, and Virginia Satir. Jackson and I corresponded about doing work together but he died before we could do it. I remember telling him that my ambition was to someday delineate the syndromes in family therapy. He thought that premature and naive. I've waited over 20 years, but this is that book.

Haley, who kept the field connected as editor of *Family Process*, began to visit us in Denver with Lynn Hoffman while they were researching *Techniques of Family Therapy* (1967). Haley told us fabulous stories of family therapists scattered around the country. We made contact with whatever other family therapists we could find and became a part of the family therapy movement of the '60s. Haley provided invaluable supervision, comparing our work with that of the other family therapists of that era. The field had not divided itself into "schools" in the '60s. We all learned from one another and taught one another. The "schools" came later, in the '70s, when family therapy had to be taught to a new generation of students who needed a simplified theory and format as a starting point. I've found each of the "schools" simplistic, but of course that was what they were supposed to be. Our techniques expectably had much in common with the later MRI Brief Therapy Project, since we cross-fertilized one another. The similarities between our approaches and those of Sal Minuchin and the later structuralists were interesting because there was no direct contact between the two groups. But we were dealing with similar populations. My background made me feel compatible with the Bowenians and intergenerationalists, and later the feminists.

What we did in Denver demonstrated that family crisis therapy is far cheaper, quicker, and at least as effective as psychiatric hospitalization for comparable patients, with far fewer long-range disadvantages. The data from the Denver Project was widely reported (see Langsley, Kaplan, et al., 1968; Langsley, Pittman, et al., 1968; Pittman et al., 1966; Pittman et al., 1971; Pittman, 1973) and strongly influenced the community mental health movement. Verification that family therapy worked was heartening to that movement too, which was gaining momentum at that time but had little data to back it up.

My subsequent experience, applying this approach on an enormous scale as director of Atlanta's public mental health services at Grady Hospital, from 1968 to 1972, demonstrated dramatically that this approach was as practical as it was effective. But, since few professions are seeking a cheaper alternative to themselves, family therapy as an alternative to psychiatric hospitalization has not been widely adopted.

In private practice since 1972, I do what we did in Denver and for Atlanta, but with families that are usually, but not always, less profoundly disorganized and less pressing in their sense of emergency. The differences between families in transition and families in crisis are less than meet the eye.

This book, while fertilized with all that I have experienced since, is rooted in the Denver experience. In Denver, in the process of studying families in crisis, we came up with a framework for understanding the state of crisis in families. That framework has kept me structured through twenty-odd years of dealing with and expanding my understanding of families in transition and crisis. I emerged from Denver with great respect for the ability of family members to drive one another sane if they must, and with the belief that the keys to mental health include responsibility and functioning. A philosophy and technology gradually developed based on family members' taking responsibility for their effects on one another and functioning appropriately.

Freeman and Simmons, in *The Mental Patient Comes Home* (1963), found that patients did better if the family was tolerant of symptoms but intolerant of nonfunctioning. By contrast, society in general and the medical profession in particular have tended to see cessation of functioning as an appropriate response to symptoms. Anxious or depressed people may be seen as suffering from excessive functional stress and encouraged to "take it easy," "take some time off from work," give up productive activity, tranquilize themselves, get out of conflictual relationships, or even, horror of horrors, go on disability. This may be appropriate for a day or even a week, but not for long. People's lives cannot be protected by sacrificing their functioning.

In the chapters that follow, I outline a way of looking at family crisis—how to differentiate the various syndromes of crisis and transition faced by families, and how to deal with each of the more common ones. The first section is on the theory and practice of family crisis therapy. The second section is on the transitions and crises of marriage. The third section looks at family disruption, infidelity, divorce, and remarriage. The fourth section examines the crises of development as parents and children go through their expectable and unexpectable transitions. The fifth section examines those structural peculiarities that make some families especially crisis prone. The last section considers the complex interplay between a family's style of caretaking and a member's temporarily or permanently disordered brain chemistry.

Weaved through this view of life's complexities are the recurrent themes of responsibility and functioning. I am trying also to impart optimism about, respect for, and trust of families, including the honor a therapist feels when a family puts its future in his or her hands. And, if possible, I hope to convey the security for both patients and therapists that comes from recognizing the absurdity of the human comedy, the realization that humor is the antidote to tragedy.

As I describe this here, after 27 years of experience, I run the risk of making it sound easy. It isn't always easy. But it is easier for a therapist who runs the risk of trusting families. If the therapist just shows the respect of assuming that families in crisis will do something sensible if they know something sensible to do, this faith will be transmitted to the families, and most will work successfully with the therapy. My very direct approaches may seem naive to the cynical, but I urge you to try them before going on to something trickier. They've worked for me and for my patients for many years.

TURNING POINTS

Treating Families in
Transition and Crisis

SECTION I

Family Crisis Theory and Therapy

Shit happens.

— Bumper Sticker, 1986

When you start dealing with real change you are talking about interfering with those who are in possession of something.

— Carl B. Stokes, *The Promise of Power*, 1973

CHAPTER 1

A Theory of Family Crisis

IDEAS ABOUT STRESS AND SNAG POINTS

CRISIS IS, according to Webster, "a state of things in which a decisive change one way or the other is impending." Crisis is the turning point at which things will either get better or get worse. It is a concept central to the understanding of change and therefore a therapy.

I've been told that in Chinese the word "crisis" is made up of the characters for "danger" and "opportunity." Certainly, crisis is a dangerous opportunity, not necessarily to be avoided. It is possible to have a crisis which does not result in change; many people, many families go through the full complement of life's crises without adding anything new to their repertoire, without learning a damned thing new. And there are therapists dedicating their careers to protecting people in crisis from learning anything from their crises and their lives. But it is not really possible to have change without crisis. At some level, there must be some awareness of impending change for people to take the awkward, often scary step of doing something unaccustomed.

CRISIS

A crisis results when a *stress* comes to bear upon a *system* and requires *change* outside the system's usual repertoire. The state of crisis is marked by nonspecific changes in the system. The boundaries are loosened, enabling a therapist or anyone else to enter and influence the way the system operates. Rules and roles become confused. Both expectations and prohibitions are relaxed. Goals and values lose importance and may even be lost altogether. Unresolved conflicts are revived and become the focus of much attention. Tension between family members is heightened.

A therapist observing a family in crisis may find the family disorganized, nonfunctional, directionless, battling over long-dead issues. The therapist may judge the family to be far sicker than it is, assume the revived conflicts to be the real issues, and overlook the stress entirely. By this time, the family members may want to remove the stress in some dysfunctional way that will reduce tension without solving the problem. They may decide to dissolve the family, ship someone off, get a divorce, have an affair (the loosened boundaries permit this), or put someone in a hospital. The pressure on a vulnerable family member may reach a level sufficient to bring forth symptoms, even psychoses. The scapegoating of one member may become the focus of everyone's attention and that member may be isolated or punished or treated. To the therapist who doesn't understand the stress, this may appear perfectly appropriate.

STRESS

A stress is a force that tends to distort. Stresses are somewhat specific to the system in question; that is, what is stressful for one family may not be stressful for another. Efforts to quantify the degree of stress have not been impressively successful. "Death of a spouse" or "bankruptcy" might be considered more stressful for most families than "fistfight with neighbors" or "Christmas," but there are families in which "going to jail" or "illegitimate pregnancy" would be routine while "family gathering" would precipitate a crisis. There are many marriages in which "spouse's death" would be far less stressful than "spouse's retirement." It depends enormously upon the values and expectations of the family and on the nature of the relationships.

A stress might be defined along several parameters: whether it is *overt* or *covert, unique* or *habitual, permanent* or *temporary, real* or *imagined, universal* or *specific*, and whether it is seen as arising from *intrinsic* forces in the family or from forces *extrinsic* and outside the family's control.

In general, stresses create fewer problems if they are overt. In a misguided effort to avoid embarrassment or pain or blame or change, many people keep secrets and thereby compound the confusion. When something happens which affects one family member and is not understood by the rest of the family, it is a bit like living in a haunted house—one member sees and reacts to forces the others don't see. If a stress is overt (the house burns down), the family can band together and outsiders can offer help. If it is covert (a secret affair or loss of money), no one knows to help.

The response to habitual or recurrent behavior is different from the responses to unique behavior. One episode of drunkenness is quite different from chronic alcoholism. One lost job is quite different from recurrent job instability. Many family battles occur over the question of whether a stress is unique or habitual. The distinction is a matter of considerable significance. The sixth failed grade, affair, arrest, suicide attempt, or episode of violence becomes obnoxious rather than alarming to the family. A person called in to help may be shocked by the irritated complacency of families who have been through it many times. The same helper, on the other hand, may later be surprised when the family reacts to the next episode in the series as if it had never occurred before.

Families may also battle over whether a certain stress is temporary or permanent. The family member pushing for change may concentrate on the permanent effects and stigmas of temporary situations like an abortion, an arrest, a failing grade, or an affair, even if a more permanent result, such as a baby, imprisonment, expulsion, or divorce, did not occur. Likewise, people who resist change may see only the temporary aspects of something and downplay long-range consequences. The mother who didn't want her son to have an earring treated the pierced ear as if it were permanent like a tattoo, rather than temporary like a hairdo. Many adolescents, dropping out of college, insist that they'll return to school in the fall. One young man, marrying for the seventh time, had nothing more permanent in mind than the dental work his prospective father-in-law could perform.

Sometimes it isn't clear whether or not a stress is real. On rare occasions, incest may be reported by a child when it did not actually occur; far more commonly, it may have occurred and been denied by both parents. The same thing may happen with infidelities. Sometimes, people destroy their children to prevent incest from being known, or convince everyone of a spouse's insanity to keep an affair secret. Yet from the standpoint of a therapist it may not matter whether the *act* occurred as much as it matters that the *relationships* and *tensions* are quite real. Sometimes a child may report an incestuous move by a new stepparent who is actually intrusive in nonsexual ways. An imagined affair may not yet be sexual but may accurately identify the direction of someone's attentions. Emotional reality may take priority over physical reality. Emotional accuracy is enormously important, even if the physical details are fuzzy.

As people go through a stressful time, they may become so self-centered that they fail to realize that this is a universal experience, an experience they share with most families. They may feel quite alone, as if this were happening only to them. Self-help organizations encourage people to recognize that others are also going through whatever they are going through. Every stage of development seems frightening indeed to someone who sees it as specific to him or his family rather than as the universal way of all flesh. Do all adolescents masturbate? Do all adolescents rape the neighbors? Unemployment is high, but is it universal? Infidelities are certainly not specific to this family, but are they universal? People need to monitor their position on the assorted bell-shaped curves of life. When experiences are more or less specific to this person or this family, that should make the family members ponder why their experience is so different from the universal one.

Stresses may arise from within the structure of the family, or a family may find itself in a stressful situation brought on by forces outside the family. In facing an enemy, it helps to know, as Pogo did, whether or not it is us. Families in which the blame is always externalized may feel no need to change the behavior which is bringing about the stresses. Parents of failing children may blame the school system, addicts blame doctors or Viet Nam, blacks blame whites and vice versa, men blame women and vice versa, and everybody blames parents, while nobody takes the responsibility for change. On the other hand, it is equally unhelpful to internalize each stress and blame a favorite defect in the family structure for whatever comes up. Children of divorcing families may blame their poor school grades or messy rooms on the marriage problems. Battling couples may blame everything that happens now on an ancient affair, on an unpleasant in-law, or some old offense. Depressed people may blame any crisis on some internal defect, constantly asking, "How have I failed?" By doing that, they miss the opportunity to appropriately assign responsibility within the family or to escape or understand difficult realities.

If these parameters can be properly defined, the stress, its characteristics, effects, and source can be understood clearly enough to be dealt with. When the stress is clearly defined, it becomes tangible and specific, and this points the way to change. When the stress is confusing, the crisis extends unnecessarily and amplifies uncontrollably. Central to solving a family crisis is the identification and definition of the stress.

Every crisis involves the interplay between the stress and the characteristics of the family which make the family vulnerable to this particular stress. I've found it efficient, as well as therapeutic, to start an evaluation of a family in crisis by focusing on the stress itself, rather than on the specific symptoms associated with the crisis state or the manifold peculiarities of the family which make it susceptible to the stress. This is not because the stress is the most important contributor to the problem, but because the stress is the most immediate factor — the last straw — and the most neutral and discernible entry point into the complexities of the family chaos.

FOUR CATEGORIES OF CRISES

Each crisis is perhaps unique, but most fall roughly into four categories, based primarily on the nature of the stress: bolts from the blue, developmental crises, structural crises, and caretaker crises. These four categories rarely occur in pure form—the overlap of and interplay between the categories are nothing for the therapist to fret over. The purpose of all of this is not to categorize accurately, but to reduce the ever changing complexity of crisis to something more manageable.

Bolts From the Blue

The first, simplest, and least common crisis is the *bolt from the blue*. The stress here is overt, unique, real, specific, and extrinsic. Someone may die, the house may burn down, the economy may collapse, the plumbing may overflow just before guests arrive, a sweepstakes ticket may win, the expressway may come through the front yard, or a child may be kidnapped. If everyone can pull together to define the stress and the changes required, the crisis may not destroy the family. Minimal change may be necessary in the family structure, depending on the permanence of the stress. The most important points about the bolt from the blue are that the stress is obvious and it clearly arises from forces outside the family. It's real. It could not have been anticipated. It hasn't happened before. It's not likely to happen again. Neither soul-searching nor blame is appropriate or helpful (though both occur). Anticipation of recurrence would be out of place (though such anxiety is almost universal). Most of the family attention can be directed toward the regrouping necessary to keep the family going.

Obviously, bolts from the blue are just about as likely to occur in healthy families as in families with all manner of problems. However, the ongoing problems and the new crisis may become confused. Once a house burned down around a family in which there was incest, drug abuse, alcoholism, and a matriarchal, intrusive grandmother. However, the fire caused the family to focus on a younger child's hyperactivity, which had been previously ignored in the large house but became intolerable in the temporary motel.

The danger of bolts from the blue lies in the search for blame—the effort to find something someone could have done to prevent the crisis. This effort will undoubtedly uncover all manner of personal and familial deficiencies to which responsibility for the crisis can be attached. As a result the real task of pulling together and adapting to the situation may be bypassed in favor of attack and defense, changing or not changing irrelevant irritants.

In a functional family, everyone joins in the effort to solve the immediate crisis, whatever the ongoing problems. It happens on basketball courts, when the game is interrupted to find a lost contact lens. The opposing teams join the search until the problem is solved, and then assume the fierce competition. There are even cease-fires during wars.

A humbling encounter with fate levels us, drains us of narcissism and petulance and the sense that we alone are being mistreated. It produces a need for one another that makes our previous differences pale. The old hurts will recur—cease-fires and time-outs don't last long, but a time-out can help heal even the most horrifying crisis. When the family cannot be distracted from the game or the war by the unique situation, when there can be no time-out or cease-fire, the family structure is in trouble and a bolt from the blue becomes a different sort of crisis altogether.

Pure bolts from the blue don't usually bring people to therapy, but they happen while people are in therapy. When someone is killed or crippled, or impoverished or enriched, or burglarized or raped, there may be some sense that this would not have happened if only_____. This is unavoidable and often useful. But people can accept only a finite amount of responsibility for the fickle workings of fate, so the more horrifying the stress, the less likely it is to serve as a useful learning experience. Guilt is useful only in very small doses. As Bob Beavers says in *Successful Marriage*, "I have a rule of thumb about guilt. It is useful if it doesn't last more than five minutes and produces some change in behavior."

Bolt from the blue crises offer an opportunity for resolving even the most resistant of structural problems in a family. When family members come together, without guilt, on an intense emotional ground, old issues can be either solved or dismissed, communication opened, and contact made without having to refight old battles. This doesn't always happen, and the blame-free window that is opened by the crisis may close quickly, but there is an opportunity for healing when the emotions about the current crisis take priority over the emotions about something in the past.

CASE 1   *The Black Sheep of the Family*

It was never clear to Shep what had happened when he was 15. All he knew was that everything he did produced uproar and both his parents were screaming and yelling at him every day. He was called "the black sheep of the family." So he told his father where he was going, moved out, got a job, lived with his boss, and had no contact with his family until he sent them a graduation invitation. They came. He learned that his mother was now an alcoholic, his parents were divorced, and his father remarried. He contacted his mother and she drunkenly raged and blamed it all on him. He contacted his father, who took him in and promised never to mention the past. Shep was relieved and never brought it up. Ten years later, Shep had gone into his boss' business, was successful enough to employ several relatives, was close to his father, and tried to tolerate his stepmother, but kept his distance from his mother and brother and sisters, and they from him.

Shep distrusted all relationships, but the therapy centered on his relationship with his wife and with the world, and with helping him overcome the sense of being "the black sheep" who stands to be isolated for his misdeeds.

Somehow the therapy never dealt effectively with his isolation from his family. That was an error, but an error soon corrected by a bolt from the blue.

Shep's father drowned during a storm on the lake. At the funeral, Shep saw his siblings for the first time in years. He mentioned something about "the family black sheep" and was shocked when his sister assumed he was referring to his father. He then learned that the father's affair with the stepmother had been going on at the time of the conflicts that had led him to flee the home and led his mother to drink. He learned that the father disappeared soon after he did and stayed in hiding for a year, taking with him the secret of Shep's whereabouts. It was not his own actions, but his father's, that had wrecked the family and that had isolated him from them.

After the funeral Shep did not go to the stepmother's house, but came by to see me and tell me the story. I had him call his mother, whom he'd thought had disowned him. The mother was overjoyed. She liked to believe the storm on the lake that drowned her errant ex-husband was "God's vengeance," and her son's return was "God's gift." Shep couldn't think in those terms, but he saw clearly that he was no longer the black sheep but the prodigal son returned.

Shep's father's death was in no way connected to the schism in the family, but it healed it. Few ceremonies in life have more power to bring people back together than funerals.

Developmental Crises

Developmental crises are universal, therefore expectable. They should be overt, but may have a few covert features. They may represent permanent changes in status and function, rather than just temporary phases. They arise from the nature of biology and society, rather than from the family structure. They are quite real. There is nothing unique about developmental crises, and above all they cannot be prevented. The usual developmental crises include marriage, birth of children, children starting school, going through puberty, becoming independent and leaving home, parents growing older, retiring, aging and dying. Some of these developmental changes are subtle and gradual; some are abrupt and dramatic. Some are biologically determined; some are societally determined.

Teenage promiscuity and pregnancies, drug use, and school deficiencies are not true developmental crises, but are so prevalent that they almost seem so. Infidelities, midlife crises, and divorce are so near-universal that they seem to be on the verge of becoming expectable crises in some segments of our society. Illegitimate children, jail, unemployment, addiction, etc., may be almost that common in other segments. All of these are of course preventable by the people involved, but strong societal forces may be encouraging just this behavior at just this stage of life, and the expected behavior may occur in families of any structure.

There are more subtle developmental crises in marriage. One is the cooling of romantic love that occurs within the first year or so of marriage as people see their mates more clearly and see that their mates see them more clearly. The honeymoon is over, usually to be replaced by a far more mature partnership. Another is the cooling of sexual intensity that occurs among men in their thirties as the drive becomes less hormonally urgent and more dependent on the relationship. In their forties men particularly become aware of the patterns of career success or failure and a rethinking of goals. Women who are oriented toward their careers go through the same thing. Women whose lives center on their children are much more crisis prone at the time of the empty nest.

Subtle developmental stages also occur in child-raising. Two-year-olds learn to say "No!" Six-year-olds work to please. Fourteen-year-olds ignore their parents' values in search of the unattainable popularity reassurances of their often cruel peers, and find manifold deficiencies in themselves. Sixteen-year-olds want freedom. Eighteen-year-olds, anticipating actually leaving home, may fear it.

At each developmental stage a crisis of some sort is inevitable. The family is called upon to adapt to the changing functional capacity or emotional state of the person who is entering a new stage of development. The family's natural response is to slow down, or even punish and prevent, the change. Problems arise when one part of the family tries to prevent the crisis rather than to define it and adapt to it. Problems can also occur when someone in the family wants the developmental changes to take place even faster or more dramatically.

A common developmental crisis centers on adolescent sexuality. Parents can go to amazing extremes to prevent their children, especially their daughters, from being actively sexual. One mother tried to have breast reduction surgery performed on her 14-year-old daughter. Adult intervention into their children's sexuality can go as far as incest or voyeurism. On the other hand, some families completely ignore it—one 14-year-old went through a pregnancy and delivery without her parents suspecting it, and that case was by no means unique.

A quite different approach was taken by another family. The parents prided themselves on their liberality. They put their 15-year-old daughter on birth control, required her to drink and smoke pot with them, and encouraged her to have "experiences." They objected only to cigarette smoking, which they thought might worsen her asthma. She refused "experiences" and sat in her room sullenly smoking cigarettes. The parents had overlooked the cardinal rule of developmental crisis: they cannot be stopped or produced prematurely; they can only be understood and thereby dampened and coordinated with all the other forces operating in the family.

Full-scale developmental crises occur when the family structure seems unable to incorporate the new stage of development. In many ways, the changes that occur in therapy are like developmental stresses and may trigger crises. As all therapists know, therapeutic change is fragile unless the family structure can change to accommodate to it.

CASE 2   *Chastity Belt*

Twink's parents were going through a divorce. The father was a teacher and part-time minister from a small city nearby, and few people got close enough to know how tortured he was. He was silent, sour, and really rather helpless. He didn't like sex, thought he should have remained celibate, and never felt up to his wife's sexual expectations. He avoided intimacy with her, as he did with everyone else. She was a gregarious, jolly, capable person — plump, vulgar, and baffled about how she married someone so inappropriate. She had had an affair, or maybe she didn't. He thought so, though she denied it, and he used that to avoid sex totally. His depressions were deep and frequent, and during them he drank and suffered and talked of suicide. He would stay up all night, usually alone, listening to Bach and thinking about celibacy. The family would try to tend to him, but would grow exhausted and hospitalize him. He would get better in the hospital, but back home the family would worry and hover and he would sink back into his patterns of pathetic, tortured withdrawal.

In therapy, his wife came to realize that her sacrifices for her husband had become part of the problem. She wanted out, and so did he, but neither was in any hurry about it. She started back to nursing school as soon as Twink was old enough. She commuted to a school in the city and then began to stay over, until finally she was a weekend visitor to the house. Shy little Twink and her stolid, detached brother hovered over the father, and strangely, his depressions seemed less intense. He even became functional around the house. He stopped drinking. The plan was working. As things got better, the therapy faded away.

The mother graduated from nursing school and started to work in a hospital in the city. The brother graduated from high school and went off to college. Twink was 14, and the mother decided that now was the time for the divorce they all wanted. She could now support herself, her son was grown and gone, and Twink was "old enough."

Twink chose to live with her father in the little town. She was much like her father and preferred the quiet life he led to the more boisterous company of her mother. She was changing though, becoming an adolescent. She showed less interest in her father as she began to date. Her father saw adolescence as abnormal and threatening, rather than inevitable. He tried to stop it. He became depressed and began to restrict her. He said he was afraid she would be sexual with her new boyfriend, who was a couple of years older and could drive. On the surface Twink passively did as she was told, but secretly she began to see the boyfriend on weekends at the mother's house. The mother accepted this cheerful boy into the intimate circle of the family, having him often for dinner, permitting him to assist with chores. The mother was busy and dating herself. She was gone overnight often and liked having the boy staying there with Twink. The father found out and was horrified. He tried to keep Twink from seeing either the boy or the mother. A court battle ensued, and I was involved again. I saw the family together and separately, but could not find a resolution quickly enough. I saw no reason to prevent Twink's visits with her mother. The father felt betrayed by me too, but, as usual, was too passive to protest openly. Before the custody case could be decided, all hell broke loose one night.

The father became desperate. He felt his integrity depended upon protecting his daughter from sex. Unaccustomed to taking action, he overdid it. He grounded Twink, refused to let her see or even speak to the boyfriend, and told her he had hired a hit man to assassinate the boy. When Twink heard this unlikely news, she stole her father's car and tried to run him down with it. The young couple ran away together. The father had the boy jailed and the girl hospitalized. The mother and I got them both released, while I worked with the frantic father, who was more terrified by his own behavior than by his daughter's effort to kill him. He came to see his drastic actions as a way of announcing that he could not control a situation he thought he should be able to control. As he realized that he didn't need to prevent the inevitable, he dropped the charges and let Twink decide where she wanted to live.

Shortly thereafter, the boy had had enough of this crazy family and took out another girl. Twink turned all her venom on the boy and gradually returned to her father's house.

When I saw Twink again a few years later, she confessed that she had not actually had sexual intercourse with the boy until they had run away together. Before that she had been afraid of sex, but she was too embarrassed to tell her mother and too angry to give her father the satisfaction of knowing. She was now, at 18, at peace with both her parents, going to college, feeling sexually comfortable, but concerned about her shyness. She loved her father, but didn't want to be like him or like her mother. She wanted to find a middle ground. Her mother remarried, and her father, still completely off alcohol, dated occasionally, but had decided that living alone gave him more peace.

In this family, several development steps were occurring at the same time—the son's leaving home, the mother's emancipation from a dead marriage, and the daughter's adolescence. Each development left the father more isolated. He tolerated, even welcomed, the first two, but his dependency was severely threatened by the last in the series. What's more, Twink's adolescence and resultant sexuality resonated with the unresolved issue in the family structure—sex. The central defect in the marriage had been the father's fear of sex, which conflicted with the mother's exultation in it, and the divorce, though welcomed by both of them, just exaggerated their irreconcilable differences about sex. The couple fought out their differences about sex through Twink, hooking her very normal stage of development to their continuing structural conflict. One parent pushed too hard in one direction, the other pulled too hard in the other, and Twink, for the first time in her life, could not please both of them at the same time.

This is the most dramatic developmental crisis I can recall, but the dynamics and structure of the crisis are no different from the many similar and more subtle cases in which an adolescent's sexuality or some other inevitable developmental stage requires the family to reconcile an unresolved problem in the family structure.

Structural Crises

Pure structural crises are those recurrent crises in which forces within the family regularly become exacerbated. Even if there are extrinsic stresses, the crisis is essentially an exacerbation of an intrinsic pattern. There may be no perceptible external stress: The crisis may be like an earthquake arising periodically from forces deep within. The crisis may be recurrent unless the first in the series is handled well enough to resolve the internal problem. The stress may be overt, but covert stresses are even more likely to bring on the crisis. If a real stress doesn't trigger the next crisis in the series, an imaginary one will do. The crisis really has nothing to do with the stress and is not an effort to avoid or understand or change anything. These families just function this way—from time to time, in response to mysterious forces in the family, they just repeat their old familiar crisis and befuddle any poor therapist who happens to be nearby.

Most truly pathological families have crises of this sort. They are the most difficult ones to treat as the crisis is not an effort to produce change but really an effort to prevent the change from taking place. Families with an alcoholic member, violent members, adulterous members all fall into this category. So also do families which contain a member who intermittently uses divorce or suicide attempts or job changes or runaways or uproars as reactions to ordinary stresses. Because of the excessive, nonspecific quality of the typical family crisis, the family may never deal effectively with the various stresses it encounters. All the family energy goes into avoiding change, no matter what stresses have to be mishandled along the way. It is as if these families have devoted all their energy to preventing some developmental transition from taking place. A family can go through decades of structural crises aimed at keeping the couple from getting divorced or getting married.

Alcoholic families are especially difficult. Nothing should be easier to resolve than alcoholism—just don't drink. But alcoholics may be joyless, difficult people without their alcohol, so families may not require or even tolerate their sobriety. Of course, even if they objected they could not completely control the drinking, but they don't have to tolerate it if they choose not to. Nor do people have to tolerate violence with its guilt-producing remorse, adultery with its disorienting lies, or suicide attempts with their threat of guilt through eternity. Yet people do live with people who do such things and let them raise their children and control their lives. It is not only dependency that keeps such marriages together, as no job could be harder than staying. It is not just protectiveness that keeps the families together either, since the spouse seems to feel that he or she is basically to blame. It must be the crisis pattern itself which is its own reward, which keeps reality from ever being considered and deficiencies from being dealt with rationally.

In families of this sort, if the therapist tries to focus on this week's crisis, the family carries on about the long-range pattern of intermittent chaos, but if the therapist tries to focus on the longstanding family conflicts, the family will carry on about the latest crisis in the series. At all costs, the family must avoid solving the very issues they complain about. Very quickly, the family will forget what they were orginally complaining about and unite against the therapist.

A typical way of avoiding change, as well as therapy, is by threatening to disrupt the family at every junction. A common structural pattern that is subject to intermittent crises of exacerbation occurs in those marriages in which someone recurrently threatens divorce. Some people have convinced themselves that their marriage is beneath them. They may see the marriage as belonging to their spouse, who uses it as a form of tyranny over them, as if they are being held captive. They take little responsibility for making the marriage work, but don't leave. From time to time, they encounter or even precipitate a crisis in which they throw the responsibility on the spouse for proving commitment to the marriage through some sacrifice or tolerance. Such people may even blame their spouse for causing them to have affairs. One such woman had several illegitimate children whom she left with her polite and tolerant husband. In another marriage, the man brought his mistress to live with the couple, telling his wife what a favor he was doing her by staying in the marriage at all since she was such an ugly woman.

Family bullies seem maddening to outsiders, but their behavior serves a function in the family. Structurally fragile spouses often suffer bullies and complain about the tyranny, but protect it. What seems to be the problem is actually almost the purpose for the family. Families which tolerate bullies and take responsibility for having caused someone else's recurrent outlandish behavior are not helpless victims but powerful accomplices. If the bully unilaterally stops the chaos, he or she may destroy the raison d'etre of the family.

CASE 3   *Friday Night at Home*

Ursula drank. Her drinking began after her son's brain tumor, surgery, and resultant disability. Actually, Uppy was in the hospital when Uppingham began his affair with Ursula's best friend. That was all years ago, and it wasn't clear then or now whether Uppy's illness, Ursula's drinking, or Uppingham's affair came first. Each liked to see himself or herself as reacting to the behavior of one or both of the others. Before the chaos of the brain tumor, the affair, and the drinking, all of which culminated in Uppingham's leaving and Ursula's suicide attempt, they had been, as they liked to recall, a happy family. Ursula had been beautiful and charming, if a bit delicate, Uppingham had been successful and protective, if a bit demanding, and little Uppy had been the bright, cheerful completion of their dreams. But after the chaos of it all, they lived together in fear. Uppy couldn't handle school or jobs and went into rages from time to time, breaking things and hitting his parents when they tried to restrain him. Ursula gave up her social activities, stayed in her room a lot, and faded away unpredictably into a secretive alcoholic haze. Uppingham kept functioning at work, but even after many months of sobriety on Ursula's part, he didn't like to go out with her. On Friday nights, he would sit in his chair, listening to sad country songs, having Ursula bring him drinks, while he bewailed the cruelty of fate that kept him tied to an alcoholic wife and a retarded son. As the alcohol enveloped him, he would tell her of his sadness over giving up her friend, his lover, and she would comfort him.

From time to time the pattern would change slightly. Uppy, having suffered some failure in another attempt at life, would tear up the house. Uppingham would go out alone, complaining that he had no one to drink with since Ursula was on Antabuse or at an AA meeting. Or Ursula would throw a drunk and threaten suicide again. One sure trigger for exacerbating it all would be when Ursula would encourage Uppy to try functioning. Uppingham would insist the boy was retarded. One of the several structural defects in this family was Uppingham's insistence that he was a victim of his defective wife and son—at every turn, this definition must be reaffirmed, and both Ursula and Uppy cooperated by reaffirming their defectiveness.

One crisis in the never-ending series occurred when Ursula defied the pattern and had Uppy psychologically tested. The psychological testing revealed the boy's normal intelligence. The father had a temper tantrum, fired the psychologist, and assured the boy he was retarded after all. Ursula then made another suicide attempt. After that Uppy managed to pass a few courses in college, but began having car wrecks which required him to withdraw from school. Ursula stayed sober for a year, and it appeared that things were looking up. But Uppingham suffered more verbally over the unfairness of his cruel fate as the guardian of the defectives. Ursula settled into a pattern of getting drunk every six months or so to make Uppingham more comfortable. If she couldn't get his attention, she would complain to Uppy, who would go into a rage, and Uppingham would have to respond.

No therapeutic effort could pry these three people from one another. During quiet times, both Uppy and Ursula would involve themselves with others in crisis and function quite effectively at taking care of Uppingham without letting him see that he was part of the problem. The most useful therapeutic maneuver was to paradoxically recommend that they live in three separate houses. They then began to demonstrate how well they could stay together.

Caretaker Crises

Caretaker crises occur in families in which one or more members are nonfunctional and dependent. The functionally dependent member ties the family down by requiring caretaking. Small children, the aged, and invalids naturally require care from other family members. The caretaking may be provided within the family, which can exhaust the family's resources. The family may require outside helpers. When a family is dependent upon outside helpers, it is subject to unpredictable stresses that arise from forces outside its control. For instance, when the babysitter falls through, someone in the family may have to miss work or school. The more serious caretaker crises occur when the help needed is very specialized or hard to replace. Caretaker crises also involve those dependent on outsiders for financial support, such as welfare families or families dependent on trust funds, alimony, or the kindness of strangers.

Families dependent on a therapist are in the same situation, as are families with chronic medical conditions. Another situation in which a family depends on forces outside its own influence arises when a single parent is in a long-term affair with a married person. In all these situations the family lives without control over those upon whom it depends. No matter how desperate someone is, his or her therapist goes on vacation in August, and that is not negotiable. Welfare families and those on alimony have no influence over the hostile forces which provide their support, and nothing is negotiable. A family with chronic medical illness is similarly unable to control its destiny, as the treatments, orders, and restrictions leave everyone dependent upon the doctors, who alone claim to understand the situation.

Some psychiatric conditions are chronic. Bipolar depression seems predominantly chemical, genetic, and outside the control of the patient or his family. The family's efforts to influence it are unlikely to be helpful and are usually destructive, encouraging the manic-depressive to control all emotions. Schizophrenia is probably at least partially chemical in origin, may well become recurrent or chronic, and is incompletely influenced by individual or family effort. The effort of the family to find a cure (to assign blame to themselves, the patient, or to one another) may prevent acceptance of the chronic or recurrent nature of these conditions. Schizophrenia can usually be managed and stabilized without invalidism, but may well require long-term medication or therapy. The family's resistance to continuing the treatment frequently results in relapse.

If a chronic disability exists, the family needs to establish a relationship with the caretaker in which the family's needs are considered. Equally important may be the family members' understanding of the nature of the dependency, the purpose of the caretaker, and the rules of the relationship. If the modus operandi of the caretaker is mysterious to them, the relationship will lose any semblance of predictability. Caretaker crises can occur when the caretaker's rules change and don't seem negotiable, or when the caretaker makes decisions without explaining them.

Caretaker crises also occur in any therapy in which the family's agenda is not quite the same as the therapist's agenda, which of course is the case in family therapy in general, when the therapist is attempting to bring about change while the family is attempting to prevent it.

A simple caretaker crisis resulted when the mother of a manic-depressive man sat through my entire explanation of the illness hearing "Librium" each time I said "Lithium." She read all she could about Librium and its addictive potential and began a successful campaign to keep her son from taking the medicine. Only after the next manic episode did she directly question my use of what she thought to be an addictive, depressing drug.

The most typical and obvious caretaker crises occur in the management of those whose physical or mental disability is recent and not fully accepted. Handling senile family members can be particularly traumatic. As we see in the following case, the specific needs must be established, so the care offered is neither too much nor too little.

CASE 4   *Housekeeping*

Winston and Winona had been in love since grammar school and had been married for 60 years. She was brilliant and imaginative, and had been successful in her own career before she retired to care for Winston. Winston was a doctor, but had retired early because of his health. They had no children and could manage on very little income. Winona adored him, and Winston relied on her to take care of him and everything else. As they entered their eighties, Winona began to let things go. Winston spent each day at a club with his friends and came home at night to cook dinner for them. They were as happy as ever, although the illnesses came more frequently and the house was a mess. Winston suggested that they move to a retirement home. Winona was overwhelmed by the prospect of cleaning out a lifetime supply of treasures that cluttered the house. She adamantly refused to move. Gradually, Winona faded and would forget to turn off the stove. She could not be left alone. She depended on a maid who came in each day and structured her.

The crisis began when Winston had a stroke and was left paralyzed on one side. He couldn't take care of Winona anymore, and she couldn't take care of him. They went to different floors of a nursing home. Winston needed around-the-clock nursing care, but Winona needed only meals and light structure. She kept her maid though, who came every day and complained about the care Winona was getting. When the maid had finally driven the nursing staff berserk with her picky efforts to prove her indispensability to Winona, the administration of the nursing home said that the maid had to go. The younger relatives agreed.

Winona, distraught over the loss of the maid, threatened suicide. The staff followed their outline of procedures and required that Winona, being suicidal, be psychiatrically hospitalized. An arrangement was made for Winona to go to a relative's house to be psychiatrically evaluated instead. She did not appear remotely suicidal, or even depressed, just a little concerned about her memory losses. And then she revealed that she didn't know how to get to Winston's room on another floor of the nursing home, and she feared she wouldn't be able to visit him unless the maid were there to show her the way.

Since the maid had kept Winona away from the nurses, she had no idea how to ask them for help. Once her need was known, she got some help with orientation, and by the time she and Winston were moved to a room together she could have served as a tour guide for the place. Winona did not need a psychiatric hospital, just directions to the elevator.

UNCOVERING THE FAMILY SNAG POINTS

Defining the stress is the easy part. The stresses can often be discovered by simply asking the family, "Why now?" There was no difficulty in these four cases in determining that it was stressful for Shep to attend his father's funeral, or for Twink's parents to permit her adolescence, or for Ursula and Uppingham to go through a Friday night together, or for Winona to lose her maid. But a crisis requires both a stress which dictates change and an inflexibility which prevents the required change from taking place.

The complex and intriguing question in crisis intervention has to do with why this particular stress is stressful to this particular family. What is the core inflexibility, the snag point, in this family which makes it difficult for family members to make the changes necessary to adapt to this particular stress? What, above all, is the change this family must prevent? What is there in this family's structure which is so precious that it must, at all costs, be protected? Even in a bolt from the blue, where the stress would be stressful for any family, adaptation to the stress may be particularly difficult for this specific family. In developmental crises, and particularly in structural crises, the stress might not be difficult for some other family. Caretaker families are carrying such a load already that they are at the mercy of all manner of stresses.

In families in crisis there is a stress, but there is also something which impedes the family's flexibility sufficiently to make the family's initial efforts at response unhelpful. As we see, Shep must never raise any questions about why his parents divorced, since he believed it was because he was such a bad kid. Twink's parents, who had been willing to divorce over their different concept of sex, could not permit themselves to come to agreement about Twink's adolescent sexuality—any agreement about sex would have invalidated the rationale for the divorce they both wanted. Uppingham could not have openly acknowledged that he had been toppled by his affair from his exalted position as hero of the family, so he chose to take the respectable position as martyred caretaker to the incompetent, even if he had to keep himself miserable and keep his family invalids. Winona, after a lifetime of basing her identity on taking care of Winston, could not admit that she was too confused to continue her lifetime job and needed a maid to guide her to him. Those little pieces of protective inflexibility were only part of the total picture, but are examples of the special features of family structure which must be protected from change, even at the price of extreme crisis or chronic unhappiness.

Each family, like each snowflake, is unique and richly complex. It would be impossible to explore all of it. Any effort to turn a particular family into someone's idea of the ideal, or even the norm, would be as cruel and crazy as the Procrustean bed. Procrusteus was the legendary innkeeper who had a bed of a certain size, and put each of his guests through the process of either carving them down or stretching them out to fit his bed. Therapists who attempt that are no more welcome than innkeepers who do so. It is quite possible, and far more respectful, to keep a focus only on those aspects of the family structure which are not working at the moment, in the current crisis.

Even then, the nature of the crisis state produces such disruption of family boundaries, patterns of role and rule assignment, goal-directed functioning, sense of past history, and tension between the family members, that it is often confusing to ascertain what is part of the current crisis and what is part of the family pattern.

In answering the question, "What, above all, does the family not want to have changed by this crisis?" the therapist has to look past the simple answers the family provides and notice respectfully the peculiarities of the family in crisis. I wish I could give you a neat formula for categorizing family snag points, and while I've devised and even published such categories, I realize that I don't really use them in practice. Those family therapists who have a more global sense of what is healthy and what is not must have categories to put families in, and therefore must choose the parameters by which they will evaluate families. Often that results in placing families along a continuum or a pair of continua, which may be valid but have little to do with the crisis at hand. Since I prefer thinking of syndromes, clusters of related symptoms and causal factors, the continua are just not applicable.

There is no right way for families to be. But there are some ways in which families are structured which leave them more susceptible to going into crisis under certain kinds of stresses. People in such families should know that they have a choice in whether or not they will change.

In evaluating a family's cherished inflexibility, the therapist notices all manner of peculiarities, and while it is polite to respect those peculiarities, it is good reality-testing to recognize them. They may or may not be part of the problem. It cannot be assumed that people know when they are behaving inappropriately, when their actions or patterns are unusual. In many families, people don't comment directly on even the most bizarre and offensive behavior. Extreme politeness is not necessarily helpful in family living or family therapy. Therapists who observe inappropriate behavior may be surprised to realize that no one has ever commented on it before.

The relevant family snag points will be exposed during the process of therapy, as the alert therapist notes the difficulties the family meets in coming to therapy, in defining the stress, in attempting to solve or not solve the problem. The family may well have already identified their pet snag points and may be fighting over them, but those are not necessarily the relevant ones. The relevant inflexibilities are those which prevent the family from making the changes dictated by the stress that triggered the current crisis. These aren't always predictable and can best be identified through the process of therapy. They may come as surprises for the therapist and the family, and they may appear as resistances to change.

The very process of family crisis therapy may break all manner of family rules and challenge certain snag points. For instance, family members may be unwilling to come to therapy at all, perhaps because they fear they will be changed, perhaps because it is against their rule to acknowledge they have problems or need help. Even when some family members come, they may be resistant to defining the family's membership and may insist upon leaving out some powerful people from other generations. Some families may object to including certain of the children, or even one of the parents, preferring to pretend that the left-out member is too perfect or too powerful to be involved. If anyone is having an affair, the affairee is a significant force in the family, but one who must be kept secret. Just bringing the players onto the field may scare the family either into health or out of therapy.

Snag Points About Communication

Expecting the family to talk about things openly and reveal secrets may be terrifying. The rules against open communication stifle problem-solving most. Early family researchers spent years analyzing fragments of family conversation in order to delineate these rules about who can say what to whom, and about what, and when. They are usually subtle and uncodified and may not even be apparent to the family members. Many family fights ignore content entirely and focus exclusively on whether people are speaking respectfully or have a right to say what is being said. The most basic job of a family problem-solver is to cut through this and let the family members deliver the necessary messages and opinions.

Families may even have difficulty laughing at themselves. I like to tell the true story of the family in which no laughter was permitted. The father had injured his facial nerve and when he smiled his mouth would droop to one side, which caused food and saliva to dribble onto his tie. Therefore, at dinner no one in the family was permitted to say anything funny. Subsequently, one of the daughters suffered acute anxiety when anyone smiled at her, which severely inhibited her socially with all but the most depressed people. This story could be told quite seriously and made to seem tragic, but my point is to emphasize its outlandishness. I tell stories like this in hopes of making people see the ridiculous positions they put themselves in when they take it all too seriously.

Families often have conflict over communication. When a man from a diplomatic, silent family marries a woman from a noisy, conflict-loving family, both spouses may be continuously uncomfortable. He may consider her "crazy"; she may call him "uptight." The two different communication styles lead to two sets of incompatible rules governing communication. The more open style does not always prevail. A determinedly silent, unemotional, noncommunicative parent can destroy all life for miles around. When a liberated child decides to open communication with a closed family, or a cautious, sneaky child enters a stormy family, the child's style may trigger crisis.

There are things that cannot be talked about, secrets the family shields from one another, secrets the family shields from the world. There are topics that cannot be discussed — sex and money are popular taboos. There are even words that cannot be spoken. To families that panic at foul language I tell the true story about the old woman who was so proper that she kept over her mantle a large sign, in needlepoint, spelling out the four-letter words that could not be spoken in her proper house.

Snag Points About Intimacy

Family therapy requires that people come together, share their problems, and even take responsibility for their effects on one another. Family therapy encourages intimacy, often a higher level of intimacy than the family can tolerate easily. There are families that can tolerate little distance, and there are families that can tolerate little closeness. And there are relationships within the family in which one family faction allies closely to distance another faction. The couple may close out the children, a parent and child may close out the other parent or the child's spouse, the children may close out the parents. As the family is required to work together in the crisis or in the therapy, these alliances are breeched. The family tension rises.

Family tension is hard to describe, but it is palpable. It may be seen as a measure of the members' experience of one another. Tension can be so low that no one feels involved in anyone else's life. Adolescents can develop severe drug habits, young adults can have affairs, and older ones can deteriorate with Alzheimer's, before anyone is aware of anything unusual.

A more visible problem is a family with a high level of tension, in which everyone bounces off everyone else and it is unclear where each emotion begins or who owns any problem. When tension is high, symptoms and emotions are transmitted rapidly. Even suicidal behavior can be contagious. There are "enmeshed" families, smothering mothers, folie à deux, "gruesome twosomes," and other ways of describing relationships in which the emotional tension is so intense that one person's emotions are felt instantly by other family members and seem owned by the reactor rather than the originator. Some people even experience others' physical sensations or think they can do so, and thereby produce various psychosomatic ills and eating disorders. Likewise, paranoids seem more aware of other people's anger than of their own, failing to notice their attacks on others but being acutely aware of the other person's response to their unrecognized attack. This leaves them feeling inexplicably attacked.

Snag Points About Roles

Each family assigns roles to its members. Some roles are functional (breadwinner, cook, banker, dumper of the kitty litter, etc.), and others are emotional (jester, family doctor, etiquette advisor, family problem, etc.). Functional role assignments are generally quite clear and obvious, though they may be conflictual. Rigidity in roles is a frequent source of crisis proneness. Well-functioning families provide some degree of backup for a member whose role is not being performed.

Some families assign roles on a gender basis, which has the advantage of avoiding discussion of such matters but prevents the flexibility necessary to adapt to change. As repugnant as it is for most of us, the "Me Tarzan, you Jane; me hunt, you cook" arrangement is as workable as any other if both parties agree. But if Jane can't hunt and Tarzan can't cook, both might starve if one ceased to function.

There are men who have been raised to be domestically incompetent, to expect to be served by women. These men may extend their functional inflexibility to their wives as well, refusing to tolerate a wife who works. By contrast, there are women who were raised to believe that they should never have to hold a paying job outside the home, and therefore have never prepared themselves for a career. Such people, when called upon to perform roles they consider inappropriate for their gender, may feel put upon. It's not easy to maintain a family which contains a prince or princess who feels too special to do the work that needs to be done.

Crisis proneness is not just the result of functional or emotional rigidity. It can also result from functional looseness. Some families prefer to ignore certain roles, as if they were not really necessary. There are families in which no one regularly cleans up, pays the bills, oversees the schedule, or determines the appropriateness of other people's behavior. Thus, when the power is cut off, or the garbage blocks access to the kitchen, or various members drift away, a crisis occurs and the situation is treated as unique. Then the member who expresses dissatisfaction is seen as the problem.

In some families, one person, perhaps an adult, perhaps one of the children, is defined as vulnerable — as one who can't help it, who must always be catered to and obeyed. Asthmatic children, who could stop breathing if upset, alcoholic parents, who could start drinking if upset, or those defined as mentally ill are prime candidates for this role. If anyone questions the vulnerability of the family patient, it is the questioner who becomes the family "problem" — the one whose behavior must be changed. The family gives its highest priority to protecting the family patient from becoming self-sufficient. Such families are particularly prone to caretaker crises.

There are other emotional roles which stifle families. If the father must always know best, if the second child must always be at fault, if the child marked for success must always be blameless in his or her failures, if mother's actions must always be seen as love, if anyone must always be anything, then nothing can ever be understood, and no change can take place.

Snag Points About Rules

Just as family roles determine who does what, family rules determine who can't do what. Family rules are even more ubiquitous than family roles, and often just as bizarre. Crisis proneness results when rules prohibit the family from functioning or from joining the world, when the rules interfere with normal socialization and development of the children or prevent awareness and discussion of problems that require change. The possibilities for stifling growth seem proportional to the degree with which the family fears the world around them.

Rules seem to be tighter in those families which experience themselves as different from the world around them. Families from minority ethnic or religious groups may bolster their identity by tightening their rules. Families who are attempting a social climb or who feel their social position threatened may become anxiously rigid, while those who have given up on achieving success in the world may give up on rules and just let life happen to them. The disheartened poor sometimes seem to operate without structure, without schedule, without standards, without rules.

Those parents who are least involved in the day to day activities of their families, such as military fathers who are intermittently away, may insist most vigorously upon rules to maintain their influence. Families who influence one another most directly and personally probably need the fewest rules — they know one another well enough to trust one another.

Snag Points About Family History

Each family has certain issues which have never been resolved and are kept in storage for an uproar whenever needed. These past conflicts fall into two categories: those that are secret or lied about, and those that are open, symbolic and past. Obviously any real issue has to be handled in some way at the time it occurs, with some people taking action and others at least accepting or tolerating that action. But secret issues can't be resolved to anyone's satisfaction, and symbolic issues exist for the primary purpose of remaining unsolved.

Secrets usually involve past rule-breaking. Someone has an affair, lies about it, and offers no explanation for his or her changed behavior, leaving everyone vaguely confused. Such problems may be shelved for years. Much energy may go into protecting a secret item of past history — a degree not earned, a debt not reported, a child given up, a marriage not acknowledged, a dread secret from the family of origin. The secret may affect behavior and decisions only slightly most of the time but, like a lightly mined field, may make a few areas hazardous. Suspicious people may know when there is a secret and may become increasingly uncomfortable around the person who holds the secret; nevertheless, they may do a terrible job of guessing what the secret is.

By contrast, certain unresolved conflicts may be known to all, as part of the family mythology. They exist to keep change from taking place and perhaps as a warning to one another of those imperfections that must never be changed. The "he never" or "she always" remarks bring up seemingly unresolved conflicts which are tolerated, while serving as warnings that no effort at change could be helpful. There are people who "keep trying" long after they have "lost hope," thus sabotaging their own halfhearted efforts. People who "realize" they have married the "wrong" person may stay in the marriage, but make sure it never works.

All history is of course severely distorted and serves primarily as a source of object lessons. An insistence upon a certain view of the past might be seen as a snag point, a way of defining things that becomes rigidifying. Crisis prone families are at the mercy of their ongoing definitions of themselves and their past.

Snag Points in Goals

People set goals for themselves, economic goals, academic goals, experiential goals, or emotional goals. Wise people adapt those goals to reality rather than hitching their wagon to a star and leaving the planet completely. When they value the goals more than they value themselves, they become depressed. When they set idealistic goals for their loved ones, they can inflict great damage. Yet it is not uncommon for people to suffer great pain when they must modify or abandon a goal which might appear rather silly and grandiose to others. When they cannot abandon a goal that is clearly unachievable, such inflexibility of goals can sabotage crisis response. High standards and noble ambitions can be snag points.

If a family sets the goal of avoiding certain experiences, and then faces one of those dreaded experience, it can be devastating. When a family dedicates itself to getting through life without anyone in the family having a divorce or an abortion or an affair or an imprisonment or a psychiatric hospitalization or even a failing grade, any overt acknowledgment that all has not gone ideally seems to destroy the purpose of the family. Families that must have only ideal experiences may feel there is no recovery from a bad experience. Some families feel little will to continue after a child becomes illegitimately pregnant, fails in school, or goes to jail or a hospital. Divorce is common after a rape or the death of a child, even when there is no blame—just a sense of unachievable perfection. The failing grade, the abortion, or the adultery marks the family for life, becoming an irradicable blot on the family escutcheon. This makes further efforts rather pointless, since the primary goal of inexperience is no longer achievable. Life rarely proceeds smoothly for any of us. Yet most of us realize that life is a comedy, not a tragedy, and no one gets through it without an occasional pie in the face.

Snag Points in Values

Some peculiarities of family structure are merely patterns the family has fallen into. Patterns may be easy enough to change and are not likely to be maintained when they are no longer working. Other peculiarities, however, are expressions of the value system of one or more family members, and those values may seem crucial to the family identity. It is the snag points most closely connected to value systems that are most relevant, most likely to become full-scale resistances to crisis response.

Inflexibilities are learned, usually from one's family of origin. People may without thinking adopt their parents' goals and values and never question them. People who grew up happily may assume that their lives, their marriage, their children, their family will be just like that of their parents. They may not take social change into account. People who learned the gender stereotypes of a previous generation may have great difficulty giving up male privilege or female protection or whatever the advantages they saw their parents enjoy. Perhaps the most common and problematic snag points are those involving gender and generation, the belief that the relationships one experienced in the family of origin between husband and wife and between parent and child are somehow the way things are supposed to be. Men, particularly, who experienced their fathers exerting authority over women and children and receiving unquestioned respect, may expect the same relationships in their own families. They may see themselves as "head of the household" and be quite baffled when others don't see them in that exalted position. They may feel cheated, and they may sabotage any change that seems to lessen their authority over others, even if that is the only way the other members of the family can grow up and become whole.

People are also influenced—far more than they may realize—by their ethnic group, their religion, and their social class. Religion may rigidify by declaring certain actions or emotions as "sinful," and therefore forbidden even if they are unavoidable or life-saving. Social class may rigidify, declaring certain actions or emotions as "low-class" or "middle-class" or "snobbish," and therefore forbidden to the members of this family. Ethnicity may rigidify, declaring certain actions or emotions as "foreign," therefore forbidden. Religion, class, and tradition are inherently conservative, holding families together as bastions against disorder, but they are often at odds with a changing society and inflexible in times of crisis.

Some people never question their reasons for believing whatever they believe. People who aren't very bright remember only the first thing they learn about any subject and reject any subsequent information which doesn't seem compatible with it. As a result, their belief and value system may be strongly held, yet never examined. Those who do think about their values ordinarily do so because what they observed at home did not seem to work for their parents, or what they learned from their parents did not work for them. When one's goals and values are born of conflict and choice, they may be held even more strongly. It has been said that "no one is fit for life until he realizes that his parents were stark raving mad," meaning that everything he's been taught is dangerously suspect and must be continuously reexamined until he is sure it is a belief of his own choosing and therefore changeable in the face of new data. Families that constantly reexamine their goals and values become more interesting and more flexible. Families that merely reaffirm their goals and values without ever questioning them can become quite rigid and stifling. Families that don't examine themselves and what they believe at all, who just don't think about such things, can have no long-range view of themselves and their place in the world.

All of these structural peculiarities can be fiercely protected by families, or parts of families. Yet they are gradually revealed to therapists who attempt to understand why the family under stress cannot take the sensible steps other families would take to relieve the crisis state and proceed with change. These inflexibilities — values to the family, resistances to the therapists — are the snag points toward which therapy is directed.

It isn't that they can't see the solution. It is that they can't see the
problem.

—G.K. Chesterson

CHAPTER 2

A Treatment Model

ORDERING CHAOS

To TREAT FAMILIES in crisis, one must have an air of calm urgency, a clear
sense of the nature of the world and how things work, impatient tolerance
for people who prefer chaos to change, and optimism that life is an exciting
series of adventurous obstacles best hurdled if you know what's going on.
One must be optimistic about life, believing the world is basically good but
frequently misunderstood. Sympathy is singularly out of place, as is passive
interest in understanding people's feelings better, disapproval of behavior on
moral rather than practical grounds, or protective willingness to join into
conspiracies.

For a therapist with such a reality base, treating families in crisis is not as
difficult as it might seem. It may be considered to consist of seven often
overlapping steps:

A condensed version of this chapter was published in Pittman, F.S., 1985.

1. Emergency response
2. Family focus
3. Definition of the problem
4. General prescription
5. Specific prescription
6. Negotiating resistance
7. Termination

STEP 1: EMERGENCY RESPONSE

An "emergency" is not necessarily a crisis. The state of "emergency" is merely a situation in which people feel the need to call for outside help. Usually the helper is called in to prevent change, to minimize damage. Still, the emergency helper is given considerable power, at least temporarily. The desired emergency response is either (1) "I'll be right there and take care of it," or (2) "Here's what you need to do until I can get there." "Take two valium and call me in the morning" is not sufficient—there must be acknowledgment of the helper's involvement. A crisis therapist, unlike a plumber, does not expect to do all the work in the emergency. Part of an emergency response is the acknowledgment of willingness to help but unwillingness to take over.

One characteristic of the state of crisis is the loosening of the family boundaries. Another is the time limitation of crisis; some sort of new equilibrium must be established within a few weeks, even if that new equilibrium is dysfunctional and will set up the system for new crises in the future. If a therapist enters the system while the crisis is fresh, he or she has far more power to prevent damage and to promote change. He can take over some administrative functions of the family during the crisis, although he would be resisted a few days before or a few days later. He has to arrive quickly and work fast.

The exception to this is the caretaker crisis in which the crisis is conceived as the opportunity for the family to be adopted by a new caretaker. Change or improved functioning is not expected, just a more personal state of dependency.

STEP 2: FAMILY FOCUS

Ordinarily in a crisis the family members choose an individual to be changed so the rest of them won't have to do so. If they are sufficiently concerned, they will be willing to be involved. But the therapist must be willing to start with whoever shows up. As Anderson and Stewart (1983) have said, "A family therapist, like a salesman, must be willing to agree to anything that will get his foot in the door." The therapist starts and then involves the others as quickly as possible by whatever means he or she can. Usually a telephone call to the missing members is sufficient, but sometimes a home visit is required. Family members may fear they will be found out, blamed, or changed. The guiltier people feel about their involvement, the more frightened they are about therapy, but a friendly, competent voice on the telephone can seem sufficiently tolerant and conspiratorial to offer some protection.

Even on those rare occasions when a family member won't come in or talk, he can be considered in the therapist's formulations. If he needs to make a change, he can be sent a specific message explaining the therapist's understanding of the situation and suggesting things he can do to make it better. He must, however, be protected from blame. Don't worry, he is already blaming himself quite enough. That's why he won't come in.

In deciding who should be included in therapy, remember that small children aren't really necessary at every visit and tend to be disruptive. All family members need not be involved. The group to be assembled is not based on biology or proximity or fault, but on power. Whoever has the power to sanction or prohibit change must be included.

Many family therapists refuse to see a family unless all members are present. I have taken a quite different stand. I see whoever comes. If someone is central and absent, I call or, if that fails, write a note. I even go so far as to set up separate meetings for individuals in the family. I like to see adolescents without their parents at least once, but I don't really like seeing the parents without the kids, even though I have to do so at times. I like to see husbands and wives separately at least once. Of course, I make clear that I won't keep secrets, which doesn't stop people from telling them to me. They don't want their secrets kept anyway—they are just so horrified by them that they fear others will be also.

Even when family members are present, they may not be involved and may take the posture of innocent bystanders to someone else's craziness or awfulness or misery. The therapist must increase the sense of family; there are techniques for doing that. The most popular is to bypass the presenting complaint and instead take a family history, focusing on either how the family came to be or what the family has gone through lately. The therapist may target the youngest child or the least involved member of the family. Or he may just calmly refuse to acknowledge the identified patient's pathology. A rather devious but effective act of therapeutic desperation is to see the identified patient separately and report back to the rest of the family that the symptoms exist only in their presence and diminish when away from them.

Family therapy can proceed without every family member being present. Likewise, all the people who are in the therapy room are not necessarily in the therapy process.

STEP 3: DEFINITION OF THE CRISIS

In the midst of the chaos, as everyone blames everyone and seeks the source of the problem in the past or the stars or the society, the therapist is the small voice that keeps repeating, "Why now?" The family may have all manner of correct and relevant information to give you, but without an identification of the immediate stress there is no way to sort out all of this data. If this crisis is a bolt from the blue, you may be told rather quickly, but you may not get accurate information about the state of the family prior to the crisis. If this is a caretaker crisis, you'll learn that fairly quickly also. If it is a developmental crisis, the information you are given may be quite badly distorted. You may, for instance, be given a story of one individual's bad or sick behavior, although it may not be the individual who is spearheading the change from one developmental stage to another. The "sick one" may be the person opposing the development or contributing to making the development a distorted one. On the other hand, the family may collar a family bystander who is trying not to be involved. With persistence and patience, you should be able to figure out who is changing and what is noxious about the change and to whom it is noxious.

Structural crises are the most misleading. No matter how often the same crisis has been repeated, someone in the family will try to convince you it is unique and brought on by external situations. Or someone may try to convince you it is a caretaker crisis in which the bully has a chronic defect outside his or her control and the world has been insufficiently supportive. One person may blame the exacerbation on some other family member's development. If the focus is sufficiently on the issue of "Why now?" and it is discovered that this is one of a series, it is a structural problem no matter how well the most recent episode is related to other stresses. So in addition to "Why now?" you must ask if this has happened before. You must also explore the past enough to find out when the family was last functioning well enough to not need you. Once you find out when it started and what the stress was, you should be able to construct a coherent description of the sequence of events.

Neither Leo Tolstoy, Sigmund Freud, nor my mother was good at short stories—all preferred three-generational explanations for every event. However, the family is likely to offer a short story here. The classic is, "The whole problem is me. I've never been any good. Just ask my parents. They'll tell you."

There are other stories: "Everything was OK until she started dating. That was when my husband began to drink. So I helped her sneak out of the house. When he found out about it he beat me up and that was when I took all the pills."

Or, "We were doing fine under the circumstances, I suppose. He's just never found a job that suited him but he's wonderful at writing and someday he'll be published. So Mother sent us a check every month to help him write, but when she broke her hip, the bills were so high that she couldn't send the check anymore and that awful woman at welfare said I should work, but he can't write if I'm not there to answer the phone and fix some food for him."

Or, "After we started our new business we didn't see the kids much because we didn't have meals. Then when he was kicked out of school, we realized he hadn't been going for months so we checked his room and found all the drugs, but he said that it was his problem to work it out since he's 16 now. Other kids do that sort of thing, don't they? I mean it is normal to get on drugs and drop out of school, isn't it?"

If the information is put together in such a way as to explain the interaction and everyone's part in it, the symptomatic behavior seems a completely understandable, if not necessarily reasonable, reaction to the situation. Until it does, keep probing, keep acting as if you don't understand. I like to flounder visibly, demonstrating my confusion and bewilderment with the situation, until the family feels comfortable enough with my powerlessness to go ahead and tell me what is going on. There is no more powerful position for a therapist than the one-down position outlined by Fisch, Weakland, and Segal (1982).

Other techniques can be helpful for teasing out a family, as opposed to individual, definition of the problem. Just keeping the identified patient out of the hospital is the most powerful way of getting the family to see how they are driving one another crazy. Home visits are extremely useful in giving perspective on past and present functioning.

My favorite, and perhaps most characteristic, technique is the reductio ad absurdum, in which each proposed definition is treated seriously and followed to its inevitable, illogical conclusion. For example, "I'll just kill myself," evokes the response, "But then you'd be dead." Or, "The affair wasn't my fault. She forced me into it" leads to the question, "What did she threaten to do to you if you refused to have the affair?" The point is to get people to translate their emotional expressions back to the concrete and practical. This is a dangerous technique for any therapist without a strong sense of the absurd and an ability to be warm and accepting on one level while being ridiculing and playful on another. Of course people who can't do that shouldn't be doing family therapy anyway.

STEP 4: GENERAL PRESCRIPTION

As soon as the crisis is defined, efforts can be made to calm everyone down in preparation for doing something sensible. You may have to sedate someone, or everyone, for a day or so, or you may just need to reassure everyone that you now understand the situation and know what to do about it. If anyone is to be hospitalized — and that can almost always be avoided —

it should be at this point or later, never prior to steps 2 and 3. Permitting an individual definition of the problem, accepting the family's helplessness and uninvolvement, creates a situation that will later be difficult to correct. I've found that Haydn chamber music, popcorn, or an air of confidence calms everyone down almost as well as locking somebody up.

Obviously, the therapist's cockiness should be at the end of the first session rather than at the beginning. The therapist should go into the first session looking confused but conscientious (the "one-down" position), flounder around for most of the interview (thereby avoiding resistance and eliciting cooperation and helpful hints from the family), and finally stick in a thumb and pull out a plum — the definition of the problem. That triumphant act is immediately disorienting and disarming to the family, but wins the family's confidence. The therapist, if he or she has developed enough good will with the family, can now cockily tell everyone to calm down, the situation is in hand.

In situations of serious pathology, it usually does no damage to prescribe medication at this point, but unless the problem is itself chemical, it is important to keep the medication from being the important part of the therapist's contribution. I once saw a woman in her sixties. She'd been depressed for a year since her beloved father's death. His death was complicated by the fact that her boss, a man she had worshipped for decades, was her father's doctor. Her husband, a worthless alcoholic, wanted her to sue the doctor for malpractice. Instead she quit her job and sank deeper into depression. She came in alone, wanting antidepressants. I teased out the story and urged her to talk to the doctor, go over the medical records with him, and settle any questions she had about it. When she insisted on medication I gave her a prescription for Elavil. She called back angrily to cancel the next appointment, leaving the message that the doctor had settled the medical questions, she felt fine now, and her doctor-boss-friend had told her that I should not have given her that awful medicine. It was my error, of course, since I let her leave thinking that Elavil was the therapy rather than an adjunct to the real therapy — the confrontation with the doctor.

With organic conditions, such as bipolar-depression, schizophrenia, and major depression, the medication is central to the treatment. The treatment of the family can't really proceed without getting the out-of-control brain chemistry under control. The lithium, the phenothiazines, and often the antidepressants are not *general* prescriptions at all, but quite *specific* ones.

Above all, the general prescription should not sabotage the therapeutic effort of change. If step 3 has failed, the time is up, and you do not have a working definition of the problem, it is hard to go on to the next step. You may have to stop, with many questions about the crisis, much reassurance, and a very early appointment. It is a little dangerous to prescribe medication before the situation is well understood and under control.

STEP 5: SPECIFIC PRESCRIPTION

Now that you understand who did what to whom and why whoever developed whatever symptom brought it to you, you can point out what you have heard. This must be done with a determined effort not to blame anyone for what has happened but with an unshakeable conviction that everyone wants to do something sensible and is perfectly capable of doing so. If family members object to your formulation, a little fancy verbal work will make it vague and supportive around the creases so no one can argue. You can then tell them what sensible people would do under the same circumstances. In order to do that, you must know what sensible people do or even be one yourself. And, since this step can't be faked, it is the test that differentiates good therapists from bad ones.

The prescription can be quite simple: "Stop drinking. If you're not an alcoholic it should be easy. If you are, Antabuse will help." "Stop the affair. You can call from here. I'll call if you're embarrassed to do so." "Don't commit suicide tonight. We'll find other alternatives tomorrow." "Go on to school/work, they'll help you if you need it." "Stay home tonight. The family needs to be together." The prescription should also be directed towards the symptom in question. When such a simple prescription is given, it is usually joined with the prescription to the other family members to either talk or not talk about the issue and to help in various ways to perform the prescribed task. Often there is conflict about who is to do what, so separate prescriptions can be given to each member of the family. These may be of the "You go ahead and hunt, and you go ahead and cook" variety. For example, "You job hunt tomorrow, and she'll write the letter to your mother." Or, "You all work together on the rules. If anyone isn't involved, he or she must abide by the others' rules. Until that is done, you (designating the youngest child or the most reasonable adult) make the rules." The important thing is that each person's task performance be independent of the others', so that one person can't avoid his or her task because someone else did.

In bolts from the blue, simple structure is usually sufficient, such as returning to normal functioning in most old areas plus handling the special tasks produced by the crisis. In caretaker crises, you've already done your job by becoming the new caretaker, but you must now assign an end to the dependency or an acceptance of it. You tell the unemployed to go to work, or the manic-depressive to get back on his lithium. In developmental crises, you side with the family authority if the change is in an adult or with the parents if the child is changing. In other words, you place the continuation of the family ahead of any individual's concerns. Once all are secure with that, you then try to coordinate the changes dictated by the new developmental phase. With children you support the theory of parental authority. Then you side with the developmental phase and have the parents accept it while they maintain control and the child demonstrates responsibility in going through it. In structural crises there is often a bully who takes no responsibility for his or her behavior. The tasks should involve ceasing the bullying and encouraging the other family members to protect themselves from it while the issues are negotiated from positions of greater equality. If you've been skillful enough in defining the crisis as one in which all are players, this shouldn't be difficult. The tasks are clearly labeled as symbolic and really tests of the members. Everyone must be given a task, even perhaps with the admonition that you know they may not perform the tasks and that's OK, because if they don't you can uncover the real problem as you find out why they didn't.

Ordinarily tasks should be assigned in the most straightforward manner possible. Most tasks are real. Some may be symbolic, particularly when the therapist's sense of whimsy meshes with that of a family member. Tasks can be made fun, with ceremonies, playlets, and a sense of adventure.

Occasionally someone's offensive or disruptive behavior is defined by that person as fun or play. Alcoholism, drug abuse, skipping school, adulteries, etc., are rule-breaking behavior defined by the rule-breaker as the pursuit of pleasure. The therapist can explore the behavior very, very seriously, earnestly seeking what is pleasurable and how much it costs. The job here is to deprive the activity of pleasure.

STEP 6: NEGOTIATING THE RESISTANCE TO CHANGE

At the next session, you'll find out who did what and why. The focus can be on the present in the form of task performance. You will probably learn much more about the family than you did at the first session. Most likely the one who is protecting the family from change is not the initial patient. New tasks, new explorations, and even revisions of the original definition are in order.

Bolts from the blue will be resolved quickly. Caretaker crises will return quickly to the point at which the last caretaker cut and ran; you may discover that the previous caretaker missed the point, giving you the chance to solve a longstanding problem. Developmental crises always require some negotiation, but they usually don't require too many sessions before the family bows to some objective outside wisdom.

Structural crises, however, can put up resistance indefinitely. These families may drop out of therapy early, try to send in only one member, or play a touch and go game. These are the families you may try to keep in therapy for a long time. These are also the families about whom all the family therapy books are written. They are a bitch. Don't expect them to change quickly. Each time one member improves, another will sabotage it. However, if you can convince just one person that change is possible, that the bully is competent, that the victims are free to get out of the pattern, the impasse is broken and change becomes possible. The question at this stage is "What, above all, do you not want to change?" The answers are often amazing and identify the snag points and inflexibilities that make the family crisis prone. These inflexibilities may not be stated verbally, but may materialize as resistances to therapy.

Ultimately the therapeutic focus moves from the stress that triggered the crisis to the family's cherished snag point which prevents crisis resolution and change. This very likely begins to impose upon the value system of the family, the family's raison d'être. Negotiating the family's inflexibilities may be a long and difficult process — and a threatening one for the family.

Therapists tend to be seen as more powerful, more threatening than we really are, presenting the threat of forcing people to be normal against their wills. There is a danger of working for more change than anyone really wants. It may also be that one member, perhaps the identified patient, is less interested in change than in a professional confirmation of his perceptions of how mistreated he or she is. It should also be remembered that a slight change in a familiar situation may seem like a profound one to the family. Every family is struggling to return to the status quo with only a few changes. This is often possible, except with developmental crises; even then the changes can be circumscribed. The therapist may have to provide constant reassurance of his or her dedication to preserving the status quo.

During the negotiation of resistances and snag points there are two pivotal characters in the family, neither of whom may be the identified patient. One is the family member who, at whatever sacrifice, feels the need to deny involvement in the problem. That person seems to believe that if all were known and understood, there would have to be profound changes in the family and particularly in his or her role in the family. That person, typically but by no means always the father, may do everything possible to wreck the therapy to prevent an assault of mental health upon his castle.

The second important character in the family is the one with the power to facilitate change. That person, often but not exclusively the mother, takes responsibility for holding the family together, for determining what is and is not appropriate behavior, what values the family will espouse. That person is already the ally of the therapy, as it was surely that person who decided to bring the family for therapy, but now that person must become the ally of the therapist. It is often difficult to support both the person who could wreck the therapy and the person who is keeping the family in therapy, since the therapy is about the conflict between the two.

The usual technique for resolving this is to support each family member's good intentions, however invisible in his or her actions, and place each of them in a situation in which good intentions can be proved by a change in behavior. This technique can be carried too far. Guilt is a wonderful thing if it is anticipatory and keeps people from messing up their lives and those of others because they accurately foresee that it would make them feel bad later. If people feel guilt for what they think and feel, if people feel excessively and self-destructively guilty for what they have already done, the guilt makes matters worse. The issue is not to give people a holiday from guilt, a free pass through life, but to teach them how to use guilt effectively.

The paradox is a popular and much overused technique for dealing with resistance. If the therapist believes the patient to be resisting change out of a desire not to be controlled by the therapist, the therapist may order the patient not to change or to change in the opposite direction. This occasionally produces dramatic results, but usually just confuses everyone. It can be disastrous with people who really don't understand what the sensible course of action would be. When a patient is particularly resistant, a paradox will just disgust him or her further with the obnoxious cuteness of the therapist. Whatever the therapeutic relationship that requires paradoxical rather than direct directives, it has little resemblance to the therapeutic relationship I try to develop, which is personal, open, and honest, but not authoritarian.

Therapy can be seen as a series of binds from which a patient can escape only by giving up symptoms and snag points — it becomes more painful and embarrassing to retain symptoms than to give them up. But there are some people with so little pride that they cannot be shamed or maneuvered into change. Perhaps they can be rewarded or threatened. Every family knows what works with its more difficult members. The therapist may even fall back upon the ultimate weapon and use a kamikaze maneuver — blast and challenge the resistant member and dramatically terminate the therapy.

STEP 7: TERMINATION

It seems to be those who need therapy least who want it most, and those who need it most who hurry to get out. In treatment of family crises, change, if it occurs, is achieved quickly; whether change occurs or not, the crisis is over in a few weeks. Let bolts from the blue and developmental crises go gracefully and they'll be back when they need you. If they don't terminate quickly enough, and if you're getting lost and bored, encourage them to try it on their own and check in later. With certain caretaker crises, especially schizophrenics and manic-depressives, someone may have to manage medication indefinitely. If there is a good working relationship with the family, the medication management can be done efficiently and on an individual basis. There is important family work in these situations. The family of a manic-depressive on lithium must learn that the danger is over and there is no need to protect the patient from emotions. Once past the psychosis, schizophrenics benefit from groups and other opportunities to learn to be normal. The family protectiveness from normality should be stopped, even if the schizophrenic has to leave home to accomplish that. Don't worry about the structural crises. They'll probably disappear quickly and return in time. After a few exacerbations, they'll make a lot more sense, and you'll understand the structure better. Eventually they may enter therapy in order to prevent crises rather than using crises to prevent therapy.

The most delicate part of termination is its timing — you want to do it to them before they do it to you. You're trying to keep them from needing you on a regular basis before anything happens that would make them reluctant to come back when they need you more than they do right now. It is delicate, but necessary, to separate termination efforts from resistance. You are very likely to keep pushing for change after the family members have achieved something they can live with. At that point, you must let them go — otherwise they can't feel safe in returning when they need to. Almost all terminations should be soft, with an open door for return. The only exception is those caretaker crises in which you are trying to get rid of a dependent chronic patient by getting the patient involved with a different therapist. You can be quite hard-nosed about that termination.

An Illustration: School Phobia

The simplest possible example of family crisis therapy would be a case of school phobia. Imagine a typical case, a 10-year-old girl, perfect in every way, who suddenly refuses to go to school, and screams, rants, raves, bites, and kicks when anyone tries to get her to go.

Step 1: Emergency Response

The mother calls for an appointment, referred by a pediatrician who found nothing wrong with the girl. The mother explains the problem. The family is offered an appointment that evening. This is an emergency, and you acknowledge it.

Step 2: Involve the Family

You insist that the entire family come, including the older brother who will have to miss football practice and the father who will have to leave work early. You have to call the father to explain why he must come. They come.

Step 3: Define the Problem

You flounder around trying to understand the situation. They tell you that the girl was home sick for a week with the flu. That doesn't explain it well enough. They tell you what she might fear at school. You keep asking why she might fear leaving home. Baffled, you ask about the marriage. The mother cries, the daughter hovers, and there is acknowledgment that the father hasn't been at home much lately since starting a new business. The mother confesses that she talked with the girl about it during the child's illness. You announce that the girl is afraid the mother will be lonely at home and is staying home to rescue her.

Step 4: General Prescription

You tell them the problem is solvable, and medication will be used if necessary, but first the father and brother must postpone their morning activities long enough to get the child to school the next morning and every day for a week. They will all work together as a family. You call the school and alert them.

Step 5: Specific Prescription

The family is to take the girl to school each morning, whatever her protest and using whatever power is necessary. If they fail they will bring her to your office instead. You'll be available by telephone for emergencies.

Step 6: Negotiating Resistance

The father says he and the boy are too busy for the family, thus articulating the snag point. The mother cries. The daughter says she's feeling sick again. You tell them they must spend the day at your office if they fail, but can merely drop by if they succeed. The father agrees, the others accept it. The next morning, the father calls from work, saying he left the task to his wife and son, and they just called him to say the girl is carrying on, the mother is crying, and the brother is threatening to hit the child. You tell the father to go home, and first comfort his wife, then announce his dedication to the family, and then pick up the girl and put her in the car. He does. All join in, and it goes well. They drop by the office in the evening, and all is well. You repeat this daily, with diminishing resistance. The father is massively congratulated for his involvement.

Step 7: Termination

The girl is fine and is congratulated for bringing the family together. She is told to tell them directly next time she's worried about their marriage, rather than putting them through this. The brother, who has learned to like this, stands ready to repeat it when needed. The parents enter therapy for a while, working mostly on the father's priorities.

When a family is in crisis, the members will usually cooperate in such a straightforward process as this. Snag points can be uncovered easily and resistance overcome quickly. It usually is just this simple.

Technique without direction is bad enough in coloratura sopranos.
In therapists and surgeons it can be disastrous.

— Pittman, 1984

CHAPTER 3

Techniques of the Desperately Resourceful Therapist

WET COCKER SPANIEL THERAPY

THE TECHNIQUES of family crisis therapy have come to be known by the unlikely name of wet cocker spaniel therapy. It was discovered on a snowy morning in Denver in February of 1966. Many of the details have long been muddled in my aging memory, but the discovery itself is as fresh and clear as if it were yesterday. Carol DeYoung was with me.

The night before a middle-aged woman (I was only 30 at the time so my sense of middle age was a bit naive — she might have been 35) had been brought to the hospital for her third or fourth admission. She was catatonic, sitting waxenly in a wheelchair, seeming displeased with the proceedings but refusing to comment in any way. She was a large, pasty woman with the lank, greasy hair of a person announcing her misery. Her mother-in-law and her young son hovered, while her husband pouted in the corner.

The mother-in-law told us that the woman had been like this for days, since learning of her husband's latest affair. The husband cried as his mother told the story and then sobbed that his wife got like this everytime he had an affair. He wailed that all the other fellows do it and their wives don't act like this. The wife did not respond.

I wheeled the catatonic woman into another room, away from her family, where she was just as unresponsive but more relaxed. I wheeled her back into the room with her family and informed them that she had conveyed to me that she was really angry and would remain this way until her husband stopped screwing around. He cried more about the injustice of it all, but agreed to go straight. Carol gave the woman a shot of Thorazine and they were sent home with the expectation of a home visit in the morning.

That night there was a fresh snowfall. Carol and I arrived at the modest home just as the husband left to take the boy to school. The woman was still in bed. We told her we were cold and wet and in need of hot coffee. We got no response at all. I explained that I was from the South and the rules of hospitality required that she offer us coffee and I did not consider it proper to fix it myself in her home. Still no response. So we picked her up, Carol put a robe on her, and we took her into the kitchen and stood her in front of the stove. We even put her hand on the knob, but she refused to move it. When I tried to move the knob with her hand, she fell to the floor. I was worn out with the situation by then.

Carol and I sat and considered our next move. It was then that we heard the scratching at the back door. I opened the door and let in the family cocker spaniel, cold and frisky and covered with fresh snow. He jumped on his mistress' chest and began licking her face as the snow dripped all over her. It seemed only a matter of seconds before she was off the floor, preparing us coffee and telling us of her anger at her foolish husband, his infantile friends, the treacherous women at his office, her meddling mother-in-law who kept protecting him from adult responsibilities, etc. The husband returned, the rules of the relationship were negotiated, and the case was soon terminated with nothing memorable happening over the three years of follow-up.

I told the story at a conference in New York a few months later. Dick Auerswald, Emery Hetrick, and Richard Rabkin were among the other "outdoor therapists" gathered at that meeting, all of us seeking reassurance that we could remain respectable even if we used nonstandard, nonpsychoanalytic tactics to bring about change in crisis situations. In the audience was a reporter from *Time* magazine, who later called me about doing an article on wet cocker spaniel therapy as a new psychiatric breakthrough. I managed to talk him out of it, fearing impressionable therapists would misunderstand the nature of crisis intervention and remember the dog as the point of the therapy. I envisioned eager therapists with snowy dogs waiting for patients willing to lie down and receive some therapeutic cold, wet, frisky licks.

I had, and still have, the fear that there are therapists who read Carl Whitaker, Mara Selvini Palazzoli, Maurizio Andolfi, and even Jay Haley, Cloé Madanes, or Milton Erickson, and remember the glittering technique but not the sanity and clarity with which those fine therapists identify the point of change.

In more than two decades since this incident, I have yet to find another situation in which I have felt the need to use a wet dog as a cotherapist. I've done many other things. In fact, once I threw a 15-year-old boy out of his chair.

The boy was 6-feet tall, a prince and a tyrant who had the support of both live-in immigrant grandmothers as he brought down crisis after crisis upon the family. In this family it was thought unseemly for any female to interfere with the actions of any male, so only the father could stop the boy and he refused to do that with the same determined passivity with which he refused to do anything else his wife wanted done. The mother wanted the father to control the boy, the father was unable to do so without obeying a woman, and the family rules and the two grandmothers would not stand for such a break with tradition. In the first meeting with the parents, the father could not understand why the mother did not appreciate the impossible situation she put him in.

At the first family visit in my office, the boy chose a chair in which one of his sisters was already sitting and demanded that she make way for him. She refused so he hit her and she tearfully left the chair. I objected. The boy laughed. I asked the father to do something. He refused, so I demonstrated for him another way of handling it. I picked up the chair and the boy and dumped him on the floor. Everyone was shocked and disapproving, and the women comforted the crying boy. I offered to give the father further instruction by letting him do the dumping next time if the boy would repeat the incident for us. The father agreed, but the boy refused. Both had gotten the point, but the grandmothers never forgave me for dispossessing their prince.

I have never again dumped anyone from a chair, so no school of chair dump therapy has developed. I did one time have a 70-year-old stand on his head. The man was Swedish and his wife Italian. Among their children was a 34-year-old son who had never worked and had been considered an invalid since he developed an obscure back pain at age 14. At that time the mother encouraged him to stop lifting weights and drop off the track team and rest. After 20 years of rest his back still hurt. His mother had decided after some previous therapy that her problem was that her husband had never been a loving, joyous person like her own father. She figured that this must be the son's problem too and decided that the son's back could not recover until the father changed. She offered to divorce him if I thought that would help the boy's back. She had always known that the boy had special talents and thought he would make a good Senator if his back got better. But in her view and that of her previous therapist all depended on the father's becoming more ebullient.

When I saw the young man with the parents, they revealed the difference between the Italian view of love as a form of celebration and the Swedish view of love as a form of suffering. I raised the image of Sophia Loren in an Ingmar Bergman movie. The father began to cry and describe his love for his son. He said he would make any sacrifice for him. He said, "I would stand on my head for him if you thought it would help." The wife smiled slightly and I assured him it would help. He got up and stood on his head. When it looked as if he were about to fall, the son jumped up and held his father's legs. The boy cried, the father cried and hugged him, and the mother laughed first and then cried, and they all hugged one another. Within a few days the boy had a job as a dishwasher, with ambitions of becoming a chef. His back still hurt, the mother reduced her ambitions to Speaker of the House, and the father dourly complained about the cost of therapy, but the couple stayed together and the boy continued to work and took up jogging.

So few Swedes marry Italians that I have never again found a situation that required headstanding family therapy. I have no foolproof techniques and no magic. Instead, I am a friendly consultant, a sane, successful, well-adjusted, intelligent expert on problem-solving, an optimistic and amused observer of the human comedy.

TECHNIQUES: NUDGES AT THE SNAG POINTS

Family therapy is ordinarily a straightforward process. The therapist brings the family members together, helps them define the problem, declares them responsible for solving the problem, assists them in outlining the possible solutions, negotiates with them resistance to change, and finally monitors the process of change. Often all that is required of the therapist is an awareness of the process, a gentle guidance back onto the path, good humor and good manners, and meticulous reality-testing. Technique is unnecessary.

Families in crisis have symptoms that result from and express unresolved family conflicts. It is the therapist's function to bypass the symptoms (offering of course the simple solution to it that most people would apply) and to uncover the conflict in the family that either produces the symptom or prevents the family from taking the sensible course of action that other families would take. This is the central process described by essentially all the great therapy theorists, but perhaps most specifically by Minuchin (1974).

Until it is clear to the therapist (if not to the family) what sensible people would do and what the inherent defect is that prevents the family from going ahead and taking sensible action, the therapist is not in a position to provoke change. The strategies and tactics of change cannot be applied until the structural defect is identified. Each family has a full complement of idiosyncracies, which might well arouse in an eager therapist the impulse to bring about change. However, in doing so he runs the risk of bogging down in a power struggle over irrelevant peculiarities of the specific family, distracting everyone from the relevant defect. I would hate for my surgeon to give me an undoubtedly useful hair transplant before he got on to repairing my ruptured appendix. The specificity in family therapy must be in the definition of the problem rather than the techniques of the therapist.

Determining the relevant defect — the snag point — in a family in crisis has been discussed in Chapter 1. Once the problem has been defined and the sensible solution outlined, the therapist can look for the forces within the family which prevent it from going ahead and doing the sensible thing that would solve the problem. What above all does the family not want to change? What problem do they insist on solving first before they can go ahead and solve this one? What do they find so valuably distinctive about themselves that they cannot change? This question is as central as the initial diagnostic question of "Why now?"

It is at the snag point that the techniques are applied. The techniques, the strategies and tactics of therapy, are just the little nudges that push people past their snag points to try something new. In the wet cocker spaniel case the snag point was the woman's open expression of anger at her adulterous husband, which was being blocked by her husband's pitifulness and her mother-in-law's protection of her son. Why didn't she tell her husband of her anger? Perhaps she could punish him more by her silence and dependency than by open expression. As she became more pitiful than he, she gained total control. But she wasn't about to tolerate more abuse from meddling therapists or cold, wet dogs. Perhaps it was the absurdity of the loving dog that made her passive-aggressive maneuver seem less than noble. I don't know — the maneuver was never mentioned again by the woman or by us.

In the chair dumping situation, why did the women tolerate the boy's bullying? The snag point was that males were seen as the only people with any power and their dignity had to be preserved. The women were waiting for the father to do something, yet they believed men should do whatever they liked. The husband would have lost his aura of power by obeying his wife; he would also be demonstrating the limitations of male freedom by restricting his son. My maneuver might have been more useful had I been female, but it at least demonstrated that all men do not believe male dignity must be protected. After the maneuver the father lost dignity if he did not control whatever needed to be controlled.

In the headstanding situation, the snag point was that the mother was not about to let the son do anything sensible until her husband could show love, whereas he only showed futile but appropriate impatience. This couple permitted their son to languish in functional incompetence while they debated the nature of love.

In these cases the technique worked. More often they don't, which is no problem, since the next moment will provide an opportunity for another technique. These techniques were not planned — they just happened. I might just as well have written someone a letter, pulled a paradox, acted helpless, gone to sleep and had a dream, or played out a fantasy scene. Those might have worked just as well. I've never gone to sleep in a session, but I've done all the other things, sometimes with success, sometimes without. In 1971, I wrote, with my colleagues in Denver, a paper on technique, including paradox, denial of symptoms, use of the patient's own symbolic language, etc. Such gentle techniques are associated with a nonblaming attitude of intolerance for the symptom and respect for the message symbolized by the symptom. From time to time the therapist may have to go beyond such gentle semantics. Wet cocker spaniel therapy is a metaphor for the desperate resourcefulness with which the therapist gives a little nudge to get the family past its snag point. Such nudges are specific and differ from more routine techniques, which tend to be unstructuring devices to stop the recycling of the same old change-preventing definition of the problem. Once the problem has been redefined and the required action perfectly clear, the nudge merely pushes a family member into doing some symbolic act which would bring about systemic change.

After 25 years in the business of family therapy, I am impressed by the infrequency with which dramatic techniques are necessary. In Anderson and Stewart's (1983) invaluable collection of techniques for overcoming resistance, almost all are straightforward and gentle. I'm quite sure any therapist could get through a career without relying on anything remotely flashy.

One danger in flashy techniques is their use at the wrong point in the therapy. A paradox might be grotesque over the telephone as someone attempts to make the first appointment, or when the family is reporting back the successful completion of assigned tasks. It would be inappropriate for the therapist to be cocky when the family arrives or to act helpless as they leave. Neither a pretend technique, a blank screen, nor a chair dump is a good routine opening gambit. And you don't hypnotize or medicate strangers or go crazy in front of them or put on a show for them. Likewise, you don't sit by calmly when people refuse to take action that would solve the problem about which they continue to complain.

CRUCIAL BUT OFTEN OVERLOOKED POINTS

First, people come into therapy in order to not change. They may be willing to change in a great many ways, as we all must, but they are now under pressure to change in some way they want to avoid. You must find out what change they fear above all and, if possible, at least pretend to join them in protecting against that change. Once that change is secured, all other changes are less threatening.

Second, change precedes insight. It is not necessary for anyone but the therapist to understand the rationale for a change. The change exists as behavior independent of the psychodynamics or the conflicts in the family. You may have to produce change prior to anyone's agreement to it. It may never again be voluntarily repeated, but it is never erased. Once a change has taken place it joins the family repertoire to be called upon whenever it is needed, whether it was initially motivated by insight, negotiation, paradox, or a wet dog.

Third, emotion is not really very important, except as an obstacle to action. Focusing on feelings in therapy gives them an importance that distracts from the business at hand. Listening to people's feelings is a social nicety that people expect from therapists before the therapist dismisses the feelings and goes on to the behavior. It is behavioral change in one individual after another which produces both structural and emotional change. Communication is behavior. So is listening.

Fourth, a family in crisis is far more open to change than a family which does feel the feared change is imminent. Techniques for intensifying crisis are quite different from those for bringing about minimal change in the face of chaos. When adapting other therapists' techniques to your own style, it is important to know the kinds of families and situations they have worked with previously.

Fifth, families are not very fragile. They have already resisted the wisdom and good intentions of everyone they know well, usually for some time prior to their coming to you. You may be able to run them out of therapy with your techniques but you are not likely to hurt them unless you attempt to protect them from one another, from change, or from reality.

Sixth, therapy is not an act of love. Therapists may well love health, the expansion of people's repertoires, or the process of change. Therapists may be as fond of their patients as surgeons are of theirs or as Michelangelo was of marble, but it is destructive for therapists to love their patient's pathology and protect it from change. Therapy is an act of aggression in which you are attacking, however gently and indirectly, the patient's most cherished pathology.

Seventh, while it does help keep families in therapy for them to like the therapist and vice versa, affection for the therapist may not contribute much to the successful outcome of the therapy. How well the family members like the therapist may not be related to how well they will like themselves after the therapy is over. If the relationship between you and the family is very good, but no change is taking place, you may do a kamikaze maneuver as a last resort. You may make yourself sufficiently obnoxious to drive the family out of therapy, but with an unforgettable clarity about what they have to do to avoid further therapy.

Eighth, most of the problems in the world are produced less by pathology in the family or in an individual than by misinformation with which people have bravely struggled onward. Your techniques are infinitely less important to you or to your patients than your good sense and good judgment.

Ninth, techniques are for occasional use. Most of the time a therapist like John Weakland, known for unobtrusive subtlety, may operate little differently from a therapist like Maurizio Andolfi, known for theatrics. There is a difference in style between different therapists, but that may be simply a matter of personality. The techniques of family therapy are available to therapists of every style.

Tenth, therapy may be seen as a process by which the therapist's sanity is transferred to the patient. The therapist calmly refuses to see the problem emotionally and instead takes a practical view, which he or she reveals to the family. This cannot take place if the therapist is acting irrationally or even emotionally to the problem. So you must not compromise your sane position frivolously. There are moments, however, when your unexpected illogic, or emotionality, or activeness, or other unexpected behavior can have a powerful impact. This is only possible if the family already trusts your sanity, your calm, your objectivity. Irrational techniques, from paradox to wet cocker spaniels, have their impact in the contrast to your usual approach.

In unraveling the dazzling array of crises inherent in the human comedy, a full armamentarium of techniques should be available to all therapists for occasional use when straightforward approaches bog down. The infrequency with which such techniques are required may be an indication of the therapist's skill. The therapist's willingness to use such techniques on those rare occasions when nothing else works may be an indication of the therapist's resourcefulness.

SECTION II

Crises of Marriage

You can't be married and right at the same time.

—Quote from someone married

Any marriage, happy or unhappy, is infinitely more interesting and
significant than any romance, however passionate.

—W. H. Auden

CHAPTER 4

The Nature and Transitions
of Marriage

ALL OR NOTHING

S WIMMING INSTRUCTORS who teach drown-proofing have learned that
drowning occurs when people are afraid of the water and struggle to stay
above it. If they could go ahead and immerse themselves in the water, they
would find they could float securely, breath comfortably, and relax totally.
The effort while in the water to keep from being engulfed by it is exhausting
and potentially fatal.

Marriage is frightening. Many drown rather than surrender themselves
to it. They try to protect themselves from it or win at it, and are therefore
doomed to failure at such a simple but completely engulfing state.

Marriages fail about as often as they succeed. Marriage is clearly fragile
and crisis prone. People couple and marry and divorce, blaming it on the
nature of marriage, or the nature of the "opposite" sex, or the nature of the

specific partner, or the time in life when they married, or the chemistry, or the stars, or falling out of love.

Few people are trained at marriage, or even think they need to be. They are told, "When the right one comes along, you'll know, and it will happen, and you'll live happily ever after." Society somehow conveys that marriage works by magic if it is between the "right" people, and if it doesn't work that means it was between the "wrong" people, who just weren't "right" for one another.

People come into marriage with patterns and expectations based upon their own previous family experience, usually their parents' marriages, which were kept somewhat private from them. If the parents' marriage was openly conflictual, it's unlikely that anyone was sufficiently objective for the children to receive helpful instruction in what works and what doesn't. If the parents went through several marriages, the children may have learned something about the impermanence of relationships or even picked up a few pointers about what to watch out for. The children of divorced families seem more likely to divorce. They may not have learned how to solve marital problems, but they have learned how to escape them.

Theoretically, previously married people should be better able to succeed at marriage than novices. They are older and wiser and are making more mature choices with appropriate caution. It does not seem to work out that way. The divorce rate for second marriages is actually higher than for first. Clinicians notice how frequently people marry the same person over and over again. It makes one think that people don't learn from their own marriages.

So people go into marriage bright-eyed and bushy-tailed, no matter how many marriages of their own and their parents they've suffered through. They hope this one will be different because they have finally found the "perfect" person. They've found someone who is either just like or totally unlike their parents or whoever. Then they react in horror when they find some quality that reminds them of their mother or their first husband or their second stepfather or whoever. They have not learned that marriage partners are not made in heaven but are the product of on-the-job training. And the on-the-job training of marriage is not very romantic.

WHATEVER WON'T BEND WILL BREAK

Marriage is most crisis prone when it is least flexible. Inflexibilities are most prevalent when the marriage involves rigidly gendered people, when it depends on the unvarying emotional high of romance, or when there is no network of supportive functional and emotional relationships to bolster the marriage and permit flexibility. Unfortunately, the very factors that make courtship intense — romance, isolation of the couple, and strong gender differences — make marriage hazardous.

Gender and Crisis Proneness

Marriage takes place between one male and female. Each has been raised to be one-half of a couple, and therefore an incomplete human being. Children are prepared for the extremely important courtship rituals as they are molded into the stereotypes of their gender. In the past, boys were prepared to be tough and sure, invulnerable, omnicompetent, unafraid to the point of being unemotional. They may well have been permitted or even encouraged—by their families, their peers, their models, and society—to be coarse, vulgar, physical, omnisexual, and dominating. The traditional masculine stereotype, when taken literally, produced something close to an obsessive-compulsive psychopathic workaholic tyrant. Girls were taught to be passive, helpful, functionally constricted, emotionally romantic, well-mannered, self-sacrificing, etc. They were trained to control relationships without letting their power show, while loyally nurturing men and boosting their confidence. The feminine stereotype, when taken literally, came close to being a passive-aggressive guilt-producing hysteric martyr and victim. Women were required to notice relationships; men were forbidden from doing so. Men were required to compete in every situation; women were forbidden from doing so directly. Anyone who became a complete person after gender training did so by accident. Those who failed to achieve their gender ideal may have gone through life ashamed and insecure. But those who achieved their gender stereotype were unfit for relationships yet unable to survive without them.

Gender stereotypes are supposed to be related to actual biological differences between males and females. These differences are, for the most part, real, however slight. Gender is more decisively a set of cultural conventions, greatly influenced by ethnicity, religion, politics, and economics. The stereotypes have softened in recent years, and they may soften further, but we are left with generations of men and women who have been strongly gendered and are disoriented by the changes in gender expectations of recent years. And we kid ourselves when we think that the softening of gender stereotypes has reached all segments of the society. We are still producing men and women crippled by their excessive sense of gender.

Gender training may do a better job of preparing people for courtship than for life; in fact, people who learn their gender roles too well may be unable to share life's experiences with someone who has received such totally different gender training. They are prepared instead for a stereotyped dance in which each performs his and her expected gender-based role, and does so automatically, independently, and impersonally. Gender stereotypes are impersonal, therefore dehumanizing. Marriage may not become personal enough to work until the gender boundaries are breached, and that is frightening because little boys and little girls have been taught that shame and ridicule await those who fail to live up to the stereotypical gender ideal.

Furthermore, if people think of their partner as "a man" or "a woman" rather than as a fellow human being, and they expect certain behavior based upon that gender distinction, they may be confused, disappointed, even indignant, when they discover the real human being beneath the gender stereotype. There are those who are so angry with the "opposite" sex that they ignore the human being and only see the stereotype. They end up believing that marriage is either "a male plot to exploit women" or "a female plot to enslave men." Such marriages don't work well.

Gender relationships cannot be truly equal so long as the economy makes divorce more disadvantageous economically for women than for men, and fashion determines that middle-aged men are considered more desirable marriage partners than middle-aged women. Women may not be able to achieve equality within marriage, but they are even less able to do so outside marriage. Our current gender arrangements mean that women must value their marriages more than men do — an inherent inequality.

These gender arrangements are in flux. The process of reevaluation and change in gender and marriage produces continuous conflict, especially when a female, who is trained to be aware of relationships, tries to engage a male, who is trained to follow rules and not notice anything so personal as relationships, not to give in to women, and not to lose any contest.

Perceived inequality between marriage partners weakens the marriage and increases the likelihood of resentment and rebellion. Even an equal relationship is perceived as unequal by those who expect their gender to be more equal than the other. If either the male or the female measures gender performance on how well one dominates the other, equality is intolerable. Strict gender roles make the marriage inflexible, and therefore crisis prone. Flexibility in gender roles increases marital adaptability and increases the openness of marital conflict, which some people find intolerable.

Romance and Crisis Proneness

Another problem with marriage is romance, which seduces people into expecting too much. Romance is wonderful. It smells like a new car and fades about as fast. But it has nothing to do with real life. Most people of marriageable age have not learned the difference between love and romance — some never do.

A romance, according to Webster, is "a fictitious and wonderful tale," therefore "an experience embodying the quality of picturesque unusualness." Obviously such experiences, however exciting, are not quite sane. However picturesquely unusual the bottom of the Grand Canyon or the top of Mr. Everest or a day at the circus, few would choose to live there. Yet society has decreed that romance should be the basis for choosing a partner for life. When people are "swept off their feet," especially by a romantic, i.e., picturesquely unusual, stranger, the intensity is so exciting that they sign on for life.

They are *in-love*, personalizing this romantic excitement and hoping marriage will make it permanent. In-love is, of course, a form of temporary insanity. Kubie (1956) describes being in love as "an obsessional state driven in part by anger." Since the intensity of the romantic excitement is directly proportional to the picturesqueness and uniqueness—and therefore the inappropriateness—of the relationship, the least workable matches are the most intense.

Many people want the magic of romance more than they want to be married. You can't have both—one is fleeting, the other forever. Inflexible romanticists cannot tolerate the intrusion of "unloving" or "uncaring" emotions; therefore, anger becomes a crisis so intense that it overshadows the problem the anger was about, thus making problem-solving impossible. Some try to keep the magic alive by avoiding the mundanity of practical reality, instead stirring up startling and disorienting experiences to provide a picturesquely unusual setting for the increasingly mundane relationship. It may hold things together, but the cost is someone's or everyone's sanity.

Isolation and Crisis Proneness

The human animal seems to be, in its natural state, a small group hunter, living communally. While monogamy seems to be natural, the nuclear family as a totally separate, independent functional and emotional unit is not natural. Therefore it takes some work.

The nuclear family as the societal ideal is fairly recent in the world's history. The nuclear family is now isolated from extended family, as well as from the small community or neighborhood of people who share a common culture, know one another personally, and concern themselves with one another's lives. Extended family and community offer support, buffers, and constraints that bolster the vital institutions, including marriage. The human animal does not tolerate anonymity, and when cut off from community and family, becomes demoralized and easily corrupted. In short, he deteriorates.

A nuclear family cannot provide all the functions required by its members. This is obvious for instrumental functioning, but it is equally true for emotional functioning. Whatever made us decide that it was good for people's mental health to break away from the constraints of family and community, and to give in to our impulses, especially the sexual ones? That trend has been a disaster. It has put all the burden on marriage, and particularly on wives, to provide cultural continuity, restraint, stability, and whatever else the community of friends and relatives used to provide. Expectably the experiment has failed.

When a couple depends exclusively on one another for everything, the deficiencies of each will become both apparent and important, and the talents of each will be less respected and more taken for granted. In a state of such interdependency, dissatisfaction will be greater and conflict more likely. But conflict resolution will be more difficult, because distance becomes unbearable since the couple is already isolated. Also, outside sources of support, outside "intimates," are likely not to be part of the community or family which is buffering the marriage. They may support the expediency of giving up the marriage rather than going to the trouble of repairing it. To those who are not personally involved it may seem reasonable and efficient to discard or exchange marriages as one would other pieces of defective or outdated equipment. In the absence of other family members in the arena, there is the temptation to establish the necessary intimacies outside the marriage, when they are needed, by sexualizing a casual relationship to make it more instantly intimate.

Life's lonely group is divergent and includes those who are unhappy and those who fear sharing control with others. Marriage rarely helps them, but they may still try it. One has to be fairly healthy to make a marriage work, yet people often marry for the very reason that they are not healthy and marriage seems a way to avoid personal wholeness. Romantics, adolescents, psychopaths, and people who are running away from home or looking for a new and better parent to marry, but may not do it very effectively or for very long. Depressives, who find life painful and exhausting, alcoholics, whose life is not their fault, obsessives, who must have everything just their way, paranoids, who can't be wrong, phobics, who must be made to face life — these people may want to be married so someone will take care of them and protect them from having to do it for themselves, but they aren't likely to want to give as much as they want to receive. Give-and-take is impossible with such people. Framo points out the confusing literature on marriage in which "it has been said by some that no one ever cured himself of a neurosis by marrying and that the neurotic problems of the two marriage partners are cumulative; on the other hand, others say that a marriage by virtue of its being unhappy can mask or prevent the emergence of a neurosis, or that the marriage relationship may embody compensatory mechanisms for seriously disturbed partners."

We naively assumed that people want equality in their marriages. Equality is an extremely sophisticated concept that requires emotional security and maturity and differentiation. Instead, many people see marriage as a contest, in which one partner wins and the other loses. They can't see that either they both win or they both lose. They want to be the one who wins at the marriage or at least make sure they don't lose. To that end, they tolerate glaring defects in their partners, defects that produce an aura of dependency, proof that they are needed more than they need. But they may not tolerate defects which give their partner a seeming advantage. People can tolerate great stupidity, cruelty, and even psychosis in a spouse, but may not tolerate thoughtlessness or nonchalant independence. The winner at the marriage contest is, apparently, the one who can best escape, and therefore has nothing to prove by doing so.

It cannot even be assumed that people want to be happy. Most people go to a great deal of trouble to be unhappily married — it is a cherished state in our society, as it grants one maximum freedom and plenty to talk about. Those who admit to being happily married are considered socially subversive — they make everyone else feel ashamed.

THE DEVELOPMENTAL CRISIS POINTS OF MARRIAGE

While the institution of marriage is inherently crisis prone, there are certain points in the development of a marital relationship which make crisis more likely, if not inevitable. These turning points are documented in Carter and McGoldrick's *The Family Life Cycle*, and have been popularized in Gail Sheehy's *Passages*. At these points, one partner may change, confusing and alarming the other partner and triggering a developmental crisis.

Falling in Love

Someone measured and found that couples talk to one another most on the third date and in the year before the divorce. There is a crisis in all courtship relationships around that third date, when one partner begins to feel an attachment first. If the other has not yet started to have romantic notions, the relationship may begin to get confusing and quite sticky. Someone has to acknowledge first that what is being felt may be "LOVE." Saying "I love you" is terrifying, not saying it is also terrifying, and not hearing it in return is grounds for suicide. Insecure people may fall apart early in a relationship, as they fear their need for love is not going to be met. They are not particularly concerned with the quality of their own loving or the needs of the other person, but only with whether the other will give them the love they fear they'll never get.

Treating insecure individuals who are out there dating can be nerve-wracking. Each day they wait for the loving response they want so badly. They often operate as if the entire "opposite" sex gets together daily to determine their relative desirability, with their date reacting to them according to their official rating. So if this person does not fall in love with them on this day, they are doomed forever to a life of loneliness and degradation. Any sane person who gets a whiff of this desperation is likely to cut and run. Getting stood up by a date is, for many, a greater crisis than terminal cancer. Most people grow up and are never again so panicky about the question of whether they are loved, but some feel the same insecurity daily and need that daily reassurance that they are indeed loved, no matter what they have or have not done.

Prenuptial Panic

If a man and woman do get past the "third date panic" and fall in love more or less at the same time, they will eventually get close to marriage. At this point, just before getting married, most men and increasing numbers of women will suddenly stop the courtship and consider the implications. He (usually) may overtly or covertly "cool" the relationship for a while. It is unlikely that both partners will experience this cooling at the same moment, so she will be jarred by it. The cooling is an effort to step back and see if he still owns himself, still can control his own life and destiny and particularly the distance he puts between himself and his loved one. Obviously, if his fiancée reacts to his coolness by panicking and pulling him tighter, his experiment has failed and he realizes he is losing himself in the relationship. He may then continue backing away from his loved one.

The woman who panics when a man gets a bit distant is accurately known as a "goodbye girl." Increasingly, it is the woman who fears marriage and the man who is eager for it, so the woman puts distance between them and we see "goodbye guys." The more insecure these guys are, and the younger, more dependent, and more unsuitable the girls they hover over and try to control, the more surely the girl will become frightened and back off.

The End of the Romance

Typically the romantic haze continues to disorient the spouses for months, until they have been married for a while. If the romance has cooled before the marriage, the wedding may still take place but one or both partners may recall that they "knew it was wrong." Some people never really feel a great deal of romance about their marriage, and don't think they should have. For them there is no crisis. But for most, the loss of that bright, shiny romantic glow is a bit sad. They begin to notice that their spouse is less wonderful than they had thought. They don't feel the sexual intensity. They may even be bored. They may be irritated by the human frailties of their partner, even by the simple humanness. They might prefer to spend an evening with their friends. They may wonder if they have made an error in marrying at all, or marrying this person in particular. Sometimes the relationship is good enough for both to acknowledge the *end of the romance*, and see it as the *beginning of the marriage*. If they see the cooling of their ardor as a betrayal, or as a problem, they may try to keep up the romantic atmosphere, which can only be irritating to all concerned. There are a few people who panic when the romance ends. They either dismiss the spouse as defective or run to a new relationship in which they can hope for a permanent romantic high.

Those who need the constant stimulation of hot romance appear to be dangerously psychopathic, but they seem to have a certain appeal and no difficulty finding partners to keep life in a continual cyclical uproar. Obviously marriage cannot provide a constant state of romance, and people who are addicted to romance cannot maintain a marriage. But everyone who marries doesn't know that. And some don't learn it even after many marriages.

The Beginning of the Family

The beginning of the family often comes along with the end of the romance. At some point the haze clears and the spouses become aware that they are part of something bigger than just their coupleship. In the past, many women were pregnant when they married and so couples were acutely aware of impending parenthood. Now, many people seem to have children before marriage — if not before marriage at all, at least before this marriage. But for those who do have a choice about having children, the decision can be conflictual. The reality can be disconcerting. And it is not only children who expand the couple into a family. The spouses must also become aware of their families of origin and the impact of those families on the marriage.

When two people marry they may not realize that they each remain very much a part of their family of origin. Often even more contact is expected now that they have grown up and settled down. The two families of origin may be very different in patterns and values, as well as in their expectations of the new couple. And the two families are not likely to be compatible; sometimes that does happen and makes it all much easier, but who is concerned with making the new couple's life easier? Some of the biggest fights couples ever have are over the conflicting expectations of their two (or more) sets of parents over the wedding arrangements. And that is followed in due time with conflict over the plans for the first Christmas or the naming of the children. The new couple is being forced to differentiate as a new family rather than a branch of the old family. This is a painful amputation, and one filled with crisis. If it is compromised, it merely postpones and aggravates the necessary procedures.

The spouses must be able to put their marriage first, without having to break off with their families of origin. They must not let the two families of origin cut them off from one another, from their parental families, or from their in-laws. Some people set up tests of love to see who they can stop speaking to whom. The jealousy through this procedure can become lethal. come lethal.

Even if relationships with both families can be kept cordial and correct, or even intimate and involved, the couple must still sort out questions of style and values. This amounts to choosing the patterns of one family or another. It can become insulting, and it can hurt. Each spouse is required to look critically at his or her own family and own origins to decide what should be kept and what should be discarded.

Relationships with friends also change after marriage. It is not easy, or safe, to maintain closeness to someone unacceptable or threatening or repugnant to one's new spouse. It can hurt to have to distance a friend, but it may hurt even more to have to go through life defending an offensive friendship. Marriages need friends who will bolster the marriage — if the marriage and the friend are incompatible, the friend must be distanced. But if all friends are incompatible with the marriage, it may be well to examine the marriage. As the marriage goes through this pruning stage, it can be isolating and lonely, and it is easy to question whether it is worth it.

Parenting

The question of whether the marriage is worth it is a question that people can't afford to answer if they are too busy with raising children. That is not an unmixed blessing: Parenthood stabilizes a marriage but parenthood also traps the parents. Becoming a parent is the clearest possible evidence that someone has moved from the child generation to the adult generation and must, therefore, give up childish behavior. Our society romanticizes childish behavior and particularly adolescent behavior. This puts the new parent in the unappealing position of having to give up all that is considered fun in life in order to become a parent and make sacrifices so the next generation can have all the fun. It is not surprising that one or both parents will bitterly resent the little brat for getting to be a child while he or she is forced to be a grownup. Sometimes both parents will resent adulthood equally, and they will join forces to protect themselves from the child, who may be battered or abandoned or left with others while the couple rebels against the child as they did against their parents or teachers or bosses or anyone else who tried to take their childhood away and make them be adults before their chosen time.

Parenthood changes marriage drastically. This most dramatic stress in the stages of marital development will be explored in Chapter 9.

Sex Drops Off

Sex is important in marriage. It can cover a multitude of sins. It can be the glue when things are drifting apart, the lubrication over the rough spots, the cushioning for the bumps. If sex is used as a reward for getting everything else right, the marriage loses its flexibility and stability. Of course, sex only provides those functions if there is sexual exclusivity. Sex has no fastening function in those marriages in which the couple gets around to having sex with one another when the preferred partners are unavailable or when everything just works out unusually well.

In previous generations, girls were encouraged to "save themselves until marriage." Little girls were taught that men who desired them sexually were being insulting and degrading to them and obviously bore them ill will. A girl would be assured that she would know when a man truly loved her, as he would make no effort to have sex with her. Even after the marriage, a sexual overture would be proof that he didn't love her. Girls were taught, in effect, to marry men who were not sexually attracted to them. The marriages that took place might be sexually incompatible and remain so for unhappy de-

cades, perhaps leading the long-married couple into therapy, perhaps leading to bad sex education for the children.

In the past, couples married without regard for their sexual compatibility.
Even couples who seemed compatible probably weren't. Sex is usually intense at the beginning of a relationship, even if it is neither efficient or
effective. Actually, couples traditionally have enjoyed their sexuality more
during the courtship than in the marriage. Traditionally, boys were required
to push for sex, while girls were supposed to hold back. As a result there was
a lot of romancing and pleasuring and foreplay and not much screwing,
which was usually a lot more fun and orgastic for the girl—and for the boy
too though he didn't realize it. Once they married, there were no barriers, so
sex became frequent and quick and devoid of romancing and pleasuring and
foreplay. It was totally aimed at the screwing—coming, ready or not.

It is not surprising that newlywed women were not too thrilled by marital
sex and developed headaches at the thought. After a year or so, the guy
would grow tired of the rejection, the battle and the lack of response, and
sex would become as frequent as necessary to keep the marriage license in
force.

Birth control permits us to separate sex from reproduction and explore it
for its own joys. However, sociologists say that men are inhibited by women
who are sexually comfortable enough to want to enjoy it. Many women who
want to explore sex find their husbands inhibited by their fear of their own
inadequacy. Many men who want to explore sexuality find their wives inhibited by what they had been taught to be proper ladylike behavior. There are
many women who do not believe it proper for women to be sexually assertive
or adventurous, before or after marriage. There are many men who see sex
as a dirty, rebellious trick brave boys pull on foolish girls. If a girl wants it, it
makes him somehow less masculine, the girl less feminine, and the whole
thing an act of servile obedience rather than the desired act of rebellion.
Most people in our society are far less interested in sex than they are in
maintaining whatever they think is necessary to fulfill the requirements of
membership in their gender. Even if their sexuality must be abandoned, they
must do what they were told was the gender ideal.

Some otherwise normal people are stark raving mad when it comes to sex.
There are people who would risk their marriage or even their life to avoid
doing what is sexually requested of them, but would then risk everything to
do whatever is forbidden. For them sex is freedom. But it serves another
function too, in that it reduces the intensity of their frightening sexual
impulses. People who are sexual "perverts," who expose themselves or who
take up with animals or babies (it is hard to consider anyone perverted
anymore, and the concept of "sexual psychopath" has vanished, as just
about anything people want to do sexually is considered proper, courageous,
and even fashionable unless it takes place with people who haven't heard

about it on TV talk shows, so only babies and animals qualify), are probably no different in their impulses or curiosities than the rest of us, but they are less imaginative in enjoying their fantasies without acting on them. The ideal marital sex is probably between two people who have been turned on by everybody they encountered all day, and saved up all those juices to expend at home, probably without feeling uncomfortable enough about their fantasies to have to spell them out.

Some people consider their sexuality shameful and act accordingly. Rather than sharing and enjoying their fantasies, they keep them secret and go through a crisis when they are revealed. There are, of course, people who just don't like sex. Some insist that they go for years without masturbating and certainly without having sex with another person. Others prefer masturbating and would rather not be bothered with someone else's intrusion into their fantasies. This seems to be a bigger problem among men than women. Some men just don't like sex and stubbornly refuse to have it no matter how much the pressure builds. Of course, once the pressure builds to have sex, they can't possibly do so — that is the way the male equipment works. There are few women who refuse sex completely, perhaps because they have the option of going through it passively, while men don't, or don't think they do.

As men age, many seem to lose their interest in sex, really quite unnecessarily. There is usually no clear physiological reason for this. They probably don't believe this but they tell themselves and their wives it is because of the wife's aging or some other pet complaint. So the wife, feeling repulsive, avoids pursuing the poor guy sexually, and everything dries up. Very soon, he thinks of himself as impotent or over the hill. The human penis, an extraordinarily phobic fellow with a mind of his own, totally refuses to function under pressure. The explanation I use, perhaps not completely scientific but fitting the salient facts, is that male hormones were produced abundantly around the clock when younger, but after the age of 30 or thereabouts they are produced mostly during sexual arousal. Therefore, if men over 30 don't use it they'll lose it. Of course, it is not enough to just have orgasms — the therapy is in the arousal. So couples who are concerned about the man's loss of libido are instructed to go through frequent and prolonged sessions of sexual stimulation, rather than trying for the accustomed desperate quick screw.

Sex, perhaps more than anything else about marriage, needs to be released from the myths that there is a difference between males and females. That doesn't usually happen until there is a crisis of some sort. Sex can be better after that.

Reaching the Summit

There are at least three separate crises of middle life, and they are often confused with one another. The "empty nest," the most dramatic, is discussed in Chapter 11. The "facts of life," the awareness of mortality and the process of growing like one's parents whether one wants to or not, should be the most liberating. "Reaching of summit," with the thought that it is downhill from here, may be the silliest, but in our narcissistic age it is the most popular. This prestigious, but by no means universal, midlife crisis has to do with people, mostly men, discovering that they have limited time to achieve whatever they are going to achieve in life. This is the point in life when people must take stock. Erik Erikson described the "crisis of generativity," the stage of generativity versus stagnation. Freud described the "success neurosis," when someone becomes depressed just at the point of achieving his life goal. Bernard Shaw said it best in *Man and Superman*, "There are two tragedies in life. One is not to get your heart's desire. The other is to get it." In either case, people think about things they have avoided until now, and consider whether this is the life they want for the rest of their life

The introspection is followed by a change. While this may be a renewed surge of ambition, there may be a change of direction toward something less competitive and more connected with the real world. Of course, there may emerge only a decision to avoid the question for a while longer, until after the young lover, the sports car, and the face lift.

This stage has been called "the male menopause," comparing it to the ovarian shutdown that renders a woman no longer fertile, as if no one can produce further after midlife. That comparison overlooks the reality that women after menopause are freer to be sexual, to pursue careers they had interrupted or postponed previously, and to fulfill whatever frustrated ambitions and dreams. There was a time, not too many decades ago, when women valued themselves, and were valued, largely for their reproductive function. Then menopause was a point of desolate barrenness and the end of usefulness and sense of worth, especially if it coincided with an empty nest. That has all changed and most women experience menopause as a part of the liberation process. Postmenopausal women are having the best years of their lives, but are not considered attractive by men going through their male menopause and struggling to hold off any signs of advancing age in themselves or in their partners. If one spouse decides to settle into a less pressured life and the other wants to keep up the struggle against age, a severe marital maladjustment occurs. A menopausal man and a menopausal woman are temporarily incompatible.

Men at the summit of their lives, whether their summit is very high or not, are likely to be depressed and self-centered and very difficult to live with. Their lives have been directed toward achieving success by whatever standards their parents set for success, which probably did not take their comfort or happiness into account. For the greater good of all, they need permission to fail and to head downhill. Unfortunately, they don't realize that is the best part of all. If they have the permission, whether they accept that option or not, all that follows can get better and better.

The Facts of Life

This may or may not coincide with the midlife crisis, while it usually comes later, it may even come earlier. It is a most important and often overlooked crisis, and often a very painful one. At some point in the course of the marriage, people come to grips with several painful realities. They are imperfect, their spouse is imperfect, their children are imperfect, they are not going to conquer the world, they are getting relatively poorer and older and uglier and shorter and fatter and less desired by others for any purpose — and it will all get worse.

This seems to occur to people as their parents begin to fail and die and they realize what is in store for them. Or it may occur as they look in a mirror or at their children and realize that they are turning into their parents. So far, they've gotten freer and more powerful every year, and it has all been uphill. Suddenly, they see they've passed their prime. At this point, they have to forgive their parents, if they haven't already done so. If they don't accept their position as the parental generation, there is nothing but despair ahead. Geriatric hippies, middle-aged cheerleaders, and over-the-hill play-boys with gold chains and their hair combed carefully over the bald spot are pathetic. They believe they won't grow old if they refuse to grow up.

As with every other stage of development, one spouse enters it first. The entry may be subtle and gradual; in fact, the partners may not notice. Suddenly, one awakens and finds him or herself married to a settled, mature middle-aged person, who is looking forward to growing older rather than struggling to stay young. This realization can be a point of panic. It is often associated with the death or disability of one of the parents, though it can occur with an illness, the death of a friend, or a crucial birthday. Whatever triggers it, it is intimately related to identification with aging or dying parents and the recognition of the way of all flesh.

The effect on the marriage can be drastic, as the partner who values youth panics at being married to someone middle-aged, someone whose powers are declining. The one who ages first may do so comfortable and naturally, while the youth in the marriage fears age is contagious and wants to get distance from this horror. Age is not just associated with dying, or even with weakness and ugliness, but with becoming like one's parents. People who are comfortable with their parents seem comfortable with growing into them. Those whose sense of themselves is still of an adolescent in rebellion may rebel against this fact of life. The only way to guard against becoming your own parent may be to escape an aging spouse, either through divorce or through an affair.

Aging

Eventually everyone must grown old — the alternative is worse. It is hard to do so gracefully though. Life is ridiculously and tragically short for most people. (There are exceptions, such as a cousin of mine who recently died at age 105, having spent 40 years in the back wards of St. Elizabeth's. I don't know, but she may well have thought life too short too.) Our society does not revere age, and no one enjoys its infirmities, although my older patients miss fewer appointments because of illness than school children do. Still, when people begin to grow feeble and can't do what they used to do, but can remember what they used to do better than what they just did, the people around them feel them slipping away. It may be sadder for those who feel left out than for those who are going through it. One spouse generally ends up having to nurse the other spouse, and both generally resent the children for not being more helpful and for not wanting to be around. It would seem a sad time in people's lives, but it usually isn't. There is a liberating freedom from expectation, from struggling, from competition. One gets to be the center of one's own attention.

This is the time of Erikson's crisis of integrity, the stage of integrity versus despair, when people look back at their lives with pride or with regret. Marriages tend to become extremely close, even when things were not so great during better times. Those who distance themselves from one another at this stage seem to suffer severe pangs of regret for doing so. Family is likely to be paramount at this stage. Going through this stage with a grandparent is perhaps the best preparation a child has for the development of his or her own integrity. This can be a lonely time, but not really desperately lonely. It does not seem to take much human contact to satisfy people who are mostly concerned with their own comfort and peace. Perhaps that is why marriages can be so comfortable finally.

People who go around asking such questions come up with the statistics that show this to be the time in life of greatest contentment. It is certainly the time of greatest marital closeness — and everyone knows that happiness is a direct result of marital satisfaction. In the home stretch, people settle in and stop concerning themselves with such insignificant matters as sexual attractiveness, sexual performance, their worldly success, their children's worldly success. Instead they can settle in to concern themselves with the business of the day, being alive and not being alone. It can be a most productive period for productive people.

People who have never been particularly interesting or involved in life tend to become even less so. There are people who sit down when they retire and expect to stay there and be cared for until they die. If a man does that, and his wife dutifully waits on him, she may have a fulltime job for a few years until he dies. She may remember these as the best years of her life and actually miss him for the rest of her life.

It is quite different for a man than for a woman, since the man can expect to die first and to be taken care of while he lives. A woman, who is usually younger than her husband anyway and less likely to remarry when widowed, can look forward to years alone and is quite likely to value his declining years as a last chance for time together. This is the period housewives have been praying for since the children left home. Many couples look forward to these years, plan for them, and are crisis struck only if he dies suddenly or she dies first. Other couples have been unpleasantly married or comfortable with the distance and don't want so much interdependency. They may dread this period and would rather leave the nursing care to someone else.

The crises I see at this stage of life sometimes involve people who are being dragged kicking and screaming into old age and are determined to hold on to all the power they can until the very end. Far more frequently, these crises involve people who are ready to give up power and responsibility, feel their job is not finished, and require permission to go off duty. Instead of anger about the past or anxiety about the future, there may be nothing more pressing in life than the effort to make the present easier and to preserve some dignity until the end.

The painful end of this period comes when one spouse is slipping away more rapidly, when one has Alzheimer's or something else that clouds the ability to respond to the present. Often the couple must separate because the mental state of one endangers the physical state of the other. The children, or grandchildren, may bring in the couple to negotiate a separation, a live-in referee and nurse, or some arrangement that will protect them from one another.

The great secret of successful marriage is to treat all disasters as incidents and none of the incidents as disasters.

— Harold Nicholson

Seldom, or perhaps never, does a marriage develop into an individual relationship smoothly and without crises; there is no coming to consciousness without pain.

— Carl G. Jung, *Contributions to Analytical Psychology*, 1928

CHAPTER 5

The Range of Marital Crises

FROM INCIDENTS TO DISASTERS

MARRIAGE, NO LESS THAN LIFE in general, is just one damned thing after another. And each damned thing can ruffle previously smooth feathers, precipitating a crisis. The greatest danger for the therapist and the couple in therapy is for the therapist to ignore the specifics of stress and the unique inflexibilities of this marriage and try to generalize about marriage. We all have our favorite problems we like to work with, but we can damage the fragile institution of marriage if we attempt to solve a problem the couple doesn't have while ignoring the problem the couple does have.

I have found it useful to think of marital crisis as falling into the four general categories introduced in Chapter 1. No marital crisis fits totally into one or the other of these categories, and eventually the structural inflexibility of every marriage may have to be approached. Nonetheless, this division can provide an orienting structure for the therapist and the couple.

BOLTS FROM THE BLUE

Couples experiencing a bolt from the blue come in with a quite specific problem. Something unexpected and unexpectable has happened and they don't know what to do about it. They can't decide on something or agree on a course of action. Commonly, the stress involves changes in the boundaries or membership of the family. For example, the spouses may discover that one of them is infertile, which raises questions of whether they should adopt children, try artificial insemination, give up on becoming parents, or end the marriage and try again with different partners.

It comes as a great shock to many who are married to previously married partners when their spouses' dimly recollected children run away from their custodial parent and appear on the doorstep to be parented. One parent may be overjoyed, while the other feels invaded and betrayed. Other couples find themselves unexpectedly inheriting siblings, nieces and nephews, or cousins. Should they take these children in? No less disorienting is the arrival of elderly parents needing care and attention.

Sometimes the bolt from the blue is the birth of a severely damaged baby. Should they institutionalize the badly deformed or retarded baby? Menopausal or otherwise unexpected pregnancies might bring up decisions about abortion. Middle-aged couples who thought their parenting days over might find a supposedly grown child bouncing back to them, perhaps schizophrenic or drug-addicted and presumably at home for a fresh start, but perhaps severely crippled or brain-damaged and at home for the duration.

Sudden and unexpected changes in the family's economic status can be extraordinarily disruptive. Marriages invaded by wealth or poverty often fail. The unattractive aspects of poverty are too well-known to belabor. But wealth is bad for marriages too. People who can afford the best of everything may have little experience in compromising and may be unable to compromise their marital expectations either. The sort of people who need to win at everything may eventually win often enough to get rich (or may be miserable if they don't). But they may want to win at marriage too, which ruins everything. Those who want to be wealthy may have little idea how to bring it about and may expect someone else to provide it; they may feel cheated if it does not arrive on schedule. If they feel they are expected to provide unattainable trappings of wealth, they may sense failure and withdraw from those they think they've failed.

There are, of course, other bolts from the blue. A son may go to jail. The family may be evicted. Someone may become disabled.

Most well functioning couples go through innumerable little bolts from the blue without requiring a therapist. Daily they negotiate rules and roles, come to grips with the past and the future, and function under varying levels of closeness and distance, varying capacities, and varying threats to the basic equality of the relationship. They may do this through quid pro quos, trade-offs that maintain the basic fairness and equality. Interestingly, it is the boundary issues that most often bring them to therapy. Expanding the family boundaries affects the balance of equality to a far greater extent than most other crises, even career-based moves. It is therefore natural that in a fair and equal marriage only a boundary decision would require the security of an outside, objective referee.

CASE 5   *The Pleasure of His Company*

Abner seemed like an inappropriate marital choice for Alexandra. She was regal—not only gorgeous but from the grandest of families. She was quite rich and had grown powerful as well. When she finally married, it was a relief, but her choice came as a surprise to her family and friends. Abner was handsome enough, and God knows he was charming and entertaining. But he was poor, and he was a social worker so he always would be poor. And he had no family status. His parents had been hardworking, God-fearing, clean living people, comfortable in their own world and humble enough not to intrude upon Alexandra's. Actually, her family tolerated Abner quite well. They lived her way in her world on her money around her family. There was, however, an ongoing, but only simmering, conflict over children. Abner wanted them and Alexandra was never quite ready, so nothing happened.

Then the crisis came. It took the form of Abner's brother, Leroy. Leroy had disappeared long ago, to everyone's relief. He had always been a problem. He'd spent so much of his adolescence in prison that he never got around to finishing high school and was not literate or civilized enough for most jobs. Lately he'd managed to support himself dealing drugs while living with a prostitute, but she had some expensive habits and his gambling luck deserted him—and so did his girlfriend. He was devastated. He drank and ingested his inventory and felt suicidal. Through his marijuana haze he vaguely recalled a brother who might be able to help out. He called, and Alexandra answered. She'd never met him, so she did the gracious thing and invited him to move in for a while. Abner was disconcerted, with understandable doubts about having Leroy too close. Alexandra treated Abner as a servant but Leroy as an honored guest, and Abner had not spent enough time around the imperious to realize which was the treatment of greater respect. During the first week of Leroy's residence, he discovered the wine cellar and decimated it, becoming even more depressed. Abner thought they needed some help and called me.

I saw the mismatched trio. The impeccably bred Alexandra properly acted as if she saw nothing unusual about this filthy, slimy psychopath beside her. Leroy, barely oriented past his own chaotic brain chemistry, seemed oblivious to any incongruity and offered Alexandra a chaw of tobacco. He talked as if he were home for the duration. Abner was frantic. He tried not to notice who and what Leroy was, but learning to ignore such odors must take generations. My emergency response, as always, was aimed at protecting the marriage, at least long enough to deal with the crisis. So I asked myself whether Leroy's presence would be good for the marriage, rather than whether it would be good for Leroy.

In considering what family members to involve, I decided it was not appropriate to include Leroy as a member of the family. So I quickly divided the trio, sent Abner and Alexandra to the waiting room, and saw the depressed, foggy, intoxicated Leroy. Leroy told the alarming (to me, not to him) story of his underground life and confirmed my initial impressions about his sociopathy, as well as about the current state of his brain chemistry. While his life was most influenced by his all-day, everyday pot habit, his current state of depression was probably attributable to alcohol.

I then saw Alexandra and Abner and attempted to define the family problem. Alexandra really had been envying Abner's career and his opportunities for providing nurturance, and she saw Leroy as a lost soul to be saved. Abner and I saw Alexandra as an amateur soul saver and Leroy as an advanced case. Abner audaciously suggested another solution for Alexandra's quandary—to have a baby. Alexandra warmed to that idea and agreed to consider it. That seemed a somewhat general prescription. The specific prescription had to do with getting Leroy in shape to move out quickly. Leroy was brought back in and the program was outlined.

Specific tasks were assigned. Alexandra, who would be at home with Leroy, agreed to make the liquor cabinet off limits to her brother-in-law and to kick him out if he broke that rule. Abner agreed to take Leroy exercising each evening. Leroy agreed to hunt for a job. The next day Leroy was off alcohol and on antidepressants. There was no negotiation of resistance. Leroy accepted all directives but one—he wouldn't give up his pot, or even be honest about it. As sociopaths do, he nodded agreeably and did what he wanted about it. A week later, he had a job. After another joint session, the couple, acting in concert, loaned him money for an apartment. He moved out and was seen individually for a couple of months; then he drifted off when he found a new girl friend and was too busy to come. He did pay back the money.

Meanwhile Abner and Alexandra used this unique crisis as an opportunity to drop some of the politeness of their relationship and deal more openly about their goals. Alexandra's resistance to having children had indeed been based upon her sense of the marriage's impermanence, rather than upon a belief that Abner wasn't good enough. As Abner became less wishy-washy about the future and pushed more impatiently, she began to relax enough to set some permanent goals. Family of origin work helped us understand why Alexandra had chosen Abner, and why Abner had cringed so before her even after she'd chosen him. Termination was soft—this crisis had opened them up, so that each new crisis could further the process of change.

DEVELOPMENTAL CRISES OF MARRIAGE

Marriage changes over time, passing through the stages outlined in Chapter 4. When people understand the life cycle of marriage, they don't get too alarmed by the various stages as they appear and unfold. But people seek constancy, and find change disruptive, and threatening, insulting, and dangerous. They want their marriage just as it was and may leave it rather than accept the inevitable and unavoidable changes that occur over time. One spouse changes, the other resists angrily and anxiously, and crisis results.

The characteristic reactions to the developmental stages are different at each stage. And of course the nature of the individuals and the structure of the marriage will play a part. In general, the more people take their marriage for granted, the more they will feel unfairly treated by these changes. Many enjoy the luxury of a marriage they aren't required to notice. When a developmental change forces them to take notice, they may not like what they see. Ongoing inflexibilities, previously accepted or ignored, are suddenly highlighted. There may be frantic blaming at such times; "you've changed!" may be hurled at a partner as accusation of extreme disloyalty.

There really are expectable phases in marriage, and one spouse tends to enter the phase first; then both partners experience distance and conflict, as if they are going in different directions. If an ingenious or experienced therapist can define the syndrome in a way that makes sense to the couple, the outcome can be predicted and thereby influenced. A diagnosis like this is powerful, a self-fulfilling prophecy, and it makes things happen, so there must be clarity about the symbolism of the diagnosis to the couple. A diagnosis of a developmental crisis is soothingly normalizing and permits both partners to take the problem less personally.

Of course, there are dangers in treating a serious character defect as a "phase he's going through," but there is little harm in starting off that way. There are even some benefits to that as a starting point. Someone is performing some action that is bothering someone else. Some people don't like being blamed, being treated as if they do indeed have control over what they do and don't do. They much prefer to treat their misdeeds as if they could not help them. They may arrange their lives around the freedom to do bad things without having to be considered "bad." Whatever they do is somebody else's fault: "He did A, therefore it is not my fault that I did B," a cute perversion of systems thinking.

The classic way of proving oneself blameless, short of believing that "the devil made me do it," is to declare oneself mentally ill. Considering behavior "sick" implies that it is outside the perpetrator's control and calls on everyone to demonstrate sensitivity and compassion by tolerating the intolerable. But calling someone's behavior a "phase" means it isn't bad in intent, though it certainly is destructive and obnoxious in effect. In other words,

"We won't blame you for acting like an ass if you will just go ahead and get it over with fast."

Obviously this trick only works when the offending behavior is fairly recent—a phase that lasts too long is something else entirely. But if the behavior fits the time limits of a developmental crisis, it can be face-saving, as well as more accurate, to so define it.

When a developmental crisis occurs, everything about the marriage must be negotiated. What emerges is a quite different marriage. The therapist must be careful not to side with the old patterns, but not to endorse the changes too enthusiastically either. The therapist, as always, maintains neutrality by siding both with the marriage and with optimism about change. Marriage and change may seem to be in conflict, and at times they are incompatible, but if the changes and the marriage are both understood they usually can be accommodated. However, the process requires more communication and intimacy than some marriages can comfortably bear.

CASE 6   *A Real, Live, Growing Doll*

Barbi was rumored to have looked just like Marilyn Monroe some 50 pounds and 20 years ago when she married Bartram. He was the handsomest doctor at the hospital, though a little uncommunicative even for a pathologist. She'd loved him so. She kept their little house and took care of their little babies and was just the sort of mother she imagined her mother would have been if she hadn't drank so much. And Bartram sat in the chair and sucked on his pipe and it was soooo romantic. Barbi didn't know why she got depressed after the fifth baby came, but she did, and her obstetrician suggested that Bartram might help her out with all the babies. She'd never seen the usually taciturn Bartram so angry. He got her a nurse instead. Sometimes it was hard for her to be as bright and cheery as he liked her to be, so she'd have a few drinks to prepare for him. She cooked magnificently, drunk or sober, and managed to take care of everything, so that Bartram never had to worry about any of it. He barely even had to see the children. He did complain a bit about her weight and put her on diet pills, which she found useless for weight control but great for setting just the right mood for Bartram's nightly homecoming. It was a wonderful marriage—everything he'd dreamed of.

They were both surprised when she got depressed again. Bartram had heard about these psychiatrists who seduce their patients, so he arranged for her to see a female psychiatrist. She joined a women's group and enrolled in law school. Three years later she opened her law office, retired from the kitchen, and informed Bartram she'd had her turn with the kids and the house—it was all his now. The time couldn't have been worse—Bartram was in the midst of writing his book (not that anyone would ever read it, but it was helpful for getting tenure at the medical school, and his medical school roommate had written a book). He appealed to her to postpone her liberation until he'd achieved his fame. She laughed at him — she'd never done that before. He begged her to consider the children. She arranged therapy for all five of them. He raged helplessly. She wouldn't turn back. The household ceased to function, the couple ceased to speak, and the children drifted. He stormed helplessly. She ignored him.

The immediate crisis occurred when Bartram refused to take the sick cat to the vet, insisting it was Barbi's job, and she refused, insisting it was his, and the cat vomited and died. The children went wild and blamed her, since she was the mother and it was the mother's job to do these things. She cried and felt suicidal and threatened to leave. For the first time, Bartram panicked and agreed to therapy.

He called — a good sign. My emergency response was, as always, to join the marriage, to reassure them both that marriage can survive with two full-scale people. Barbi was skittish about the therapy, so I had to reassure her that I was not going to send her back to the kitchen, no matter how tightly Bartram and the kids lined up against her. I decided not to involve the whole family, and to see the kids just once. I did not want to align myself with the children, as they were totally opposed to their mother's emancipation in view of their father's domestic incompetence. (They liked him but saw him as merely decorative.)

I then defined the crisis as a stage not in Barbi's development but in Bartram's. She already knew how to function skillfully at home and out in the world. His refusal to learn domestic skills was endangering his family — they'd all be lost without her. I blamed her for going through these changes without telling Bartram. I even blamed her for not having taught him how to be a total human being when he was younger and could do it more gracefully.

The general prescriptions involved going to movies together and having her explain to him how gender issues have changed over the past 20 years, while he was in his pathology lab seeing people only after they'd died. Male and female bodies had changed little over the decades, so how was he to have known that their roles had changed?

The specific prescription was severalfold. First, Barbi was to stop threatening the marriage — that was too hard on her, him, and the kids. He agreed to do anything if she'd just stay. Second, she was to turn over most domestic chores to him, with temporary supervision. Third, he was to reassure the children that it was OK for him to do these things and to tell them to come to him for everything. He was to make sure he was available to them at his office. Fourth, Barbi was to cook one meal for the family each week, on Sunday night. This would be a festive occasion, a chance for Bartram to lavish praise on Barbi. Fifth, they were to join a couples group so he could learn to be a human being and she could learn to sympathize with his developmental crisis.

I expected that the resistance would show up and require negotiation in the couples group and did. Bartram displayed an amazing array of techniques to try to scare her back into subservience. He gradually came to like his new relationships, and as he did Barbara (as he now called her) came to like him again. However, termination may never be total.

CARETAKER CRISES

Therapists expect change and improvement in competence. Caretakers may not expect increased competence and may even settle for or value incompetence. Caretakers can be professional or amateur; however, the most crisis prone situations occur when an amateur caretaker is struggling and competing with a professional therapist to prevent anything therapeutic from moving someone toward competence.

Some marriages are actually caretaker arrangements. The word "marriage" is best reserved for those relationships that are, at least in spirit, more or less equal. Some marriages are determinedly unequal and are therefore particularly inflexible and crisis prone. The inflexibility is named and institutionalized. Some partners are not equal — not even close. Their marriages may not even maintain the semblance of negotiation and trade-offs between equals. There is no quid pro quo. Some like it that way and keep it that way. The couple may have entered marriage with the understanding that it would not be equal, as when a rich old man hires a young female nurse by marrying her. Or when a couple makes a prenuptial agreement to the effect that one owns everything and the other nothing. Some people just don't want to share their lives with anyone else. They won't even let someone else play with their toys.

More commonly, people are attracted to chronically needy depressives or schizophrenics. "He (she) needed me" is a common explanation for why a person married someone rather thoroughly messed up, incompetent, dependent and crisis prone. People who are struggling out of their own adolescence and messy family situations may find themselves attracted to others who seem to be only a few steps behind in the same process. However, many of the kids who marry prematurely are not just slow developers, but very crazy; they are looking for some security and stability in the institution of marriage, but they are so insecure and unstable themselves they can only find comfort with others no better off than themselves. Sanity is not much valued until later in life — it seems too much like parental behavior to be popular in adolescence. Like clean clothes on singers, it implies something innately boring or civilized.

People who are overly impressed with gender differences may find the other gender so mysterious and intimidating that they can't accurately assess the character or even the sanity of a member of the other gender — all men or all women are equally frightening. It is particularly difficult for genderists to accurately assess such stereotypical extremes as a brutal, paranoid man or a psychopathic, hysterical woman. Naive people may find such gender-related psychopathology to be in some bizarre way sexy, ergo attractive and desirable. Thinking they've gotten hold of the cream of the gender crop, they marry quite sick people.

Others marry emotionally damaged people who reminded them of their similarly afflicted parents. The marriage then represents another in their lifelong series of exercises in mastery of the affliction in question. Rescue fantasies run rampant. For instance, the children of alcoholics tend to marry alcoholics over and over again. Some guilt-ridden people marry crazy people in order to make life difficult for themselves, much as one would wear a hair shirt.

A marriage to an incompetent person is threatened by any increase in the sanity of either the competent or the incompetent spouse. Successful therapy may bring a merciful end to these irremediably unequal marriages, but not before inducing an horrendous crisis. Of course, the therapist may misunderstand the quid pro quo of the situation and be considerably more alarmed by the inequality than either spouse. It is tempting to jump in to protect one spouse from the other. Much delicacy is required to avoid threatening a marriage while increasing the competence of each partner at unavoidably different rates.

One spouse's incompetence is not always part of the initial marital bargain. Some people have a workable marriage for years and indeed merge their lives; then one tragically slips out of sanity. Usually in longstanding marriages both will try to hold the marriage together, at least after the first psychotic episode. If it seems unique — and there is every effort to make it seem unique — it may be reacted to as if it were a bolt from the blue. Yet, even if recovery seems practically complete, there results an unavoidable inequality, with one spouse always subtly suspect and the other nursily vigilant. The enduring marriage requires focus on the uniqueness of the episode. If that sense of uniqueness is lost by recurrence, the marriage becomes a caretaker arrangement, which may be uncomfortable for both partners.

If a spouse chooses to remain in a marriage to an imperfect partner with a chronic or recurrent disability of whatever degree, that spouse is going to have to do some caretaking. Caretaking skills should be in everyone's trousseau — everyone, male or female, must enter marriage with the expectation of doing his or her share of caretaking over a lifetime. Remember "richer or poorer, in sickness or in health?" Caretaking can be gratifying, especially if one feels appreciated for it. If one is being blamed instead of appreciated, caretaking can be an incredible burden.

Marriages with an incompetent member are understandably crisis prone. The marriage may be thrown into crisis when the patient-spouse gets worse, commands an even larger share of the caretaker-spouse's attention, or ceases to provide whatever small contribution has become customary. If the patient-spouse is particularly helpless or demanding or unpredictable, the caretaker-spouse needs considerable support and a second level of caretakers to care for the caretaker-spouse. Any failure in that backup system may trigger a crisis. Bernheim and Lehman (1985) outline the nuts and bolts of treating caretaker marriages. It is different, and it is delicate.

Most caretaker relationships are thoroughly benign and involve an amateur caretaker with the noblest of souls and a faulty instruction book. Crises occur when one spouse must take care of the other and doesn't know how. There are supposed to be professional experts who can explain the nature of, for instance, schizophrenia and what the spouse can do that would make it better or worse. If the therapist can't explain the condition and the therapy, therapy becomes confusing and deservedly suspect. When the mental health professions can't figure out how to treat schizophrenia, it seems grotesque to blame a family member for not figuring it out.

Family therapists tend to treat the family members as co-patients and confound or paradox them without enlightening them. It can never be assumed that the caretaker-spouse has been given any sensible idea of how to provide the indicated care. And without operational instructions, the caretaker-spouse is likely to come up with some properly ignorant ways of dealing with the problem and then to find the whole business frustrating as well as unsuccessful. Therapy for caretaker-spouses may provide little support or supervision, instead causing blame and guilt and anger. It may undermine the nobility of the caretaker-spouse's effort, thereby threatening a marriage already made tenuous by the patient-spouse's condition.

Therapists may set out to destroy marriages they know little about. They may be under the sway of theories that assume symptoms arise from the other spouse's need for the symptoms; ergo, stamp out mental illness by stomping on marriage. And why not? It's been traditional to treat children of any age by stomping on mothers.

Competent spouses, theoretically, can fire incompetent professional caretakers who are threatening their own competence, but professional caretakers can do enormous damage before the couple catches on. It is the therapist's job to induce change by triggering "therapeutic" crises; it is hard to assess the ultimate outcome of these crises as they are occurring. People may feel far safer if their therapist does nothing therapeutic (i.e., change inducing) and settles for caretaking (i.e., change preventing).

Therapists may sabotage caretaker marriages in another way too, i.e., by therapeutic nonchalance toward the marriage. Individual psychotherapy has somewhat the same effect on a marriage as an affair. Or the treatment may be too expensive or inconvenient to permit the family's survival. Marriage is hard enough without some therapist who is only sensitive to the effect of the marriage on the therapy and takes no cognizance of the effect of the therapy on the marriage.

CASE 7 *Going Out Together*

Carl and Carrie didn't look as if they belonged together. He was casually dressed, lounged around the office, and treated me familiarly. As I entered the waiting room, he was chewing an unlit cigar and scraping the mud off his boots. A builder, he was accustomed to dealing breezily with all manner of people in all sorts of places. Carrie must have seen the visit as an occasion of some sort. She was overdressed, in her Sunday-go-to-meeting clothes, and fresh from the hairdresser, weighted down with hair spray. She might have worn little white gloves. Through her makeup and social smile I could see tight facial muscles. Her posture had that unmistakable phenothiazine rigidity.

After relaxed pleasantries with me, Carl suddenly snapped to attention and devoted his total attention to Carrie's care. She clearly liked it. He made a big show of hovering as he helped her walk into the office, settled her into the chair, and began cueing her to list her symptoms for me. I tried to get some control of this recital, but he would not stand aside and let me deal with her. He had decided that she was to be hospitalized and given shock treatments, since the medication she was taking had not helped. I assured him it had been 20 years since I'd run across anyone I'd needed to shock electrically. I was trying to give an emergency response that said, "Look, I see what sort of shape she's in but I can probably handle it if you'll give me a chance. Go off duty." He did, resuming his casual, sleepy approach. I was baffled by his brief show of hovering, and said so.

Carl opened up about what his life had been like during the year of Carrie's depression and how he wanted her back the way she used to be — staying up most of the night cleaning and sewing and canning things and running organizations like a "natural woman." He admitted she'd had several episodes like this before, but it was just like her mother so he didn't worry about it. The other times he'd been too busy to pay much attention, and her mother would come over and help out. But this time her father was sick and her mother unavailable and his business was going so well that he just decided he'd stay with her himself. It had been awful. He couldn't leave the house. I didn't understand that, but he explained, "Anytime I'd leave the house without her, she'd whimper and it sometimes looked as if she were going to actually cry, so I just stayed home with her. The psychiatrist — the only time he talked to me, a year ago — told me not to leave her alone, just to let her rest, and to give her Mellaril any time she got upset. Actually, I kinda enjoyed being home with her, but there's some problems with my business and I'm desperate. I've got a business to run and she won't get well." She smiled and told me how wonderful he'd been to her.

I immediately called the former psychiatrist. He didn't remember his instructions to Carl. Nor did he realize that Carl was still bringing her to her appointments with him. She had seemed calmly serene in his office, but since she described getting upset a lot he would increase her medicine again.

I then called Carrie's mother. There was a strong family history of manic-depression, and Carrie's own history left little doubt. The mother described Carrie's moderately severe manic interludes between the depressions. She'd been on lithium off and on through the years, but always discontinued it when she got better. The crisis was defined. Carry was mildly manic-depressive, but her emotional life had not been one of Carl's interests until her mother was unavailable and he had to go through one of the depressions with her. He was so frightened by her emotions and she so enjoyed his hard-to-get attention that she had been overmedicated and understimulated.

The general prescription included making Carl less alarmed by Carrie's emotions. I laughed at her display of symptoms, which disoriented him. It disoriented him even further when she laughed back. I pointed out the difference between her pleasant banter with me and her clinging misery with him. He agreed that she didn't need shock treatment as much as she needed a more entertaining therapist. I thought she also needed a more easily entertained husband, one whose attention she could get without having to be miserable.

The specific prescriptions included reduction of the phenothiazines and antidepressants, and insistence on exercise and activity. I told Carl that if she complained of feeling depressed, he should send her on a two-mile walk, accompanying her by automobile if necessary.

By the next week, she hadn't complained of being depressed, but had come up with a new symptom — agoraphobia. If she drove she would become disoriented and see flashing lights, so Carl had to take her to the store or the beauty parlor each day. This struck me as a resistance, but Carl was alarmed by it, so we scheduled a neurological workup. This reassured everyone that Carrie was normal. Only then would he let her drive alone. Instead of driving with her, he would wait at the destination. She did fine.

It gradually became apparent that he wanted to spend more time with her but needed justification. We decided that he should only spend time with her if she were feeling well. He was toxic and his presence made her worse if she were a bit depressed, so if she were depressed he should promptly leave and go to work. She was then to exercise herself out of the depression.

Gradually they learned how to center their relationship on pleasurable activities rather than caretaking, something they had never figured out before. They didn't look as if they belonged together for a reason — they had led parallel lives, not dressing similarly because their activities had not overlapped. It was nice watching that change as they did more things together. Carrie continues on the lithium and has had no major highs or lows for some years now.

STRUCTURAL CRISES OF MARRIAGE

Some people proudly sob or boast that they are unhappily married and spend a lifetime making sure they keep it that way. (Does religion promise a special corner of heaven to reward the unhappily married? Do they assume everybody is unhappily married and they don't want to be different? Or do people make themselves unhappily married just because it is stylish and gives them something to talk about with their friends?) There are no limits to the inflexibilities that couples can institutionalize to keep themselves unhappily married.

Everyone who has written about unhappy marriages has come up with some way of classifying them, using one or more continua. Minuchin offers two categories—"enmeshed" or "disengaged." Sager (1976) has come up with 49 categories or "partnership combinations," matching up his seven "partner profiles." Since every marriage is at least as complex as Sager describes, and that's only for starters, I've avoided trying to classify marriages. Still, it is convenient to think of "enmeshed" and "disengaged" couples.

Structurally defective marriages, those subject to regular crises of exacerbation, might be seen as falling into two very broad categories—marriages that are explosively close and those that are shakily distant. Sometimes a marriage will ricochet back and forth between these two extremes, or one partner will be frantically intimate with someone who is being desperately distant, the Pepe le Peu syndrome (named after the cartoon skunk, oblivious to his own noxious odor, who romantically pursued with ever more inflamed ardor an accidentally striped housecat who was trying to escape him).

"Enmeshed" couples come in because the conflict is escalating. The marriage is too intense. One spouse is fed up with something the other is doing or not doing. The other usually acts helpless. No one wants to end the marriage, but one person may want to change it and the other is not so sure. These couples fight, and the fighting can get frightening at times. The fighting is over someone's job performance, or housekeeping, or parenting, or sloppiness, or party behavior, or eating habits, or handling of money. An impasse is reached. Sometimes they fight over several different issues. They see the marriage as basically good, but they just can't resolve certain conflicts, which they have to fight over even if it does no good.

"Disengaged" marriages are not really less conflictual. The more distant spouse puts a great deal of time and attention into the business of avoiding the marriage and then focuses all his or her anger onto the little bit of time and attention squeezed out by the other spouse. Conflicts that do occur may be merely passive-aggressive tricks to avoid some conversation they need to have about some problem they don't want to solve in order to make the marriage closer than they would prefer. It takes enormous energy to avoid one's marriage — it really is much like trying to stay above the water in which one is immersed.

One certainly gets the feeling that these people are either fighting or not fighting for the sole purpose of keeping the relationship from getting too close or too distant, and therefore keeping it "enmeshed" or "disengaged." As one observes the unpleasantness, it is hard to avoid the sense that these people could achieve the same effect by discussing it and, using Stuart's (1980) tokens or Jacobson and Margolin's guidelines, agreeing on the amount of closeness or distance they wanted. Of course, that is the sensible solution they devote their lives to avoiding. Why would people spend their lives avoiding agreeing, even when they are in agreement? Most of these unhappy marriages have in common a lack of gender equality and an impersonal set of role assignments based on gender. Much of their therapy consists of overcoming gender stereotypes. Is it possible that the basic problem with many of them is that they must not come to agreement with a member of the "opposite" sex?

The point of all of this is not to bring about change or even to make sense, but to find a justification for distance and for being "one up" in the marriage. These are people who are trying to win at marriage by defeating their partner. If they succeed in making the other feel just inferior enough, they gain control over the closeness and distance of the relationship, as well as the rules. They may have to reinforce the little humiliation from time to time. The best time is around their friends, since that is most efficient. This is the characteristic counterphobic behavior of men who fear closeness and dependency in their marriage. They show off to their friends that they can torment the woman and therefore must not be very dependent upon her. Women do this too, of course, but less characteristically. More often, the wives follow social custom, bite their lips and are supportive in public, but let loose the criticism in private.

In counterpoint to the "one up" position of power is the even more powerful "one down" position of being an innocent victim of something or other. The victim position permits people to spend their lives acting helpless and demanding that others either obey and take care of them or suffer guilt for their callousness. There is no tyranny like the tyranny of the weak. The source of victimization can range widely. Quite obviously, the ideal is for the victim to have been victimized by a villainous spouse. The current spouse is not really a good choice, since leaving the villain would solve the problem. Also, the spouse could eventually make amends of some sort. The ideal is an unspeakable past relationship that haunts with immeasurable sorrow and no hope for repair. An ex-spouse is an excellent choice; a parent is even better and far more appealing to therapists. There is a gender difference here in that the world gets fed up with men who suffer too long, but women are permitted, even encouraged by men who want to weaken them, to suffer for a lifetime.

Many people, usually men, can only operate comfortably within a narrow emotional range and they may require a spouse to stay within that range. Somewhere long forgotten I came across the concept of the "homoclite," a particularly dangerous type of human being. A "homoclite," believes that (he) has the correct or normal set of emotional responses and anyone who reacts differently is incorrect, abnormal, or defective. Since he permits no independent emotional reactions, he can drive someone who takes him seriously quite mad. However, since he seems so secure, correct, and normal, he attracts people who doubt themselves and feel security in his supposed strength. They attach themselves to him and grow increasingly insecure as they find themselves reacting "incorrectly" to life's events. "Homoclites" may sound paranoid or appear obsessive-compulsive, but they are totally comfortable and find it unfortunate that everyone close to them sinks into a state of dithering despair. "Homoclites" make disastrous spouses, parents, friends, bosses, and therapists — they are the Typhoid Marys of insecurity.

Structurally defective marriages have a set of ongoing misdefinitions that keep the defect alive. Such self-diagnosed barriers to marital happiness always consider the problem permanent and unsolvable, like ethnic differences or gender myths or some unforgivable past offense. (A nice example: A man said, "Of course I can't love anybody. Nobody's ever loved me. Those that tried either gave up or pissed me off.") If the therapist buys that definition, the therapy will be unsuccessful as usual. The therapist must first find the specific inflexibility that produces a recurrent snag point that prevents crisis resolution and serves as a longstanding barrier to happiness. Then the therapist must redefine it.

The center of the treatment of structural defects of marriage is the definition of the structural inflexibility. Defining a structural inflexibility can be among the most creative acts a therapist ever performs. The range is enormous and each is idiosyncratic; they cannot be finitely listed or even categorized. How they are expressed is important too. A few definitions: "It is against her rules for him to be angry with her, yet he has found no other way to get her attention." "She wants romance and emotions before she can be sexual, but he is uncomfortable with emotional and feels secure with unemotional sex." "She wants her mind read, which requires his total attention, but he wants to satisfy her efficiently while he proceeds to have the financial success that he thinks will give him control of the relationship." "He's made money and bought respectability, but she married a ragamuffin and resents having to play the social game she married him to escape." "He's reminding her more and more of the father she married him to torment." "He wants stimulation, she wants peace." "She wants him to stand back and let her pursue her career and avoid mothering and nurturing and all those things she's never been good at, but he feels cheated and constantly angry because he expected marriage to provide the nurturing his family refused to give him." "He wants her to stand back and let him pursue his career and avoid fathering and nurturing and those things he's never been good at, but she feels cheated and constantly angry because she expected marriage to provide the nurturing her family refused to give her."

If one is determined to be unhappily married, he or she can always find some defect upon which to blame the unhappiness. Some item of past history, some cultural difference, some physical imperfection, or even some difference in taste can be sufficient to produce an exacerbation of the conflict and bring about the desired level of closeness or distance. If all else fails, the one who desires to be unhappy can resort to magic and say, "I just don't love you anymore."

CASE 8   *Greetings*

David was a good Catholic boy. In fact, he suffered from what John Lutz calls the "St. Joseph Syndrome"—he worked hard, showed no emotions, and tried to keep his wife a virgin. He was a college professor, the soul of propriety. He surprised himself when he got into the affair. The affairee, Sheba, seemed such an unlikely choice. She had only a sixth grade education, was quite ugly, and would have been an object of pity had she not been so extraordinarily unpleasant. She was just out of the state hospital after her latest suicide attempt. She'd given her children to the latest of her brutal husbands and had decided she'd try to support herself. She found a job as a waitress in the cafeteria where David ate breakfast. Somehow they ended up on the couch in his office. It isn't even clear that they actually consummated the relationship, but whatever went on was more sexual than David felt was proper, so he divorced his wife and children and married Sheba. Sheba thought it a mistake—she never could understand anything he was talking about, and she'd tried marriage before without success. But no one before David had ever thought of her as being so sexual, so compellingly "woman." So she married him.

Once they were married, David began to treat Sheba as he had his first wife. He worked and avoided emotions and rarely showed an interest in sex. She had a child and got back one of the children she'd given up before, but she'd never let his children enter their home, for fear they'd return to their mother with criticisms of her. She devoted herself to perfecting the children and the house. She wouldn't let anyone come in until it was just right. She went on a plastic surgery kick, trying to make herself look better than any of the other faculty wives. Her clothes were a constant concern. She was sure David would take up with another woman, so between nose jobs she would spy on him. She still couldn't get an answer to her continuing questions of what in the world he saw in her. She made a suicide attempt. He arranged individual therapy for her. Everyone told her to get a job. She insisted upon working in David's office. He continued his impersonal adoration of her, never noticing anything about her, telling her only what he thought she wanted to hear but reassuring her, whenever asked, that he was totally in love with her. She was baffled—if he loved her, why didn't he want her sexually?

The crisis that led to their seeing me occurred when David went to the card shop to buy a birthday card for his grown daughter by his previous marriage. Sheba saw him looking through cards and felt a surge of jealousy. She drove her car through the window of the store. David calmly got her out of jail and took her back to the individual therapist, who suggested that the couple should be seen. This baffled David, but, being the dutiful husband he was, he went along with it.

My emergency response was to reassure them that we could find simpler ways for her to get his attention. I then told her that her trick with the car and the store window had been crazy and obnoxious behavior and for her not to do that anymore. I told him that he was a dishonest son of a bitch for not telling his wife that he was, of course, corresponding with his daughter; he should do whatever he thought best with his daughter but not lie to his wife anymore. They both seemed relieved.

The problem, of course, was that poor Sheba had only one talent, sex, and David prided himself on how little he was interested in that. It would not have helped to define the problem as Sheba's—everyone had done that all along without success. My new definition of the problem was that David was letting Sheba down by not appropriately appreciating her sexually. The core inflexibility in this marriage had to do with David's disapproval of sexuality, a strongly held value that lust was disrespectful and dangerous. The specific prescription for that was for David to pursue Sheba sexually. Surprisingly, he did it, or at least he made enough of a gesture in Sheba's direction for her to feel entitled to proceed. (Most men who don't like sex are extremely resistant to initiating it; the more pressure the more resistant they get. But most of the sexless men in the world are not as lucky as David, to be married to Sheba.) This was Sheba's area of expertise and she made the most of the least overture.

The most therapeutic part of the therapy was, as is usual in structurally defective marriages, the general prescriptions and the person of the therapist. I treated Sheba with great respect, except when she was emotionally intense, at which time I'd tell her she was making me nervous, and ask her to please tone it down for me. My patronizing approach to Sheba embarrassed me at first—it seemed unctuous—but she glowed from it, and I liked that. Then I'd fuss at David for having been so unresponsive that she had to overdo her attention-getting maneuvers. Most of my attention was devoted to opening David up in front of her and then translating him to her. She never had understood the way in which he'd been raised and what all his guilt was about. She, like so many people raised in desperation, had no concept of the emotion of guilt. For Sheba life was simple—one was either loved or not loved—nothing else mattered.

David had never thought much about his emotions, much less talked about them, and it was hard. I had to go through my usual posture of being nonverbally warm and verbally attacking as I tried to make it secure for him to talk about how he felt. Once Sheba trusted me, I could see David alone and sort through things he was afraid to tell her about. He'd been so frightened by Sheba's emotions early on that he tried to keep her calm by making himself totally flat. As soon as he got out of neutral, Sheba began to feel stronger. I don't know that she ever really understood any of it, but he became a real live human being and she stopped doing crazy things to get his attention.

Termination came after a year or so when they moved out of state. Years later, I got a card telling me that Sheba had a good business going, that she had met David's older children and it went OK, and that sex was still great. I had wondered whether I'd done anyone any favors by getting this mismatched couple back together, but they seemed to think so.

Well, who made the magic go out of our marriage? You or me?

—Cartoon caption by James Thurber

CHAPTER 6

Treating Marriages

THE DELICATE BALANCE

T REATING MARITAL CRISES is far more difficult than treating crises involving more than one generation. The brittle institution of marriage can be broken by a clumsy therapist. Therapists who have a standard definition of the problem and a standard expected change can create new problems while overlooking the problems at hand. The uniqueness of each marriage, and each crisis, must be respected.

A marriage therapist must believe in marriage. There are many therapists who don't. They might believe in ideal marriages, and may even seek them or dream of them, without believing in the sort of imperfect marriage that succors and structures us normal, imperfect human beings. Patriarchal male therapists, often supported by religion, have believed in marriage where women are subordinate to men. Recently, certain feminist separatists have seen marriage as a male plot to enslave women; they seem to seek opportunities to liberate women from this enslavement. They may do this openly or subtly or even inadvertently. There are many other therapists, particularly individual therapists, who find marriage a barrier to personal flexibility and "growth." Such therapists can wreck marriages without even seeing it as a problem.

In treating the manifold crises of marriage, the therapist must be careful to protect the marriage when no one else is doing so. The marriage seems oppressive to one or both partners, and the quickest solution to the latest crisis might well be to split the combatants and try to keep them apart. Such an approach not only would be cavalier, but also would, of course, fail. Then the couple, back together after their marriage was treated with such offhanded disrespect, might well find therapy dangerous and the therapist treacherous. A decision about a marriage is a weighty one, one best approached between crises rather than in the thick of one. No matter how loudly people insist they want to divorce, they are in your office, not that of a divorce attorney, and your job is to protect the marriage so the spouses can be freed to struggle with one another and with themselves. The marriage is in your hands.

Step 1: Emergency Response

One or both partners have contacted you because they feel a threat to their marriage. Someone has left, or is threatening to, or is thinking about it, and someone else is trying to hold things together. The sensitive part of a therapist's emergency response is not in demonstrating involvement or concern, but in demonstrating neutrality. One spouse always calls for the appointment and often "brings" the other. The therapist must join the marriage without joining the caller, which is extraordinarily tricky and never quite right. One partner wants therapy more than the other. One partner wants the marriage more than the other. The therapist's name was obtained from someone closer to one spouse than the other. The therapist, even before the initial call, has no perceived neutrality. And of course nobody enters marital therapy hoping for fairness or neutrality — what's desired is confirmation or alliance, so neutrality, even if achievable would be a disappointment. Marriage therapists have to be humble and get good at the one-down position, so even if they can't get totally neutral, their power can seem harmless.

Step 2: Family Involvement

The couple may come to tell you about one of the children or one of the grandparents, and family therapy may already be underway. When it is clear, or even suspected, that the problem at hand is a marital one, the rest of the family may be a distraction, causing embarrassment and slowing things down.

Marital therapy is usually conducted without the children and other relatives. Yet many times spouses seek therapy for themselves by requesting help for or with a child. The family enters with the children, but the therapy quickly switches over to work with the marriage. When the spouses come in for themselves, the children may not be seen at all, unless they are introduced as problems. If the children are no problem at all, it is generally helpful to see the couple with the children once, or maybe a few times. If the children are uncomfortable around the parents, the children may even be seen without the parents. In the midst of a disruptive family crisis, when one of the adults is falling apart or the marriage is threatened, the children benefit from being oriented to the situation. The danger of continuing family therapy after the marital problem has been defined is that the children may be enlisted as buffers or stabilizers or distractors, which could do damage to them and interfere with the couple's learning to deal with one another.

Usually the two marital partners are seen together. Often one will come to the first appointment without the other, even when they are specifically instructed to come together. Sometimes one comes alone to tell a secret, in hopes, one must assume, of sabotaging any chance for therapy. More often, one comes just to check you out and make sure the marriage can be entrusted to you, since the spouse is less committed to therapy and won't try too many therapists before giving up on the idea or will only come if the other spouse is clearly defined as the patient. That's all right. The therapist, upon discovering that only one partner has arrived but the marriage is the patient, can call the other spouse and proceed with one in the office and the other on the phone. Or if the missing spouse is unavailable, the therapist can call him or her later. If one spouse is dealt with separately, the other should be also, in person or by telephone.

One spouse may be terrified of therapy, as if problems don't exist unless the therapist diagnoses them. The attitude is comparable to that of small children who seem to believe that they become invisible if they cover their eyes — if they can't see, they can't be seen. Becoming invisible to therapists, not being seen by them, makes one, by omission, mentally healthy. Anyone who fears therapists must have never met one — we really aren't very imposing or scary — so a telephone conversation can cure the phobia.

I have found it helpful to offer one separate individual session for each marital partner. Most jump at this opportunity to charm me and tell me their secrets, even though I make clear I won't agree to keep the secrets. People just need to check out the safety of revealing things in their fragile marriage.

The grandparents may well be integral to the presenting crisis, perhaps as caretakers, perhaps as stabilizers, or perhaps as flame-fanners to a bolt from the blue. Their investment in maintaining a structural inflexibility may keep the crisis exacerbated. Or they may be central to a developmental shift in the marriage.

When a couple is in crisis, there may be pressing reasons for seeing parents or other relatives—siblings, grandparents, whatever. Often the spouses have separated and one or both have gone home to momma and daddy, or the parents have moved in to "help." The parents' visit may have made a chronic situation acute or may have initiated the therapy. The parents may be providing the financial or emotional support for one spouse to finally do something about a longstanding problem. Or the parents may be trying to separate partners who tolerate their lives fairly well. When the parents are part of the crisis, they should be part of the therapy at the beginning and eased out as the couple comes together to stabilize the relationship. When parents are trying not to be involved, when they are working at neutrality, it may be best to respect that. They don't have to be in the therapy just because they are there. In marital therapy, particularly at the beginning, there should be a reason for bringing anyone beyond the couple into therapy.

In prolonged therapy, after the crisis has cooled and the couple begins to negotiate their resistance to change, it is extremely useful to see families of origin once, in whatever sequence or configuration develops normally, with or without an acute crisis. Every Christmas I find myself scheduling visiting parents of ongoing couples. I find it works best to see parents after you know the couple very well. Obviously, seeing the families of origin regularly tends to overwhelm the therapy. Framo (1980) calls family-of-origin work with couples "the major surgery of family therapy." It is a powerful, delicate operation and requires that both spouses trust the therapist. The spouses may become rather childlike around their parents and be quite different from the way they are when they are the older generation. They may expect the therapist to be equally intimidated by these powerful parents. When the therapist reacts to the parents as if they were peers, and only human too, that may serve as the model for the couple to achieve peerdom with their parents.

Sometimes other generations must be involved in marital therapy just enough to be excluded. A brief telephone call may provide enough reassurance and explanation to permit them to stand back and let you and the couple take over. Therapists who deal with families of origin notice how rarely family members are destructive once they know what is going on and what they can do to help—even if it means staying out of it.

STEP 3: DEFINING THE CRISIS

Almost always the bulk of therapy with couples is in defining the problem—the solution is usually obvious and often already agreed upon, and the resistance takes the form of obstructing the definition process. The presenting definition is usually either (1) "We can't communicate," or (2) "I want a divorce," also phrased as "I don't love him/her anymore." The first implies that the couple wants to stay together and would like to overcome some barrier to intimacy and tranquillity. The second implies that one of them wants to leave, but the other doesn't. These are deadend definitions in that no helpful action flows directly out of them. A useful definition of the problem must move from the emotions to the expectations and must be rather specific. "We can't communicate" might well mean "Everytime I bitch at her about her drinking, she hits me," or it might mean "Every night he sits there in front of the TV and won't entertain me at all," or even "No matter how many times I tell her, she still puts starch in my shirts and serves me food I'm allergic to." Any of these definitions is specific and concerns acts rather than emotions.

Spouses who are frightened of their anger at one another can avoid dealing with the anger by trying to find a neutral, impersonal, "nonblaming" definition of their conflicts. They may feel better about declaring themselves "out of love" than "angry." They may prefer a "problem in communication" over "a disagreement." I realize that family therapists, under the influence of Bowen, have encouraged "I" statements. It is far more polite and respectful to take full responsibility for one's emotional state by announcing it as something arising from within, rather than something poured on by someone else. However, it is important for marital partners to explain to one another what they like and don't like and how they react to one another. It should be a simple matter for competent persons to change their actions, their schedule, and their habits. Although it is an overwhelming task to "fall in love," "be entertaining," or "stop feeling that way," it should be easy enough for someone to "have sex more often," "take me out for the evening," and "tell me when you're angry rather than put on a show."

Equally problematic are definitions that diagnose the spouse or determine the spouse's character defects. Name-calling is unhelpful not because it is unpleasant but because it is not specific. The definition of the problem is the process by which people remove the labels from their state of mind and get specific about the things they don't like in the marriage. Saying "You are an alcoholic" is not as helpful as saying "I can't stand your drinking" or even "You're disgusting when you drink." Saying "I'm an obsessive-compulsive and am only comfortable in an orderly environment" does not help as much as saying "If you leave your stinking socks on the dining room table again, I'm going to throw them out." Couples can read all the books about wonderfully respectful marital communication later; in the midst of crisis what is needed is direct, specific outlining of the conflicts, reducing the overwhelming impasse to its component parts.

In defining the problem, it must first be established whether anyone is having an affair. This should be asked directly, although you often know the answer just from the way the spouses sit in the waiting room. The infidel will sometimes lie about it but in some way convey the truth, either in the session or by telephone later or by requesting a separate individual session. Otherwise, the therapy will proceed and be mysteriously sabotaged or disorientingly ineffective, and the question will have to be asked again. If there is no infidelity going on, the couple's definition of the problem is usually either specific or concerned with "communication" and other such vague interaction dissatisfactions. When someone talks about the absence of love or wanting out of the marriage for some vague but compelling reason, that is practically diagnostic of infidelity—current, recurrent, or anticipated.

Bolts from the blue are easiest to define. The couple comes in to explore a specific problem which they can define but not solve. They reassure you of their good marriage and their determination to keep it good, and you can see it. You know they have lived together, really together—they joke and banter with one another in a personal and familiar manner, rather than being polite or cautious. They can isolate the problem and place it in time and space. They know when it arose and how. They just don't know quite what to do about it. They may be defining it clearly, but want a third person to assure the equity of their solution. They may be able to pinpoint the situation quite nicely, but be ignorant and naive about possible solutions. These crises are not necessarily easier to treat than others, just easier to define. The question "should we have children?" is far easier to ask than to answer.

Identifying a developmental crisis is based upon the familiarity and expectability of the situation to the therapist. It is customary to overdiagnose developmental crises, even when the stage of development is not a familiar one. It reduces alarm nicely to diagnose a syndrome—we all are more comfortable with horrors we can name than we are with nameless ones. Even burglars or pterodactyls are less scary than the things that go bump in the night.

Structural crises are not always easy to diagnose, as the spouses like to reassure themselves that the problem has some unique features, that it isn't really as bad this time as it seems, that, "gosh, nothing like this ever happened before." So the therapist is misled into believing a structural defect is a developmental crisis. The determinant question is whether this has happened before. If the therapist identifies the developmental syndrome before getting the history of past episodes, the situation can be misunderstood. That's OK. It does no harm to accept the more optimistic definition, at least for a while. It won't take long to realize that a longstanding problem is going through a stage of exacerbation or has developed into something worse.

Of course, many of the marriages with structural defects have those defects because one or both partners are defective. This may be the source of continuing conflict, without much progress, as if the conflict is the purpose of the marriage and has the desired result of keeping one partner from changing while the other is martyred and protective—an amateur caretaker. All spouses of incompetent people are not caretakers. The caretaker may be another family member or even a professional who maintains the incompetence by either mystifying or ignoring any forces for change in the family. Individual therapy is not always a caretaker arrangement, but individual therapists who refuse to deal with the family may well foster, however unwittingly, a caretaker situation in which the basic inequality of the marriage is either produced or maintained by the untherapeutic therapy.

Structural crises and caretaker crises overlap. The distinction is in the equality and functional capacity of the two partners. Structural crises occur regularly in marriages between two reasonably competent people who keep their distance from one another, intermittently threaten the marriage, and arrange recurrent crises to underscore the fragility and inadequacy of the relationship. Caretaker crises occur in marriages in which one person is incompetent and the other is enslaved, but it is clear they are together forever, no matter how awful it gets. There is a big middle ground between these two extremes—marriages in which one partner is defective and the other isn't quite committed—and the intermittent crises jerk the marriage around, sometimes seeming to threaten it and sometimes seeming to make it impossible for the more competent partner to leave.

There are not many times when someone is truly helpless, no matter how often one feels that way. Some problem definitions increase one's sense of helplessness, while others empower even as they challenge, by suggesting an action that could be taken to change things. But if people are to be empowered to take action, they must accept responsibility for whether they act or not, whether they have acted or not. In our zeal to make sure no one feels any sense of blame for the messes and failures of one's life, we may leave people feeling helpless. There really is no difference between blamelessness and helplessness except the time frame: Blamelessness implies there was no action in the past that could have changed the situation; helplessness implies there is no action now that could change the situation in the future. The most important thing a marriage therapist does is empower people in order to overcome their helplessness about their life. If they must blame themselves in order to give up their helplessness, so be it.

People must recognize they are not the victims of their marriage. They can leave it or they can change it if they don't like it. But they must also see that it is *their* marriage. It belongs to them. It is not the property of their spouse. There are men who see marriage as belonging to the wife, as a kind of feminization of their lives. And there are women who see marriage as belonging to the husband, as a form of institutionalized slavery. And if they define it that way, they will be influenced by that definition and make it so, or wreck it in order not to make it so.

As always, the center of crisis therapy is the definition of the crisis. In marriage the point is to empower and to make sure people see their marriage as belonging to them, even if that means seeing it as their fault.

Step 4: General Prescription

Marital therapy may work largely because of the nonspecific factors. By its very format, marital therapy assumes the equality of the two partners and the equality of the genders — this is a matter of enormous importance. There really are important differences in how men and women are socialized, how they react to things, and what they expect from one another. However, any stereotypical notion of MAN or WOMAN may be widely divergent from the man or woman here in this marriage, this situation, and this office. The therapist, even though committed to marital equality and extremely sensitive to gender differences, has to be careful not to confuse this man and this woman with MAN and WOMAN.

The therapist is respectful, even of rather startling and outlandish ideas and behavior, and shows alarm, disapproval, or disrespect rather carefully and studiedly. The therapist is the therapeutic tool. The therapist's comfort with marriage, with men, with women, with responsibility, with conflict, with emotion, and with the absence of emotion can be a revelation.

Nonspecific prescriptions for marriage in general have been institutionalized in Marriage Encounter and various communication and "enrichment" processes, which may rigidly refuse to deal with specific problem areas while they teach couples a less inflammatory language. Family therapy has likewise tended to favor the nonspecific approaches to marriages. Sending people home again or off to the cemetery to face family of origin issues, however specific to the individual's development, is actually a general approach to marital conflict, and they work particularly well for structurally crisis prone marriages. In fact anything that helps people see themselves as others see them, or even to get some distance from the terror of their marriage, can be generally therapeutic to the marriage.

By respecting two seemingly divergent and quite intense viewpoints, the therapist exerts a powerful effect. A startling and therapeutic trick is for the therapist to hear two utterly incompatible stories and insist upon believing both and even explaining how they are not emotionally incompatible. The therapist is trying to respect the marriage, the commitment of both partners to the marriage (even when it doesn't show), the good will and basic humanity of both partners, and the honesty of both partners with the therapist.

But it is not necessary to respect anyone's unpleasant or destructive behavior. There are limits to positive connotation. Violence, dishonesty, and adultery, for instance, should not be positively connoted. In fact, one of the more effective nonspecifics of marital therapy is the therapist's acceptance of any emotion or lack of emotion, in contrast to the therapist's horror at the dishonesty of marital partners with one another. With one hand the therapist is endorsing the full array of human emotions and their expression within the marriage, while with the other hand the therapist is requiring that the couple treat one another with respect and equality.

This requires the well-mannered therapist to be studiedly impolite and encourage others to be as well. Politeness is a distancing technique, similar to the letting-lie technique recommended for people one assumes to be sleeping dogs—the avoidance of saying unexpected things or acknowledging feeling or noticing anything out of the accepted ordinary. There are people who are so terrified of openness and intimacy and gender equality that they don't enjoy exposing their marriage to a therapist. If the therapist respects that too politely, no therapy can take place. The therapist is in the awkward position of having to push the limits of politeness and probe the sensitivities of the couple. This is impossible to do without breaching those limits and pricking those sensitivities. Some patients will be offended and frightened. Any therapist who doesn't send an occasional patient screaming out of the office is probably being too cautiously polite.

Blamelessness is essentially the same as helplessness—it assumes that the individual could not have brought about a different outcome through a different set of actions or attitudes and therefore cannot do so in the future when the circumstances recur. I've not found that reasonably competent people object to taking responsibility for their actions, even when they insist upon blaming their emotions on others. Those people who do require blame-lessness are sick, and their determination to be innocent bystanders in their lives is their problem. In dealing with such paranoid or psychopathic people, the therapist may temporarily accept the convention of holding them blameless. However, the therapist must be alert while taking such condescending approaches—an act of emotional dishonesty by the therapist can erase his or her personal involvement in the therapy and sabotage the therapeutic relationship. As a corrective, the concept of innocence may be carried to a literal extreme that will parody the attitude and render it absurd and amusing. That will bring the players back into contact.

There are some severe limitations to a generic approach to marital crisis, primarily because the couple may not have the therapist's favorite generic problem, and may, in fact, have a problem that requires specific information or specific action. The specifics of a bolt from the blue can be dealt with directly, and a caretaker crisis requires specific attention to the condition forming the basis for the caretaking disequilibrium. A developmental crisis can be dealt with generically, but the developmental stage must be clearly defined and understood. Structurally defective marriages are often treated generally rather than specifically, or the specifics of the individuals are dealt with by distracting everyone from the problematic interaction.

Step 5: Specific Prescription

In the presence of any structural defect one specific effective directive is to tell each partner to stop doing what he or she is doing that threatens the marriage. Whoever threatens the marriage is then "blamed," if you will, for doing so. If that blows the therapist's neutrality, so be it. Even if the therapeutic task is to evaluate whether the marriage should continue, the therapist must then first observe the marriage as it operates when no one is threatening it. Once it is clear what each partner wants the other to do differently, the requisite changes can be prescribed. The changes, unimportant in themselves, are examples of dedication to the marriage — which is considered a virtue. It certainly does no one harm to develop new marital skills and get experience at fulfilling another's expectations. Once the attitude of cooperation is established, the specific requests tend to lose their magic. While this is going on, the therapist is distracting the spouses from their conflict by focusing on the history of the marriage and especially on the history of their families of origin.

Specific directives consist of simply telling people to behave differently. This may seem shockingly simplistic, but it works much of the time and conveys optimism about the voluntary nature of behavior and the capacity for change and development. It also fixes the therapy in time and place and gives it direction. Sometimes destructive behavior is not really representative of inflexibilities or values that are strongly held even when they don't work, but is merely an indication of patterns people have gotten into, never questioned, and can change at will.

There is a convention whereby one partner is never given a directive for change without the other also being given a directive. At the beginning of therapy this can help protect the therapist's neutrality until trust can be developed, but it need not be adhered to after things become comfortable and cooperation is assured.

Caretaker crises require that the therapist diagnose and explain the disability and supervise the caretaker. All three must understand the condition and what to do about it. This can be formalized into psychoeducation and lends itself to group approaches, but it also fits nicely into the usual approach to family crises.

Caretaker relationships may require the specific prescription of ceasing to magnify the disability by providing unnecessary care. The amateur caretaker must be specifically instructed to give up power, and the disabled one must be specifically instructed to take on responsibility. And the whole process must be explained so that everyone will understand the change of direction.

In developmental crises of marriage, the important specific prescription is to stop threatening the marriage and instead to explain the emotional process. The emphasis is on the emotional aspect of the stage of development. Typically, if it can be communicated and understood, it does not have to separate the spouses from one another. The partner who is threatened by the changes in the "developing" one must likewise explain what it feels like. As the spouses explain and reexamine their history and their family history, they get a perspective on this latest stage of development. The vital specific directive is to stop threatening, sit tight, wait it out, talk about it, and get a long-range perspective on it.

The threatened partner may have to make some complementary changes to remain in synchronization with the developing partner. If the stage of development involves the end of the romance and one partner wants the relationship more functional and friendly and less flirtatious and playful, it may have to go that way. If the relationship has been gender differentiated and the husband notices that he likes women who are competent rather than decorative or the wife notices that she likes men who think and feel and talk and listen rather than just barking orders, somebody is going to have to change. The therapist may have to dictate who is going to adapt to whom, so the therapist's value system becomes part of the therapy.

These developmental conflicts frequently center on values and a definition of emotional and marital health. Is the new stage moving toward or away from that ideal? The therapist must be clear about it. The therapist's own longings and romantic fantasies can get in the way of the therapy, and a frustrated therapist can live vicariously through his patients, unleashing them to do the risky things he himself wouldn't do. Burnt-out therapists can easily idealize freedom and unrootedness. The recently divorced seem to need company.

Bolts from the blue generally involve a decision. The therapist may get by with defining the quandary to be decided, but may have to give a specific directive on what decision to make, for instance when one partner wants to make a sacrifice that would not benefit anyone but would relieve some neurotic guilt, or when a course of action has serious disadvantages that are being overlooked. Usually the specific prescription involves the collection of information, especially having conversations that have been dreaded and avoided.

The therapist's specific prescriptions should flow directly from the crisis that has been defined, not from the therapist's concept of the ideal marriage. The therapist can retain a neutral, reassuring commitment to the marriage while still supporting change and dealing with the resistance to change.

STEP 6: NEGOTIATING THE RESISTANCE

Whatever the type of crisis, people will be people and will resist doing the sensible thing. This may be most apparent in structurally defective marriages, where people devote their lives to making sure their marriages produce as much smoke and as little fire as possible. And it may be least apparent in unique crises, where people are trying hard not to let the crises of life threaten their marriage. But everybody, married or single, has a repertoire of behaviors that are thought to have worked in some past situation and which must be applied to each new situation. The therapist may find this as exasperating as the rest of the family does, but it is traditional. It resembles Scarlett O'Hara, who had one solution to each of life's crises.

Even when Rhett Butler left her, her response was the same, "I'll think about it tomorrow, and meanwhile I'll go to Tara."

There may be resistance to coming to therapy. If the therapist insists on seeing the couple together or not at all, the partner who is phobic for change is given all the cards. The resistant one may show up for therapy, declare it "courteous" to be there, and then refuse to be involved. That maneuver can drive the therapist (at least when I am the therapist) berserk. It really is possible, and sometimes necessary, to do marital therapy with one member of the marriage. There are many marriages in which the responsibility for the marriage is carried by one person; in some ethnic groups the full responsibility for the marriage is a wedding present given to the bride. It isn't ideal to see just the wife in those situations, but the therapist may have to settle for less than equal involvement in the therapy and work toward "greater" rather than "absolute" equality.

Resistance to solving marital crisis centers around the specific inflexibilities that make the marriage crisis prone. Since these may give one partner power over the other and maintain the desired level of closeness or distance, they may be quite strongly held. Inflexibilities may lead people to resist conflict, to recoil from genderless functioning, to abhor emotionality, and to persist in idealizing their parents. It may take years in a couples group to teach people to fight without fearing the marriage will fall apart or to treat one another as individuals rather than representatives of the enemy gender. It may take a great deal of family of origin work to get people past the fantasies they have about their parents, themselves, and how life is supposed to be. As long as two people can keep sharing with one another their reaction to the experience of living, they can handle just about any crisis.

STEP 7: TERMINATION

The process of marital therapy can be long and tedious, particularly for a structurally defective marriage, whether the couple stays in therapy continuously or jumps in and out with each new crisis. If the couple can be coerced into staying in therapy for a while, the threat can be relieved and some health can be learned. The same sequences of behavior keep recurring at each new crisis point until the couple finally begins to catch on to the inescapable nature of marriage—it belongs to you, you can't win at it, you can't be partway into it, and the roles and rules have little to do with anything so impersonal as gender.

issues:
  intimacy
  equality

SECTION III

Disruption of the Family

Cuck'old (kuk'uld) n. someone whose mate is unfaithful (derived from cuckoo.)

Cuck'oo (kook'oo) n. 1. a large greyish brown bird given to laying its eggs in other birds' nests.
2. a silly or addlebrained person.
3. someone who is being unfaithful.

CHAPTER 7

Infidelity

THE SECRET INSANITY

O F THE SERIOUS STRESSES that disrupt families, none is more common than infidelity (Humphrey, 1983). Not only is the marital affair the most common disruptive force in families, but it is also among the most devastating. Infidelity is the most universally accepted justification for divorce. It is even a legally accepted justification for murder in some states and many societies. The crises that follow infidelities fill the offices of family therapists. I doubt if there is any problem on which we all devote more energy, yet the literature on affairs is scanty and confusing.

As Framo points out in his 1975 paper on "Husband's Reactions to Wives' Infidelity:"

It is difficult to make generalizations about affairs because they have different meanings and determinants in each situation. Exploration can reveal that the affair was an act of desperation, that it had little to do with the mate at all, that it was consciously designed to arouse the mate's interest, that it was based on revenge for real or fancied wrongs, that it was destructive in intent (aimed at getting rid of the mate), that the third party was a way-station on a route back to the mate (and in this sense the affair revived an empty marriage and was therapeutic), that the affair was set up by the marriage partner, and so forth—the individual and interactional motives are infinite."

WHY PEOPLE SCREW AROUND

Obviously the reasons for affairs are complex and varied and the same phenomena can be attributed to forces within either the system or the individual. Still, it is somehow assumed, by both family therapists and by society, that affairs are caused by forces within the marital system. In at least a quarter or a third of affairs, the marriage is so stormy and conflictual, or so sexually or emotionally dead, that the marriage's contribution to the situation seems overwhelming and determinant. There may be marital factors in many other affairs too, but individual and perhaps cultural reasons seem too prominent to dismiss. By keeping their focus steadfastly on the marital contribution to the problem, family therapists may severely limit their understanding and helpfulness in this common situation.

After an act of infidelity there is guilt and fear which turns quickly into anger at the spouse and an effort at justification and blame. Adulterers, on their way home from their affair, define things in such a way as to place responsibility on the spouse, of all people, who probably wasn't even there! They decide there is something wrong with their marriage and then proceed to create a problem in the marriage that will both relieve their sense of responsibility and maintain sufficient distance to permit the affair to continue. The spouse, confused, may assume the infidel is temporarily insane, which is not too far off. The infidel is indeed disoriented in the most important structure of his or her life.

The data on the frequency of infidelity are fairly consistent. About half do and half don't. Traditionally, more men than women were adulterous, but the women seem to be catching up. The misleading aspect of the data has to do with the pattern of the infidelity. Much of the infidelity takes place in the last year of the marriage. Whether the deteriorating marriage causes the affair or the affair causes the marriage to deteriorate is a controversial question. Intact, continuing marriages are far less adulterous. Infidelity of some sort takes place in at least 70% of marriages—that's a lot of infidelity. Some of it is occasional and infrequent ("unique affairs"). Some is a rare but intense passion that threatens the marriage and feels like love ("caretaker affairs—falling in-love"). Some infidelity is open and hostile and part of the marital battle ("structural affairs"). Continuous, recurrent infidelity ("developmental affairs—philandering"), considered normal behavior by the adulterer and perhaps by the spouse, may occur in no more than 20% of intact marriages. Much of this habitual adultery is by no means secret, and some is with the active cooperation of the spouse. It would seem that most people in intact marriages are not being secretly adulterous. When someone is being secretly adulterous, it should be considered a problem specific to those involved rather than behaviour typical of a gender or an era or a society. If adultery were dismissed by a therapist as expectable, typical behaviour, its specific meaning could not be explored. If adultery were anticipated by a spouse, that would interfere greatly with trust and intimacy in the marriage. Most people believe strongly in fidelity, certainly for their spouse, and generally for themselves. It remains the ideal, even if it is not always achieved. Therefore, it is not only more accurate, but also more helpful, to consider infidelity to be out of order and symptomatic. The important issue is to determine what it is symptomatic of.

Most of the reasons for affairs have to do with the ego state of the person having the affair. The reasons range from "hobby" to "politeness." Even if someone did not love the spouse, an affair would be a rather complicated and indirect way to say so and an inefficient way to approach the problems in the marriage. The feelings one spouse has for another are complicated from the beginning. The degree of complexity of the emotions in longstanding marriages is staggering for even the most experienced family therapist. To reduce this complexity to a question as adolescent as the presence or absence of "love" is idiocy of the highest order. That question is best left to the petals of daisies. The therapist, and if possible the infidel and the cuckold spouse, must recognize that marriage abounds in love, hate, lust, disgust, envy, guilt, pity, loathing, admiration, dependency, fear, and all other emotions known and unknown.

The most obvious assumption about adulterers is that they are angry with their spouse. Anger at the spouse is popularly assumed to be a constant feature in the motivation of secret affairs. Anger is of course an essential ingredient in the emotional stew of every marriage. I don't know that people who have affairs are angrier than those who don't, but I am impressed that those contemplating affairs are not as angry with their mates as those who are justifying the affairs in which they are already involved. The anger, however inevitable in marriage, however moderate objectively, however seemingly unwarranted, seems compelling to the spouse experiencing it.

Perhaps even more often, adulterers are angry with the institution of marriage, seeing it as depriving them of something. Some people indeed are too angry and passive-aggressive for fidelity and must either negotiate some other arrangement or live a life of secrecy and basic enmity with their partner.

Everyone feels deprived in some way, at some time, but people have very different expectations of marriage. Some people expect marriage to meet all their needs, either as their natural due or because of their manifold sacrifices to the marriage, including perhaps their own fidelity. They may feel deprived by things other people might consider trivial. Some expect unadulterated attention, others impeccable service, still others uninterrupted romance or the status that comes from being married to someone who arouses envy in others. The deprivation over "ring around the collar" or the gift of an imperfect rose may be far stronger to those sensitive to deprivation than the deprivation felt by more stolid and sacrificial types after years of no sex, months of no money, or weeks of no conversation. Those who are expert at feeling deprived may not be very good at getting, or even defining, what they want, much less negotiating the give and take that will keep it coming. But even if the deprivation were far beyond the tolerance of most of us, a secret affair would be an unlikely solution. However, an open affair is an effective attention-getting maneuver and may bring things to a head — and the couple to therapy. Sometimes, an affair is tried and revealed, and the "depriving" cuckold avoids the problems, uses the affair as an excuse for further distance and deprivation, and sets up a lifetime of punishment, or a marriage made tolerable only when unilaterally open.

If one spouse is fed up with the marriage but is not quite secure in going ahead with separation or divorce, an affair might be chosen to break the bond of the marriage, give security that there are possibilities for life outside the marriage, and perhaps even provide a smooth transition into another marriage. The affair partner might be the object of magical expectations and rescue fantasies. The affair becomes a dry run for the divorce. Often in such cases the affair cannot hold up under such expectations. When the affair breaks down, the marriage may temporarily reconcile until the insecure adulterer can find a sturdier rescuer. Throughout this process, the cuckold spouse may have little sense that there are problems in the marriage.

An affair might be a message to one's mate — perhaps a request for more attention, perhaps a suggestion of what the adulterer would like for the cuckold to emulate, perhaps an effort to infuriate the spouse into leaving. However an affair is a rather circuitous and nonspecific message, made even more confusing by secrecy.

Perhaps the most specific personal reason for an affair is revenge for a mate's affair. In the aftermath of an adultery, a counter-adultery has a strangely compelling logic. The primary emotion is vengeful anger, but there is also a search for orientation and for reassurance. The cuckold, most often the wife, may feel her security shattered, her desirability assailed, her principles ridiculed. She may feel freedom from the usual constraints. The rules are off, the barriers down. The mouse can play because the cat has been discredited. An affair begun with such anger, confusion, and doubt is not likely to be very pleasant, and the adulterer may be asked to take the blame for the pain of his or her affair plus the pain of the spouse's. The guilty infidel may even assist the cuckold in having an affair. Revenge affairs don't seem to clear things up very well, as they may leave everyone uncomfortable and ashamed, but a good affair in the revenge mode may mean the end of the marriage. Revenge affairs may not even stop the awful self-righteousness of cuckoldry, since the original adulterer may then have to take responsibility for destroying the marriage and making the spouse both a cuckold and an adulterer. And if the cuckold is now an adulterer too, the original adulterer has permission to repeat the process, while the problems never get approached at all. Marriages based on revenge affairs may look like French farce to outsiders and may contain some elements of adventure, but they don't seem to last long. Perhaps the most hostile form of revenge, short of suicide or murder, would be for the cuckold to have revenge affairs but do it secretly, while continuing to punish the original adulterer self-righteously. This has been done.

Sometimes one spouse will encourage the other to have an affair. The reasons may be kinky (the desire to watch or hear about it), benevolent (the effort to assure sexual satisfaction for the other person), or defensive (to escape the guilt for one's own affair). The usual path to an "open" marriage is through one spouse having an affair and then encouraging the other to partake also. Open marriage (O'Neill & O'Neill, 1972) was an influential concept a decade or so ago. It was tried by many people and must have worked for some of them, but many crises were triggered, and I have never seen it work for long. Some couples who tried it were disappointed in their inability to overcome jealousy, feeling that to be a serious and depressing character flaw. They saw jealousy as such a primitive emotion that its emergence at the orgy was disquieting; it was as though they had grown tails and begun swinging from trees. They were uncomfortable with the idea that humans are instinctively monogamous, albeit imperfectly so, and inherently jealous once bonded in a committed relationship. Believing affairs inevitable, they directed their efforts at control toward the jealous reaction to the affairs. One man "forced" his wife to have affairs until his jealousy could be overcome. She left him for one of the other men. Another man came in with the problem that he was often impotent during spouse-swapping episodes with another couple; he disliked the unattractive wife while his wife was much taken with the husband. A more common crisis for swinging couples occurred when one spouse would meet secretly with someone from the other marriage. Apparently even open affairs have their problems.

Some problems which should be solvable within the marriage just don't seem that easy to those involved. Some of the simplest sexual problems seem baffling to people with little successful sexual experience. One spouse may prefer that the other become sexually expert, so he or she won't have to struggle with inhibitions and awkwardness. Sometimes one of a sexually inept couple will go out for training and experience that can be brought home. If the experience is being shared it can be helpful, even though the gratitude is often diluted with some of the more expectable emotions. However useful it sounds in theory, in practice it doesn't always work. Often the affair is kept secret and is used by one partner to reassure herself or himself that the sexual problem belongs to the other spouse. The sexual knowledge gained from the affair may not even be imparted. On the other hand, if the affair is known, the sexually repressed cuckold may use the infidelity to avoid sex even more stubbornly. One young woman, still a virgin after a year of marriage, suffered from severe vaginismus at the sight of her clumsy, oversized husband. She petitioned at work for surrogates with small penises, auditioned several, and finally chose one she thought just right for the job. The husband knew of the process but was not informed of its success, as she chose to leave him instead.

A marriage does not have to be bad to drive someone into an affair. Some people cannot tolerate the intimacy of a good marriage. The better the marriage gets, the more comfortable and happy, the more frightened they get. An affair may be a protection from being engulfed, from becoming too dependent. Obviously the person who has an affair for this reason does not identify this as the reason, but it may not be as rare as it might seem.

Most reasons for affairs seem to arise from within the individual, rather than from the marital relationship. The marriage is important, not because it produces affairs, but because it fails to prevent affairs. If one partner is willing to sacrifice a marriage (and perhaps a family, a home, a fortune, and whatever else) for a sex act, why is the marriage worth so little, the sex act worth so much? Often the major irritant about the marriage is that it interferes with affairs and becomes the source of guilt and punishment for them.

Unquestionably, the major reason for infidelity is the cultural expectation of it, perhaps simply the cultural lack of expectation of fidelity, perhaps the cultural requirement of infidelity. In some societies there is no expectation that either gender will be sexually exclusive; in other societies the females are supposed to be faithful but the men aren't. If the society ridicules fidelity and vigorously encourages affairs, fidelity might well be a symptom of timidity or inhibition or even rebellion, rather than a character flaw or an indication of the spouse's inadequacy. Our society as a whole endorses fidelity, yet there are powerful forces which actively encourage infidelity. There is a general cynicism about marriage, based on the high rates of infidelity and divorce, and from this cynicism emerges a belief that one's own infidelities are a defense against the infidelities of one's spouse. *Cosmopolitan* and *Playboy* magazines espouse such philosophies. Marriage is seen as the problem.

Many people don't like whichever sex is seen as opposite. In fact, the fear of the opposite sex may become so intense that affairs are chosen to deny the dependency of the marriage and to treat the phobia through desensitization. Phobic adulterers are more likely to be compulsively promiscuous than to develop intimate affairs. Many, sometimes I think most, people prefer not to be happily married, to retain some limits on the intimacy and "togetherness." They work at maintaining just the right distance in the relationship. The affair may be an aid to that distance. Although the spouse's affair may create an undesirable state of distance, the end-of-the-affair reunion and post-affair problem-solving might produce an undesired state of closeness. The danger of bringing an affair into the open is not that the infidel becomes more likely to leave, but that the infidel becomes more likely to stay and to try to get close.

Reassurance of one's attractiveness or desirability or sexual prowess is a little different from the counterphobic maneuvers of those who fear the opposite sex. The anger is less intense, the affairs are spottier and less compulsive and may even be friendlier. There may or may not be problems in the marriage that contribute to the need for reassurance. It depends on what the adulterer needs reassurance about. One man needed to know he could be attractive to younger women who didn't know how rich he was; one woman needed to know she could attract primitive, uneducated, unsophisticated men.

Some people manage to maintain heterosexual marriages supplemented by homosexual affairs. They can perform sexually with the opposite sex and prefer the benefits of a heterosexual marriage and life, but have greater sexual and emotional comfort with their own gender. It is often a workable compromise and may occur with the knowledge of the spouse; more often it is kept completely secret in a marriage that is rather formal and distant and sometimes, but not always, sexually cool. Some of the men in my practice have for many years led an undercover homosexual half-life, while avoiding closeness with either the sex partners or the spouse. Others, male and female, choose intense, intimate homosexual affairs after many years of bored heterosexuality and then blame it on the spouse. Still others, sexual hobbyists, intersperse heterosexual adventures with homosexual ones. In my practice those with the most sexual experience have seen little difference between adventures with men and adventures with women. The less experienced, more generally inhibited and guilt-ridden see the homosexual activities as somehow non-adulterous. Interestingly, when such affairs came out, the spouses also tend to see them as "queer" rather than "cheating," as compulsory rather than voluntary. In general, homosexual affairs are no different in motivation or process than heterosexual ones, but have less disruptive impact on marriage. I have known several men whose homosexual dalliances were known to their wives, but who then precipitated a divorce threat by getting into a heterosexual affair.

For those who are phobic for the opposite sex but diffident about homosexuality, there are orgies and gang bangs, in which the sex is hetero but the stimulation for the activity is the sharing with same-sex friends. A more subtle form of showing off sexually involves competitive seductions, perhaps of the same person at work. Even more subtle, but still the same, is the seduction of people who are or will be the object of rivals' lust. Texas oilmen marry glamorous movie stars as status symbols in a competition with one another similar to contests over who has the biggest derrick or the steadiest gusher.

There are some for whom sex and seduction are a hobby. They collect experiences, not for show and tell or to impress anyone else, but because they enjoy doing it as a primary recreation. Those who choose sex as a hobby may be as compulsive and obsessed as any other hobbyist. For them the process is conflict free, pleasurable, and unrelated to anything else, such as marriage satisfaction. The affairs such hobbyists have may be fun but are not very personal; they may pose little threat to the marriage.

At the opposite extreme is the need to be "in-love." In-love is a kind of high that can escalate to craziness. Our society protects the in-love experience as if it were real, valuable, and certainly unnegotiable. Those who are in-love may be so bewitched they will kill or die to maintain the bond of mutual dependency. Inevitably such love cools, and it cools for one person before it cools for the other. The one who is no longer in-love can find the engulfing in-loveness of the other, so delightful a short time ago, suddenly irritating. The state of being in-love can barely be influenced by good advice or logic, but at least it is temporary. It seems no less intense at 40 than at 14, but for those in midlife it lasts months rather than weeks. If it only lasts days or is dispelled by consummation it seems to be called "infatuation" and is not valued.

For most people, the illogic and danger of in-love become apparent before they are out of their teens. Others only realize it after a few months of their first marriage when the romance palls and the honeymoon is over, when they realize that relationships do not occur automatically and must be tended and at times tolerated. Some people go through a marriage or two before catching on to the imperfect relationship between the intensity of in-love and the duration of it. Those who become addicted to being in-love are not likely to be satisfied with marriage or with any affair for very long, requiring a change of partners at regular intervals. For these people, the in-love experience is so intense that anyone with whom they are not in-love, such as the spouse or ex-mistress, is the enemy. Marriage is unworkable for people who must be in-love at all times.

While affairs involve sex, they are not usually about sex. Affairees tend to be different from the spouse in some significant aspect, but that significant aspect is more often than not something functional rather than something physical. And the function is not typically sex. One woman chose a lover simply because he didn't seem superior to her as her husband did. Men with domestic wives seem attracted to career women, while men whose wives are involved with careers seem attracted to domestic types. Doctors' wives choose shepherds, nymphs frolic with stockbrokers. The choice of an affairee seems based on the other person's *difference from* the spouse rather than *superiority to* the spouse.

One surprisingly common reason for an affair is politeness. Little girls are taught to answer "no" to sexual requests, but little boys are not, and the refusal of a sexual offer from a female would be not only un-macho but also impolite. When a man gets into an unfamiliarly intimate situation with a women previously identified as a friend and now clearly a friend in need, it would be impolite, even ungallant, to turn her away. Men who can't say "no, thank you" gracefully are at risk for pity affairs with depressed women who have recently lost a lover and need reassurance of their attractiveness. Once an affair is consummated, its motivation may be misunderstood by all involved.

Some people have affairs out of nothing more complicated than curiosity. After years of fidelity in a sexually stimulating society, they may want to see what they are missing. The motive is so innocent that the crisis may come as a shocking surprise.

In unraveling a crisis of infidelity, it is important to know why the affair was begun. Certainly the reasons for an affair are far more important than such details as "who?" "where?" "when?" and "how much?" "Why?" is a far more subtle question, nowhere more subtle than here.

Unique Infidelity—Almost a Bolt From the Blue

Almost a third of the adulterers I've seen have claimed to have had only one affair. Some of these have had only one adulterous sex act. Many others have had only rare, widely spaced one-night stands. The affairs or dalliances may have occurred accidently, perhaps while drunk. Perhaps on these occasions the infidel is curious, or too embarrassed to say "no" to someone seductive, or too polite to say "no" to someone dependent. Perhaps the infidel is alone and needs a friend, or is unhappy and frightened and needs reassurance or someone to help him or her through the night. Perhaps he or she really does go a bit crazy, a manic episode for instance.

The behavior is unique and situational. It just happens, somewhat like a bolt from the blue, unplanned and surprising. These people do not consider their behaviour appropriate and they do not blame their spouse. They usually try to keep their affairs secret from their spouse, as they don't want to threaten their marriage or bring about any change in it, and they have no desire or expectation to repeat or continue the experience. Their marriages, as any marriage, are boring sometimes, frustrating sometimes, infuriating sometimes, but not to the point that the infidel seriously considers getting out of it. There may be the sense that the dalliance would not have occurred had the marriage been stronger. Generally, they are committed to making it stronger. The defect is experienced as residing within the infidel or the affairee, not in the cuckold.

The relationship with the affairee may have been friendly before the sex and now conflictual, embarrassing, or downright hostile. It may be protective, the secret alliance of partners in crime. There may even be a panicky sense of inextricable, and not completely welcome, bonding with the affair partner. Although there may be a clear attraction to the affairee, that is seen as a danger rather than love. If, in the aftermath of such a dalliance, the infidel justifies the act by defining the situation as "in-love" with the affairee, which sometimes happens in the postcoital confusion, that changes the situation drastically.

The crisis following such an affair may center on fear of being exposed, fear of it happening again, or concern about one's own stability. One man recognized that he must be manic-depressive like his father when he found himself in bed with a strange woman for the first time in his long and happy marriage. All manner of individual symptoms occur under such circumstances, with several myocardial infarctions and a few suicide attempts. Agoraphobia is a classic aftermath of a unique infidelity, anxiety attacks are common, as are obsessive-compulsive symptoms with a fear of venereal disease or pregnancy. The usual pathology is depression, often with considerable agitation.

The marriage is unavoidably affected. There may be revised expectations, even a somewhat inappropriate effort to blame a previously satisfactory marriage. If the dalliance is known to the spouse, the cuckold may focus on possible defects in the marriage, which may confuse the issue enormously.

Certainly, there are far more affairs of this sort than ever come to light. Most of these produce only mild discomfort to the infidel and little perceptible confusion in the marriage. Years later they may be remembered vaguely and with little guilt or anxiety, with justification based on their situational nature. There may even be pride over the infrequency with which such incidents occurred. Or there may be regret that there were not more of them, since the memory may be rather pleasant. Often though, the memories fester, the guilt increases, and the incidents take on more and more significance with time. This is especially likely if the marriage grows more and more intimate with time. The long past affair may seem to be a barrier to the desired intimacy, openness, and honesty of the developing marriage.

If such affairs are unique, situational, and now long past, should the therapist encourage revelation? Obviously, if the affair is suspected by any family member, if the individual crisis is severe, or if there is danger of emotional blackmail from the affairee or anyone else who knew of the affair, it must be revealed. If there are problems in the marriage, or the desire for greater intimacy, it should be revealed.

On the other hand, if both partners are satisfied with a less intimate marriage, then secrets, caution, and the anticipation of recurrences would assist them in achieving that increased distance and decreased bonding.

In general I encourage revelation, and I am willing to work individually with someone who is not yet ready to make that revelation. Interestingly, when I do see the spouse and raise questions about infidelities in general, he or she usually already suspects the affair and is willing to continue the marriage nonetheless, thus dispelling the infidel's fears.

There are marriages in which it is just assumed that extramarital sex will occur sometimes. Neither wants to talk about the details, but someone's anxieties may be relieved by restating the unadorned principle that it is not a problem. In those cases, the specifics are unimportant to anyone, and therefore not part of the crisis, unless one spouse has decided that a closer, more intimate and honest marriage would be preferable. Exploration of the other's wishes in the matter might help determine whether the revelation would be an unwanted intrusion.

I've seen a few infidels who had brief, secret affairs and chose not to reveal the affair to the spouse. Though most of them were determined not to repeat the experience, their marriages were damaged and became confusing for a time, with inexplicable distance and dissatisfaction, which could not be approached in therapy. The decision was to be faithful but not to be completely open. A distant marriage may not be damaged, but a close one will be.

One young man, previously happily married, had such a sexual episode and quickly stopped it. But he decided he wanted a more distant marriage and the option to be unfaithful if he ever wanted to do so again. He did not see a problem in his marriage, but he did now believe monogamy restrictive. He decided he liked the sense of independence he gained by having a secret. It made him feel one-up on his wife, a little more powerful, a little less dependent. He did feel a little lonelier, but he thought the trade-off was worth it. I have no doubt that such a conclusion has been reached by many who choose to live with such secrets. The damage to the relationship may be slight, if the spouse also is comfortable with the distance.

In my practice those who reveal their dalliances have triggered major crises by doing so, but no cuckolds have left permanently, and all of the marriages have become more intense, closer, and more communicative, whether that was desired or not. One wife revealed a brief old affair that had worried her for years. Her husband was furious, primarily because he felt she was coercing him into revealing his ancient dalliances. He considered those to be none of her business. She was clearly trying to get closer than he would prefer.

The truly serious difficulties occur when an affair is suspected but vigorously denied. Several cuckolds have been brought in and labeled paranoid by their adulterous spouses. Some have even been hospitalized for their jealous delusions. I have encountered several children who knew or suspected affairs which the parents denied and suffered considerable damage as a result.

The decision about revelation must be individual for each situation, but revelation is usually both safer and more ethical. The choice seems to rest with the question of whether secrets or therapy would be more productive in the long run.

CASE 9   *Tennis, Anyone?*

Eve had an anxiety attack. She called my office, referred by a relative I had seen, and told me she was dying. She was hyperventilating and in panic. Her husband, Egbert, a dentist accustomed to such reactions, rushed in (the maid had called him) while we were talking on the phone. I sent her out for a walk with him. A second phone call was far calmer. She was scheduled for an appointment the next day. She insisted on an individual appointment, which of course suggested the diagnosis. The next morning she called to cancel it, saying she had decided to divorce her husband and move to California later in the day. Betsy, my partner, talked her into coming in anyway, by gently pointing out that she was obviously upset about something embarrassing, perhaps an affair or some other secret, and we were accustomed to dealing with such things.

Eve came in alone and confirmed our suspicions. Eve was 30, had been married ten years, and had three small children. Her parents, though wealthy, had not considered college important for her. She went for a year, made her debut, and got married, still a virgin. Her husband, Egbert, was five years older. Egbert was a large, quiet, handsome man, who worked long hours as a dentist. At night his feet hurt. He was nice to her and gave her whatever she wanted. She had three children, a Mercedes, a big house, a maid, and a tennis court.

She hoped she could get Egbert to exercise and was taking tennis lessons so she could play with him. The tennis instructor, a college student, gave her a book to read. She'd never read a book before, nor had Egbert. She tried to get Egbert to read it too, but he preferred the *Wall Street Journal*. She talked about the book with the tennis instructor. More books followed. Finally he gave her *Fear of Flying*. By then they were talking about things she'd never talked with anyone about. It was a hot day and he asked if he could take a shower and she just stood there as he walked out of the shower naked and they fell into bed, for a few frantic seconds. They both felt foolish. She hurried him out and had an anxiety attack.

Eve tried to act calm when Egbert came home, and he didn't notice anything untoward. She called the young tennis instructor and asked him what she should do. He acted helpless and begged her not to tell her husband. She fired him, rehired him, and fired him again. He left his phone off the hook. She went to his apartment to take him back his books, then feared Egbert would notice, and went back to get them. That night she seduced Egbert and it was, as usual, good. She felt some relief but she didn't sleep all night. The next day she had another episode of hyperventilating. That was when she called me.

She told me the story and calmed down. She had already told Egbert she was going to divorce him, but wouldn't tell him why. I told her to tell Egbert the whole story and bring him in a few days later. She came in alone. She hadn't told him, she hadn't slept, she wanted sleeping pills, and she'd planned an escape to California. I told her I wouldn't see her without him.

She brought Egbert in. She had now told him she wasn't going to leave. He was baffled by her plan to leave him since he thought the marriage wonderful. She'd never complained before. Now she wanted to talk about things and have him read things. He preferred to solve problems rather than talk about them. He wanted to know what to do. As he saw it, Eve had gone crazy. The dalliance was not mentioned and he left more confused than before and rather hostile about the pointless confusion.

That night she told him everything. She felt great relief. He was angry for a few minutes, then felt panic with the fear that unless he changed to be more like the tennis instructor he might lose her. She was so comfortable that she suggested rehiring the tennis instructor. He actually cried for the first time in his adult life.

By the next appointment, he felt more secure that she would stay and playfully threatened to have affairs of his own. Mostly he was awkwardly, frantically responsive and attentive, offering to take her dancing, offering to read the books she'd read. She loved it, but he was sweating.

They spent six months in a couples group, while she tried to teach him to communicate about the things she had learned. He gradually became a little more playful, but not too much, as she basically liked him as he was. They quit coming to the group when a new couple came in and he could not face the embarrassment of reviewing the affair again. He saw the problem as solved.

A year later she called to report that he was working less and enjoying it more. She was happy, he was happy. She was glad the whole thing had happened. She could get his attention very easily now.

There was no question that Eve's reaction to her dalliance was too intense to permit it to go unexplained. The result of the confession was mostly positive. A marriage which has survived such revelations is not always better for it, but it certainly can be.

HABITUAL INFIDELITY—
A DEVELOPMENTAL PATTERN

Some people just don't believe in fidelity. They never expected to practice it. Their parents didn't practice it. They view it as a perversion, akin to celibacy, something belonging to a previous era or a foreign culture or a strange religion. There is little conflict in their mind about it, little guilt or anxiety. Yet, even if they brag about it to their friends, they must keep it secret from their spouse. If that's OK with the spouse, it may not produce many crises. In a society which does not permit divorce, and which expects men to have more freedom than women, the women have some security in their restricted position. But in our world, in which marriages can be blown away by the next sexual attraction, the cuckold has no security and can not accept this double standard blithely. This old-fashioned double standard is a source of conflict if one partner insists upon it and the other finds it threatening. It is a source of distance if the philanderer knows it is unacceptable to the spouse, does it defiantly, and keeps it secret.

Philanderers are usually male, may have cultural or religious support for their views, and may not see their infidelities as related to marital problems, though the wife is nonspecifically the enemy since she is opposing a sacred male perogative. He may be angry at marriage and place responsibility for the marriage on the wife, as if the marriage belongs to her and is used against him to prevent his appropriate freedom.

Some defiantly determined philanderers are multi-married and adulterous in each marriage. Rather than marrying someone who encourages his hobby, or pursues her own, he marries someone whose security requires fidelity and is devastated by his philandering. Such men may be angry with wives for objecting to their infidelities or for failing to satisfy them so completely that they won't want affairs. There is a peculiar religious support for blaming the cuckold in those fundamentalist sects which consider adultery in the heart identical to adultery in the flesh, and which may even go so far as to consider acting out the impulses a possible cure for the mind wracked with lust. One notorious philanderer said, "It is wrecking my life. No matter what I do, I still want other women. No matter how hard I try, I can't get my fill. I can't make it go away. If my wife will just stick it out, maybe when I get older the desire will go away." It had never occurred to him that one's actions are based on decisions rather than inclinations.

If a man marries a woman who accepts this pattern, as his mother and grandmother did, the marriage may stay together. She may take courses in being a "Total Woman," and both may get what they were expecting out of the marriage. There is little current societal support for this pattern. Fewer and fewer women are tolerating it. The men may be quite confused by their wives' failure to accept a pattern their mothers never questioned. Such men gripe to one another about liberated women.

Apparently there are societies and ethnic groups in our own society in which this pattern works. The wives understand and accept it, even expect it, and they may keep their own sexuality suppressed in order to avoid interfering with it. But our society no longer supports such a double standard. Most men have come to expect equal partners in their marriages, and equal partners are not likely to tolerate this pattern lying down. Those who do accept this don't come tell me about it.

Most of these men are stuck in early adolescence, still struggling with their fear of women and female control, and proving their manhood by defying women — just as they did at 14, when they sneaked out of the house, defying their mothers, so they could try to get laid. They use this bad little boy act as proof of masculinity.

Infidelities begin early, even on the honeymoon. They are not necessarily more frequent during periods of marital conflict. They may even stop when the marriage is threatened. In-love, if it happens at all, doesn't last long. The affairees are often humiliated, rarely valued. If the pattern is known and the spouse tries to circumscribe it, with a weekly night out or separate vacations, the infidel is likely to defy the pattern. There is great resistance to domestic control.

A few men do not seem to quite fit this defiant pattern. They are obsessive, conforming workaholics who adapt themselves precisely to their masculine society at work. They don't really defy women; they don't think of women's feelings at all. They partake of women sexually, either obsessively or competitively, but without concern for the relationship with the woman at the motel or the woman at home. They may like sex, or consider it healthy, but women just don't matter to them. Emotions of any sort are to be overcome or ignored—emotions just don't fit into the equation. And they can get their sex less emotionally away from home.

Some women follow the same pattern, although it is far less frequent. Their fathers were adulterous too, and they disdained the weak mothers who accepted it, while they admired and emulated the fathers' seemingly greater strength and independence. There is some societal support for the female philanderers too, but infidelity works no better for women than it does for the men. The spouse is the enemy, the divorce rate is high. The relatively few female philanderers I've seen have had fathers and husbands like this and assume it is universal among men, so their similar behavior is a blow for equal rights. As one such woman put it, "All married men screw around. Everyone I've ever been to bed with did."

CASE 10 *Puppy Dog Tails*

Fritz and a woman from work were arrested for soliciting an undercover policewoman to join a sexual threesome. The arrest was shown on television, and cost him his job. Felicia didn't know how to react. She assumed she must leave him if she acknowledged knowing about it. She felt that he had broken the trust, not by having other women, but by doing it so publicly that she would have to acknowledge it. Fritz had humiliated her. She asked him not to come home quite yet while she thought it out. All her friends and family knew about it. They urged her to divorce him; she resisted. His parents called to tell her she was making too much of it; "Men are just like that." His friends urged him to lie, but he couldn't think of a lie to tell.

Finally the depressed, confused Felicia made an appointment, came in alone, and described her quandary. Felicia had known, at some level, that Fritz screwed around. She tried not to ask him about his job and all his traveling, because she didn't want to have to face the possibility that he was involved with other women. She had always known, at some level, about his philandering, and she knew that he knew she knew. Even if she hadn't known it before, she certainly knew after he gave her herpes. They had never talked about it. They never talked about anything that personal. They kept their distance from one another. Felicia enjoyed a quiet domestic life like her mother had had after her father had left. She considered herself lucky that Fritz had stayed married to her, even if he was only home on weekends. She liked being at home with the two babies, and Fritz was fun on the weekends. She'd often said that she had the ideal life of a single mother—enough money to stay home all day and a regular Saturday night date.

I called Fritz, explained Felicia's plight, and asked him to come in with her and reveal all. We negotiated his resistance to participating in therapy, and he could see the logic of my suggestion; he could also see that he had no alternatives. He did not want to lose Felicia and his little children. He agreed to come in.

At the appointment, they were terrified. Neither wanted a divorce, and each feared talking about it. Felicia didn't want him to talk about his affairs, but I talked Fritz into telling her the whole truth. I assured her that she had lived with his philandering for all these years and could continue to do so if she chose to, but she should know what she was choosing to live with. He opened up eagerly. He told her about his immigrant father, so proud of his latest mistress that he took Fritz and his brother to meet her when he was 14. He described his mother's resolute refusal to acknowledge even the most blatant infidelities while she nagged about everything else. He told her about his window peeking compulsions in adolescence. He explained how his first wife had reacted to the discovery of his affairs by having one too, so he left her and his infant daughter. He described the orgy at the bachelor party before he married Felicia, and the repeat of it when they returned from their honeymoon. He confessed the competitive escapades when he and his friends would show off for one another with prostitutes. As he described this, he sounded less frightening and more pitiful. He cried about his help-lessness in the face of his sexual impulses. He told her he loved her and needed her. He wasn't sure he could change.

She said she couldn't divorce him, but couldn't live with the affairs. I pointed out that she had, and indeed could. She asked him to stop em-barrassing her. He told her she could have affairs too if she liked. But he told her he couldn't change the pattern. He feared that he would become impo-tent if he didn't have variety. He explained everything he could think of about himself, revealing more than he ever had, and it was pitiful. She became sympathetic with him. He reassured her eloquently that the problem was his and that she was not to blame. She believed him and became secure with that. Suddenly he was not afraid of her.

They terminated too quickly, and have called with other crises, but still don't want to change drastically. They have become friends for the first time. He began to share everything with her. Their sex life improved. His whole relationship with the female gender changed. He even made contact with the daughter from his first marriage. But he began to spend more time with Felicia then she wanted, and she didn't want her life changed that much. She did not object to the few episodes of slippance he had over the next few years, as long as they were discreet. He could understand the virtue of honesty, but the concept of fidelity seemed weird to him, and Felicia did not really require it. She encouraged him to resume traveling.

Fritz had been taught that men are defined by their sexuality but that women can't tolerate male sexuality. His father believed that, his mother lived it, and his first wife confirmed it. He had no concept of women except as confirmers of male sexuality or enemies of it. Once the intensity and fragility of his own sexuality had been accepted by Felicia, he could be friends with her, but still not faithful to her. He doesn't fear her, but he can't bring himself to bond with her—in part because she doesn't expect or require it. His comfort with women has extended into his relationships with all the other women in his life. The crisis point for Fritz was when Felicia could no longer deny the infidelities. The turning point came when she, and then he, recognized that you don't have to get a divorce when you acknowledge that sexuality is not always perfectly controlled.

This couple was able to use a potentially disruptive crisis to become friends. I have little optimism that the marriage will stay together forever. Now that Fritz is less afraid of women, he is at risk for a more romantic and personal affair, and that would be more threatening to the marriage. Felicia feels better about herself now, and could leave him if that happened. The prognosis for the marriage is poor because Fritz still can't make a full commitment to fidelity, and there are many hazards out there.

Most marriages with this pattern don't turn out well. Felicia and Fritz found an acceptable, though hardly ideal solution. Some philanderers keep their marriages distant through constant hostility, others through steely politeness, and if the pattern remains constant, the marriages may continue for a lifetime, distant but unthreatened, and maybe even polite. The silent acceptance of the pattern of counterphobic philandering keeps the distance constant, and the marriage cautiously stable. But that constant politeness is tiring, and makes the philanderer need reassurance from other women all the more. These men are guilt-ridden bad little boys who don't know what to do with their sexuality. It takes a secure and sexy woman to live with a man whose sexuality scares him this much. She can't afford to let it scare her. But first it has to stop being secret and that seems dangerous. It is. Few people would choose to live with this pattern, if they knew they had a choice. They need not take the philandering personally; philanderers are not personally involved in either their marriages or their affairs.

When these marriages don't last, the ultimate problem may not be the sexuality, but the man's fear of getting too close to a woman—thus his constant counterphobic defiance, distrust, evasion, and belittling of women. It is not that he likes sex that much, but that he fears women that much.

STRUCTURAL INFIDELITY

Some affairs do arise from forces within the marriage. The preponderance of emotion remains within the marriage, although much of that emotion may be anger. Some of these marriages may be almost or completely sexless. Some may be stormy. Some may be distant. The affair is known, sometimes explicitly, sometimes with permission, sometimes defiantly. Both partners are aware of the problems in the marriage and have made various efforts to find a solution. The affair is part of that process, sometimes an effort to dramatize dissatisfaction, sometimes to find an answer, sometimes to find a way out, sometimes to find the courage to continue. While an affair may ruin a good marriage, it may hold a bad marriage together. There are cuckolds who can't tolerate intimacy, but who do enjoy a good fight. They are not about to end a good fight by turning a devalued and despised adulterous spouse over to a rival. The affairees are not usually valued much and the affairs aren't likely to be long-term. They may well stop once they have been dramatically confessed and the cuckold blamed for them. Sometimes they are kept up for a while as the infidel gains more control in the marriage.

These affairs are quite different from those in which the infidel operates secretly. Even if the secret infidel's marriage is terrible, there is no concerted effort to change it or end it. The hallmark of this group of affairs is the attitude of "look what you made me do" or "look what I'll do if you don't do what I want you to." In covert affairs, whether unique or habitual, the infidel takes responsibility for the affair and tries to protect the marriage from ending or changing. In overt affairs, the marriage is intolerable and must change or it will surely end. Some of these marriages have already passed the point of decision and the infidel is holding on until the kids grow up or the next spouse can be found.

These marriages may have overwhelming interactional problems, or they may have only an insoluble sexual problem. Each situation is different. But the affair arises directly from the structure of the marriage.

CASE 11   *Sex Manuals*

Gilda was the prettiest girl in town. She was pursued by all men, but almost kept her virginity. Not quite. She gave in once and it was awful. She didn't try again. After college she worked briefly for an airline and married a banker. Grover was perfect but he was stuffy. He was satisfied that Gilda was beautiful, talented, and intelligent, that she gave him three beautiful, and intelligent daughters, that she became president of the garden club, and that she started her own successful travel agency. But her flirtatiousness bothered him. He acted morally superior, criticized her for flirting, questioned the appropriateness of her taste. His putdowns were unending. She pretended to be amused. She wasn't.

They never quite learned to have sex effectively. He told her she was frigid. She believed he was right and began to dress more outlandishly, which alarmed him even more and brought forth more criticism. After 15 years of marriage she had never had an orgasm or won an argument or been told she was good enough.

She read a book on sexuality and got up the courage to tell Grover that the sexual problem might be his rather than hers. Incredulous, he promptly had sex with another woman. He told Gilda and insisted the other woman was satisfied with him. She then seduced a married neighbor, who specialized in such matters, and found sex quite different and satisfactory. She suddenly felt whole and free. She told Grover about the affair and tried to teach him what she was learning about her own sexuality. He became impotent with her and developed incapacitating anxiety. He tried other women and was impotent there too. He knew of her affair and raged about it, but she wouldn't stop. She taunted him with it. She feared that she could never live with him and wasn't sure she wanted to, but she felt guilt over the affair and agreed to try the marriage. She broke off the affair. Grover improved. Sex was finally good. But Grover now criticized her for her affair as well as for everything else. She decided he would never let her be his equal.

At this point, six months too late, they entered couples therapy. He tried to stop his parental behavior and accept her infidelity, but the humiliation was too intense. He kept punishing her, just more subtly. He couldn't trust her. He saw her affair as proof of incompetence rather than as a successful problem-solving process. She no longer cared. She knew now that she was OK and that Grover had been keeping her from growing up all these years. He didn't want her to leave him and criticized her for it, but she left him anyway. She was determined never again to marry someone who didn't like her.

The sexual problem in Gilda and Grover's marriage was solvable and was solved as soon as Gilda ceased to accept Grover's definition of it. It had been used for 15 years to maintain a marital structure that reinforced Gilda's view of herself as a sexy-looking, but sex-free, child. It protected Grover's view of himself as a totally controlled, mature man. Gilda's solution solved the sex problem but reinforced the view that she was not really competent and was in need of a supervisor. However, once she felt truly sexual, she didn't think she needed one. This is the quandary I've previously described in "The Doll's House Marriage" (Pittman & Flamenhaft, 1970).

In cases of structural infidelity, there are several layers of problems. The top layer, the affair, is usually easily ended and of course must be. The second layer is the immediate problem the affair was intended to solve. That too is usually easily solved. The third layer, the structural problem, is the fear of intimacy and equality. Seldom do both partners get that resolved at the same time, so that the marriage often ends as one partner becomes capable of a real marriage. Sometimes such marriages flounder along for a lifetime, with one partner maintaining control and distance and overlooking the other's known but undiscussed affairs. These people want to be married, just not to one another. Sometimes therapy can work, sometimes not. That depends on the marriage, not on the affair. Keeping the couple together is not a therapeutic success. They can do that on their own, even if one or both is destroyed along the way. Marriage cannot be a game in which there is a winner and a loser.

FALLING IN LOVE—A ROMANTIC CARETAKER

Isn't love grand? It grants clear immunity from the rules of logic, the pressures of reality, and the responsibilities of living. In a culture which romanticizes love, it becomes an explanation for anything. In the German Romantic tradition and in 19th century Italian opera, the most desirable consummation of love was death. Only by dying at the point of most intense love could the love be made to last. In real life, love fades. Some people don't like that reality. Just as they resist the fading of youth and beauty, they resist moving on to the next stage of the human life cycle. They like being in love, and when they marry they expect to be in love forever. It isn't the same a few years later. It may be better, it is surely saner and more efficient, it is probably friendlier and more accepting, it may even be more fun and closer—but it isn't as intoxicating and it doesn't blot out reality as completely.

There are some people, as often male as female, who can't live comfortably without the in-love experience. They are a little like the habitual philanderers. Their irresponsibility is just as innocent. They are more dangerous because they take it all so seriously. Their marriages don't last long enough to get into therapy, and they don't see it as a problem anyway—they're not sick, they're just in-love.

The crisis of "in love" affairs comes in longstanding marriages. These people have been married for a decade or more, have had few if any previous affairs, and have maintained workable though sometimes placid marriages prior to the affair. The infidel has no complaints about the marriage, but no longer feels "in-love." Usually, the spouse feels no need to feel "in-love" and instead feels the comfortable love and unquestioned commitment of longstanding marriage. The lack of "in-loveness" doesn't seem much of a problem until the affair begins.

The affair may have been sexualized quite accidentally, just as in a unique affair, but the postcoital reaction is different. Usually the relationship is already intimate—a friendship, or a close working relationship, or an old lover from youth. Unlike the sort of guilt-relieving sexual misfits chosen by habitual philanderers for temporary bouts of "in-love," these affairees may be reasonably appropriate mates. Not always of course—people looking for someone to fall in love with can pick real dillies. Often the chosen lover is a dependent and desperate person in the midst of a domestic crisis. Somehow the relationship gets sexualized and in the effort to explain it the infidel decides that he or she is unhappily married and now in love. Some infidels leave the marriage immediately, before the intoxication wears off. Most stay at home, torn between the spouse and the affairee, producing some of the toughest problems a marital therapist faces.

The marriage, which may have been just fine, will suddenly develop such severe problems that it looks like a structural affair. The previously sensible, efficient, independent, competent spouse will be told a few lies, kept at a distance for a while, misled about the infidel's obvious emotional crisis. In no time, the spouse is dependent, confused, unsure, and irritatingly intrusive. Anything the spouse does is wrong and makes the situation worse. Before the secret is out, the spouse's efforts at closeness and nurturance are irritants. After the secret is out, the spouse's anxiety, anger, depression, and efforts at guilt production are obviously irritants. If the spouse is cool and understanding, even that is an irritant. Before the revelation, the spouse is the enemy in fantasy. After the revelation, the spouse is the enemy in reality. The distinction is not made between the enemy of the person and the enemy of the "love." To people in love the whole outside world is an intrusion.

Fortunately love fades, but the months before it does are horrible for the cuckold. Cuckolds in such situations lose 20 pounds, get doctorates, have nose jobs or boob jobs, start jogging, learn sexual tricks, make every improvement ever mentioned, and solve all problems ever dreamed of. But none of it works, at least not yet. If the cuckold attempts suicide or homicide, or becomes as obnoxious as possible, that won't work either. The cuckold no longer exists for the infidel, except as a faceless enemy, a representative of the world that is not part of the "love." Any effort to break up the affair just strengthens it.

CASE 12   *The Nurses Station*

Hubert and Helena had been married for 25 years. Their children were grown, but they both were youthful and energetic. Hubert worked out at a health club several times a week. Helena dieted steadily and had had her eyes fixed. Indoors she could pass for 28, though she was near 50. Hubert had not been quite as successful as she'd hoped, and he traveled more than she liked and he preferred business to personal entertaining. She loved to entertain and had a perfect home for it. She was a good shopper and an inventive cook, so their wealthier friends didn't know they weren't quite as well off as they seemed. Hubert's brother was a Cadillac dealer, so they got nearly new demonstrators cheap. They could charge their vacations to the business and no one knew.

They had been almost completely faithful to one another all these years. Sex had not been very important to either of them, and Hubert did not complain about Helena's lack of interest in it. She assumed that if he wanted more he would have it out of town. He really didn't — it wasn't important to him either. They tried sex every couple of weeks, when either was getting uncomfortable about how long it had been. If either wanted it the other was agreeable. In fact, they were agreeable about everything except guest lists for parties. Helena wanted the social leaders, Hubert the business leaders. They always compromised and there was never a problem. Even the children had been agreeable.

Then Hubert got fired. He was depressed for a while but Helena was supportive. He got a new job. His boss, Boots, was a somewhat younger woman with more status and more clout in the industry. She was aggressive, efficient, socially crude, overweight, ugly, styleless, sexy. She could not have been more different from Helena. Yet she had the aggressive qualities Hubert wished he had in himself.

Boots had just gone through a divorce. Her husband had caught her in another affair and after the messy trial had gotten custody of the children. She wanted Hubert and she took him. He didn't stand a chance.

Helena didn't notice for months. She never liked to talk about business. Although Hubert had more and more meetings and traveled more, she only noticed when his work interfered with their social schedule. He was making money and she was pleased. After a month or so without sex, she decided it was time and told him so. He wasn't interested. She waited another month and tried again, but again he wasn't interested. She got suspicious and raised the question of whether he was involved with someone else. She was shocked when he told her he wanted a divorce. He denied having an affair. She never suspected Boots, who had been so awkward the one time Helena met her at a party.

She decided they needed therapy. He was agreeable. When they came for the appointment he told her he wanted a divorce. I pointed out that he obviously was in an affair. He acknowledged that he was in love with Boots. Helena listened incredulously, cried softly while he supplied tissues, and then blew up at him. He didn't know she cared. He said he would move out. Helena ordered him out, then begged him to stay. I suggested that he move slowly, which suited him fine. I then set up individual appointments for each of them.

Hubert came first. He described the excitement of having someone with whom he could discuss business. He said he'd always wanted more sex with Helena, but she never seemed very passionate, just agreeable. His successes had never seemed sufficient for Helena, but his talents were much approved by Boots. He'd never been particularly unhappy in his marriage, but he'd never been as happy as he was now in this new business with this new woman. I suggested to him that he tell Helena everything and tell Boots that he had told Helena everything. I said that if he couldn't break off the affair he should bring Boots for the next appointment.

Helena came next. She was frantic, depressed, emotionally labile and without direction. She didn't want anyone to know what was happening. She hadn't slept since the last appointment. I suggested she (1) take antidepressants, (2) shut up about the affair, (3) acknowledge she had failed Hubert, (4) seduce him nightly, (5) tell him why she wanted him, (6) remove all threats and tell him she'd wait it out for a while, (7) plan a career, and (8) wait.

By the next week, she had taken the antidepressants for two days, hated them and stopped them, but slept fine and was no longer crying and shaking. She had seduced him on schedule and had applied to graduate school. He had told Boots what he was doing and told Helena everything. He was startled by the change in Helena; he liked it but thought it too late. He liked the sex with Helena but hadn't told Boots about it, as it would upset her. He was confused by his mistress' anger. She had expected him to divorce Helena without telling her why. She was uncomfortable about Helena's knowing of the affair. She was furious at the suggestion that she come to therapy. She did not see why she should be involved in Helena's mental problems. Hubert realized that Boots did not understand the gravity and complexity of his life and situation, as well as his responsibility for Helena and his family. Reality was setting in. I suggested that he tell Boots a lie. Perhaps he could keep his sex with Helena secret from Boots.

Hubert did the only thing a gentleman could do with that paradox. He became impotent, which he related to his drinking. He stopped drinking at home and Helena could arouse him. He kept drinking each afternoon with Boots and avoided sex with her. This didn't last. He told Boots of the sex with Helena and she told him to stop. He tried, but Helena seduced him anyway. Hubert's anxiety increased. He was under pressure at home and at work. His marriage had never been better, but he still felt in love with Boots. Boots would not come to therapy. He began to avoid appointments, as Boots set his schedule and sent him out of town each time an appointment was set. The unchanging situation seemed permanent. Helena was feeling stronger, sexier, more independent. She wasn't quite enjoying herself, but she liked herself.

Hubert acknowledged that he was afraid to give up the affair with Boots, for fear his job would be endangered. He also was afraid of Helena's reprisals when he was back fully in the marriage. He was more afraid of Boots than of Helena. He told some more lies to Boots about sex with Helena, but couldn't break off the affair. Helena demanded that he leave. I agreed it was time. He wasn't sure this was the right thing to do, but he planned a move into a temporary furnished apartment.

When Boots found out he was leaving Helena, she finally called me. She wouldn't come in but agreed to a telephone appointment. She wasn't sure she wanted him after all. She didn't know what to do. He seemed so weak and pitiful. She didn't understand why Helena hadn't just stepped aside back when things were good. She couldn't believe they loved one another. I tried to explain the nature of marriage. It had no meaning for her. She had begun to see herself as a mother or a nurse to him, just helping him out of an awful marriage. I tried to explain that the marriage wasn't awful, just dull, and that this was as much Hubert's doing as Helena's. I told her they were still having sex. She was furious. Hubert had lied to her. She saw it as an infidelity. She raged and blamed me for ruining their affair. She accused me of being unethical. I was supposed to break up marriages, not affairs.

She then explained what a nice person she was, how respectable her family had been, and how she was not a home wrecker. She told me she would never refer any patients to me and hung up.

Meanwhile, Helena arranged everything for Hubert's move, cleaning up, choosing the extra furniture, and putting down shelf paper. Hubert moved. That night he and Boots had a fight and he had a heart attack. Boots took him to the hospital. The hospital called Helena, who was there within minutes. When Helena saw Boots, she screamed at her for killing her husband and hit her with her purse. Helena and Boots had a fistfight in the Coronary Care Unit. Boots was furious; Helena was exultant; Hubert was sedated. Fortunately, it was a very mild heart attack (I believe he was merely hyperventilating).

Two weeks later, when Hubert left the hospital, Boots had quit her job and married the man named in her divorce suit. Hubert went home with Helena and was promoted into Boots' job. Within a few months the relationship was back as it always had been. Hubert blamed his lack of interest in sex on the heart attack, although it did not interfere with his exercise routine. Helena did not go on to graduate school. They had no interest in continuing therapy.

I don't think Hubert will have another affair. As with Hubert, Helena, and Boots, these triangles are a mess. They seem interminable and it is hard work to keep everyone alive and sane through the whole process.

TREATMENT OF CRISES OF INFIDELITY

Step 1: Emergency Response

Most often, the secret is out, someone is threatening divorce, and all hell is breaking loose. The therapist is given a wonderful crisis in which to operate.

The cuckold may come in alone, even if advised to bring the infidel, for the first appointment. The cuckold is angry, fearing loss of control; sometimes incredulous, doubting his or her own sanity; usually depressed, sometimes severely; always anxious, fearing the inevitable encounters and potential family disruption; and often ashamed, reviving every conceivable personal failing and insecurity. Suicide and homicide threats may have been made, divorce screamed about and lawyers hired, friends and relatives polled for advice. The cuckold knows about the affair, probably before being told, but keeps hoping the infidel will deny it and experiences the disorientation of believing neither the confirmation nor the denial. The cuckold needs emergency attention before he or she can realize that this is a common problem and one that is solvable gradually. Action need not be taken immediately. Medication, particularly antidepressants, may be in order. The infidel should be contacted right away, probably by the friendly therapist, who recognizes he or she is out of control, undoubtedly anxious, ashamed, defensive, and fearful of the therapist's criticism.

If it is the infidel who comes alone for the first appointment, he or she may be anxious, sometimes depressed, unable to tolerate the secret of a sexual dalliance or in a quandary about an ongoing affair he or she is unable to leave for a marriage he or she is unable to face. The spouse may have no idea of the affair or may be doing desperate detective work in the face of the infidel's denials. The infidel, in an attempt to hide the affair the affairee is threatening to reveal, may have suggested divorce without offering reasons to the confused spouse.

In every case of ongoing or suspected infidelity, immediate confirmation of the situation is recommended and perhaps accomplished by telephone at this point. Inevitably the reaction is less serious than anticipated. So far, in over 25 years of practice, I have not seen a single suicide or homicide from the confession, although there have been some severe responses to the continuation of confessed affairs which were sworn to be over and weren't.

There is another question which may be more relevant. What happens if the affair is not revealed? Perhaps then the crisis can be avoided, the opportunity for problem-solving forgone, and the distance, with its guilt and anger, maintained. But the marriage, for what it is worth, is saved, not just saved from the threat of divorce, but saved from the threat of intimacy. Therapy with a couple with a secret is very difficult. If the adulterer keeps the secret, the therapy is a charade, the therapist the enemy, and the affairee is the competing therapist in a plot against the cuckold and against the marriage. That frequently happens, and the therapy tends to end quickly. If it doesn't, it can become horribly confusing. If the couple keeps the affair secret from the therapist (that has actually happened), the therapy can only be an effort to demonstrate that therapy wouldn't work. If the therapist is sucked into an alliance with one spouse to keep an affair secret from the other spouse, that has to be a plot to drive someone crazy. If the affair is over, or long past, it is sometimes denied and becomes a focus of conflict.

At times the adulterer will strive diligently, and even successfully, to prove that the cuckold is paranoid to believe an affair took place. One wife became suspicious that her husband was not jogging each evening when his running clothes never got sweaty. She went to his secretary's apartment and found him naked in the secretary's closet. He told her she had gone crazy and was hallucinating the entire episode; then he brought her in for therapy.

It would be arrogant and infantilizing for a therapist or a spouse to protect someone from the opportunity of deciding what he or she is willing to live with. The secret does not belong to the adulterer or to the therapist but is the property of the marriage. The couple can and must decide what to do about it.

There are dangers to revealing an affair. The infidel usually feels great relief immediately. The cuckold, however, is angry, hurt, humiliated, betrayed, distrusting. He or she may engage in emergency behavior, which at first gets lost beneath the infidel's relief and realization that the response is not as intense as feared. The cuckold needs enormous support and reassurance at this point. Violence, separation, and counteraffairs are possible responses if the infidel is insufficiently contrite and reassuring. Confessions of affairs are best made when everyone is sober and in a supportive atmosphere, rather than in a car, during a drunken brawl, or at gunpoint.

Step 2: Bringing Everyone Together

If the spouse knows about the affair, he or she should be immediately included. If the spouse does not know that an affair is part of the current crisis, he or she should be immediately informed and included.

There may seem to be two exceptions to the rule of revelation. One is the situation in which someone is leaving a marriage for a current lover and does not want to prejudice the divorce against himself or herself. The infidel wants to leave the cuckold temporarily disoriented and guiltily preoccupied with some irrelevant deficiency so he or she can gain a financial advantage in a "friendlier" settlement. The affair will eventually be known, and the cuckold will eventually realize he or she has been "had." The short-term advantage will have long-term disadvantages. Couples therapy is impossible, but individual work may be done to help the departing spouse with the crisis of "in-love," which overlooks the long-range picture.

The other exception is the unique affair. Sometimes an infidel comes in with anxiety over a brief sexual dalliance, now past, and unsuspected by the cuckold. Many factors about the marriage might be examined before a decision is reached about whether the issue would be best explored between the spouses or individually. It may depend upon whether the infidel desires a closer or a more distant marriage. He or she cannot keep the secret without losing some intimacy and cannot reveal the secret without a commitment to greater intimacy and vulnerability. The revelation would certainly "hurt" the cuckold in the short run, but the secret might have worse long-range consequences. Couples therapy would be difficult, probably impossible, if the therapist knew but the spouse didn't.

The concept of privileged communication should not apply in marital therapy, and both partners should understand this from the beginning. It should be standard to reveal the affair, and the reasons not to do so would have to be compelling. At least there can be the acknowledgment that, during a previous period of marital conflict, indiscretions took place, even if the details are buried. Anyway, it rarely comes as a surprise. Spotless monogamy records, like spotless driving records, may be desirable, and affairs and wrecks dangerous, but it takes more than a fenderbender to lose your license.

If possible, in "in-love" affairs, the ongoing affairee should be included in the therapy. Ideally, the husband's mistress or wife's mister should be considered part of the family system and included in the therapy sessions. After two decades of attempting to include the mistress or mister, I've only been successful eight or ten times. More often the affairee will come in with the infidel, or alone, or will consent to telephone interviews. Whether the affairee is included or not, the persistent request for such inclusion clarifies and dramatizes his or her centrality in the family. Sometimes the infidel is shocked at the idea of such openness. Quite often the affairee will protest that affairs are supposed to be exempt from therapy. There does seem to be an unwritten rule among family therapists that mistresses and misters will be granted immunity from responsibility for their involvement in the system. Whether the affairee comes in or not, the cuckold should feel free to contact the third person in the marriage bed. The cuckold does not have to operate within the infidel's rules, and the affairee has no right of immunity. Even if the infidel is paralyzed between two relationships, everyone else need not be stupefied by the indecision.

The children may know what is going on, often before their cuckold parent does, which is a terrible burden. Children, being inherently selfish but also intolerant of suspense, may bounce back and forth between their parents, terrified of the outcome while offering desperate and invariably unhelpful advice. If the affair drags on they must be told something. Adult children, parents, other relatives and friends always seem to know and are often inappropriately, but understandably, impatient with the seemingly interminable process.

Step 3: Defining the Problem

Often a couple comes together, talks about all manner of confusing matters, and denies affairs when asked. One or both will then call to confess an affair and ask whether it should be revealed. It should of course, and inevitably is at the next appointment if not before. The first appointment is the infidel's sly attempt to have his or her spouse's sanity assessed before risking the revelation.

Therapy can begin as soon as the secret is out. All that precedes the revelation is merely a flirtation.

Once the secret is out, the reasons for the affair must be explored. The definition is rarely accurate since many affairs really do just happen and the dissatisfaction with the marriage follows rather than precedes the onset of the affair. The cuckold should not be too quick to take responsibility for causing the affair, unless he or she has deprived the spouse sexually or recently had his or her own affair. Most of the nonsexual dissatisfactions of marriage are best approached through some maneuver other than infidelity. In the effort to focus on factors specific to the marriage, the more common nonspecific factors should not be overlooked. What is sought is a definition of the marriage problem that provides the cuckold with an opportunity to demonstrate a willingness to make changes for the sake of the marriage, even if the problems being approached are only peripherally related to the affair.

As with any stress, the definition requires evaluation of the degree to which the affair is real or imagined, overt or covert, intrinsic or extrinsic, unique or habitual, permanent or temporary, specific or universal. The syndromes often overlap, particularly in structural affairs, since there are always structural dissatisfactions in marriage, and the infidel, the cuckold, the affairee, and the therapist all seem to blame all affairs on marital dissatisfaction. Placing the affair in one of the syndromes described earlier may take a little time — not just exploring the history, but also seeing what the couple does after the first interview.

Step 4: Calm Everybody Down

The sense of emergency can best be relieved by ending the affair, ending the marriage, or reinforcing commitment to the marriage. Seventy-five percent of affairs end at or before the point of revelation. The most important part of the calming procedure is the affirmation of commitment to the marriage. In unique affairs that can be done automatically by the infidel and usually just as quickly by the cuckold. In in-love affairs, the infidel leaves the continuation of the marriage in doubt. In habitual affairs the cuckold may do so. In structural affairs it may be more reassuring to leave the outcome in doubt until the marital problems can be better understood and a new marital contract negotiated. The therapist may have to offer the reassurance, by having them agree to stay together at least until the situation can be explored.

In those cases in which the affair has been denied and the suspicious "cuckold's" sanity questioned, the confirmation of the affair and of the "cuckold's" sanity is invariably calming. When the "cuckold's" sanity is confirmed without immediate acknowledgment of the reality of the affair, the crisis continues but is less disorienting. If it is apparent that the "cuckold" is mistaken, that the affair is not real but imagined, the "infidel" can offer reassurance by ending the nonsexual threatening relationship or behavior. If the "cuckold" is paranoid (and determined to feel betrayed), all efforts at reassurance and explanation will be even more infuriating. In this case phenothiazines are in order, though often angrily refused. Of course, the mates of paranoids are sometimes unfaithful too, and sometimes the therapist is mistaken about who is lying and who is crazy, and maybe both are true.

Step 5: Find a Solution

The solution is usually obvious. In unique affairs, the affair is over, the secret is out, and the task is to strengthen the marriage and learn to live with fallible human beings.

In habitual affairs, each affair is, in itself, meaningless, but the pattern expresses a reluctance to entrust one's sexuality to a marital partner. The couple has the choice of accepting some extramarital activity, which often makes the activity unnecessary, or working on the philanderer's problem with intimacy and the barriers the cuckold puts up to it, or ending the marriage. That cannot be an immediate decision, even if promises or threats are made in the wake of the crisis. The usual suggested solution is that the infidel try fidelity for a finite period while the therapy proceeds and the infidel shares his adulterous fantasies and impulses.

In structural affairs, the couple can agree to fight out the issues without the affairs. I believe, not too secretly, that many of these structural infidels are really philanderers trying to remain unhappily married, so the suggested solution is a test of that. Some of the cuckolds may continue to refuse sex even if that is the problem defined by the infidel, as if they too want to believe it is an habitual pattern. They might prefer bypassing an effort to work on their problem with intimacy by permitting the marriage to be unilaterally or bilaterally "open," especially if they know that solution rarely works.

When the infidel is in-love, the solution revolves around the infidel's making a choice. If the infidel chooses to end the affair, the crisis is dealt with as a unique or structural crisis. Sometimes the infidel will choose the affairee without question and then reconsider that decision later after the romance fades. If there is any ambivalence, the infidel is urged to go slowly, while the cuckold attempts to correct the dullness and routine of the long-standing marriage. When the secret is out and the decision made to break off the affair, the infidel may call the affairee from the therapist's office and end the affair. The couple may feel closer than they have in years and may work effectively on the problems being defined.

Step 6: Negotiating the Resistance

Unique affairs are already over when revealed, but the cuckold may have great resistance to accepting the infidel back into the marriage. The anger and rejection become the problem rather than the dalliance, and other reasons for the rejection should be explored.

Structurally adulterous couples are being asked to fight out the issues without resorting to affairs. The denial of marital problems can be a resistance. The existence of marital problems is universal but not necessarily related to the affair. There must be movement on both sides to demonstrate commitment to the marriage, so the marriage is saved by negotiating and effecting changes, even if the changes are not specifically related to the motivation for the affair. Therefore, while the infidel must control the adulterous behavior, both must be willing to change for the marriage. The most problematic resistance is the premature termination of therapy, most often by the cuckold, who is avoiding intimacy by declaring the problems solved. On the other hand, the infidel may avoid intimacy by declaring problems insoluble, a setup for more affairs. If the infidel has further secret affairs, that may amount to a decision to terminate the marriage.

Philanderers are asked to forgo affairs for a time while talking to the spouse about their sexual impulses and sexual past. The philanderers who see their sexual pattern as specific to themselves may thus end their long-standing isolation and sense of helplessness over their sexual impulses, and may be ready for an honest partnership. Those who see their philandering as universal or culturally required may resist such openness with a wife and may attempt to save the marriage by agreeing to fidelity without believing in equality. If the pattern is well established and has continued through previous crises, the infidel's reassurances that he will change his ways may ring hollow. Some do change, and most do with age, but is difficult to change a cultural pattern for the sake of a long devalued relationship with someone who is the enemy in fantasy and now in fact. The cuckold may be weary and may not expect or even desire a change. Efforts at control are not just useless, but actually inflammatory, as one of the reasons for philandering is to escape, overpower, and degrade women, by defying one and possessing another. Some of these men, however, are powerful, charismatic people. Such people may be sufficiently rewarding to live with that a dependent but self-content spouse may attempt it for years or a lifetime, and be glad she did (the Rose Kennedy syndrome). Many cuckolds want more from marriage and finally leave. Most women feel great relief upon escaping such men and most such men prefer to start over with a less angry (perhaps less equal) woman to whom they owe less emotionally.

The most obvious resistance is in the romantic affair. The infidel may feel unable to end the affair immediately. Some therapists refuse to work with couples who are in ongoing affairs. That is understandable. It can be treacherous to operate in a family full of lies. I am sympathetic with the idea that as long as an affair is continuing, a therapeutic separation is a reasonable suggestion. In fact, if the cuckold is dependent, and that dependency is an irritant to the infidel, a therapeutic separation might be the most corrective maneuver. When, however, the cuckold is so dependent that suicide or psychosis seems a real danger, separation may be too stressful; the finality of divorce may be less suspenseful and may elicit more support from relatives. If the couple stays together during the no longer secret affair, the cuckold has the opportunity to correct any behavior seen as contributory. That is a hard task, being constantly sabotaged by the infidel; it might be workable for only the most resilient and resourceful of cuckolds.

The infidel may be suffering severely and often drinking heavily at this point. The affairee too, often a family friend, close coworker, or even a relative, may be going through hell. The alternative to working with the situation might be individual therapy for each, which produces dangerous temporal malalignments, as each makes decisions independent of the other's decisions. Nevertheless, postponement of separation may not be as polite as it seems. I sometimes tell the story of the man who loved his dog so much that he cut off the dog's tail only an inch at a time.

Romantic affairs are by far the most difficult. The crisis may go on for months or years at total stalemate while the infidel tries to avoid a decision, stall the therapy, and prevent change. The cuckold may try to control the situation instead of working toward his or her own independence.

Usually (75% of my cases) affairs stop very quickly once they are overt. The end of the secrecy removes both the power and the purpose for continuing the affair. Some affairs continue for years if secret. Few open affairs can continue for many months without either society's or the spouse's acceptance. But those months may be difficult for all concerned. If the infidel cannot decide what to do, he or she may be advised, while telling the complete truth to the spouse, to tell a few lies to the affairee. By this time the infidel, under just as much pressure from the affairee as from the cuckold, may be doing that anyway.

In my experience, about 25% of adulterers continue an affair after revelation. About a third of those leave home to try it with their in-love partner. They may marry quickly and make little sustained effort to return to the marriage. The failure rate of these romantic remarriages is high. Another two-thirds continue the affair for some time after the revelation, unwilling to end the affair and yet not quite willing to leave the marriage. Half of those finally leave, after periods ranging from a month to 30 years. Half of those return. The remaining third finally give up the affair. It doesn't seem to matter statistically whether the cuckold carries on wildly or sits at home blithely, has counteraffairs or makes suicide attempts. Anything the cuckold does is a vague irritant—all the emotional energy is in the affair. Overall about half of those who can't make up their minds go with the spouse and half with the affairee. A few of these bounce back and forth for years. Sticking it out is not easy and may work no better than separating. In general, if the affair can't be ended within a few weeks, a separation may be a relief. But, just in case the romantic affair does have a structural element, it is probably best for cuckolds to take the time to show themselves at their very best before embarking upon a separation—just to demonstrate to the infidel what he or she would be missing by ending the marriage permanently.

While it may be possible to live with a philanderer, it is not easy to live with someone who is "in love" with someone else. The cuckold's anger is a problem. The infidel already feels guilty enough, unless he or she is already immunized against the spouse's anger. Any effort to compound the infidel's guilt is counterproductive, since the affairee is trying to reassure the infidel he or she is doing the right thing in continuing the affair. Guilt and shame feed affairs more often than anger. The cuckold's sympathy is amazingly therapeutic, and in any good marriage it is there beneath the anger. But it dissolves instantly at the sight of another lie.

If the infidel is being honest, but still in the affair, and the cuckold is demonstrating a commitment to change, the couple may well decide they don't want what they thought they wanted at all. Some people don't want a very intimate marriage. The cuckold may well have decided the pressure of changing, tolerating, and holding on is too great, the anger is too strong, and the love or whatever was holding the marriage together is beginning to fade. It is helpful to know whether all the effort is directed toward saving the marriage or toward keeping it from changing. Some distance may be more helpful than further efforts at change. A separation may be in order. A separation at this point is often ultimately helpful, since it is now apparent that the marriage can be far better than it had been.

Often the spell of the affair can be broken during the separation, as the reality of that relationship is intensified and the sacrifices of a divorce made graphic. If the cuckold continues efforts at revenge and punishment, any benefits of the separation are lost. If the cuckold starts dating at this point, the infidel's sudden jealousy may come as a therapeutic surprise. Often the affair ends at the point of separation but the infidel still prefers not to continue the marriage. As noted earlier, it is typically the infidel who chooses to end the marriage, and he or she does so about half the time. The infidel does not usually marry the affairee, and when it happens, it does not usually go smoothly.

Step 7: Termination

Crises of infidelity don't end quickly. There may be years of guilt, doubt, continued rehashing of the crisis, and punishment that sets the stage for future affairs.

Even if the marriage seems to end, it is commonplace for the infidel to make an effort at reconciliation just before the divorce becomes final, as reality finally sets in. And it is just as commonplace for the cuckold to have lost interest by then. It is not uncommon for these attempts at reconciliation to continue for many years.

Affairs seem too frivolous and confusing to serve as the basis for ending a marriage. Cuckolds usually discover this in time. Infidels often don't. The infidel must know that he or she is temporarily insane. The affairee should know that the situation and the loyalties and repercussions are far more complicated than they seem. Divorce can save lives but is too risky to apply during something as disorienting as an affair.

infidelity
bolt from blue — 1x
habitual — developmental prob
stral — from prob in m.
falling in love — crazy

. . . rather bear those ills we have
Than fly to others that we know not of

—William Shakespeare, *Hamlet*

Why is happiness such a precious thing? What have we done with
our lives so that everywhere we turn, no matter how hard we try
not to, we cause other people sorrow?

—William Styron, *Lie Down in Darkness*

CHAPTER 8

Divorce and Remarriage

FRAGMENTS AND EMULSIONS

D IVORCE, LIKE AMPUTATION, undoubtedly saves lives. It has always been
considered an extreme, desperate measure—sometimes necessary but rarely
desirable. Its recent popularity is startling. I suppose a society can get used
to a high murder rate, a high rate of infant mortality, and high rates of crime
or alcoholism or pollution, but it pays a price. Trust and security are lost.
Living in a world one perceives as noxious or untrustworthy, in a family one
sees as treacherous and impermanent, causes a hardening of the individual,
a callous determination not to be distracted from survival issues by the
concerns of others.

DIVORCE: EVERYONE GETS HURT

Divorce is an awful thing to go through, an even more awful thing to
inflict on one's children. And it doesn't work. It certainly doesn't stop a
battling couple from battling, and it does not get the children out from

under the conflict between their parents. People who react to one another that intensely can't seem to give one another up. Most people try to stop the divorce at least once before it is over. A surprising percentage of people who go through it get back together to resume whatever imperfect marriage they wanted out of anyway. And survey data do not lead to the impression that divorced people are any happier or that second marriages are any better than first. It is not a matter of replacing one's youthful mistakes with mature choices. In fact, the divorce rate for second marriages is even higher than for first. Apparently people don't learn from their marital mistakes. The divorce process itself may make it difficult to learn from mistakes, since it is an adversarial process in which both partners are out to prove the problems were not their fault.

The divorce process is at best unpleasant. More often it is downright devastating for everyone in the family. It is usually distressing for relatives and disturbing for friends. It is probably more traumatic than a death in the family, since it tears family members apart rather than bringing them together. Few family crises produce such profound changes in so many lives.

The majority of divorces come as a direct result of someone's affair. At the time of divorce, most often one of the marital partners is in-love and wants to marry someone else. The divorce comes as a liberating adventure for that partner, but is experienced as a betrayal and desertion by the other partner and by the children. The departing spouse is emotionally out of synchronization with the rest of the family. He or she celebrates while the rest of the family mourns — and the better the departing one feels, the angrier it makes the mourners. The combined crisis of infidelity, divorce, and remarriage to the "homewrecker" can devastate everyone in the family, while the infidel/deserter is baffled that the family does not share his or her happiness over the romance of it all. Fortunately for all concerned, the affair usually ends just as the divorce becomes final and remarriage becomes possible. But if the infidel's timing is off and a marriage to the affairee does take place, this collaboration with the enemy is unforgivable by all generations and produces a remarriage under siege.

Thus many divorces involve one partner who is having a wonderful time and another who is miserable and absorbing all the emotional energy of the family. The children must give vigorous support to the deserted partner, even though they would prefer the company of the merry adulterer, who may be depraved but at least wants to have fun.

This contrasts sharply to those less frequent divorces that occur after the marriage has gotten so awful everyone is impatient to get it over. When both parents are clearly miserable over this long and eagerly awaited coup de grace, the children, the friends, and the relatives can all be wonderfully supportive and everyone can enjoy suffering/celebrating together.

But that doesn't happen often — at least not in longstanding first marriages with children. Divorces do sometimes occur in such marriages when no one is being unfaithful, but in my practice they are atypical. Separations occur, but the spouses generally get back together quickly because the bond is not broken and they have no other home to go to.

Divorces that do occur in longstanding, monogamous marriages some-times involve one partner who is unreliable, perhaps alcoholic, nonfunction-al, psychotic, or just "sorry." Such divorces are more likely to occur early in a marriage, when a naive and unsuspecting bride discovers what her new husband is really like, when the manic phase ends and the depressive phase begins, when the party is over and the partying continues, when the money runs out and no one goes to work, when the romance is over. There may be no children yet, and the family is still not formed.

If the marriage has produced children and a period of family life, even if it would seem unbearable to outsiders, it has been tolerated and has to some extent worked. Getting out of it is difficult and painful, however necessary.

In second, third, or subsequent marriages, in which the children are from previous liaisons and perhaps live with various former partners, the mar-riage isn't quite the family center it is with a "nuclear" family and it is easier to leave. Subsequent marriages are more likely to end in divorce, and the divorce that does occur can be far less traumatic. Some second and third marriages never quite gel and can end rather pleasantly, in somewhat the way people settle a minor traffic accident and drive off.

But divorces in second marriages can have their own special traumas. The stepparent, whether departing or deserted, may expect to lose any future relationship with the children and may regret that loss. While children can hope to maintain some relationship with departing natural parents after a divorce, they will probably lose beloved stepparents totally and finally. They may not care, of course, and may be delighted to be rid of one another. The biological bond is by no means essential to an intense parent-child relation-ship, but after a divorce the nonbiological parent-child relationship does not often survive.

Divorce has become so prevalent that many consider it a normal part of the family life cycle, a developmental stage families go through. It isn't. It is aberrant. It cannot be anticipated in a healthy manner; in fact, the anticipat-ing and preparing for it might well bring it about. Marriage can work only if it is treated as if it were permanent. If it is treated as if it were temporary, it will be protected against and entered only partially, and the pair will each keep an eye open for future marriage partners.

If divorce is not unique in the family, the crisis may not be so intense, although a family which divorces habitually must be structurally unstable. After a divorce has occurred in a family, there is understandable insecurity and doubt about the stability of family life. This carries over to the children of divorce, who tend to approach their own marriages desperately yet suspi-ciously, which must be confusing to their new bride or groom.

Likewise, if a divorce has a temporary feel to it, if a reconciliation seems a possibility, family members do not go ahead and react and get on with it; instead they go through awkward maneuvers to get the couple back together again. The fantasy of reconciliation can paralyze a family and is particularly destructive to children. This sense of temporariness can continue even as the parents remarry, with the children treating their stepparents as usurpers (as in *Hamlet*).

If a divorce is not "real," if the couple goes through the legal procedure but continues the relationship, it can be confusing for everyone. By that time, the affair may have become overt and somewhat like a marriage or engagement, and the marriage now becomes a covert affair. Or the divorcing couple may be dating and keeping it secret from their own parents. The children may be called upon to keep a strange array of secrets as the cast of characters expands.

It can be even more confusing if the divorce itself is covert, if a couple is trying to keep the children from knowing or from telling their potential sources of support, or if they are hiding it from their parents and friends. Yet people do such strange things. They put their children through this most disruptive of traumas, demanding that the children not acknowledge the trauma is going on and not get any support from anyone. They say in effect, "What we are going through is so embarrassing that you would be ostracized if your friends knew about it. It is so shameful you can't mention it. But we're going to do it anyway, and you must not complain."

A family going through a divorce is very much in crisis, a kind of structural unique situation with the worst features of both. Everyone feels responsible, and guilty, as they examine their contribution to the disaster, but they can't stop it. All manner of awful things happen to everyone in the family, and people fall apart in every direction. It is not unusual for every family member to become symptomatic during a divorce.

If the mother and children stay in the family home, as is the usual temporary arrangement, the father is displaced and feels it. Initially, this separate father may have the worst time of it. As a recently separated father, he is at high risk for suicide and for violence, even homicide. He may also drink a great deal. Strangely, the trauma is intense for him whether he left the family eagerly or under protest. He is lonelier than expected. His married friends shun him. His single friends are not having as much fun as they had led him to believe and don't include him in it anyway. His life is disrupted and unstructured to a far greater degree than anticipated. He tends to devote more time and attention to his children than he has previously or will subsequently once he gets his life scheduled enough not to need his children as babysitters for him.

The separated father tends to be jealous of his estranged wife, regardless of who was having the affair that led to the separation. If it was his affair, he may sabotage it by collapsing dependently upon it, displaying all those bad habits and helplessnesses that did in his marriage. If he was not in an affair, he may find an earth mother to help him through the divorce. These are women who are afraid of marriage and equality in such a way that they specialize in intense affairs with recently separated men, taking them in and nurturing them while they fall apart, and then feeling rejected as soon as they get well enough to cross the street alone.

The recently separated man may find that his standard of living is reduced, and his life is rather spartan at first. (He will recover financially in time. His contact with his children will drop off drastically as soon as he gets involved with his next wife, and he will devote more attention to his stepchildren than to his real children. He doesn't know that yet, but the children seem to, and all his current attention seems insubstantial to them.)

Initially, the mother is in the family home with the children and usually has the support of the friends and relatives. Her life is disrupted far less than her husband's. And she gets most of the children's support because she is there, she is the one who stayed rather than the one who left, and she is the one who provides emotional security (even if she actually kicked their father out so she could more easily pursue her affair with the meter reader). If she is older, married longer, and unemployed, she is likely to lose her identity and security and become seriously depressed, even suicidal, collapsing dependently upon her children. She may desperately encourage the children to spy on their father, or reject him, or play tricks on him. She may even encourage the children to become symptomatic in her effort to make her husband feel guilty enough to come home.

Being "supportive," her friends' husbands will come over and make passes at her, which will then prompt her friends to shun her. She may find no single man to go out with. She is likely to feel unattractive and to devote herself to dieting, exercise, and self-improvement. She may go back to school or work, or may try to get her first adult job, discovering that the world sees her as unskilled and marginally employable. As she gets busy, she'll have less time for her children. She'll get her life reorganized before her children do, but won't be available for them.

As the process continues, the divorcing woman will become more dependent on her divorce attorney; she will fight with her husband about more and more things as she feels stronger and realizes her rights. She and the children together will end up with less than half the family resources, but her former husband will complain bitterly about that amount (and his new wife or girlfriend will complain even more about it). She will have a lower standard of living than he, be less socially sought after, and somewhat less likely to remarry. If she is over 40, her chances of remarriage are markedly lower than her ex-husband's. But she will have a far closer relationship with the children than he. No one will care much who was the "guilty" and who the "innocent" party in the divorce. But she, noticing that she gets the short end of the deal, will devote much energy to refighting the divorce and may drive her children away as she tries to keep them from forgiving their father.

Divorce is another in a series of contests between two people who chose one another for the game, at one time thinking they were ideally and equally matched. They may delight in the ongoing post-divorce battle over who was the good guy and who the bad, who the villain and who the victim, who the saint and who the sinner. It may become the center of their post-divorce life. When people divorce, they tend to give up all the good things about their marriage together and keep all the bad—that's why they got a divorce instead of just having a fight and changing the bad things. Divorce means never having to say you're sorry. It is legal proof that you don't have to compromise or do anything sensible you don't want to do, that the law will protect your right to continue your bad habits even if no one can live with you because of them.

So the divorce frees the parents from having to be loving or accountable or reliable with one another, but protects their right to keep fighting and to nurse their hatred of one another until the end of time. It may seem as if one person chose to divorce and the other tried vainly to hold on. Rarely is that unilateral; usually it is ultimately bilateral. In almost every divorce, the departer makes a pass at returning. The pass may be halfhearted, even just a test or a provocation, not well intentioned at all. The pass may mean only that the departer would return home if the deserted one would accept all faults without attempting change or guilt. The deserted one has her or his pride, rejects the offer, and can (and does) explain why.

This whole crazy unstructuring of everyone's life may be desired by the parents. It may even be desired briefly by occasional adolescents who would like to confuse and distract the parents sufficiently to get by with something or other. But it isn't often desired by children for very long, and it is they who ultimately suffer most. The myth of Medea has psychological accuracy. In it, Medea's husband Jason takes up with another woman. Medea is enraged and decides to punish him. She kills their children and presents them to him. Medeas can be male or female, and their methods are usually psychological, although one frequently encounters newspaper reports of men and sometimes women who kill their children in a rage over a marital desertion. It is commonplace for fathers to reject and avoid their children when they separate from the children's mother. Meanwhile mothers may abuse, physically or psychologically, a child who most resembles the husband who got away.

Children lose in other ways too. Both households are poorer, so there is economic deprivation. The family usually has to move, which is never easy for children. Children are usually embarrassed and can even be discriminated against, as if their birth were invalidated by the revocation of the marriage which produced them. They lose grandparents and extended family as their standing in the family is compromised. The children may even be separated from one another by custody arrangements. The fortress of the family has been breeched; the family has fallen and one parent may be, quite literally, in enemy hands. The child's security is lost.

But the most important effect on children is the change in their relationships with their parents. The parents are either depressed or distracted, preoccupied with the changes in their own lives, and not likely to be available to the children. They may even be collapsing dependently upon the children, even quite young children. The mother will have to go to work or take a more demanding job and take care of things that were the father's responsibility. Or she may be the one to leave, and the father may have to take care of things he had never dreamed of taking care of before. The parents will require a set of social activities outside the house. They will be dating, which is incredibly time-consuming and distracting, as well as irritating to the children. The adults will be developing new skills, facing new situations, feeling new anxieties, encountering new difficulties. They will be insecure, distracted, and overwhelmed.

The children will be called upon to grow up quickly — what the household clearly needs is fewer dependent children and more competent grownups. Some children respond by becoming more mature (or more pseudo-mature) and learning to parent their parents. Most children seem to be baffled by this abrupt and uncalled for end to their childhood. They may rebel by regressing and demanding more parenting. Or they may attempt to be little adults and, failing at it, become even more insecure, depressed, and dependent. Characteristically children regress, develop symptoms, and cling. They punish their parents and get even less, so they demand even more. It can get bad.

Actual data on the crisis of divorce have been gathered in longitudinal studies by Wallerstein and Kelly (1980) and by Hetherington (1979). Both studies show that everybody suffers horribly and for a long time. Wallerstein and Kelly document the intense regression of younger children and the depression and developmental delay of older ones. Children of all ages seem to have at least a bad year. The younger ones suffer most, particularly the preschoolers who are most dependent on their parents, and they may evidence difficulties for years. (In my experience, divorce is hardest on early adolescents, but then everything is. The point is that everyone suffers.)

Hetherington found that about three-fourths of divorced parents regretted the divorce at the end of the first year. (They were lonely, their marriage-wrecking affair was over, and many of them were returning to the marriage.) However, after two years of divorce, only one-fourth were still regretting it. (Most people who divorce remarry, and by the second year most of the parents were loving someone new while still fighting with their ex.) Successful post-divorce adjustment — perhaps unfortunately — seems to depend primarily on the establishment of a solid liaison with a new partner.

The experts disagree about whether divorce is a catastrophe or merely a disaster. Beal (1980) examines the data on divorce and describes the awful effects on the children. Cohen and Jones (1983) examine the same data and take issue with the antipathy toward divorce, finding that a divorced family may still be preferable to an "unhappy" one and noting that people still believe in marriage as long as it isn't marriage to the current spouse. Even Cohen and Jones find divorce a major crisis for children, the degree of stress directly related to the loss of involvement of the departing parent.

Ahrons and Wallisch (1986), studying a nonclinical sample of divorced families, found that half the divorced spouses continue in "conflict and anger that is negatively correlated with the continued involvement of the noncustodial partner," thus working against the best interests of the children. They urge the idea that divorced couples would be more cooperative if divorce were considered non-pathological and a normal phase of development, thus warranting community support. Joint custody seems desirable to most experts, even though it forces the divorced couple to cooperate with one another, an activity at which they are obviously not expert. Frequently after a divorce, fathers will attempt to function as parents for the first time in their lives, which might be lovely but might intrude threateningly upon the mother's familiar territory. A mother may resent sharing her children with a man who didn't want to share his life with her.

In contrast, Goldstein, Freud, and Solnit (1973) believe that each child should have one psychological parent and that the other should be kept peripheral. Most experts seem to disagree, but what they are suggesting is indeed what usually happens, i.e., after a divorce, the children end up with one psychological (and functional) parent and one peripheral parent.

The crisis of divorce is extraordinarily prolonged; some sort of resolution takes at least a year—and often much, much longer. In those states in which the legal divorce process is quick, the marriage may be legally dissolved before the family has reacted to it at all. In those states in which the legalities drag on for years, the emotional divorce must drag on accordingly. The emotional process takes longer if the marriage is of long duration, if either partner is reluctant to get the divorce, or if the children still hope for a reconciliation. Everyone may operate as if the divorce is not real until, a few years later, one of the partners remarries and makes it seem final.

DIGGING OUT OF THE WRECKAGE

Boundaries

Divorces most often occur because the marital boundaries have already been breached. When there is a romantic affair that has brought on the divorce, the marriage and divorce are no longer en famille, and the anger and sense of betrayal are greater. There is an emotional discontinuity about the whole thing, along with permission to breach the family boundaries further. Once the divorce process starts, however, the family boundaries disappear, and all manner of people enter the arena, while others leave. Still-married friends scatter; single ones gather. Helpers of various sorts arrive, especially the divorce lawyer and frequently a therapist or two. The parents' parents and other relatives may become closer. Soon everyone is trying to pair off, including the teenaged children, who cling to their own enamoratae and tend to sexualize their relationships prematurely.

Usual Patterns

The survivors of the divorce must reassign tasks and renegotiate all rules. Generally, the remaining parent is overburdened, and the children are required to function more as adult. The generational bounds seem to crumble, as the survivors turn to one another for support. The departing parent may be even more overburdened, but still find time to come by and stir up trouble by trying to maintain authority over rules and roles in the family he just left. He may even be invited back for that purpose. It is never very clear who is making the rules in a family in mid-divorce. Role functioning for all family members generally nosedives during the process.

Goal and Values

The most depressing aspect of divorce is having to bury all the cherished plans for the future. Survival is about all that can be worked toward—less pressing goals may get lost. Values must be reexamined too. The revelation that a divorce is in the offing usually involves the revelation of some rather unsettling secrets. Even if the marital couple has been aware of the extent of the problems, the children usually haven't been, at least not consciously. The family members' sense of themselves must change. Not only have they lost their security and ceased to be a fortress, but they have also lost their virtue and ceased to be a paragon.

Revival of Past Conflict

All the hurts over the life of the marriage flash before everyone's eyes. There is no past conflict too insignificant to be fought over during the divorce process, no little secret too sordid to spread, no little guilt too petty to defend. The totality of the life together must be discredited and the history rewritten to make each the hero and victim of the villainous ex-partner. During the divorce, the couple may fight the fights they needed to fight before and even reveal the secrets that have kept them apart. Some longstanding problems may be solved. There are many people who are afraid of conflict and revelation; they must institute the divorce process in order to have the dreaded, necessary battle that can either make or break their marriage.

A civilized divorce, in which one partner bows totally to the other or both put politeness first, is spooky to observe. It cannot solve anything or teach anything or liberate anyone. The divorce battle is vital and should not be postponed. But it is not just between the divorce partners. Everyone else is dragged into the fray. It can be horrible for the children, who may be called upon to referee, or to betray or desert a parent, or just to listen to all the dirt. It can also be horrible for the parents of the divorcing pair, or the friends and relatives, or clients and associates. One advantage of divorce is that it strips away all dignity and brings everyone down to human size.

Tension

There are few times in anyone's life when the tension is higher. No one can be comfortable during a divorce in the family. Everyone is so sensitive to everyone else that anyone may be the first to develop symptoms, and any member of the family may be the patient, and any symptom is possible. The initial anger is followed by anxiety and then by depression. The deserted spouse may be suicidal. Or the deserted spouse may fear that the departing spouse is psychotic, or severely alcoholic, or suicidal—and that may be correct. Divorce is at least as traumatic for the departer as for the deserted. Or one of the kids may fall apart, run away, or make a suicide attempt. The symptoms can develop more slowly, with one or more family members performing poorly at school or work or just deteriorating. Ordinarily, every member of the family is suffering and most are symptomatic. And it does not get better quickly. The wounds fester for months, even years—and the scars remain forever.

TREATMENT OF CRISES OF DIVORCE

Step 1: Emergency Response

It is not difficult for a therapist to join a family from which one of the parents is suddenly departing. The boundaries are quite open. The therapist is not in a position to assure the continuance of the family, but must convey optimism about the survival of the individual members. The departer may have to be contacted separately and reassured that marital reconciliation is not mandatory when some family member develops symptoms, that a decision about marriage or divorce is too important and affects too many lives to be made on the basis of something temporary like an affair or a suicide attempt or a psychosis or a temper tantrum.

Step 2: Family Involvement

Any member of the family may be "the patient," but when a divorce is in progress it can be assumed that the symptom bearer is seeking help for the family. The therapist should offer to see the whole family, including the departing spouse. Often, the departing one is in individual therapy, from which the decision for divorce emerged. Every family undergoing a divorce needs therapy, although many would prefer to avoid it. There is the fear that the therapy will make the family stay together, so the one who wants the divorce will be the one who objects most strenuously to therapy. The departer has already chosen the therapy, i.e., divorce—if possible even erasure—and is too angry and frightened to consider alternatives. Obviously, often the therapist must deal only with the deserted members of the family.

There are even times when the therapist is left with only one member of a dissolving family and can do little more than hold that member together as everything around falls apart. It seems a meager task compared with holding a whole family together, but it is still a vital task, and someone's got to do it.

Step 3: Define the Crisis

Everyone must understand that the marriage is ending, which is not difficult to explain, and why the marriage is ending, which is very difficult to explain. I feel it is neither necessary nor appropriate to keep family secrets from the children when these secrets serve as the basis for such a disruptive decision. The children must live with both parents and therefore must not be distanced by secrets or anyone's guilt and continuing fear of exposure.

It is difficult to define the reasons for a divorce. It is not sufficient for the parents to mouth clichés about not being in love anymore, especially to children who are being taught not to torture their siblings whether they like one another or not. Everybody except divorcing parents knows that people must be loving to their fellow family members whether they love one another or not.

Each family member must understand the history of the marriage. Everyone needs to understand the reality, uniqueness, overtness, permanency, and structural nature of the divorce, or the separation, or the efforts to avoid the divorce. The children must understand the issues at impasse, from both sides. They should know of any affairs in progress. In fact, I have difficulty thinking of anything the children categorically should not know. The parents, at this point in their marriage, are not in a position to present a united front and need not even try.

It may seem unnecessarily burdensome to tell people the truth, to reveal the secrets that would explain how the world works and why the unexpected happens. I don't know that it is especially good for children to know of their parents' misbehavior, but it is distancing for them not to know.

Steps 4 and 5: Prescriptions

Just talking about the divorce clears the air. Just seeing that there are at least two sides to the problem permits the children to be closer to both parents. It is vital for the children to know that they did not cause the divorce and that there is nothing they can do to stop it.

The couple is given the opportunity to reconsider just what their decision involves. Many divorces could be prevented (for better or worse) by a good fight, but hiring lawyers to perform that domestic duty expands the fight and makes reconciliation more difficult. The divorce process should be slowed down (in Georgia, the waiting period is only 30 days, and the divorce may be final before the couple can get in for the second appointment with the marriage counselor), but not called off. One partner wants to end the marriage and that should be respected. Nevertheless, people who are choosing such a drastic process deserve to know what their alternatives are.

Couples contemplating divorce should know the facts: Most people regret their divorce at some point during the first year; many couples get back together during or after divorce; there is no such thing as total divorce for couples with children—they must deal with one another forever; most children of divorce are back to normal after a few years; the divorce process is awful and people should be prepared for the worst; a million people a year in our country divorce and survive it—most marry again and most of those go on to divorce again.

In assigning specific tasks the therapist's job is twofold: to demonstrate what would be involved in going through with the divorce and to point out the changes that would be required to prevent the divorce. Everyone should know what they are purchasing for the price they are paying. Put in those terms, it may or may not be worth it. Most important is the clarification that the parents could take steps to salvage the marriage, but the children can't. (On those occasions when the children could do something to change the situation, they should be given that information and that opportunity.)

Step 6: Negotiating the Resistance

As the spouses begin to add up their physical and emotional losses in the divorce, they may recoil in horror from the task and consider reconciling. An effort at reconciliation may be a sincere awakening of reality or merely a resistance to taking responsibility for such a drastic decision. As the negotiation proceeds, the couple tends to bounce back and forth between the two extremes of being married and not being married—there is no midpoint, no arrangement somewhere in between. The decision to be married requires agreement; however, the decision to be divorced can be unilateral.

It seems preferable not to be too hasty in getting the decision made. As with all difficult problems, the solution lies in reducing the problem to a series of simple tasks, actions that could be performed to signify change. If an affair is going on or has just ended, the infidel should cease all contact with the affairee. If someone has an offensive habit—from cracking one's knuckles in bed to chaining up love slaves in the basement, from heroin addiction to leaving dirty gym socks on the dining room table—the behavior might be discontinued to demonstrate the effort to make oneself acceptable to one's mate and to establish the priority of the marriage. If someone chooses to end the marriage rather than to give up the offending habit, that is either a decision or a diagnosis. Agonizing about whether one's spouse is ideal or not is a depressing exercise in narcissistic romanticism; it is rather different from the nitty-gritty choice between one's marriage and one's bad habits. At heart, people are being called upon to give up their determination to demonstrate that "nobody can tell me what to do."

This set of negotiations may take place with the couple living together or apart. In general, if the relationship is too intense, a separation may be in order. If it is too detached, a separation may be desired but counterproductive. If one person wants to separate, that must be respected, even if the other is bitterly opposed. The spouses may postpone the divorce, but stay apart for a while, while they negotiate the changes needed before the departing one dares return home. It is not up to the therapist to tell people whether to live together or apart. But it is up to the therapist to tell people who are divorcing that the legal advice they are getting is for the purpose of protecting their property rights, and that following that advice may wreck the possibility of reconciliation. People must know whether they are married and fighting, whether they are courting and testing one another, or whether they are divorcing. The approaches are quite different.

It may finally become clear that the couple is not negotiating reconciliation, but is divorcing. If there is serious doubt about whether they are marrying or divorcing, they are divorcing. Many people are reluctant to acknowledge that they want a divorce, but they make no effort to repair the marriage and passively permit their partner to divorce them. They seem to value the position of "the aggrieved party," so they continue their obnoxious behavior while blithely insisting they don't want their spouse to pursue the inevitable divorce.

Once it is more or less clear that the couple is divorcing, the therapist may have to switch from being the guardian of the marriage to being the guardian of the divorce. Couples may resist being divorced as imaginatively as they have resisted being married. They tend to hang on, with one persisting in wielding authority and the other persisting in collapsing dependently. One (either one) may produce crises which require the other's intervention. One may insist upon supervising, or controlling, or just checking up on the other. The couple may continue fighting. If they are only fighting over money or the wedding presents, this may seem harmless enough, however extravagant, as they go back to court over and over to replenish their addiction to one another's abuse. But if they fight instead over the children, they encourage the most destructive behavior imaginable.

Keeping a divorced couple divorced can be a challenge to the therapist, especially when the children and perhaps even one of the spouses persist in dreaming of reconciliation. That hope of reconciliation can keep a family enslaved for a lifetime and a therapist tied up as a mediator interminably.

Step 7: Termination

Even if the couple is happy to keep refighting the marriage forever, the therapist may have to split up the therapy, providing ongoing support for one of the partners (sometimes both separately), or remaining available for the inevitable crises. Some couples can never negotiate even the simplest post-divorce conflict without a mediator, and the therapist is a far safer mediator than the children. A marriage is never over, a divorce never complete, and the therapist may have to remain in the wings indefinitely.

REMARRIAGE

Most people marry for the first time in a giddy romantic haze, without much thought for why they do so—it is just the way of all flesh. One is expected to marry, and there is a race to "fall in love" at just the right time in one's life. Questions of "why?" come up if someone does not do so. If Mr. or Miss "Right" does not come along, they marry as soon as they can anyway—less "in-love" with their mate than "in-love" with love. Myths of romance are so seductive it is somehow assumed that almost any problem can be solved by "falling in love," getting married, and "settling down."

Subsequent marriages are not so inexorable. Only the most foolish (and the most foolish are abundant) retain their belief in romance. Still, the human animal is just not comfortable alone—the couple is the basic social, functional, and biological unit. And there are practical reasons for remarrying. Raising children is best done in pairs, two can live as cheaply as one, and sex is more efficient when it's done at home. Many divorced women with young children and a worthless ex-husband can hardly survive—functionally, emotionally, or financially—without remarrying. The prospective husbands or fathers may not be a promising lot, and there may result a series of disastrous marriages to itinerant psychopaths, always looking for a comfortable, though temporary, ready-made landing spot. Horror stories abound in my practice and everyone else's.

The world and the mental health profession beg people to wait several years between marriages. People need to know that they can live singly before they choose what, if anything, they need from another marriage. Of course, it is the people who tolerate the unmarried state least who will be most dependent, demanding, and desperate in subsequent marriages—and therefore most unsuccessful.

People who remarry in desperate panic because being alone seems unbearable are not likely to choose any more wisely the next time than they did the last. But when they choose badly, they may cling helplessly to someone quite destructive to them and to their children. The worst marriages seem to have the greatest endurance, because they include someone who believes that the marriage is crucial to survival and all must sacrifice to keep it going at any cost. Such blind dependency seems to bring out the worst in bad people.

Likewise those who get along quite nicely without being married may be "confirmed" bachelors (male or female) and inflexible spouses, resentful of sharing their lives. Marriage is total, and some people just want a standing date for Saturday night or someone to supplement the family income or do the less appealing household chores. The ranks of the multi-divorced include those who don't really want much marriage, but dabble in it from time to time.

There are many who can't tolerate being alone, but who have little capacity for intimacy. They marry the first person who is willing, and then divorce when the first domestic battle looms.

Marriage is not for everyone. There is much to be said for the idea that everyone who divorces should have therapy before marrying again. Unfortunately, therapy does not work well unless it is driven by a crisis which produces a willingness to change—and the change most single people want is another marriage.

Remarriages are not quite like first marriages. After a first marriage that produced children, subsequent marriages can't start with a couple and expand from there. There is no honeymoon period. The new marriage doesn't even signal an end to the previous marriage—it just supplements an already complex family network. Needless to say, each divorce just increases the likelihood that the next marriage will end in divorce too. Surely people don't enter fourth or fifth marriages with enough confidence to change the monograms on their underwear, much less their silver. Most second marriages end in divorce. An even smaller percentage of third and fourth marriages hold. Yet some of the best marriages occur after a series of failures. Eventual marital success is rarely the result of finally finding the Mr. or Ms. Right, but of some more basic change. One friend of mine (a psychiatrist) insists that the fifth of his seven marriages was the best. I've known at least one quite successful 11th marriage (someone finally put the poor man on lithium).

Of course, some remarriages are functionally first marriages, in that the very first marriage was just a brief childhood escapade that never quite "took" and left no residue beyond embarrassment and wedding presents. A marriage that produces no children does not have the same glue as one with children. Childless marriages may be closer, and may even be more satisfactory because they are less demanding and more flexible, and in time may be just as difficult to leave, but once they have been left subsequent interaction may not be necessary. When there are no children, divorce can be clean, without unfinished business.

Blended families—remarried families with children—are inherently both cluttered and shaky. They can work, but they require more attention and compromise. Things don't happen naturally. The members of the stepfamily network must cooperate with one another without really wanting to be part of the same network. Stepfamilies are unwieldy at times of crisis.

The remarriage itself can be a major crisis. Just putting on the wedding can be a public relations nightmare. Remnants of past families are present and unblended. There are inevitable embarrassments and slights.

If the previous marriage ended in death rather than divorce, the dead spouse will haunt the proceedings—it becomes both a remarriage and a refuneral. The children are made especially aware of their dead parent and may be determined to keep him or her very much alive. Cherished in-laws may be uncomfortable, even heartbroken. Losing a widowed son- or daughter-in-law to another marriage can be a major loss to parents still grieving the death of their child. The remarriage probably also means a loosening of ties to their grandchildren.

One of a pair of divorced partners will inevitably marry first (with luck to someone other than the affairee who triggered the divorce). The ex-spouse is likely to make an awkwardly timed, and probably insincere, effort at reconciliation or he or she may just create a scene to avoid being overlooked. The children may attempt to block the marriage, developing any imaginable symptom. One teenaged boy seduced his father's fiancée, and told everyone about it. A little girl climbed to the roof of the church and threatened to jump if the marriage took place.

Even if the ceremony goes off on schedule, with everyone behaving reasonably well, the children can sabotage the honeymoon with a well-timed crisis. They seem determined not to be overlooked, even if they have to go to jail or the hospital to get the bride/mother's or groom/father's attention. Usually a prominent sulk is sufficient to prevent the new marriage from getting off on firm footing. Children who try to stop their parents' remarriage may be enforcing the will of the other parent. Or they may be expressing their own selfishness or their legitimate anxieties. But often they are responding to the ambivalence of the marrying parent.

It is not surprising that people tend to enter second marriages somewhat ambivalently and tentatively, sometimes going so far as to draw up prenuptial divorce agreements, or just postponing the wedding a time or two, or marrying abruptly after years of wavering about it. The remarriers, having been hurt before, are wary. A second marriage is not the fulfillment of childhood fantasies and biological destiny, but a way of making oneself as comfortable and secure as possible after one's naive dreams have been shattered.

Remarriages also don't get the familial and societal support that first marriages receive. Becoming someone's second or third or fourth husband or wife does not automatically make one a member of the family—it may take a while.

For the children, the parent's remarriage is a significant crisis—both a danger and an opportunity. As Sager and his colleagues (1983) say, "In the remarriage of one or both parents, children often find an additional parental figure who may effectively complement or supplement what cannot be secured from one or both bioparents. The entire process can be one of growth for children and adults—or it can be a disaster—or anything in between."

Emily and John Visher (1979) outlined seven problem areas arising from the complexity of stepfamily characteristics. These are:

1. There is a biological parent outside of the stepfamily unit and a same-sexed adult in the household.
2. Most children in stepfamilies hold membership in two households.
3. The role definition for stepparents is also ill defined.
4. The fact that "blended" families come together from diverse historical backgrounds accentuates the need for tolerance of differences.
5. Step-relationships are new and untested and not a "given" as they are in intact families.
6. The children in stepfamilies have at least one extra set of grandparents.
7. Stepfamily financial arrangements . . . take on many emotional overtones.

Treating a crisis in any remarried family requires excruciating sensitivity to the complexities of the family structure; at the same time the crisis process must cautiously sidestep a revival of all the past conflicts and unending battles. While there is no one standard structure for a first marriage, there are no maps at all to the structure of "blended" (or more usually "emulsified") families. Nothing can be taken for granted. Each stepfamily is truly unique. Stepparents may be the same as parents, or they may not be. Children from previous marriages may be ex children, and divorced bioparents may be ex-parents. After a divorce or two, people tend to choose their own parents or children, rather than letting the choice be made by either biology or someone's sexual preferences of the moment. A multi-married man may have lost all contact with his biological children, yet be a wonderful father to stepchildren of a current or even a former marriage—perhaps even marrying someone with children of just the right age or gender to replace those he lost in a divorce. Women who have not had children of their own may marry a man for his children and then keep the children after the marriage fades. Children of multiple marriages may attach themselves to one or more of the parents or grandparents that have flitted through their lives. The biological relationship is usually the strongest, but that is by no means always the case.

Blended families have more crises than other families, and each crisis is more disruptive and dangerous. The structure is more complex, the cast of characters includes at least a few unwilling members and perhaps unstable members as well, and there is usually less committment to keeping things structurally stable. The relationships may have an evanescent quality. Family disruption is an ever-present threat—it's been done before.

SPECIFIC CRISES IN BLENDED FAMILIES

Intrusions from Previous Spouses

If there are children, if there is alimony or child support, or if there are continuing close ties to former in-laws, there will be contact with the previous husband or wife. This contact can be unpleasant and threatening, dangerous at worst, disconcerting at best. It is always awkward for the new spouse, and some jealousy is unavoidable. The divorced partners can neither fight nor be friendly without discomfort. The old intimacy must be replaced with cordial and cautious distance, while everyone's fantasies and memories run rampant. The ex-spouse may be out to break up the new marriage, or to compete with the new spouse, or to continue the old punishments and justifications. Ex-spouses may want to keep the old dependency going and call on one another in times of need.

An alcoholic man, whose wife had divorced him years before, would phone suicide threats to her each time he went on a binge. She would ride off in all directions to rescue him, which greatly displeased her new husband. The new husband brought the ex-husband to therapy, and the three were seen together briefly to break up the pattern.

Threats to Continuation of the Marriage

There is always some doubt about the permanence of a remarriage. One or both of the partners have left a previous spouse or been left by one. Divorce threats are more frequent and seem more real. They know they can do it.

One woman insisted that her new husband keep his furniture in storage for seven years while she tested out whether this marriage would work better than her previous one had. She wouldn't let her new husband move anything in the house; there were even things he wasn't allowed to touch. A crisis came when he inherited some antiques from his father and wanted to move them into the house.

Wranglings Over Finances

The previously divorced often want to keep their money separate from one another. They may even have freer financial dealings with the previous spouse than with the current one. Sometimes the family is dependent on alimony from a previous marriage. It is not uncommon for a woman to set aside everything she owns in an estate for her children from a previous marriage; sometimes a man will do that too. The financial complexity of remarried families can be mind boggling. There is no set of standard rules for setting things up fairly, so each family is breaking new ground. Their possible arrangements can be bizarre.

One man left an invalid wife and eventually married a younger woman, who was expected to continue the support of the ex-wife in the event of his death. She was also expected to provide nursing care and handle the ex-wife's finances, but was not permitted to refuse anything the invalid ex-wife requested. The new wife rebelled when the old wife demanded and got a new sofa while the younger woman couldn't afford one.

Another couple lived together for years as husband and wife, but could not actually marry because the woman's generous alimony would cease if she remarried, while the man's payments to his ex-wife would actually increase if he remarried.

Children Moving In and Out

Children of divorce may have two, or more, homes and families and may be incompletely at home in each. They may move back and forth between the two households, spending weekends in a neighborhood quite different from the one in which they go to school, thereby disrupting peer relationships. The absent parent, usually the father, may be lax about visitation, may stand the kid up, promise things that aren't delivered, frustrate the mother's social schedule, and then expect the kid to subordinate to the father's series of women friends. As adolescents, kids may be able to control the rules of the household with threats to go live with the other parent. It can be tragic for a mother to see her 14-year-old son leave her to live with the psychopathic father she divorced in order to keep him from influencing the boy. At times the child will spend years dreaming of attaining an age at which he or she can go live with the other parent, only to find the seductive offers of a home quite empty.

A cowboy had not seen his 16-year-old son since his wife left him soon after the boy was born. After her latest divorce and his latest marriage, the mother had the boy call to see if he could live with his father. The father was delighted until the boy arrived. The son was the spitting image of his father—except that he wore an earring and sexually ambiguous clothing and expressed the ambition of becoming a hairdresser. The father was ashamed to show him to his friends, his wife's family, or even to his therapist. He became so depressed that his new wife (who found the boy "creepy") threw a series of scenes and demanded that he be sent back to his mother. The father was so distraught he began drinking heavily and left the marriage, blaming his new wife. But he refused further contact with his son.

Different Authority Over Different Children

The rules governing children of different marriages may be quite different. Stepchildren traditionally have been in the Cinderella position, but they may have the seeming advantage of another part-time home and part-time parent. If they threaten to go live with the other parent, they may gain some inappropriate authority over the rules governing them. The expectations of the blended family may come from different backgrounds and experiences, as well as different ethnic or religious affiliations. Children of the same age may be totally different in their relationship to authority and to the world.

Both husband and wife had three sons, all adolescents. The poor, dumb husband had raised his sons brutally and insultingly, while his first wife was off in mental hospitals. The boys stole, lied, were often in trouble, fought with each other constantly, and failed in school. The wife's sons had been dominated by a successful, obsessive father, who permitted no self-expression and required perfect performance, and usually got it. The wife hated her martinet ex-husband and his influence on her neat, lifeless sons. She wanted her sons to learn from their three unruly new stepbrothers. Instead the two older boys recoiled in horror at the chaos and moved in with their father. The youngest accepted the challenge and devoted himself to bringing the unruly boys under control. He turned into a copy of his own father before his mother's eyes. She felt she'd lost all three of her sons. But the bad boys turned out fairly well, and the poor woman was back in an orderly household against her will.

Different Financial Realities for Different Children in the Same Household

There can be rich kids and poor kids in the same household, and it can influence behavior, expectations, and relationships. The financial difference can be slight but embarrassing, as when one father pays child support and another doesn't. It can be seriously disruptive, as when a father makes sure his natural children are favored over his stepchildren. Or it can be absurd, as when one child is lavishly subsidized by an absent father or a trust fund, while the other children have none of those advantages. Usually families try to even out these differences, but that can cause crises too.

A husband's daughter and his wife's daughter were exactly the same age. The husband's daughter had grown up in poverty, on welfare, caring for her psychotic mother. She was a perfect student, neat, ambitious, hardworking, and cold. The wife's daughter had a fabulous trust fund from her grandfather and was assured of the best in life. She was charming and friendly, failed in school, and lived in the fast lane. The two girls lived in the same house and attended the same school for years without becoming friends. The poor girl worked three jobs for her spending money and won a scholarship to college. The rich girl dropped out of college to await the maturation of her inheritance. She'd tried for years to be friendly with her stepsister and never could understand why the poor girl didn't want to play with her.

Children's Efforts to Break Up the Marriage

Children, displeased over the loss of a parent to death or divorce, may cling to the remaining parent. The reduced family may get along quite well, with the children and the remaining parent forming a rather satisfactory functional unit. The children may resent a remarriage, as they lose their remaining parent emotionally and lose their advanced functional status, perhaps to someone who fails to appreciate their position. Stepparents often make the mistake of trying to get a parental and rather independent adolescent "under control," which is about like putting toothpaste back into the tube. The children, singly or in concert, may then try to oust the new stepparent. Their efforts may be subtle or may take on an air of desperation. The new stepparent, baffled and threatened, may overreact by assuming an authority that escalates the battle and requires the natural parent to take sides. Everyone suffers.

A new stepfather, having read books and taken courses in blending families, set up family meetings with his new wife and her adolescent children. The children were coldly polite. He tried to force them to talk about their hostility. They politely refused to acknowledge any anger. He grounded them until they would do so. The mother finally intervened on their side, which the stepfather saw as a betrayal. He pouted. She packed up the kids and left.

Parents' Jealousy of Children's Allegiances

If the children do make friends with the new stepparent, the absent parent may feel threatened and attempt to undercut the new relationship. The parent may view the child's tolerance of the stepparent as an infidelity and react accordingly.

A father had been a ne'er-do-well and adulterer, but he did not want his wife to leave him. He and his new fundamentalist church considered it unChristian of her to disobey him — her God-given husband, Lord and Master. She left anyway, taking the kids. In due time she remarried. Her new husband was a kind, stable, and gentle man. The kids liked him. They began to avoid their brutal alcoholic father and his succession of women. They began going to the stepfather's church. The father proceeded to convince the children that the stepfather was homosexual (he must not be a real man — he rarely drank, kept no other women, and never beat the kids the way a real man would). He even convinced them that if they went to the stepfather's church they would go to hell. A holy war erupted that tore apart the rural community in which they lived.

Loosened Sexual Boundaries

The incest taboo is so weak in remarried families that some experts (notably Sager et al., 1983) don't even use the word "incest," preferring the less inflammatory "household sexual abuse." The "Lolita syndrome" draws its name from Nabokov's novel about a professor who is so enamored of a nymphet that he marries and murders her mother so he can gain access to her. Stepfathers frequently cross sexual boundaries with their stepdaughters, and while mother-son incest is rare, stepmother-stepson incest is far less so. (The classic case is Eugene O'Neill's *Desire Under the Elms.*) Adolescent stepsiblings may feel little incest taboo. They may carry sexual flirting and teasing rather far. In some families the stepsiblings may openly "date"; in other families the parents try to enforce an incest taboo, with varying degrees of success.

A girl's father had died, and her mother remarried when she was quite young. The incestuous relationship with her stepfather began early — she was eight. She didn't reveal it until she was leaving for college and was concerned about her eight-year-old half-sister, the natural child of her mother and the incestuous stepfather. The stepfather was embarrassed about the revelation of his secret sexual relationship with his stepdaughter. But mostly he was horrified that anyone would think he would be incestuous with his *own* daughter. The mother had difficulty accepting that distinction, and left him.

Different Grandparental Relationships With Different Children

Grandparents, concerned with their heirs, may find stepgrandchildren an intrusion between them and their "real" grandchildren. Of course, if they have only stepgrandchildren, they may grandparent them royally. When the grandchildren come in both the "step" and the "real" varieties, the grandparents may make more of a distinction than the parents do between the two varieties, thereby fostering unpleasant resentments and triggering crises.

A boy, from his mother's first marriage, had been adopted by his stepfather, and had seen himself as his father's son no less than his natural siblings who followed. But he had always noticed the meagerness of his Christmas presents from the paternal grandparents. The crisis came when he found he was left out of the grandparents' wills.

Remarried families come to therapy for all the same reasons, with all the same crises, as are found in original families. In addition there are these messy crises around the blending process. The therapist must explore the complexities of the family structure before proceeding. The family may be a maze of alignments and loyalties, and no relationships can be taken for granted. This must all be understood early on or the therapist may blunder seriously. What may seem like a parent and child, or a pair of siblings, or a married couple, or a divorced couple, may be something else entirely—and the therapist is always the last to know.

CASE 13   *No Bed of Roses*

Bud and Rose had been married for 20 years, and had two children, 18-year-old Leif and 13-year-old Blossom. Bud was having an affair with his coworker, Aphid. No one knew about Aphid, so Bud's desire for a divorce baffled Rose and the children. Marital therapy had gone very badly, as Aphid had been kept secret, and Bud was hopelessly confused about his mission in the therapy, so nothing made sense and all the efforts to save the marriage just did more damage. At the time of the divorce, Rose was pitiful, leaning heavily on her own mother who offered financial support in exchange for Rose's helpless dependency. Bud married Aphid. Rose, in desperation, married the first man she could find—Thorn.

The older son, Leif, found Thorn prickly and moved in with Rose's mother. Thirteen-year-old Blossom, however, decided to stay with Rose and Thorn and break up their marriage. She reported wild stories of abuse to her grandmother, her brother, and her father. Bud kept quizzing her on whether Thorn was making sexual overtures toward her. She finally told them that Thorn had exposed himself to her. The family couldn't agree on what to do next, so they had Blossom psychiatrically hospitalized. A fight ensued between the adults about who would pay for it. Aphid refused to let Bud pay anything, and Thorn said he was broke. Bud thought Thorn was lying, so had him investigated and found unmentioned past marriages, income tax discrepancies, and an old warrant for his arrest. Gleefully, Bud turned this information over to the police.

The hospital, exasperated by the financial dealings, arranged to discharge Blossom if I would work with the family. The first session, my first contact with the family, was to include Blossom, Rose and Thorn, Bud and Aphid. Thorn disappeared with Rose's money and flatsilver on the day of the appointment. Not knowing any of this, Blossom accused a staff member of making sexual advances and ran away from the hospital the hour before her discharge. Rose, Bud, and Aphid arrived for the appointment, which focused more on Thorn's disappearance than on Blossom's future. Rose decided to move in with her mother, but the grandmother would not accept Blossom. Bud convinced Aphid it would be cheaper for them to take Blossom in than to keep her in the hospital.

Thorn went to prison, leaving much chaos in his wake. Even with Thorn out of the picture, therapy was complex. Aphid's children were not very tolerant of Blossom's joining the household—they were busy trying to kick Bud out. Blossom didn't want to live with Bud and Aphid. She worried about Rose, and feared Thorn would return and Rose would take him back. Rose was trying to live with her mother and Leif, who was disgusted with all of them and offered no support. Rose felt stifled. Eventually, Blossom blew the arrangement apart by accusing Aphid's son of making sexual advances toward her. Aphid kicked her out. After complicated negotiations with Bud and Aphid, with Rose and her mother and Leif, it was decided that the other adults would assist Rose in setting up housekeeping for herself and Blossom.

The therapy was directed toward teaching Blossom how to seek successes in her own life rather than continually sacrificing it to protect her mother. Aphid was enraged that Bud would help support Blossom and Rose. Rose's mother was finally cajoled into permitting Rose to go to work rather than collapse helplessly. Rose did go to work, for the first time in her life, and Blossom settled down again.

A year later, things were going well enough, believe it or not, for the family to drift out of therapy. Bud and Aphid's marriage was shaky, even without Blossom, and they found their own therapist through their church. Blossom was seeing a school counselor regularly, and Rose was complacent with the progress that had been made. She had decided she liked to work, and had taken a second job.

The next crisis occurred after another year when Thorn got out of prison and Blossom feared he and Rose would get back together. Rose by this time was having successes at work, was managing financially, and had a new boyfriend (whom Bud had investigated and declared OK). But Thorn made Rose bloom. When Thorn reappeared, Blossom acted up again—she got tattooed and ran off with a motorcycle gang. This time, Bud and Aphid's marriage was too insecure to tolerate another round of Blossom, but Aphid had sucked Bud dry, and had lost her grip on him. He arranged to send Blossom to boarding school, and to pay for it, whether Aphid wanted it or not. Perhaps because it displeased Aphid, Blossom opened up to the plan!

My final contact with the family (except for Christmas cards from Blossom) was with Rose and Thorn, who decided not to remarry. Bud and Aphid had separated, but Rose didn't want him back either. Rose recognized that, whatever suffering Blossom had experienced, she herself was a stronger and happier person than she had ever been, and didn't need Thorn, or Bud, or Blossom, or Leif, or her mother, to take care of her anymore. They were all relieved. Thorn wasn't up to going through it all again either. This was my first meeting with Thorn. He was charming, but his check bounced.

SECTION IV

Crises of Development

There are only two lasting bequests we can hope to give our children. One of these is roots; the other, wings.

—Hodding Carter

Parents are the bones on which children sharpen their teeth.

—Peter Ustinov, *Dear Me.*

CHAPTER 9

Parenting

THE FLIP SIDE OF CHILDHOOD

THE BIRTH OF A BABY is considered the most blessed of life's events. It isn't of course. Babies leak, won't follow anyone else's schedule, and give nothing in return.

PREGNANCY AS A CRISIS

Some people don't like babies at all, while others find them inconvenient, but might like them at some other time. Raising children has ceased to be a high status job. And it offers very little job security. Consequently, almost as many pregnancies end in abortion as in babies.

Babies don't hold marriages together very well either. Women used to have babies to provide fulfillment of biological destiny, while men wanted babies to prove masculinity and insure immortality. As women increasingly want their identity to come from their careers rather than their marriage or children, men seem to affirm theirs through seductions or the accumulation of wealth and toys. It is even difficult for a grown woman to find a grown man to impregnate her. She has to consider the likelihood that she will be a single parent (in spirit if not in fact) and that either her career, her marriage, or her child will be sacrificed to her husband's interminable adolescence.

Pregnancy can bring forth all manner of fears, most of them basically fears of growing up. The most common may be the fear of becoming like one's own parents, of suddenly evidencing the parental deficiencies so resented during one's own childhood. Guilt-ridden expectant parents may fear their children will carry the marks of their own inadequacies, or even be born deformed as a mark of God's punishment. Insecure expectant parents may fear the baby will destroy the marriage, either by pointing up their inadequacies or by competing successfully for the other parent's favors. Women may fear loss of their physical attractiveness, while both men and women may fear, perhaps appropriately, the loss of vocational and social mobility. The greatest fear is of making the marriage permanent — once a couple has had a child together, they are tied together forever.

Actually, while educated women who have some sense of the investment required to raise a child seem to obsess over the decision until all is perfect or until it is too late, more and more babies are born to underprivileged, unhappy teenage girls who want to love and be loved, who want someone of their own and can't find that someone in their family or their world.

Pregnancy is frequently unexpected and undesired. The option of abortion makes it less automatic than it once was. Practically all single females consider abortion when they become pregnant and many married ones do as well. I have not noticed that abortion produces nearly as much guilt as giving up a child, but it sometimes haunts a woman for a lifetime, especially if she does not have children later. The abortion decision can tarnish a relationship (married or otherwise) and leave it with a destructive shared burden of guilt and blame. Abortion can also be a bitter blow to expectant grandparents, damaging potential sources of support. The process of a secret pregnancy and abortion is not a pleasant one — it is quite isolating. No one brings presents, or sends flowers, or even talks about it. Few important life events are so secret, so lonely, and so uncelebrated. Post-abortion depressions are common.

By contrast, most pregnant women manage to get a high level of support from family and friends during the pregnancy, even if the father of the baby feels a little put upon and left out during the process. Pregnancy does produce a period of great imbalance in a marriage — a pregnant woman is a "we." Pregnancy can be a threat to a man's narcissism and centrality, just as it is for other children in the family. The first pregnancy may also call for more adulthood from a man than he feels prepared to give. It is not unheard of for an expectant father to enter an affair, plan a divorce, or even disappear during a pregnancy.

THE TRANSITION OF CHILDBIRTH

Both parents have fantasies about the unborn child, attaching personality and physical characteristics to it, naming it, and even planning its future. There are fantasies of glory and perfection, as well as fantasies of monstrous infestation. There are women who fear childbirth and men who fear the child is not really their own, as well as parents of either sex who fear the child will be horribly deformed. Usually childbirth is less terrifying and the child more acceptable than feared. In the end, the birth of the child is a relief.

But not always. The typical developmental crisis of childbirth is disruptive enough at best, but there can be other factors which contribute to making childbirth an even more disruptive event. Syndromes involving crises of childbirth include (1) postpartum depression, (2) child abuse, and (3) despair over an imperfect baby.

Postpartum Depression: A Caretaker Crisis?

Postpartum depression is not well understood. It has some features of a caretaker crisis, in that the mother is temporarily in need of caretaking, but the infant needs even more attention and everyone looks to the mother to provide it. The most common family explanation for postpartum depression seems to focus on the father's sudden cessation of interest in the mother as all attention shifts to the child. The new mother then presumably demands everyone's attention and resents the child's stubborn refusal to parent her. I have seen severe postpartum depressions in mothers who had a family history of violence and child abuse and feared that they would abuse the child themselves. I've also seen depressions when there was no such history and no such fear. Postpartum depression rarely occurs immediately, usually requiring six weeks or so to develop. Probably chemical factors are involved. Such depressions respond well and quickly to antidepressants, unless the mother and child are separated by hospitalization of either, which prolongs the fears of maternal incapacity and inability to care for the child, thereby producing a phobia of the child. Psychological explanations for postpartum depressions abound in the psychoanalytic literature, but don't explain why one mother would react to childbirth with depression while another would not.

The diagnosis of postpartum depression is obvious. There may be considerable family pathology, or there may be none. A constant feature is the mother's belief that she can't care for the baby alone. The treatment consists of providing her with assistance in caring for the child. The husband, the grandmother, or a nurse may provide this assistance. Hospitalization is strongly contraindicated. Antidepressants may be necessary and usually work.

Fathers may have a variant of postpartum depression, in which they feel overwhelmed by the responsibilty of parenthood and the loss of their own childlike position. They may run away from home, quit their job, have an affair, or go into a classic depression. Unlike the depressed new mother, the irresponsible new father is not likely to get much sympathy or assistance from the family and may skip out entirely. Fathers who are babies themselves and accustomed to intense caretaking from their wives are clearly most at risk.

The immediate postpartum period is a major turning point for marriage, one that frequently requires grandparental involvement and support. A family with a new baby may have too few caretakers to go around.

Infant Abuse: A Structural Crisis Likely to be Exacerbated

Child abuse can begin at birth. The usual explanation is that the mother resents the child's getting better parenting than she got in the past or is getting now; there is also likely to be considerable anger at the husband for neglecting her. The father or mother's new partner may resent the mother's increased attention to the child and subsequent neglect of him. Either of the parents may unleash anger on the demanding child, as if to beat the child into passivity or even to bully the child into becoming a parent. The child, of course, responds by becoming uncomfortable and even less responsive and more demanding. Fairly soon, there is a cranky, rejecting baby who is even less gratifying for the parents, therefore even more subject to abuse. A horrifying pattern can then develop in which the parents pull their relationship together by torturing the child in tandem.

These family dynamics are sufficiently consistent to serve as the basis for diagnosis and treatment. Infant abuse can be considered the first of a series, indicating a structural defect that may be exacerbated. This is a dangerous pattern, likely to be repeated with this child and with subsequent ones. Since infant abuse is rarely a one-time event, a single episode is sufficient to call forth emergency procedures to protect the child. Violent, abusing parents may have to be separated from their child for a time or even permanently. Such decisions about separating babies from their abusive parents are extremely difficult and painful, since the abusive parents may be desperately dependent upon the love they had hoped to get from the child and may go to great extremes to keep the child they are brutalizing so horribly.

If there is some stability in the family, as well as some assurance of cooperation with the therapists, the decision may be made to leave the child with the abusive parents. The pattern can be changed. But this is a scary decision, not to be made lightly. Ongoing supportive, almost parenting therapy of the parents is needed until the child becomes less demanding and old enough to provide some self protection.

Imperfect Babies: A Bolt From the Blue

Some babies are obviously damaged, a few quite severely. But any birth defect changes the situation drastically. Even if the child is premature or one of twins, this fact can become the total identity of the baby and cause for such hovering and anxiety that the child is likely to be protected, and therefore resented, by the parents, and ignored by others.

The birth of an imperfect baby is a major crisis for the family. The parents may blame themselves or may blame one another, dredging up guilt from past misdeeds. Birth defects may be blamed on drug abuse, emotional upsets, past abortions, sinful thoughts or actions, or on defective genes from one or the other family. A damaged baby greatly increases the likelihood of postpartum depression in either parent or in a grandparent. Even rather slight defects can trigger massive reactions, and major defects can be devastating.

The child may have a disfiguring birthmark, a crippled limb, or a cleft lip, cause for concern as well as disappointment. But, as always, the more obvious the defect, the less disorienting the crisis. The child may have the frightening condition of Sudden Infant Death Syndrome, without visible defect but in danger of stopping breathing during sleep. Parents of SIDS babies must monitor the child's breathing around the clock for many months, living with the very real fear that the seemingly healthy child could suddenly die without warning. Asthmatic children present a similar fear. Hydrocephalic babies, after surgery, are left with shunts which may become blocked from the slightest pressure. Even more horrifying are those babies with Tay-Sachs or other genetic chemical disorders. The child-raising process consists of a vigil over a dying baby. The prolonged preparation for the death of a child who can never grow up can become a total obsession for one or both parents. Children with Down's syndrome or brain injury will never grow up to be normal, but can be gratifying and affectionate children. Yet they still tend to isolate the parents, consume their emotional energy, and leave them pessimistic about the future.

Some genetic or birth defects may cause the child to be a frightening and exhausting burden for the parents, leaving them isolated from the rest of the world and sometimes even from one another. Subtle or confusing defects, as well as those which appear gradually as the child grows older, may trigger a series of caretaker crises as the family attempts to understand what is wrong with the child and what to do about it. With any abnormality, it is vital that the parents and grandparents be well educated about what to expect and what can and cannot be done. Raising damaged children is more of a challenge than raising perfect ones; it can be just as rewarding if the challenge is acknowledged and if the damage is not seen as the parents' failure.

It is hard for parents to start the long haul of raising the baby they have rather than the baby of everyone's dreams. All children are a disappointment to their parents, and all are less perfect than originally imagined. Parenting is a fabulous pursuit rather than a competitive sport, and the payoff is in the process rather than the product. One of the wonders of child-raising is the opportunity to understand what your own parents went through and to forgive them. The snag points typically involve unresolved issues in the parent-grandparent relationships, so crises of childbirth can be a marvelous opportunity for all three generations.

MARRIAGE AND PARENTHOOD

Nothing changes a marital relationship quite so definitely and permanently as parenthood. Parenting, like sex, tennis, and making beds, is best done in pairs, and it is the best part of life when the two are working well together. But it usually doesn't happen that way. More likely, one parent will enjoy parenting and center her (usually) life around it, while the other will try to escape from parenting, compete with the child(ren), and feel deserted by his wife. The anti-parent may find the increasingly adult behavior of his spouse to be offensively parental, something to rebel against. When the anti-parent is male, he may escape into his work and to playing games with the other boys—there are special clubs for men who play golf all weekend to escape their wives and children. Among the less advantaged the boys go to bars to drink beer and avoid coming home until the kids are asleep. The new father may become a workaholic or take a second job. His wife, housebound, may lose any skills she ever had in talking to grownups, and become "only a mother," talking daily to her mother and other mothers but losing the other facets of her identity, particularly her marriage. A recent movie, *Mr. Mom*, showed a young mother returning to work after years of staying home raising children. At her first business lunch, she automatically leaned over her boss' plate and cut up his meat for him.

In such marriages the conflict may center on one or both partners' recognizing that the wife is becoming only a mother. They may or may not notice that the husband is becoming one of the kids.

If it is the husband who throws himself into parenting, he may become the grandmother, supervising his wife in her child care but taking no direct responsibility; after a while she might rather do it all herself. He may, of course, become the primary deliverer of child care; although that is becoming more common, it is still rarely thought of as the masculine ideal and is downright threatening to many men and to some women. If he does become the nurturing parent and the one who takes care of things, it may be with his wife's blessing and enthusiastic encouragement or it may be quite offensive to her. Most often, father is lavishly praised for the least little parental effort, and it is as much trouble to get him involved at all as it would be for the beleaguered mother to do it herself. Non-domestic men are a luxury few families can afford, though many men were raised to expect such pampering and feel cheated when they don't get it.

However the couple assigns the parenting tasks, it becomes apparent to one or both of them that the nuclear family is just not big enough to support a home, a marriage, two careers, a child or more, and a nonfunctional prince. Something gets shortchanged. Usually the woman's career, the home, the marriage, and the children are sacrificed to the man's career and his ego, while he demands all the parenting. Some couples can afford servants or have relatives who can fill out the family to functional size if the husband is frightened of domesticity. But most often, it just remains a frustration and everyone suffers. Single parenthood, despite its obvious disadvantages for the child, may be far more pleasant for the single parent than staying in a marriage to someone who insists upon being one of the children rather than one of the parents. This is a societal quandary that has not been adequately addressed; the spouses may run the risk of thinking their difficulties are unique, and blame one another for the problems that arise.

As the child grows older, one or both parents may strongly identify with the little tyke and react to the other parent as the child does. If the mother yells at the child, the father may experience it as her yelling at him. If the father neglects the child, the mother may feel herself being rejected. If he is authoritarian with the child and seems to put the child down, the mother may feel the putdown. As each parent goes through the various parental activities, the other parent may reexperience his or her own parents and react accordingly, reviving that childlike sense of being little and helpless in the face of big, powerful grownups.

It is a disconcerting experience to watch a lover/playmate suddenly turning into a parent/authority. It becomes even more disconcerting as the child becomes adolescent. Grownups remember themselves as adolescents so much more vividly than they remember themselves at any other age, even yesterday. We all identify to a disorienting degree with our adolescent children, especially with their struggles with their other parent. This is worst when the other parent is an ex-spouse, but it is bad enough even in the best marriages. People who have had difficulty with their own adolescence, who have never gotten past their rebellion against authority, are likely to encourage their child's adolescent rebellion, rebel against their teenage child's more adult parent, and choose this point in their marriage to start an affair or end their marriage.

An enormous percentage of our society's children are not growing up with both their parents. A few of these have two functioning parents, living apart but parenting cooperatively. But most live with single parents, who, whether married, remarried, or truly single, are at a disadvantage in raising children. When there are too many roles to be filled, one or more of the children may become parentified, a position that has both advantages and disadvantages. More distressingly, a single parent may be forced to either live in poverty or neglect her child, or both. Single parents may call on therapists to assist in the parenting process and may make therapy somewhat permanent. Parenting is too complex a job to be done alone. Yet, I'm amazed at how well some people do it.

CRISES OF CHILDHOOD

Family therapists may see children as family barometers, developing symptoms as the family tension rises. Children's symptoms are often dealt with as if the child is merely registering what is going on in the family. It may seem impersonal and even inhumane to see the child as putty in the hands of the parents; moreover, it grows increasingly naive as the child approaches puberty and becomes a power to be reckoned with. But in crisis situations it works well to acknowledge the enormous power inequities between adults and children and to assume that parents must change in order to bring about change in the child.

Normal children are controllable but not perfectable. It is normal for children to prefer play to work, to eat when hungry or when food is available, to explore the world full of flora and fauna and phenomena like fire, to be too busy for a bowel movement or urination before bedtime, or want "what he wants when he wants it," and still to expect total approval and attention and tolerance. If the parents are alarmed by such normality and recoil in horror, or identify the child in terms of that behavior, or feel defeated by it, or induce shame and guilt for it, they will bypass the opportunity to simply stop it.

Amateur parents, or those spoiled by a previously "perfect" child, may have great difficulty understanding that they must control and structure children. Children must be reminded and directed and overseen as they do their homework, perform their chores, and otherwise learn to take responsibility. When a four-year-old second child does not behave as the parents remember a six-year-old first child behaving, the parents may decide the child has a character flaw and try to punish it out of him. Most of the crises of childhood result from just this pattern. Small children are baffled by threats and punishment, yet respond readily to continuous structure and benign control. Parents who don't understand this produce insecurity and rebellion.

Raising children is a slow, gradual process. Quite normal children are frustrating, particularly if their normality is not understood by anxious parents, who want a super kid or a less troublesome one. If some element of parental anxiety causes the pace of parenting to be accelerated, that does not accelerate the child's development, but merely confuses the child and ultimately thwarts his or her development. Second children, having missed all the tolerant attention granted first children, are especially at risk for parental impatience.

Parental anxiety is usually the result of some forces outside the child. The mother may be bored with mothering (especially if she feels alone with it) and ready to get on with her life. The father may resent the responsibilities of fatherhood, the continuing preoccupation of the mother with the child, or the mother's lack of attention to the child. There may be marital or financial crises that affect the parents' patience and therefore the child's development. Yet the effect on the child may not be immediately apparent. Botanists can look at the rings in the trunks of ancient trees and determine weather conditions years ago, severe winters, forest fires, and diseases. Child development experts should theoretically be able to do the same, evaluating the age or stage of development at which the mother had an affair, the father lost his job, or the grandmother got sick. The rings are likely to remain, although the child seems to continue to grow and prosper — at least until adolescence. Then all hell breaks loose.

Most children brought to therapy are quite normal, but not necessarily average. Parents may err in either direction in their sense of acceptable norms and may damage their children by fixing that which ain't broke or by overlooking and accepting that which is. The therapist to a family with small children must be an expert on the range of normality. Parents are too invested to know the difference between that which is less than ideal and that which is a reparable problem. The therapist may have to rely on objective, impartial determinations and should not bypass psychological and developmental testing or neurological workups.

Caretaker crises occur when children are not physically normal. Often this is known from birth, or even before. In a way, the lucky children are the ones whose disabilities are most obvious. If the imperfections don't show, the effort to raise the child normally can be frustrating and destructive. Hyperactive and learning-disabled children seem normal, but are realistically unable to do things well that come easily and naturally to other children. Their very real defects may seem to be character flaws. The tendency of parents, teachers, friends, relatives, and babysitters is to increase the pressure and to use shame and even guilt to bring about the self-control or initiative that seems missing. By the time these kids are seen by therapists, they are insecure and rebellious, the parents are exhausted and furious, and the adults are fighting with one another over which one's futile effort should be made next to accomplish a goal that is unachievable. Mistaking a neurological weakness for a character weakness leaves everyone frustrated.

Some children just don't fit in. They may seem normal or even exemplary to their parents, yet may deviate just enough from the ideal to be unacceptable to other children. Fat little girls and unathletic little boys may or may not be embarrassing to their parents, but they are almost guaranteed to be unpopular with their peers. They know they are unpopular, and they know why, and everyone tries to get them to diet and exercise by humiliating them further. They feel so out of it that they see the task of self-improvement as monumental and not worth trying.

Hyperactive kids are a trial for everyone who values peace and order — not just their parents, but also their siblings and other relatives, and even the neighbors. They are not tolerated well by peers, even at a very early age. They produce conflict between the parents, when the mother (or whichever parent has the job of maintaining order and quiet for the other parent) is unable to control the child, and the father blames her. A parent whose job is to play with kids briefly and intermittently may see no problem with the child. Once the child starts school, the problems are magnified, as the teacher calls exasperated, the other children shun the hyperactive one, and the kid can't seem to concentrate long enough to get any homework done.

Learning disabled kids may be undiagnosed until years of school problems have exhausted everyone. They may conscientiously struggle to learn things the family believes to be simple, yet do quite well in many other areas. All the disciplining and screaming the parents can attempt can't make the child a good student. The child feels worse and worse, finds almost everything embarrassing and frustrating, and exaggerates the disability. The learning-disabled often fail to catch on socially too, becoming objects of ridicule for other kids. In their struggle for acceptability, they may react defensively and withdraw or deliberately turn themselves into class clowns.

Child development involves a few inherent crisis points, such as weaning, toilet training, and starting school, at which the family will have to adapt to changes in the child's functional status or requirements. Ordinarily, however, it is the child who has to do the adapting, growing up in a family of a certain structure which goes through its usual exacerbations of conflict, facing with the rest of the family whatever bolts come out of the blue to affect the family, and adjusting to the often cavalier disruptions of caretaking arrangements within the family. The child may or may not be considered as the family moves, divorces, remarries, changes child care arrangements, has more children, and goes through whatever crises they go through. Children seem to be amazingly resilient in the face of life's crises. They react and then they adapt. But that very adaptability leaves them at the mercy of their environment.

The world is frightening to children, and they reflect what their parents fear, as well as what their parents have taught them to fear. They also must face their awareness of their helplessness and dependency on their parents. Among children phobias are common. Perhaps the most common phobia of childhood is fear of separation from the parents. If the parents are also a bit frightened of separation, they may stay home from the party because the child is upset or let the child sleep with them if the child has a nightmare, thereby magnifying the child's phobia. Parental hovering does not in any way reassure the child that separation and nightmares are safe. Temper tantrums may even be seen as a form of phobic behavior, in which the child is frightened of his or her own anger and panics over it. If the tantrum is frightening to the parents and is punished rather than controlled, that just increases everyone's fear of the child's normal anger.

The prototypical crisis of childhood is school phobia. School phobia constitutes a true psychiatric emergency. The central issue is probably separation anxiety rather than something symbolic. The child generally describes some teacher or fellow student who triggers the fear, and since the parents don't actually know what is going on at school and may be a little uncomfortable about having their baby exposed to unpleasantness, they may magnify the problem by letting the child stay away from school until they all feel better. Usually the phobia follows an illness or some break in the routine that keeps the child away from school legitimately for a time, so the child's plea of illness or upset may be accepted at face value. The child may seem perfectly well and calm and happy and cooperative until time to return to school, at which point the child turns into something out of *The Exorcist*, screaming and kicking and vomiting split-pea soup and throwing things around and threatening everyone who tries to take him or her to school.

This well-known syndrome is often attributed to maternal depression, paternal distance, and a child who feels protective of the mother and is afraid to leave her. It is generally treated by having *both* parents involved in forcing the return to school, over whatever objections the child may muster. Ordinarily the child calms completely upon being overpowered and has no problem once inside the school building. There may be all manner of family pathology, but often there is not. All mothers of school phobic children are not depressed, and all fathers are not uninvolved, and many school phobias require minimal therapy after the child is returned to school. It is frequent, however, to discover that one of the parents was school phobic and that the child is enmeshed, perfectionistic, and intolerant of anything being out of control.

Children do become depressed over losses and threatened losses. Depressions are normal in childhood as children become aware of their dependency, their insignificance in the universe, their limitations, and their own mortality. If a child's concerns are openly dealt with and the parents are reassuring, the depressions tend to be short. Obviously, children are dependent on their parents and any threat to the continuation of the family will depress them, sometimes severely. In the midst of marital conflict, the parents may think they are providing reassurance by pretending the children don't know what is going on and therefore not discussing the problems with them. Parental silence just increases the child's insecurity and depression. Children know, at some level, what is going on but need the words to say it.

There are many things that can go wrong in the child-raising process, from bolts from the blue like molestation to structural realignments like divorce and remarriage. Children can be exposed to horrible influences and great traumas. Usually they survive them fairly well—they react, and then they adapt. Incidents don't affect children as much as patterns do. The patterns under which children grow up will affect them for the rest of their lives. However, there are a few family patterns which seem to bring about symptoms much more quickly, producing symptomatic children.

The children who are growing up in the worst families are not identified as patients and are not brought in for therapy, except sometimes as an afterthought during the treatment of one or more of their various parents and stepparents. Surprisingly, they don't often develop symptoms—perhaps they realize that no one would notice if they did. Certainly they are being shaped by their parents' dysfunctional, inappropriate, or disruptive behavior, and the effect will show up in adolescence or later. But children in truly awful families frequently grow up strong and stable, perhaps by distancing themselves from the family at an early age. It may be an advantage for children to know their parents are stark raving mad. Certainly it is preferable to believing the parents are perfect and wise, and correct in their concern about the child's imperfection. Every child needs some adult who thinks he or she is wonderful. A doting grandparent can be a Godsend. So can an aunt or uncle, an older sibling, a maid, a friend's parent, or a teacher.

Therapists can't be there to protect children from most of what happens to them, but therapists can remember to consider the children as the adults go through whatever crises they have chosen in life.

There are several structural patterns of parenting that don't work very well. The problems may begin to appear in childhood or may not appear until adolescence or even later. Children being raised in these ways may not be brought in as patients unless someone else begins to object to the pattern. Typically, someone will intervene and declare a problem neither the parents or the child had defined. The school, a new stepparent, an older sibling, a grandparent might trigger a family crisis by objecting to the pattern. More often the pattern just continues throughout childhood, and the problems appear in adolescence. These patterns correspond to the six syndromes of adolescent crises and are their forerunners. If they can be caught and reversed in childhood, some of the horrors of adolescence may be dampened.

Unsocialized children, marked for failure, are growing up in families which don't function well in the world and are raising kids with unattractive habits which are acceptable to the family but unacceptable to the world. These parents just can't get it together well enough to train their children in social skills. The children may be obese or bedwetters or just extremely shy and unsocial. The parents may not notice since they aren't very different themselves and are too passive and defeated to do anything about it if they did notice. These parents feel defeated by the world and aren't surprised that their children feel the same way. The snag point for these parents is their sense of helplessness with the world's expectations.

Often, a child is marked for failure by his or her family because of circumstances of birth, resemblance to a family pariah, or some childhood action. The characteristic the family reacts to may be admired or dreaded — it hardly matters — the point is that it becomes the child's identity, a reason for being "different."

Anxious children, who fear they are imperfect, are growing up in just the opposite situations. Their parents also fear the world, but they believe that success is possible if everything is done just right. They may hover anxiously over everything the child does and says, attempting to perfect it so the child can be successful in the world. The child, fearing both the world and the parental disapproval, may develop anxiety symptoms or obsessive-compulsive ones, and may cease to function altogether. The snag point for these parents is their dedication to the idea that perfection can be achieved and must be achieved for security in a demanding world.

Sneaky children, destined to be sociopaths, are growing up in families in which the parental conflict takes place on a more underground level. Dishonesty is encouraged as the child operates within a web of deceits and alliances aimed at undercutting authority. The battle may be between the parents and the world rather than between one parent and the other. This pattern is also a possibility in one-parent families in reduced circumstances. These very difficult parents have as their snag point the belief that the rules of the world and of one another exist to be broken or circumvented, since authority of any sort is the enemy to be overcome.

Parental or rescuing children, typically the oldest child of a depressed parent, may learn to hover protectively and cling to the pathetic parent. These children may be perfect in every way, and may actually become parental to their parents at amazingly early ages. These children may become symptomatic with separation anxiety, including school phobia. A less toxic form of this pattern is fairly typical in single-parent families. As they get older, in their efforts at rescuing their parents from marital crises or desperate romances, they can develop even more serious symptoms. The snag point here is that the parent feels incapable of parenting without the child's support.

Neglected children, those who will eventually go underground, are growing up unattended in incompetent families. This pattern is typical of poor, single-parent families, but it also occurs in rich, busy families. There is no one to see to the child, as the parent or parents are too busy surviving or succeeding. There just may be nothing at home for these children. The snag point in these situations is that the parent takes no responsibility for the child.

Rebellious children, "brats," are so busy fighting with their parents that they don't adapt very well to the rest of the world. These may be dependent frightened children growing up in stormy families; the children may be caught up in parental battles in which it becomes impossible to please both parents at the same time. These children may have temper tantrums to distract the parents from their rather similar behavior. There may be no consistency, as the parents operate from the rule that they must not agree on any course of action involving the children — or anything else. These parents' snag point is their inattention — they don't respond to subtleties.

To raise children successfully, parents may have to overcome their despair, their anxiety, their own rebellion, their dependency on their children, their irresponsibility, and their inattention. They may even have to make peace with one another and with the world. Therapy may be directed toward just that.

TREATMENT OF CRISES OF CHILDHOOD

Step 1: Emergency Response

There are few true emergencies of childhood. Even when the parent who calls feels threatened and urgent, the appointment may have to be postponed because of dance lessons or soccer practice, which puts the sense of emergency into perspective. One exception is school phobia, which is a true emergency and must be handled quickly.

Step 2: Involve the Family

Both parents and any resident stepparents should be included in the first interview. As always, the ideal may not be achieved. It may not be necessary to see the other siblings, but it is always helpful and rarely destructive. Grandparents and other resident adults should be included too. Reports from the school and the pediatrician are usually important and worth the trouble, since it is crucial for the therapist to know whether the child is neurologically intact and whether the problem is present in other settings as well as home. Parents may insist upon seeing the therapist first without the child. When I've gone ahead and pampered the parents a bit, actually auditioned for them before seeing the child, I haven't noticed that it created problems, as it does sometimes with adolescents.

Step 3: Define the Crisis

Families in crisis characteristically call for help by increasing the intensity of the crisis until one of the children becomes symptomatic and then sending the child out for help. Many of the children identified as patients are just finding a therapist for their parents' marriage. The parents or the child may tell you this right away, but it will often be discovered later in the therapy.

At other times, though, the child is not alarmed by the parents, but the parents really are alarmed about the child. The list of things that children can do that will alarm parents is endless. Often the parents are imagining a problem with no reality to it at all, which is indeed a problem. Parents may be seeking reassurance that their child is not abnormal, despite an upsetting experience or an intense emotional reaction. Variations of normality may be magnified into problems by the anxious parent. There may actually have been some misbehavior or peculiar behavior on the child's part, an episode of fire setting for example, which is treated by the parent or someone else as cause for alarm, as if the unique behavior were habitual.

It must be clear whether there is a neurological or physical defect in the child. The diagnosis of learning disabilities and hyperactivity is inexact to the point of chaos—all opinions are suspect, and even neurological and psychological testing produces only hunches. Yet the diagnosis is vital. It is undoubtedly safer to underdiagnose these conditions temporarily, while remaining willing to shift directions with experience. Actually, the parents and teachers who see the child over time may assess the subtleties of neurological intactness better than the best experts who see the child only once. Unless there is clear evidence to the contrary, it is best to assume the child is normal and is behaving in a manner that makes sense in the context of the family.

If there is a habit disorder in the child, or a pattern disorder in the parenting, that must be clearly defined. If the initial focus is kept on the behavior of the child, the structural problems in the parenting or even in the marital relationship will soon become evident in the resistance to solving the problem. Parental helplessness, perfectionistic anxiety, rebellion against authority, dependency on a child, irresponsibility, or inattention may show immediately, but are most fruitfully approached as they interfere with parenting functions. It is not a good idea to diagnose the parents initially.

Step 4: General Prescription

The therapist can relieve tension by giving the child the opportunity to explain the alarming behavior without danger of punishment or hysteria. The very format of family therapy, the democratization of the family, is tension-relieving for the child, with everyone getting a chance to talk and even the most powerful parents being assigned a child's role in comparison to the powerful therapist. The posture of the therapist is crucial and tricky. He or she must be more powerful than the parents without being too powerful for the child, must support the parents' authority and the child's right to be heard.

Step 5: Specific Prescription

The usual prescription is twofold and is directed toward the offending behavior. The child is told to explain the behavior and its reasons, and the parents are told to understand the child's feelings and stop the child's behavior. It is an interesting diagnostic process to watch the child attempt to explain the behavior and the parents to try to stop it, since most often the parents have devoted themselves to explaining, or even diagnosing, the child, while demanding that the child control himself or herself. The child may even be able to explain the behavior and at the same time give the parents hints about what they can do to get it under control. It is refreshing, and generally accurate, when the beleaguered child explains to the parents, "I'm just a kid." The parents might have to be reminded that they, and the therapist, did similar things when they were "just kids," until someone either stopped them or recognized the behavior as normal.

When the problem involves either the child's behavior or the child's emotions, the parents are told to control the child. This may mean stopping the child's school refusal or temper tantrums or stopping the child's depression or anxiety. The child is told to do what the parents say. The parents are not told primarily to change themselves, but they will have to do so in order to parent the child.

Step 6: Negotiating Resistance

There is certain to be resistance to anything that challenges the family's traditional values, and in fact, the very format of therapy may challenge those values. The family may have inflexible rules against the father's involvement in parenting, against criticism of the mother, against the child's talking about feelings, against anyone noticing the marriage, against any adult acting parental and controlling the child. Most families will do all they can to solve the problem with the least possible change, and they can be quite creative, and often successful, with a plan much modified from the one agreed upon in the session.

The usual resistance is for the family to avoid doing any of the prescribed tasks and, once back at home, to (1) not mention the tasks, (2) fight about the tasks, (3) pretend not to understand the tasks, or (4) talk only about the deficiencies of the therapist and belittle the tasks, a quite likely possibility if the therapist uses paradoxical approaches too early in the therapy. The child may even sabotage the therapy by giving up the offending behavior before the parents get the experience of working together, or another child may grab the spotlight before the index child gets cooperative attention. Each family will resist change in its own unique ways, and the second session is likely to be far more revealing than the first — and nearly always surprising.

The parents have been given the task of stopping the offending behavior, if possible without threatening or punishing the child. Behavior is either voluntary or not, and is either forbidden or accepted. If a child does something that is voluntary and forbidden, it may be punished. But first it must be established that it is voluntary and that it is forbidden. Parents may fight between themselves, or with the child, over specific punishment, and may threaten all manner of things and carry on wildly and terrifyingly, without making any effort to understand or control the behavior in question.

Most of the six snag points that lead to structural patterns of ineffective parenting are challenged by asking the parents to understand and then control the child. Once the parents accept the job of controlling the child, the offensive behavior generally changes, as does the focus of the therapy. The parents will then struggle with their helplessness, anxiety, rebellion, dependency, irresponsibility, or inattention as those parenting habits prevent them from effective parenting.

If the symptomatic behavior continues, the parents can work together to find ways of stopping it, and the therapy may focus on their difficulty in working together. The therapist, in negotiating this parental cooperation, may support a plan the parents come up with, elicit a plan from the child or the child's siblings or grandparents, or offer an approach that worked with the therapist's children or previous patients. It is probably more important to get agreement on the plan than to get the right plan. The most amazing and unlikely plans have worked, if they produce cooperation.

Often the therapist faced with a family complaining of a child's depression quickly uncovers parental marital conflict which becomes the focus of therapy. Overly parental oldest chidren often get their parents into therapy via their own depression. In such cases the therapeutic task may well be to leave the child out of the rest of the therapy and out of the parents' marital troubles.

Step 7: Termination

Most of the crises of childhood are resolved rather quickly. Structural habit disturbances may take longer. Even if the parents are willing and trying to change the patterns, the child's response may be slow and uneven. One of the toughest jobs for parents and therapists is to get fat kids to change eating habits or uninspired students to keep up with school work. Parents will make changes for their children they will not make for one another or for their infuriating adolescents. As the situation improves, the interval between sessions can be extended, and the decision about whether the sessions are held at all can be left to the child, who is permitted to come in ad lib, but required to come in if the symptom continues or returns. Often marital therapy then proceeds without the child.

Children have few decisions to make, few choices, other than to do what their parents tell them to do. If that is unclear, it is the parents who'll end up being seen regularly over a period of time. If the parents are so unreliable and destructive that the therapy becomes impossible, the child could, as a last resort, be removed from the home. Individual therapy of a child is not an antidote to a toxic family.

SOME CHILDREN IN CRISIS

CASE 14   *The Baby's Bottle*

Ida, 10, informed her father that she could not adjust to his remarriage. After a stormy marriage, her parents had divorced when she was five. She had lived with her mother and stepfather and baby half-brother, but her real relationship was with her father, whom she saw often. When he remarried, Ida tried to go on the honeymoon and carried on wildly when she couldn't. During the first therapy visit, she sat on her father's lap, sucking her thumb and brushing his hair, while he purred. The new young stepmother sat on the other side of the room looking embarrassed and disgusted. They were both librarians, logical and unemotional. Ida treated them as semi-animate objects. I tried to move Ida to her stepmother's lap, but the father wouldn't let go.

I called the real mother, a rambunctious lady who reported that Ida was very helpful with the baby and acted appropriately mature with her. She confessed that her ex-husband sometimes sucked his thumb too. I suggested that the stepmother involve Ida in the work around the house. At the next visit, Ida, back in her father's lap, thumb firmly in mouth, described her adventures with baking cakes and sorting papers with her stepmother. The stepmother then complained that Ida still sucked a bottle, given her by her grandmother. I discussed the inappropriateness of this with Ida, but the father protested that it would hurt his mother's feelings if Ida gave up that special bottle. Ida came up with the idea of calling her grandmother and explaining that she wanted to stop being a baby and grow up to be someone like her stepmother instead. She called from the office and felt quite proud of herself, and then sat down beside her stepmother rather than in the lap her father offered. At the third visit, Ida and her stepmother were quite close and loving and the father confessed some relief that he wouldn't have to continue providing all the loving. He did report that his mother was shattered by Ida's efforts to grow up and was pushing the newly married couple to have babies. The stepmother said she didn't want children, but pointed out that if her husband would let Ida grow up, he might some day have grandchildren.

I saw them once more. Ida was still demanding, but was behaving more maturely. I saw Ida a few years later with her stepmother at a movie. She proudly told me she was wearing her first bra and would not be spending the summer with her father as she was going to a co-ed camp. She seemed willing to turn the job of caring for her poor father to her stepmother, while she got on with her life.

Comment: When the offending behavior occurs in some situations but not in others, the capacity is there, but the directive has not been given. Frequently, an outsider, sometimes a stepparent, a grandparent, a teacher, or a therapist, will have to give that directive for everyone to cut the nonsense.

CASE 15   *The Belly of the Whale*

Jonah, at 11, was the fattest little boy I'd ever seen. He also had the worst report card in his class. Everyone called him "whale." The school had insisted on therapy. He and his equally obese parents sat and cried over the world's intolerance. The father was helpless and inept, the mother phobic for work and barely involved with anything other than fighting with the school over Jonah. They described an evening in their house. After dinner, they would beg Jonah to do his homework. He would shake his head and cry, while his mother brought him food and his father looked helpless and watched TV. The 15-year-old brother, who had recently slimmed down and shaped up, was embarrassed by Jonah and picked on him until he cried. The mother would then fight with the older brother and Jonah would leave his homework, take his munchies, and join his father at the TV. I set up a plan. The father would oversee Jonah with his homework for an hour each night. If he hadn't finished, they'd exercise for an hour and then finish it. Dinner would not be served to anyone until after the homework was done. If the father didn't comply with this, the mother would fuss at him, not Jonah.

The next week, everyone had performed as directed and all were bouncy about it. By the next week, all were still performing as directed. All my efforts were directed toward helping the flaccid father continue the structure and keeping the frantic mother from sabotaging his pitiful efforts. The father would keep it up for a while and then go limp. He'd cry, Jonah would cry, and the mother would go to battle with either me or the school to take the pressure off poor Jonah. The brother would take over the structure and the mother would attack him, and he'd pick on Jonah, and Jonah would cry, and the father would cry, and I'd feel fed up with them all. Finally we sent the mother back to school herself and she was too busy to either force the structure or obstruct it. Jonah discovered a new trick. He'd do the homework and then not turn it in. The brother came to the rescue, forcing Jonah to turn in his homework or beating him up if he didn't. This time, Jonah defied the brother by finally doing his homework and his exercise on his own. The brother went out for football, but promised to take over the structure anytime Jonah faltered.

Comment: Families who aren't careful raise children who are like themselves. When they spend a lifetime protecting and defending their own inadequacies and idiosyncracies, their children are likely to emulate them. In some families, there is no health to draw from and no pre-crisis state to return to, so no magical maneuver that will bring about the keystone change. It is a hard pattern to break, but the therapist's best ally may be a family member who has somehow stumbled out of the family pattern.

CASE 16   *Mother in Distress*

Knight was 12, the tallest boy in his class, but just a little kid. He had been such a beautiful child that he'd been kidnapped at two from a shopping center. His mother had rarely let him out of her sight since, and he played only with the boy next door. She was not so attentive to her cold, taciturn husband or her gregarious younger son. She had left the husband, which pleased Knight, but then she had gone back to him. When the father had moved from Wyoming to Atlanta, the mother had delayed joining him when Knight did not want to move. She had finally come and they had been in couples' therapy for much of the year in Atlanta. The mother had been depressed, and the therapist had tried to teach the father to respond. He didn't, but the mother recovered anyway and decided to stay in the marriage. Knight's response was to write suicide notes and refuse to go to school. The mother called the therapist, who asked me to see the family.

Knight cried through the first session, calling himself a freak because of his height, raging that nobody liked him and that everyone expected too much of him. It was unclear whom he hated most—his brother for having friends when he didn't, his father for loving his brother and avoiding him, or his mother for holding him so close. He offered not to commit suicide if the mother moved back to Wyoming or the father kicked the little brother out and spent time with him instead. The mother felt hurt. The father, busy stifling the little brother's playfulness, gave no response at all. We spent that first session trying to teach the father how to hold a crying 6'-tall child. He looked terrified and talked about his own childhood with a manic-depressive father. From an early age, he had been the mainstay of the family and had learned to keep all emotions tightly controlled. He wanted Knight to do the same, but he feared him, having nightmares that Knight would kill his little brother.

The crisis was easy. The father was directed to either keep holding Knight or take him back to school. He went to school the next day. After a few good days, his father went on a trip. His mother left her job and kept Knight at home to catch up on his school work. I screamed at her. He continued to get rejected and to try to get some response from his father, only to have his mother intervene. His sniveling made his father shudder. Knight had been completely kidnap-proofed — he could drive away anyone who tried to get close. I even went to school with him to supervise his social skills. But the only really effective move was having the mother punish him instead of cuddling him when he got himself rejected by other children. Then I had him fight physically with his brother in the office, preventing the father from intervening, as Knight demonstrated the flamboyant choreography with which he could make it appear he was killing the boy without actually hurting him. In time Knight and his brother became friends, and Knight gave up on getting any sensible response from either parent. At least he stopped fighting with the world.

Comment: When the obvious road to health (in this case the father's involvement) is hopelessly blocked, an alternative route may be required (in this case having the mother punish rather than reward the symptom).

These cases display a wide range of childhood symptoms and various levels of family stability. In each case, the child's symptomatic behavior has been tolerated, accepted, or even encouraged for some time before someone has objected to it. The objector may be the school, or a new family member, or an old family member who suddenly gets sick or well and now requires something different. The child will resist the change as long as one or more family members share in the protection of the child from normality.

This protection from health is most likely to stubbornly persist in single-parent families and in those where there is serious marital conflict. None of these families was severely dysfunctional, so the therapy could be tightly focussed. When one parent is psychotic and alone, either because the other has left or has given up, the therapist's job is far more difficult. Even the hardest working therapist requires at least one reasonably sane and active family member, and may have to create one before the child can be changed.

A few years ago adolescence was a phase; then it became a profession; now it is a new nationality.

— Donald Barr, *Who Pushed Humpty Dumpty*, 1971

Why can't they be like we were, perfect in every way?
What's the matter with kids today?

— Lee Adams, *Bye Bye Birdie*

CHAPTER 10

Adolescence

THE TIME OF NORMAL PSYCHOSIS

ADOLESCENCE IS A PERIOD of normal psychosis. At no time in a person's life is there such awareness of crisis and change. Adults may romanticize this period, recalling it fondly as a time of glamour and pleasure and heroic achievement and closeness to peers, epitomized by the senior prom or the big game. For a few adolescents, high school is life's high point. For most, it is the pits. There is intense self-consciousness and awareness of the slightest personal deficiencies. There is constant preoccupation with peer status. Adolescents feel too much. Moods come and go with lightning speed and intensity. Every moment, every mood seems forever. And there is little ability to act contrary to one's impulses or moods, even in the interest of one's survival, much less in the interest of one's future.

Parents seem useless, perhaps even the enemy. They cannot possibly follow the styles and monitor the social instability. Even more, the parents can't track the mood swings — even at best, they are always a mood or two

175

behind in their responses. Nor can parents easily understand the priorities which control the lives of teenagers. For adults the task of the adolescent is to prepare for adulthood (and bolster parental pride) by performing well at adult-approved skills. For the adolescent, the task is to survive another day by arranging sufficient emotional support from peers, or whomever else can soothe the stings of social humiliation.

There is no time in the life of a family when greater stability is required than during the adolescence of one of its members. Yet the adolescent offers no stability at all. The adolescent must derive stability from his or her family — it can not come from within nor from equally unstable adolescent peers. However, if the parents are seen as thwarting change and growth toward independence, rather than tracking it, the parents cannot provide stability. Nor can the parents provide much stability while they are making their own marriage and life chaotic.

The adolescence of one family member arouses in the parents a revival of their own adolescent struggles and fantasies, calls into question the parents' values, disrupts the accepted family patterns, makes the usual rules obsolete, and challenges and exposes the usual roles, shatters the parents' goals for their rapidly changing child, and increases family tension enormously. Adolescence is a crisis for all concerned.

Adolescents need their parents. It is not frivolous to suggest that children (and they are still children) between 12 and 18 need parenting more than they did between six and 12, and perhaps in many ways as much as they did between one and six. There is a tendency for older adolescents to deny their need for parents and for the parents to forget that the adolescents need them more, not less, than a few years earlier. It is not easy for the adolescents to coordinate their fantasies with the world's realities, as imperfectly represented by the parents. But it is even harder for the adults to go through the process of rethinking everything they thought they knew about life and the world as the adolescents challenge it. I'm not sure people are truly adult until they have been through adolescence from both ends and have relived those stormy years in the positions of their own parents, observing how the choices and value patterns that have been guiding their lives were actually chosen. Those years of their children's coming of age can be a more vivid experience than a comparable period of psychoanalysis, and often bring them far closer to their own parents.

The strength, beauty, energy, and sexuality of adolescents, not very impressive to the adolescent who is awed by the parents' power, wisdom, grace, and security, make the parents feel weak, ugly, tired, and impotent. Adults and adolescents make one another feel disquietingly inadequate and dissatisfied, contributing indirectly to the parents' midlife crises. Adolescents' idealism and impatience with their imperfect parents can turn minor marital or vocational dissatisfaction into something major. Adolescents also can dash parental fantasies of glory and make the sacrifices of parenthood seem wasted. After 14 years of dutiful parenthood, any parent deserves something better than a normal 14-year-old.

Parents cannot provide expertise on matters of adolescent *style*. What is socially and stylistically acceptable or unacceptable for one generation may not be for the next. Parents may try to be trendy and to understand the taste of their children in music, dress, and etiquette, but unless they are willing to turn that into the full-time preoccupation their children have, they are not likely to get it right. They'll end up appearing foolish to their children. Parents must let their children be the experts on style; they may notice and comment on the differences, but without considering stylistic differences to be substantive differences.

Parents must provide expertise on matters of *substance*. Morality, particularly sexual morality, does have its stylistic components. A decade ago swinging was considered trendy, today it is frowned upon. Virginity, at least for females, was once admired, but is now more often suspect than prized. For a while homosexuality was more acceptable than it had been, but now it is losing popularity. Our society still presents certain ideals for sexual behavior, but tolerates some deviance from the ideal. Parents must understand this; otherwise they disqualify themselves as experts in less controversial areas of morality. It has been said that no one can grow up successfully until he realizes that his parents are stark raving mad, at least in a few areas.

Parents may have a clear notion of their ideal adolescent but little sense of the variations within the normal range. They may not know that normal adolescents get drunk, get laid, get depressed, smoke pot, tell lies, wreck cars, throw temper tantrums, keep messy rooms, wear tacky clothes, listen to barbaric music, talk on the telephone interminably, feel attraction to disgusting people, and don't like to visit relatives they don't know well. This behavior, while normal, may not be a good idea, and may require parental comment, control, or intervention. The dialogue between parent and teenager must be maintained, and it can't be maintained if parents believe adolescence is a character flaw rather than a series of hurdles along the track to adulthood. It is the parents who must maintain the overview of the temporary nature of all of this adolescent chaos — adolescents view everything as permanent. If parents do so as well, no one has perspective on it all. This requires an atmosphere of honesty, directness, and openness.

In some families, honesty, directness, and openness are valued; in others they are punished. There are even families which accept and reward cheating, lying, theft, and, on rare occasions, murder. Children who follow the world's rules may have to break the family's rules in order to do so, and vice versa. These substantive issues must be explored by every family and are difficult for most. Many people preach and teach one system of values while practicing another. They expect their children to follow the teaching, not the practice. Children have the responsibility to make parents aware of the discrepancies in their own system of values. During that unavoidable process, the parents may see the child who questions the parents' values as bad, disrespectful, impolite, rude, and rebellious — and they may, of course, be right. Some families tolerate these confrontations better than others. Some find the process so threatening that they see the child as defective when there is any deviation from the parental values.

THE ADOLESCENT UNDERGROUND

When puberty begins, most kids become obsessed with privacy. This first involves hiding their enlarging genitals from their parents and developing a sense of shame about their bodies. Physicians are the only adults that ever see naked 13-year-olds, and they have a struggle with it. At that age, pubertal children fear parents, perhaps believing the parents would prevent maturity if they knew it was occurring. Masturbation and whatever other sexual activities adolescents engage in are shame-inducing and hidden. Adolescents play at being adults, but are embarrassed and try to do it furtively.

Actually, sex is properly considered private, and parents should encourage or require some secrecy so the adolescents can pursue their groping in the dark and protect the parents from any impulse to control, direct, or prohibit it.

As adolescents partake of "adult" pleasures, such as alcohol or drugs, that too is often kept secret. Even kids from open, honest families feel pressure from peers raised less openly, who require that activities be part of the adolescent underground. However, once a child becomes part of the adolescent underground, the parents become the enemy and nothing makes sense. It should be obvious to even the most dim-witted parent when a kid has gone underground. Some parents don't notice, however, and a child can become drug-soaked, alcoholic, or thoroughly enmeshed in criminal activity before anyone reacts. And once it comes to the parents' attention that a child is dabbling in these pursuits, the parents, having had little knowledge of the child's life for years, may assume the problem is bigger or smaller than it is and either over- or underreact.

As soon as a crisis hits, the child may fall back on the parents, discover they aren't really trying to take his or her puberty away, and trust them a little more for the remaining few years. These little crises are crucial to the parent-adolescent relationships. If the parents are unhelpful or punitive and restrictive or guilt-producing or naive or hysterical, it may be years before they are given another chance.

The adolescents who come into therapy do not typically come from placid families. A hefty majority comes from divorced families. Even among the intact families, a majority lives under the threat of divorce, usually because of one or both parents' affair, sometimes because of alcoholism. The children are inescapably aware of the instability of the parents' marriages, usually aware of the affairs, and often parties to the process and decisions. The parents may not be available to them during this time when they need their parents most.

Some kids have little choice but to live out their adolescence underground. The luckier ones have other adults in whom they confide — grandparents, friends' parents, teachers, aunts and uncles, coaches, ministers, older siblings. Other kids, more ashamed of their activities, may choose unsavory characters or foolish adults or restrict their confidences to their peers.

Quite a few children become heavily involved in drugs during these years. I don't see drug-soaked kids as frequently as I did ten years ago — only about 20% of my adolescent identified patients are drug-soaked. While many, if not most, kids have dabbled in drugs, most do not make drugs the center of their lives, as was the style in the late '60s and early '70s. Some still do.

DRUGS AND THE ADOLESCENT UNDERGROUND

The drug most frequently abused by adolescents is alcohol, which is also the drug most frequently abused by their parents. Because it is familiar and usually socially acceptable, some drinking is expected and many kids are taught to drink in whatever fashion the parents consider appropriate. Alcoholism runs in families, with both heredity and environment contributing. Parents who use alcohol daily may encourage their children to do the same, without realizing the depressant effects of daily alcohol use.

Adolescents discovering alcohol are little different from the way they were a few years earlier with Halloween candy — they promptly overdo it and make themselves sick. Some learn from this experience, in part because it is a difficult one to hide. The effects of alcohol are well-known to the parents and easily identifiable, if the parents are paying attention. There do seem to be some adolescents who are biologically alcoholic. They receive some sort of euphoriant effect less evident to the rest of us and become quickly addicted, with alternating periods of depressive withdrawal and elated intoxication each day. They are willing to give up much else in life for the sake of alcohol. Other kids, on the childlike principle that more is better, try to squeeze more pleasure from the grape or the grain by drinking themselves silly every time they pursue pleasure. These habits are hard to hide, but some manage.

Marijuana is more subtle. It has become somewhat socially acceptable in the last decade. Even the youngest children and the densest adults know that it is fairly harmless if used infrequently. But many users, most nonusers, and some who treat users or try to raise them don't seem to know that it functions not only as a euphoriant but also as a mild hallucinogen, which somewhat paralyzes the user's ability to control the focus of his own attention, thereby significantly diminishing learning and the ability to structure oneself and to order priorities. Any beginning smoker knows that the effect on attention, motivation, and structure persists for several days, leaving the user in a mental state somewhat comparable to mild schizophrenia with a learning disability, but vaguely serene and free of anger. Anyone who knows a heavy user recognizes that smoking even several times a week soon leaves the smoker with a persistent burned-out mental state, characterized by lack of interest in learning, relationships, schedules, or proprieties. Even after discontinuing a heavy marijuana habit, the user may remain unstructured and unmotivated for many months.

The greatest danger of marijuana is for kids who are already learning-disabled, for whom learning even with full attention is a frustrating struggle. For schizophrenics, marijuana is a disaster, enhancing the chemical disorder, thought disorder, social isolation, and other symptoms. The best-known active ingredient of cannabis is THC, an hallucinogen similar in structure and effect to LSD and, presumably, to whatever mysterious natural brain chemical causes schizophrenia. For reasons I don't understand, schizophrenics are much attracted to hallucinogens, including marijuana, and find they relieve anhedonia, even as they increase passivity and withdrawal from stimulation and striving. Heavy pot smokers are difficult to differentiate from schizophrenics and the learning-disabled. Stronger hallucinogens are far less popular than they once were, but are still around, and mimic or induce schizophrenia far more dramatically.

The press tells us we're in the midst of a cocaine epidemic. So far I've seen a few adolescents addicted to this drug, although I have encountered many adult users. Cocaine is so rapidly addicting that kids (or adults) can run through a fortune, withdraw from all activity and wreck their physical and mental health in a matter of weeks.

SYNDROMES OF ADOLESCENCE

Some adolescents present with crises carried over from an earlier age, such as school phobia and incest. Others suffer from syndromes usually associated with a later age, such as anorexia and bulimia, homosexuality, and schizophrenia, all of which are uniquely baffling problems, in which the family's etiological contribution is unclear or perhaps even nonexistent. All of these syndromes, at whatever age, have great specificity. But the typically adolescent syndromes, like everything else about adolescence, are not specific, however intense. The symptoms may wax and wane, although the pattern is tangible.

The family literature doesn't try too hard to make specific diagnoses of adolescents. Goldstein et al. (1968) did define four symptom groups based on social adjustment: (1) aggressive antisocial, (2) active family conflict (rebellious), (3) passive negative (underachieving), and (4) socially withdrawn (anxious, dependent). Stierlin (1973), examining adolescent runaways of the "runaway culture" of the '60s, described three transactional modes: (1) binding, (2) expelling, and (3) delegating, corresponding to emancipation from enmeshment, casual wandering away from neglect, and adventurous rescuing of the family from boring inhibitions. In general, the family literature assumes some families are too tight and others too loose, some adolescents loved too much and others too little. The specifically adolescent developmental syndromes are very much a part of the family matrix in which they arise.

I find it helpful to define six developmental crises of adolescence, six syndromes of symptomatic behavior, each with a fairly specific family structure: (1) underground adolescents, (2) sociopathic adolescents, (3) rebellious adolescents, (4) adolescents marked for failure, (5) imperfect adolescents, and (6) rescuing adolescents.

Underground Adolescents

Underground adolescents may continue to live at home, or at least sleep at home and receive telephone calls there, while avoiding involvement with the people there. They may go to school or pretend to go to school, and they may have jobs of an undemanding nature from which they derive enough money to finance their rather independent existence. They may steal money from their parents' purses and wallets, or sell or pawn family items, all without being noticed. They rarely talk to their parents, going straight to their rooms when they come home. They may not even come home at night. They may miss family meals, if there are such meals, and eat heated-up leftovers at a later hour. Conversations may consist of nothing more than "Where are you going?" "Out." "What are you doing?" "Nothing." "When will you be back?" "Later." There may be protest if the questions are pursued further.

If the adolescent has problems, they are not brought to the attention of the parents. Report cards may be intercepted or forged. Large sums of money may be borrowed or loaned. Some of these kids have large secret bank accounts from a healthy drug business. Many have furtive abortions, hidden automobiles, even unknown apartments away from home. Some go through pregnancies and even deliveries without their parents' noticing. Some have not been to school for months, even a year or so. Some do run away—the running is unnecessary, as no one chases. Some move back and forth between the households of their divorced parents, with long periods unaccounted for.

The life of an underground adolescent may be singularly unstimulating— hanging out and smoking dope, alone or with equally bored friends. They avoid interacting with adults, as they have too little activity and too many secrets to make for conversation.

The families of these kids are distracted. Usually the parents are divorced. Sometimes the parents are together and both work. Often there is a semisecret affair going on and everyone is afraid to question anyone's comings and goings, for fear of revealing a secret they don't want resolved yet. These parents don't want to have any problems at home to demand their attention. Their interests are elsewhere. They are tired of being parents, perhaps frightened of it, and want it over, however it ends. They prefer to consider their child's secrecy to be proof of maturity and independent functioning. Most parents realize that if an adolescent is not telling parents about problems, it does not mean that the problems are small, but that they are too large.

The adolescent underground begins sexually and may involve some major sexual secrets. Homosexual dabblings are common, though not universal, in early adolescence. Most partakers go on to heterosexual dabblings in due time. Some do not, for various reasons, and are left thinking of themselves as homosexual. Parents may know nothing about this undercover concern and may interpret the child's lack of heterosexuality as shyness or virtue or religion. It may come as a major shock when their son announces that he has decided he is gay. Whatever adolescents are doing with their underground sexuality, it rarely conforms to their parents' fantasies about it.

The parents provide and protect this undercover life so their children can be sexual in private. Some parents may fail to provide birth control information. Someone may get pregnant and try to keep that secret for months. Others get involved with clearly unsuitable relationships, with prostitution, or with promiscuity to a degree unsuspected by the parents. I don't know why parents assume their children will use their freedom and distance from adults to make better sexual choices than mature, experienced adults make. Parents who forbid sexual activity are naive, but may encourage their anxious children to feel guilty about the sex they do have. In general guilt does not improve judgment.

The hallmark of underground adolescents is not that they are out of control but that they are uncontrolled. Blowups are likely when the parents, or anyone else, attempt to control these kids. The kids have had little experience with following the rules of the adult world. They are not often happy with their life, but they see nothing tempting in their parents' lives and know that they don't want to grow up to be their parents. The parents know that whatever else they want in life, children are not it. After the initial blowup when the parents take notice of them, the kids may become pitifully dependent and revert to the stage of development at which the parents had effectively deserted them. At this point, the parents, resenting the sudden dependency and need for nurturance, may belittle them and boot them back underground.

It is not easy for uninterested parents to resume parenting after they have thought themselves past that task. Obviously, many of these parents received less parenting than they might have liked. Many were underground adolescents themselves, or married early to get away from home, and have little sense of how much postpubertal parenting people need. They wish the kids would just grow up somehow and produce no crises that require a parental response.

Sociopathic Adolescents

All normal adolescents break rules at times. But all rule-breaking kids are not alike. Some kids are neglected and go underground. Others are bad and have learned it at home. The two groups are not easy to tell apart when you see just the kids. The family patterns are quite different. Underground kids grow up without parental constraints, but also without parental protection. Sociopathic adolescents may have close relationships with their parents. The parents may like the kids just fine; it's the world they don't like. The parents may be antisocial themselves — lying, gambling, cheating, having affairs, underpaying income tax, pulling shady business deals, fixing speeding tickets, pilfering at work, and amassing power and connections they use to protect themselves from societal consequences. They may not think of themselves as criminal; they may see themselves as "smart." And they teach their "smart" approach toward society's rules to their children.

Children in these families grow up noticing parents' antisocial actions and learning how to do these things themselves. Or alternatively, the kids grow up with such parental protection that they never have to face the world's consequences. They are taught that the rules are to be broken, that the law is the enemy. The children are taught how to lie to anyone in authority, how to take advantage of others, how to avoid obligations, and above all how to escape consequences.

The crisis occurs when the child gets into trouble outside the home. If, when their child is caught stealing, or cheating, or lying, the parents support the world's authority, the child may feel betrayed and may resent the parents' reversal of standards, especially if the parents don't reevaluate themselves. The child may then attempt to force such a reevaluation, which may be unpleasant for the parents. Still, that is the corrective maneuver. It may have to be repeated a few times before the child learns that the world's rules are different from the family's rules, as well as less negotiable and more powerful. It may take a few more examples before the parents learn that lesson. Family therapists may not see such families — the families correct themselves.

More commonly, the child breaks the world's rules and the sociopathogenic parents protect him (or her) from consequences. Sometimes the parents blame the world and treat the child caught shoplifting or cheating or whatever as a martyr or victim, as they devote full attention to helping the child beat the rap. This approach seems particularly common among the very rich and the very poor, who do not identify with the authority figures of the middle class, such as teachers or policemen.

The parents may respond in a manner only slightly less destructive. They may acknowledge the need for punishment but declare the world too untrustworthy to provide that punishment. So they arrange to avoid the legal or social consequences and turn the incident into a family matter, applying family punishments to social offenses. A child may be grounded for skipping school, even as the parents protect the child by writing a dishonest excuse to keep the school from punishing him. The parents might discover the child has been picked up for shoplifting, have their lawyer get the child off, and dock the child's allowance. The parents may even seek psychiatric intervention to protect a child from drunk driving or drug dealing or rape or murder. One shocking family contained parents, both psychologists, who debated whether to ground their 15-year-old son for a week after he raped a neighbor and transacted a mammoth cocaine deal. The child may react with gratitude toward the parents, and the incident may make the family closer and the child more dependent upon the parents' authority. The problem is that it undercuts the child's relationship with the world and its rules and authority. This manner of turning children into psychopaths is particularly common among the very rich and powerful families in our society. The police and the school almost expect it. It is also common among the very poor, who make no identification with a society that has treated them so shabbily.

These families bring their sociopathic adolescents into therapy after years of life without consequences, when the parents' power to protect has finally become overextended. Often the adolescent is in more trouble than the family can handle, and the request for help is a sham. The real desire is for a legally relevant psychiatric excuse—a letter to the judge that the poor child can't help it. Occasionally, the request for help is valid. The family recognizes that their adolescent is not turning out as expected despite their many sacrifices.

Some of these parents have worked hard at being controlling and punitive with their children, even as they kept the children from ever facing the world. They are not likely to see the connection between their own dishonesty and that of their children. The parents may have been in conflict over the child for some time, with one parent being punitive, the other protective and permissive, which further undercuts respect for authority. As the parents fight, the kid slips through the cracks once again. A therapist entering this situation can quickly polarize the family against the therapist, just by indicating that the adolescent needs consequences. The therapist then becomes the authority against which the child must be shielded.

In one family, the 16-year-old son had stolen all the family jewelry and watches to sell for drug money. The father laughed about his own adolescent misdeeds and seemed proud. The mother, who kept secret records on what had been stolen, was careful to leave her purse heavy with money and lying around open. She pretended to be asleep when her son greased her finger to slip off her engagement ring. I was called in after his arrest for burglarizing the neighbors. The parents decided they had erred in not giving him more spending money. They were going to fight the charges. When I suggested that jail would be appropriate and helpful, they warned the boy to run away.

He did, taking the camping equipment with him. I told the father to find him. The father ambivalently rented a helicopter and located the tent. He told the mother of its whereabouts. She baked a tin of brownies to take to her son with the message that he should move and camouflage the tent. They fired me, and I don't know the final outcome.

Rebellious Adolescents

In contrast to underground adolescents, who hide their antisocial behavior from their parents, and sociopathic adolescents, whose parents protect them from the societal consequences of their antisocial behavior, rebellious adolescents anxiously follow the world's rules but stay in open conflict with their parents. Rebellious adolescents make sure their rule-breaking is known by the parents, usually beforehand, sometimes afterwards. The conflict is not between the child and the adult world, but specifically between the child and the parents.

All adolescents rebel against their parents. They must, to bring about awareness of the need for rule changes as they age and develop. The rebellion may be intense at the start of puberty, but normally cools with age and is only intermittent after 16 or so, by which time both parents and adolescents have learned a lot and have reached some compromise. Some parents fear their children's adolescence and actively oppose it. The children of such parents may attempt to go underground, but can't, as the parents are watching too closely. They may be able to maintain some underground life, which the parents may welcome, but their emotional life is primarily consumed by fierce battles with their parents over rules and punishment.

Adolescent rebellion is a term applied to all manner of normal and pathological behavior. All normal adolescents must run a few steps ahead of their parents in order to become independently comfortable with the world. The ideal might be for the kids to break the rules, have the adventures, and report back to the parents what they have experienced and learned, so the parents can change the rules accordingly. There are occasional parents with whom adolescent adventures can be negotiated beforehand. Often, such efforts merely produce explosions and restrictions. The parents might prefer the children to go underground, but the children are too frightened to do so. Either phobic parents or phobic children can produce the syndrome of adolescent rebellion.

Rebellious adolescents learn what will get them the exact blend of freedom and dependency they desire. While the battle may seem an effort to attain freedom, they seem to spend most of their time under some form of restrictive punishment. Obviously, the punishment must be part of the reward. Since these adolescents are growing up in families frightened by their freedom, the adolescents learn to fear it too and arrange to have it restricted. They can do this by pushing obnoxiously for more freedom than they can possibly achieve, while making a mess of whatever freedom they get.

Adolescents who spend their teen years grounded are not rebelling at all—
they are hiding from a world they fear as much as their parents do. But to
cover the fear, they put their family through the torment of temper tantrums
that will ensure punishment. If there are no real restrictions, the adolescent
can dramatically run away and thereby produce some.

Rebellious adolescents can do a good job of magnifying parental conflict.
They often divide parents into the classic permissive-denying split, but instead of accepting the permission they get from one parent, they go into
battle against the reticent parent and produce such a furor that the permitting parent is forced to recant. If the parents cannot be divided, the rebellious adolescent can pick fights with a sibling, which will throw the family
into sufficient crisis to limit the adolescent's freedom.

Adolescents may rebel in a variety of ways. One involves clothes and
grooming. Kids like to dress in a manner that tries to counter two fears: that
people will think the parents still control the child's appearance, and that
people will think the child is trying to appear like a real grownup. Kids may
therefore choose to appear sloppy and outlandish in a fashion no sane
parent would approve, just daring the parents to make an issue of it. This
demonstrates to the world that the adolescent is independent of the parents
but not yet adult. On those occasions when a child dresses as a grownup, the
child slips into grownup attitudes and postures, which may feel great around
adults or other teenagers similarly dressed, but is embarrassing around teenagers dressed in the non-child, non-adult fashion of youth.

Parents who understand the child's fear of dressing in a childlike fashion
may still misunderstand the child's resistance to impersonating grownups.
An adolescent must be extremely secure or extremely insensitive to break the
adolescent dress code—a code no parent can conceivable understand or
appreciate. After a few battles over clothes and hairstyles and makeup, the
child ceases the drive toward earning adult appearance and remains arrested
at the earlier stage of proving that the parents are not dressing him or her.
The clothes then do become a form of rebellion, making, like most adolescent rebellion, a statement to the effect, "I don't feel secure enough yet to act
like a grownup."

Adolescents rebel in other ways too. They may refuse to keep their rooms
as the parents would like, they may refuse to carry on conversations in the
parentally approved manner, they may refuse to follow the parents' time
schedule, they may resist visits to relatives. Some even resist domestic chores
(though this is unusual if the parents provide reminders, supervision, and
praise for the work the kids do). Much of this is normal adolescent disor-
ganization and immaturity—few adolescents can tell time or arrange schedules without supervision, and their social priorities are different from the
parents'. But much of this refusal and resistance is an effort to get the
parents to negotiate priorities.

The parents may naively assume the child wants more freedom and arrange to provide it, which magnifies the conflict. More often, the child

wants more structure, but structure which considers the child's anxieties about the issues the parents are taking for granted. It may be difficult for phobic parents to recognize their child's outlandish carrying-ons are motivated by fear of the very activities the child claims to want desperately. Anxious people rarely notice the anxiety of others.

Certainly there are families in which the parents are unwilling to let their children do normal adolescent things. Such parents are unlikely to produce children who are comfortable with normal adolescent things. Socially anxious parents produce socially anxious children, and socially anxious children are not socially acceptable to other adolescents, so they are not included in the acceptable adolescent activities. Thus their rebellions take on a special awkwardness and desperation. When parents base restrictions on an exaggerated sense of caution, they disqualify themselves as experts on the dangers in the world and produce counterphobic reactions in an adolescent who would be as comfortable as adolescents can ever be, i.e., willing to face any danger to attain peer acceptance.

All adolescent rebellion, of course, is not a counterphobic response to parental restriction. Some adolescent rebellion begins as the normal and necessary effort of the child to learn to be under his or her own control, rather than under parental control. But if the parents react anxiously to the adolescent's quest for independence and determination to experience the limits, the child has three choices: to live within the limits of the parents' anxiety, to rebel and throw the parents into crisis, or to proceed cautiously and reassure the parents. Older adolescents can learn to do the last of these; younger ones rarely can. Still, it works best to assume all rebellion is counterphobic, whether parental anxiety is magnifying it or not.

Rebellious adolescents have to be taught to have their sexual adventures before midnight, to call home when too drunk to drive, to bring their unacceptable friends home for dinner, and generally to explain their discomfort to their parents. When children consider their activities unacceptable to their parents, they become anxious and don't use the good advice they've been given. They may stop the open rebellion and go underground, which is far more dangerous. If teenagers feel free to call home at crisis points in their adventures, many dangers can be avoided. When adolescents need help with birth control, or drunk friends, or stolen goods, or drug habits, or frightening romances — without fear of punishment for having gotten into the situations — their best source of help should be their parents. That assumes rational parents.

One awkward girl who had never had a date was forced by her parents to go to a school dance with a date they'd arranged, but in a dress that was too sedate for the occasion. She arranged to get drunk before the dance, throw up on the dress, and spend the night with the boy. She came home at breakfast, dressed in the boy's clothes, still sick with a hangover. The parents forbade her to date again.

It would rarely be misleading to assume that all adolescent rebellion is fueled by anxiety. The task is to determine who is anxious about what and how that anxiety can be firmly and safely overcome. Not infrequently, adolescent rebellion is helpful for all concerned and understanding it may be more therapeutic than stopping it.

Adolescents Marked for Failure

Unlike the underground, sociopathic, and rebellious adolescents, who are primarily unhappy with the world around them and demonstrate that unhappiness by breaking or ignoring the rules of the world or the family, there are many other adolescents who accept and respect the world but don't like themselves. Those who behave badly don't like themselves either, of course, but they don't experience it or act it out that way. The miserably unhappy kids, who hold out little hope of finding a place for themselves in the world, are somewhat different. These adolescents see themselves as marked for failure. What they do in life is give up and make a show of failing. These kids are unacceptable to other kids, whether their parents like them or not. Usually the parents dislike these kids as much as the world does.

These children are marked for failure by their families, by their peers, and by the world. The decision that these kids aren't going to have success in life is made early on, usually before adolescence, sometimes in early childhood, rarely even before birth. Some of these are obviously damaged children, with sensory or motor impairment, physical handicaps or disfiguration, or retardation. Interestingly, the more obvious the defect (blindness, dwarfism, paraplegia, etc.) the more likely the world will be supportive and accepting. Minor deviations from the norm are more confusing and more likely to produce parental disappointment and social discomfort. In adolescence, cerebral palsy is less of a social disadvantage than moderate obesity.

By adolescence kids marked for failure by hyperactivity, learning disabilities or some other characteristic that makes them different expect rejection and relieve the suspense by currying it. They may dress or behave in a way that will bring it quickly. Some pretend they don't care, dramatizing the not caring with obnoxious behavior. Others whine and pout over rejection, spot it easily, quickly and often inaccurately, and thereby make themselves chronic victims, punishing anyone who gets close by acting picked on and inducing guilt. Others, starved for relationship, will engulf anyone who is humane or desperate enough to tarry too close too long. Some of these "losers" automatically dislike anyone who is also considered a "loser" and put everyone who tolerates them in that category. Rather than banding together, these unattractive kids remain isolated, each yearning for some miraculous invitation into the "popular group." They may have crushes on more popular kids and do foolish and daring things to get their ideal's attention.

Adolescence for these children consists of one social crisis after another, interspersed with desperately inappropriate efforts to get attention — everything from dressing weirdly to getting arrested, from disrupting the class to suicide. They may join up with far older or far younger people in intense, stormy, or sexually exploitive relationships. Homosexuality, in reality or fantasy, is common. Unattractive girls may attempt sexual promiscuity as a route to popularity. Unattractive boys may do the same, but usually homosexually. Unpopular adolescents are more often drug involved than popular adolescents, more often antisocial, and generally more likely to do unpopular things.

Kids marked for failure are usually depressed and usually have no place to turn. They are embarrassing to their parents and siblings. They are often in trouble at home or school. Adults find them unappealing too. They cling so desperately that sometimes even therapists find them a trial.

Sometimes the parents are as socially obtuse as their children. They either ignore the desperation of unpopularity because they themselves have known nothing else or punish and reject the unattractive behavior because they have only known popularity but don't know how it is produced. Parental social savvy is extremely important, but hard to find. If anyone can bring himself to like these children in their imperfect state, it can work wonders, but the kids must also be taught the secrets of social success. It is difficult for one person to perform both tasks at the same time. Unquestioned acceptance and social relearning can not take place at the same time.

The classic kid marked for failure starts as a fat little girl with a glamorous mother and a gorgeous sister or brother and a father who is absent, distant, or ashamed of her. The sibling ignores her as much as the father does, and the mother battles punitively with her over her diet. At the dinner table, the child is belittled and insulted until she runs in tears to her room to hide with her furtive bag of cookies.

This painful situation can go on for years until some crisis hits during adolescence. The crisis may be triggered by the child's antisocial or grossly inappropriate behavior. More often the child develops severe depression. Suicide attempts are common, and while they are usually damaging and manipulative, they can be fatal. The pain of social rejection cannot be underestimated, even if the actual rejection is slight. It must be taken seriously.

The family therapy is aimed at involving the family in the adolescent's awkward struggle to learn how to establish relationships, both inside and outside the family. The parents may have to reveal and reexamine their own long forgotten efforts to find their way through the social maze. The parents must accept the reality of the rejection and the pain, must understand the process of social learning, and must avoid their tendency to blame either the child or the world. What the parents like or dislike about the child may or may not have any correlation with what the world reacts to.

Social acceptability is never total, but social unacceptability isn't either unless people are so sensitive to it that they make it so. It is the therapist's job to keep social failure from being total, even if he or she can't maneuver the family to provide that buffer.

Imperfect Adolescents

A rather different group of adolescents are those who succeed with the world reasonably well but are not quite accepted within their families. Each family has a system of values by which it determines what is good enough. It is rare for the family's concept of what is good enough to correspond to the world's assessment of baseline acceptability. Families may tolerate behavior the world could not (as with sociopathic kids and many kids marked for failure). Conversely, there are families which expect their children to excel in a manner deemed important by the family.

I know a family in which the children and their cousins are so competitively successful that only one failed to be either a valedictorian or a state champion in some sport, and that very normal child was considered unacceptable because of it. A boy with an I.Q. of 140 was considered mentally defective in a family in which his sisters were Phi Beta Kappas and his cousins "off the charts at Harvard." A girl, who led her class, was the only one of her siblings to score under 1600 on the SAT's, whereupon she became suicidal.

In other families, all but one child became 6-feet tall, or a millionaire, or a born-again preacher, and the child who did not achieve these things was considered a failure. Imperfect adolescents may include kids with stormy tempers in placid families, sloppy kids in neat families, homely kids in beautiful families, quiet kids in noisy families — people whose characteristics are not considered defects outside the family but are much criticized and fretted over within the family.

The imperfection in the child may be overlooked by the parents but rubbed in by siblings or grandparents or other relatives. A grandparent may set up competitions between cousins. Aunts and uncles may undercut an envied niece's or nephew's confidence by finding defects others have overlooked. Siblings are particularly hard on one another — the more successful a sibling in the eyes of the world, the more determinedly a less favored brother or sister may seek the hidden defect. If no one in the family can find an imperfection, one's best friends will surely do so. Someone can find a defect in anyone. No one escapes this process completely and we all grow up feeling at least a little flawed. It probably helps when the flaw is overt and clearly outside one's control.

There are worse fates than imperfection. Some people grow up without accepting their imperfectness, still intolerant of anything less than the ideal in themselves or others. They may merely defend themselves against awareness of personal failings and become hostile, defensive people. Or they may continue to believe perfection is required and become severely depressed over failures others would take in stride. I recall a man who had grown up on Little League teams which had never lost a game — he was unfit for the real world.

Adolescents are all imperfect, innately so self-conscious that they stay normally preoccupied with their defects, real or imagined. They rarely need parents to call attention to their shortcomings, particularly in those areas that are being tested by the world (academics, athletics, social) or are observable by peers (physical, interpersonal), although adolescents' contributions to their failures in those areas may well be sympathetically dealt with when crises arise. Parents may have to call character flaws to their adolescent's attention, as part of social learning, since other adolescents are amazingly unconcerned with such matters. Teenagers can forgive one another for murder quicker than they can for zits. But social learning must be tolerant of error or it will be discounted as picking or rejection or just some old-fashioned quirk of the parent. While kids need information on matters of ethics and morality, they don't benefit much from condemnation.

Imperfect kids sometimes learn to discount their family's values, as they get all the acceptance they need from the world. The parents' picking, when unsupported by the world, is merely alienating and may even drive a child underground.

All manner of pathology has been attributed to parents' trying to help a child to overcome a small problem, thereby magnifying the problem. Stuttering has been considered the result of parental overcontrol of the child's speech, encopresis the result of premature toilet training, obesity, anorexia, and bulimia the result of parental preoccupation with weight and dieting. Homosexuality has even been attributed (probably erroneously) to excessive parental concern with gender identity. In general, parental picking has rarely received favorable reviews from mental health experts.

In one memorable family, the father's children were adulterous, promiscuous, or homosexual—all of which was acceptable as long as it was not mentioned. But the new stepdaughter spoke openly of her masturbation and was instantly ostracized, thus precipitating a major crisis of values between the two halves of a blending family.

The crisis of the imperfect adolescent appears most frequently when one or both parents become obsessed with some real or imagined imperfection. The child may be battling with the parents over it, or the parents may be battling between themselves over it while the child tries to get some healthy distance. The child may be nominated as "patient" and come in for the appointment furious and defensive. The family needs help, but the presenting complaint must be quickly undercut or the therapy will be destructive. The therapy is likely to be brief, whether it should be or not; it is important that it not fall apart while everyone believes the imperfect child is indeed a defective child.

Much of the family therapy literature seems based on the syndrome of perfecting parents/imperfect children, and much that goes on under the name of family therapy seems an effort to protect normal kids from parents who want better than normal kids. These are the kids who need to leave home and the parents who need to go back home to understand where they found their values. Popular literature and film find this syndrome particularly appealing and, like the family therapy literature, tend to see it as the basis for all intergenerational conflict. It isn't. These cases are not more common than the other syndromes of adolescence. They are, however, the easiest to treat and usually the most responsive to family therapy. The greatest danger is that the therapist will perform an unnecessary parentectomy before building the foundations for the intergenerational tolerance that will permit parent and child to support one another and learn from one another for a lifetime.

Rescuing Adolescents

Another adolescent syndrome much discussed in the popular and professional literature is the situation which arises when the parents are in trouble and a child develops symptoms to call attention to the marital problem. These adolescents are offering to sacrifice themselves in order to rescue their family. They have a painful time of it, and some don't make it through, but the survivors include the next generation of family therapists.

Alcoholic families are the most reliable source of rescuing adolescents. When one or both parents drink or use drugs to excess, someone must remain on duty. Even if one parent stays in the home and remains straight, sober, and stable, that parent can't take care of an out-of-control mate and a house and family too. One child, usually the oldest female but often the oldest child of either gender, becomes the adult for the family during the periods of intoxication or unpredictable absence from the home. These kids are expected to take care of the house, the younger children, and the disabled parents, without instruction, explicit permission, or acknowledgment and appreciation. In fact, the adolescent caretaker may be criticized or even punished for acknowledging awareness of the role assignment.

The rescuing adolescent must lie for the substance-abusing parent and may never call for outside help or otherwise let the secret out. It is a frightening job, and a thankless one. Sometimes there are several children who can form a workable team to secure the family of alcoholic adults. But often the parentified child is as unappreciated by the siblings as by the parents. The rescuer's social life suffers — the child can neither leave home nor have friends visit. Relationships with grandparents and other relatives must be kept distant also, as the parent's misbehavior must be kept secret. Rescue becomes a fulltime job and a fulltime worry. These kids often leave home at the first opportunity.

Parents don't have to be knee-walking, toilet-hugging, gutter-dwelling drunks to render themselves incapable of functioning as parents. Those who have a few "cocktails" before dinner or a joint in the evening are sufficiently off duty to require the undercover supervision and monitoring of their ignored but alert children, who may do little more than protect the grownups from the minor crises of the day, while they take care of themselves and one another and consult with one another about the relative clarity and availability of the parents to handle whatever needs to be handled.

The children of schizophrenic or manic-depressive parents or chronically physically ill ones may also become caretakers and guardians to the parents, as well as parents to their younger siblings. Even if a competent parent is in the home, the presence of one who needs protecting from the child's crises deprives the child of much of his or her childhood and particularly of his or her adolescence. Hypermature adolescents may grow up to be cold, joyless martyrs or bossy, intolerant martinets, proud of their strength but angry over their sacrifices.

In violent families, in which one parent regularly brutalizes the other, a child who has observed this process for years may finally be old enough and brave enough to pull the gun off the mantle and shoot the brutal parent. Those families in which the children murder the parents are usually violent families under threat of divorce.

During parental affairs, one child after another may develop symptoms that will keep the parents involved with one another. Small children may bed wet, older ones fail in school, and adolescents may shoplift, involve themselves deeply in inappropriate relationships, or even make suicide attempts. Adolescent runaways are particularly common during times of conflict in the parents' marriage. During that suspenseful period after a parental divorce, when the children still hope the parents will get back together, they can produce every known crisis to pull them together. They will make any sacrifice for the marriage.

As families dissolve, adolescents who have been previously identified as imperfect may show the greatest change in their behavior, since they frequently identify themselves as the cause of the parental unhappiness and disruption. They may even be identified as the problem by the parents. While some may use the opportunity of a threat to the family to improve the presumed defect, most seem to exaggerate the offensiveness so that they become the center of everyone's concern. If they have had experience with bringing the parents together in alliance against them, they will surely attempt this trick now, when it could be useful.

After the divorce, kids may set up battles between parents and stepparents or orchestrate crises that will disrupt both households, as they move back and forth between the two parental homes. Previously well-adjusted adolescents often spend a few stormy years in the wake of a divorce, while others shield themselves from the whole situation, using perfectionistic, obsessive-compulsive defenses. They turn themselves into unfeeling machines, investing little in relationships and expecting little in return.

In one-parent families, the single parent is often (not always) bitter, lonely, overworked and underloved. She is eager for the children to become both more self-sufficient and better able to give emotionally and functionally to the parent. The child may be pushed into premature adulthood, yet not permitted much adolescence. The child is expected to be self-reliant yet remain dependent and involved with the parent. The child may alternate between rebellion and rescue as the guilt and anger build. The latchkey aspects of the child's life are of small effect compared to the conflicting emotional burden. One horrible temptation is for the child to rescue the parent by becoming competent at home and incompetent in the world, able to help out but unable to leave.

The classic rescuing adolescent is the runaway. When the parents are fighting, or even when another sibling is in trouble, this adolescent unites the family by dramatically running away. It is effective for the family, and it reduces pressure on the runaway herself (or himself — while adolescent runaways are usually thought of as female, I've seen just as many boys who pull this trick). Certainly some of the kids who run away in times of family crisis are schizophrenic, but many aren't — they just have a low tolerance for anxiety. The runaway calms down long before the frantic, searching family does. It's really not a bad trick, unless the runaway stays away too long. Some become frightened and get into trouble or expose themselves to dangers, hoping to be rescued themselves but afraid to go home and face the consequences. I've seen kids run away during a family fight, a family funeral, a sister's abortion, a financial crisis, a parent's affair, as well as after an embarrassing failure of their own.

Some rescuing adolescents become suicidal. In the midst of the family fight, they may threaten suicide and run into the bathroom and lock the door. They may leave a suicide note and hide. They may actually stage a suicide attempt. I've seen at least one family in which an elaborately staged suicide attempt actually worked, because the girl's sister forgot to give the parents the suicide note that was intended to save the girl and the family in the nick of time.

Rescuing adolescents may become violent. One girl, while the parents fought, got in a car she didn't know how to drive and ran it into a tree. Another hired a hit man to kill her father to keep him from divorcing her mother. Still another tried to poison her father's mistress.

Usually rescuing adolescents do something more subtle. Most often they merely become depressed and begin to fail in school or withdraw socially. There is no specific symptom associated with this syndrome. Kids whose parents are threatening the continuation of the family can develop any symptom at all. Even anorexia was at one time considered an expression of this situation, and schizophrenia is often attributed to it. Little Hans was in this family situation when he developed his famous phobia for horses, as were several of Freud's cases of adolescent hysteria, although Freud was looking under a more convenient streetlamp for his explanations at that time.

The rescuing adolescent may not be aware that he or she is reacting in a rescuing fashion. The parents may not even relate the child's symptoms to the adults' problems, and may seek individual therapy for the child rather than do what would relieve the child's suffering — seek marital therapy for themselves.

EVALUATING ADOLESCENT CRISES

Contrary to popular thought, all adolescents in crisis are not rescuing their parents or rebelling against them. Much adolescent turmoil has little direct connection to the parents, even though they may handle it badly. Evaluating the family with an adolescent crisis is made a little more complicated than other family crises because adolescent norms are so diffuse and because every adolescent is caught between three sets of powerful and conflicting forces, all in flux — the self, the world, and the family.

Certainly all adolescent crises don't fit into my six syndromes, and many don't fit neatly or for very long in any of them. But these syndromes are far more common than those that receive most of the attention on adolescents in the literature. Ninety percent of the adolescents I see fit somewhere into these groups. The more often discussed symptoms of adolescence, i.e., schizophrenia, anorexia, incest, are less common, but may well fit into these six structural categories nonetheless. These six syndromes must be differentiated because they are directly related to treatment.

When someone becomes alarmed over someone else's behavior and calls for help, the relevant question is, "Who believes there is a problem? And why?"

The first factor to evaluate is whether the concerns about the adolescent are *real* or *imagined*. Imperfect adolescents are perceived as problems by the family but not by the world. Sociopathic adolescents are perceived as problems by the world, but not by the family. Outside information may be required to get perspective on the degree to which these kids deviate from the world's norms. Still, it is not a majority decision. The therapist must take the responsibility, even if he or she remains a voice in the wilderness and convinces no one immediately. Just because the world, the adolescent, and one of the parents sees no problem, the other parent's belief that a problem exists may well be correct. Moreover, when the adolescent believes there is a problem, there will be in time — an adolescent's call for help must be answered, even if the therapist's job is to convince the kid of his or her normality. Likewise, if the family believes there is a problem, the problem may not be real, but the belief is real, and the belief may become a real problem. Fixing something that isn't broken will surely break it. The therapist's job may be to uncover whatever is behind the belief that there is a problem, i.e., the need to have a problem.

The family can be the patient — the locus of the problem — and can be

changed with therapy. Society, by contrast, can't be. Society's views are not
negotiable in therapy. So, if the world sees someone as a problem, the reality
of the deviance must be accepted. The world is not much concerned with
individuality and attempts to limit it. If one teacher, or neighbor, or judge
sees a problem no one else sees, that may be negotiable, but if the offending
behavior offends more than one individual, negotiation is not possible.
Everyone must develop the ability to conform to the world's rules, even if he
or she chooses the limitations of not doing so. Deviant behavior is not just
an issue between family members — the world is also involved.

The *overt-covert* parameter is particularly crucial with adolescent crises
because parents and peers encourage so much covert behavior for adolescents. With icebergs there is a constant ratio of eight parts covert to one part
overt. With adolescents one can be sure there is some part underground; the
difficulty is establishing how much. All sane adolescents keep some things
covert. Yet they usually want some of these things out in the open, and
eventually the covert is made overt. Most parents have some idea of what
their kids are up to, and the kids know it.

When a secret becomes problematic, it is rarely helpful for the therapist to
conspire to keep the secret, and the adolescent rarely requires it. Adolescents
frequently want to consult privately with the therapist about a secret, to be
reassured that it can be revealed, and they are usually relieved when it is.
Ordinarily a therapist can tell when there is a secret, even if it is unclear what
the secret is, and individual sessions may be far more helpful than harmful
at such times.

Parents too may have secrets, which of course are equally destructive and
produce all manner of family pathology, but most dangerously call forth
rescuing behavior from the kids. In one case the kid's secrets may block
understanding, while in another the snag is the grownup's secret; in either
case, the problems can't be solved until they are overt.

In general, when things don't make sense, the therapist can declare that
there is a secret, and someone will reveal it, although it may take an individual session or a furtive telephone call to do so. I can think of a few situations
in which the maintenance of a secret within a family would be helpful. This
even extends to the current sexual secrets of the parents and the children.
Certainly the parents would be more helpful if they knew their children were
sexually active, were sexually inhibited, or were in sexual trouble. I believe
the children need to know that their parents are sexually active, especially
when an affair is threatening the family — otherwise the reactions to the
affair will be baffling to the kids.

I'm not sure it is necessary for the parents' sexual inadequacies to be
common knowledge, but they usually are suspected even if not revealed, and
I see no point in protecting the children from them. Adolescents are strongly
affected by parental attitudes and should know the parental kinks that
determine those attitudes. I must admit I have been a bit squeamish about

revealing such things as a father's intermittent homosexual dalliances, or a mother's abortion efforts during a child's pregnancy, or some ancient affair, or the true paternity of the child of an adulterous mother. I've tended to keep such secrets at least until they were definitely relevant to a current problem, though I'm always tortured by them and am never clear what the best course of action would be. I'm left without a clear formula. But it is rare for me to believe the covert should be kept covert at the price of any confusion.

Adolescents tend to see everything as *permanent*, while their parents hope everything is a *temporary* stage of development. This works fine: The kids get upset; the parents reassure. Problems of *temporary-permanent* definitions arise when the parents stop reassuring, when they begin to see permanent deficiencies in their children. They may suddenly find the child imperfect, or go into battle and try to overcontrol, thereby producing rebellion. On the other hand, parents may define sociopathy or social failure as temporary and refuse to deal with it except protectively or let the kid remain underground and not deal with it at all. Just as the norm for healthy relationships is for the adolescent to be alarmed about him- or herself while the parents soothe, it is commonplace in problem families for parents to be alarmed at what they see as permanent defects in their children while the children deny any such significance. Less commonly, the child will try to get help for a problem the parents see as temporary and insignificant.

In any case, it is vital to know who sees the problem as a stage of development and who sees it as a portent of doom. Errors in either direction can compound the problem. The therapist is characteristically on the side of cautious optimism, seeing everything as surmountable, but nonetheless significant.

In evaluating adolescent crises, the therapist must differentiate those behaviors and conditions that are *unique*, and therefore no problem, from those that are *habitual*, and therefore cause for therapeutic concern. The question must always be asked, "How often does this happen?"

This parameter probably produces more domestic arguments than any other and leads to more rebellion. Since parents are the experts at spotting trends, and the kids see each of life's adventures as having a unique set of justifications, kids are able to find some reason for every act of forgetfulness or failure, some reason why the activity of the moment is an exception to the usual rule. Kids will attempt to explain the unusual reasons for coming in late or not doing their chores or blowing up when criticized. Parents will talk about how the child "always" or "never" follows the rules or shows respect or control. The truth follows a pattern that is somewhere in between. The pattern of rebellious behavior, or any other behavior, must be clearly outlined to be understood.

By contrast, parents may tend to see sociopathy or failure as unique when it is clearly habitual and consequently consider it not a problem that requires attention or concern. When both parents and kids insist upon defining habitual behavior as unique, no one may come for help until the world, the police, the school, or the neighbors step in and define a problem the family has been ignoring. Therapists, employed by the family rather than by the world, have less success in defining problems the family doesn't want to deal with — the therapist, unlike the police, can be fired. Still, the therapist can call attention to the repetitive nature of behaviors and, after some time with the family, even the frequency with which such patterns recur.

The most difficult part of evaluating crises of adolescence centers on the issue of *intrinsic* vs. *extrinsic*. This differentiation involves several issues. Does the problem reside in the particular child who is growing up badly? Does the problem lie in a society that fails to respect the uniqueness of this child? Does the problem lie in a society that encourages the child to differ from the parent's wishes? Does the problem lie in the family that is creating problems for the child? Does the problem lie in the child who is creating problems for the parents? "Where have we failed?" "Why won't they leave me alone?" "Why can't they be like we were, perfect in every way. What's the matter with kids today?"

The family, soul-searching and struggling over these issues, may have had more conflict over the definition of the problem than over the problem itself. In general, it is singularly unhelpful to decree that society must change before someone can grow up or have some peace. It may be true, just unhelpful. For most of us, there is not an alternative society any more than there is an alternative planet, so the world and its rules must be taken as "given." More apropos is the question of whether the problem is the adolescent or the parents — if they have decided it involves both, they may have already solved it. Typically, at the beginning, the battle is reduced to a simplistic issue of whether the kid or the parents are at fault. With few exceptions, adolescent crises must be considered as having both aspects.

The situation of adolescence is difficult at best, even without the aggravation of the specific family structure. Any effort to underestimate the situational potential for crisis makes the expectable problems difficult and the idiosyncratic problems of the particular family insoluble. All normal adolescents have some underground secrets, some antisocial impulses, a fair amount of rebellion, some failures, some concern about imperfections, and a wish to rescue their parents. How far these tendencies will take them depends on the family structure. If parents are distracted, protective, controlling, socially inept, critical, or dependent, the corresponding tendency of the adolescent can be magnified into one of these syndromes.

The therapist who is evaluating the family crisis must be accurate in all other parameters but foggy in this one. Either extreme is dangerous; either blaming or rescuing the kid or the parents makes interactional change more difficult. Adolescence is a process of mutual adaptation; as the child inevitably changes, the family structure must also change and must be thrown into the therapeutic blender along with the behavior of the child. Even when the family structure is clearly and even admittedly a part of the problem, with rescuing, imperfect, and rebellious kids, the adolescent must be considered part of the equation rather than an innocent victim who has no choices but to react as he or she does. Likewise, those families in which a kid goes underground, or becomes sociopathic, or fails socially must not be seen as passive recipients of all this adolescent unpleasantness. These are all, however subtly, interactional syndromes in which the family structure is part, but not all, of the problem.

TREATMENT OF CRISES OF ADOLESCENCE

Treating families with crises of adolescence is usually, but not always, one of the joys of being a family therapist. It is particularly gratifying when compared to an individual approach to adolescents in crisis.

Step 1: Emergency Response

Adolescent crises tend to come in like a lion. Most typically, the mother will call to set up an individual appointment for a child who is in trouble and in conflict but does not really want to come in. There may have been a big fight, the kid may have run away, the school or the police may have called, drugs or sexual secrets may have been discovered, a suicide note may have been found. There is a sense of emergency. If an appointment can be made right away, the family is likely to cooperate fully.

There are exceptions, particularly with the mildly depressed failing and rescuing adolescents, when no one seems quite sure whether there is a problem or not and the family is a little embarrassed about the whole thing. Occasionally, a family member will call to report a very serious problem and then seem reluctant to make an appointment. It can be disconcerting when an adolescent attempts suicide but can't be seen because the appointment time would conflict with a ballet lesson or beauty parlor appointment! It can also be disconcerting when a child has been in trouble for a long time and the family is only now willing to be involved to avoid jail.

Adolescence is a time of such craziness and such rapid changes that no one is very good at differentiating emergencies from non-emergencies. It is best to assume that time is of the essence. A fairly safe rule of thumb would be: (1) If the caller's complaint is about behavior, put the parents firmly in control; (2) if the caller's complaint is about the child's emotional state, urge that the child's feelings be given top priority. Needless to say, I've gotten into trouble following even this rule of thumb.

Step 2: Involve the Family

The parents sometimes ask to be seen before the adolescent, so they can charm the therapist and tell him or her how awful the child is and how hard they have tried, etc. I tend to distrust this and discourage it, even if an occasional parent will take offense and go elsewhere for help.

I ask the caller to bring the "whole family," stressing importance of this. Usually there is some resistance to this; in fact, I never know who is going to show up. Obviously both resident parents should come, and usually do at least once. I encourage, but don't insist upon, nonresident parents at the first visit. I prefer having siblings of similar age present, but don't push it too hard, especially if the identified patient would prefer not to expose him- or herself to siblings. I go ahead and see whoever comes, but if the missing member is a parent, I get him on the phone. Sometimes I call missing siblings too.

The problem of the missing father is often commented upon. I've never had much trouble getting fathers in, but mothers still keep telling me the fathers won't come. I think they are merely afraid to ask or willing to ask only if the father wants to come in. When I call the father and explain the necessity for his presence and then try to respect his schedule, he comes.

If the adolescent requests an individual appointment, that means there is some secret; it may well be best to give in and see the adolescent alone first. It is rare that the adolescent, after revealing the secret to the therapist, will insist upon keeping it from the family. If it is clear from the beginning that no privilege exists within the family, the secret will come out anyway. But the child may need to test the seriousness of the secret with another adult before risking telling the parents. Adolescents can feel enormous shame until some adult, any adult, tells them it is not as bad as they are fearing.

Once the crisis is defined and the initial chaos calmed, the number of family members who show up for therapy tends to dwindle; that is sometimes OK, and sometimes not. If the family spends the time talking about whoever isn't there, clearly the therapy is misdirected and someone needs to be called. But there is usually much work to be done with whoever is there.

Steps 3 and 4: Defining the Crisis and Making a General Prescription

The situation is evaluated and determined to fall into one or more of the six syndromes — underground, sociopathy, rebellion, failure, imperfection, or rescue.

The format of family therapy resolves many of the problems by getting the secrets out, confronting the problems, eliciting everyone's concerns, outlining the realities of adolescence, and stopping the either-or definitions of the problem. Ordinarily, no matter what else has gone on, the family is closer and more open and more secure after the first family interview than it has been in some time. Even a bumbling therapist cannot completely dispel the magic of a first family session over an adolescent problem—unless, of course, the bumbling therapist tries to rescue the adolescent from the family.

Step 5: Specific Prescription

The specific changes the family can make to solve the problem depend, of course, on what the problem is. It is not the symptom or behavior that determines the specific change. One poor grade or sexual excess or drug involvement or family fight or runaway or lie may mean something quite different from the same behavior in another context. However, while there is no formula based on the symptomatic behavior, there is a specific solution to each syndrome of adolescence.

Underground adolescents require parental monitoring and a far closer involvement with their families. The kid may have to be put on a kind of probation, with the parents responsible for awareness of and control over the child's activities. The siblings can be involved as monitors also. Secrets and confidences must not be honored—they have been abused. The rules are to be determined and taped to the refrigerator. Interestingly, the parents are more likely to sabotage this effort than the underground kid himself, by pushing the problem into either the overly protective posture that produces sociopathy or the overly restrictive one that produces rebellion.

Sociopathic kids may or may not have someone who is making them distrust their ability to conform to the world's rules, but they nearly always have someone who is protecting them from the world's consequences. That is easy enough to determine. The task with antisocial kids is to arrange, or at least permit, consequences and to cease all protective efforts. The adolescent may rebel against this, unless the acceptance of consequences can be accompanied by redemption into the family. This is difficult for parents who distrust the world and prefer to undercut the world's consequences, gloat over their victory over society's authority, and then never let the child live down his or her misdeeds. With sociopathic families, this may be a long-term struggle, often accompanied by conflict over the therapist's bill. The parents may well rebel against the therapist's insistence that the child's illegal activities be dealt with by the legal authorities and may run from therapy as they do from all other representatives of the larger society.

Rebellious kids are a great deal easier. Here too the task is to make the rules clear, as well as the punishments for breaking those rules. The parents and child should negotiate these family rules, but it helps to let the adolescent write them down or make the first draft. They are usually amazingly reasonable, basically agreeing with the parents' rules in most respects. Involving other siblings in this is particularly important. The goal is ordinarily to undercut parental overreactions without undercutting parental authority, and this requires an authority structure to which all family members are committed.

Social failures require a slow, painful therapeutic effort. They must have support from someone while they learn how to be acceptable. The task involves accepting the reality of their unacceptability and arranging assistance in the two-pronged process of practicing acceptable behavior. Eliciting hope that will permit risk-taking is the primary task for the adolescent; an end to the denial and protective-rejecting stance is the primary task for the rest of the family. The specific tasks involve overcoming the specific behaviors that produce social rejection. The process remains delicate until some social success is achieved. Individual therapy, group therapy, diet groups, tutoring, exercise programs, camps, etc., may be started right away.

Imperfect adolescents are the easiest of all. The task is simple—more realistic expectations—though the change in parental expectations may require some time to affect a child's expectations of self. Parental revelations of their own failures and inadequacies can be useful meanwhile.

Rescuing adolescents require permission to be more concerned with their own lives than with their parents' lives. Therapy for the parents, without the child, may be the best solution, but preferably after the first visit or two. Merely leaving the child out of the parental unhappiness and turmoil may frighten the child. The child can't go off duty until someone else takes over.

Step 6: Negotiating Resistance

Most parents are willing to pay attention to their children, tabulate rules, punish more gently, give support, cool their overreactions, reveal their imperfections, and even leave the kids out of parental unhappiness—if they are getting support and direction and if they get response. Most kids are willing to reveal their secret lives, accept consequences, follow the rules, make some efforts in their own behalf, learn their parents' peculiarities, and even tolerate some family insecurity—but only if they can feel some security and acceptance. The resistance is often negotiated by having each generation notice the subtle improvements in the other and making sure neither awaits the perfecting of the other.

Most of the prescribed tasks for resolving adolescent crises are well accepted by the parents. The most resisted task is likely to be with sociopathic kids—legal intervention into sociopathic behavior. It is hard enough to convince parents to respect authority sufficiently to leave crimes against society in the hands of society. Compounding that, the legal authorities are so accustomed to parents' protecting their kids from punishment that they often turn their own responsibilities back to parents who seem stable and interested, even as the parents are trying to get societal and legal reinforcement for their authority over their children. Official probation, so life-saving for out-of-control kids, is not easy to arrange. The alternative task, a very poor second choice, is to kick the kid out. Strangely, that is often more acceptable to sociopathic parents, but it is often a trick to get the therapists off their backs so they can slip out of therapy and resume the protection of the child from consequences.

Resistance to taking the prescribed action may pinpoint the family pathology and become the focus of therapy. Resistance may develop to convening as a family, to seeing the problem as a family problem or as a problem at all, or to revealing the problem within the family. Sometimes a family will make a brief all-out effort and then give up. Some aspects of family treatment of adolescent crises are frequently resisted. Trust—between the parents, between the generations, and between the siblings—may be sadly lacking, sometimes deservedly so amidst the alliances and secrets of a lifetime, and these trust issues may have to be dealt with before the specific problem can be approached.

It is perhaps surprising how well adolescent crises bring families together. This may be the reason why so many family theorists see all adolescent crises as having a rescuing function. Nevertheless, parents can resist aspects of therapy. Some parents have difficulty acknowledging the good intentions of the other parent, defining differences in approach or in the definition of the problem as proof of the other's destructiveness. Some have difficulty exposing themselves to their children and prefer to sacrifice their children than to disillusion them. Often there are family secrets that are being protected by one parent or another, even when the kids know or suspect the hidden information. This resistance then becomes the focus of the therapy and the revelations and exposures become major breakthroughs. Witnessing a powerful parent exposing himself and throwing himself on the child's mercy is as heartening as seeing a parent in need of rescue becoming competent and independent of the child. It seems precious and squeamish of therapists to attempt to bypass or cover up the deficiencies of the parents or their marriage—no one can be more aware of these than the adolescent children who live with them and are required to react to them without acknowledging them.

Ideally, parents get a second chance at reexperiencing their own adolescence through their children—not, one hopes, by acting out a second adolescence and thereby competing with the real adolescents and depriving them of real parents, but by rethinking what they learned the first time, and how, and why, and how that might be modified now. Reexperiencing and rethinking of values and identity are central to a successful outcome for all parties, and yet the process is frightening and becomes the aspect of the therapy that is most often subtly resisted when the pressure of the crisis is most intense. Frantic parents may prefer action of some sort to making alliance with their children through identification with the adolescent experience.

Step 7: Termination

As the therapy works, the adolescent loses interest and gradually drops out. Fine. With adolescent crises, exacerbations, often in strikingly different form, are to be expected. Change is usually rapid, as are all changes in adolescence, but it may be alarmingly temporary unless it is reinforced. Adolescent ex-patients tend to drop by for retreads off and on for years, and that is to be encouraged. Adolescence is, in itself, a series of crises, and hard terminations are unrealistic and destructive. The successful therapist may stand in the background indefinitely, like a grandparent or godparent, without ill effect. The usual failures occur in those families in which the parents continue to protect their children from growing up. It eventually happens though. Most adolescents do grow up, and become alarmingly like their parents, despite everyone's best efforts. But the lucky therapist may find just a few traces of him- or herself in there.

The proverbial minister, priest, and rabbi were debating the point at which life begins. The priest said, "Life begins at the moment of conception, when the sperm invades the egg." The minister insisted that "Life begins at birth, with that first breath of God's air." But the rabbi, older and wiser, said "You're both too young to know this, but life doesn't really begin until the kids leave home and the dog dies."

CHAPTER 11

Emancipation

EMPTYING THE NEST

THE MYTHOLOGY of the empty nest syndrome at its most dreadful assumes a little grey-haired, menopausal lady, who has rarely left home and never worked outside the home, who has served her term as PTA president, has darned socks and knitted sweaters and baked birthday cakes and driven car pools, and has sent her children tearfully off to college or the army or marriage, armed with brownies and good advice. Her husband, who has slept in the other room since the first child left home, plays golf when he isn't working or with his mistress. Her husband's mother is in the spare room gazing at a blank TV and the children don't write. She sobs softly when a letter doesn't come, sweetly conspires to make them all feel guilty, considers suicide, and has another drink instead.

The lives of middle-aged women have changed, and the empty nest syndrome is no longer common. It still occurs, though. Women who have developed little sense of a personal identity, apart from being someone's wife, someone's mother, someone's daughter, may now find themselves lonely, with little to do and no one to care. In a society that values youth, particularly female youth, women may be concerned with their appearance, with the competition from younger women. Their identity is most dependent on their husbands, just when their husbands are most involved with work, least involved at home, and most desirable to younger women. It is no surprise that alcoholism among women increases during this period.

A woman sitting on an empty nest is in a bit of a bind. The obvious solution to her crisis is to become closer to her husband and/or more involved in her own career or other interests. Either direction may trigger marital conflict, which may prevent the just launched child from feeling up to pursuing independence. A more intimate marriage is often not desired by a busy husband, unaccustomed to paying much attention to his wife. The same husband, on the other hand, may not like having to take care of himself or share household tasks while his previously domestic wife is busy elsewhere. He may well desire less intimacy and better service. One solution is for her to care for aging parents until the grandchildren arrive. That solution may be unavoidable and, while it does not sound very self-actualizing, it at least protects her husband from either intimacy or domestic competence. These women flock to graduate schools and marriage counselors, but it may be too late for many of them to save both their lives and their marriages.

This is a time when many forces are operating. Men are at greatest risk for infidelity. These are called the "dangerous years," the time of "male menopause." Men may feel cheated and trapped, worried about their health, noticing the decline in physical strength, and hoping to make one more push for the success that has eluded them or to enjoy one last fling to capture a youth that is fading. Successful men, long alienated from life at home, may become more involved with the work and play with which they have busied themselves for years while their wives were involved with home, children, and possibly, aging parents.

Fathers too can have empty nests, especially when they have been the only parent or the primary one. It is not unusual for fathers who are involved with their children but not with their marriages to spend years seeking their next wife, get into a longstanding affair, and get a divorce when the children are finally out of the home. Still, the usual crisis for fathers occurs when the mother suddenly decides that she must spend the rest of her life involved in her marriage, and the father has long ago given up on his marriage and views the launching of the children as redoubled freedom to be uninvolved at home.

And, of course, leaving home may be frightening for the children. They are leaving their familiar world, their family, their friends, a boyfriend or girlfriend, their pets. It is scary, and many if not most will seriously question whether they should follow through with the plans they have been making. Perhaps they should go to college closer to home, or postpone it a year, or go where their friends are going. Typically, high school seniors find themselves clinging closely to their classmates, and their families. As they perceive adulthood looming, they stop their rebelling and pouting, and prepare themselves to join the world. When they attempt greater closeness at home, the family, perhaps finding the children likable for the first time since puberty, may be reluctant to let them go. Parents may experience renewed hope that they can perfect the child before emancipation. They may send subtle or not so subtle messages to the child that perhaps staying closer to home would have some benefits. The child, already normally anxious about leaving, may give up and settle in at home.

There is no societal agreement about the appropriate relationship between parents and their emancipating children. The prevailing cultural stereotype centers on interfering parents, who want to know what their children are doing and make the children feel guilty for not including them in their lives. There seems to be a belief among many family therapists that parents have no right to be involved after the age of 17 or 18, and that such involvement runs the risk of being destructive to all concerned. The parents are expected to pay for education, and often for therapy, but other financial involvement is considered infantilizing and ultimately guilt-producing. In Georgia, perhaps elsewhere, parents have no court supported authority over their children after the age of 17, but are still legally responsible for their children's support and debts until 18. The assumption seems to be that the parent-child relationship should be worked out early, and parents should keep hands off after that.

This hands off approach runs counter to my own experience, clinically as well as personally. The healthiest families I know maintain close intergenerational relationships for everyone's lifetime, with lots of involvement, lots of conflict, and lots of interaction around the conflict. The parental home and resources provide a buffer and sanctuary as the children establish themselves. Leaving home becomes a gradual process, highly individual, and never complete. The dependency slowly shifts from one generation to the next, ideally with a long period in which both generations are self-reliant, intimate peers.

Like most other ideals, this one is not always achieved. The process is skewed if the younger generation stays too dependent too long, or if the older generation becomes too dependent too soon, or if the two generations conspire to prevent the necessary period of peerdom — by the older generation's refusal to accept the younger generation's self-reliance, by the younger generation's refusal to achieve it, or by an arrangement whereby the older generation remains emotionally dependent upon the younger and the younger financially dependent upon the older.

CRISES OF LEAVING HOME

A crisis growing more common than the empty nest occurs in those families in which young adults either don't leave home or fail repeatedly in their efforts at emancipation. Leaving home crises fall into three syndromes: (1) the cozy nest, in which the young adult is at home unemancipated and the parents are comfortable with it; (2) the crowded nest, in which the young adult is at home unemancipated and the parents are uncomfortable with it; and (3) fatal flights, in which the young adult makes a mess of emancipating but won't return home.

Cozy Nests

Sometimes one or more of the children is not leaving home, but the parents are not particularly concerned about it. This is not an uncommon pattern, and it may not be a problem. Family therapists' commitment to intergenerational separations can be overzealous. Certainly, a child who cannot function away from home, or a parent who cannot survive without children at home, or a marriage that cannot return to a twosome lacks the flexibility we would consider ideal mental health. But the pattern, however limiting, is not necessarily destructive. Crises of the cozy nest may be iatrogenic, in that the therapist creates the problem by declaring a problem when the family feels no symptoms. While the cozy nest pattern is characteristic of schizophrenia, alcoholism, and retardation, it is also characteristic of certain ethnic and cultural groups in which there is no pathology at all. In our economy, this pattern is becoming more common. Kids who finish their lives at home may work successfully, have an active social life, and eventually marry. But they don't have to do so, and therein is the problem.

Cozy nests are particularly characteristic of single parents, either fathers or mothers, and their youngest or only child. The young adult who is not leaving home does not have to work up any pathology to justify not growing up. He or she can be rewarded for staying home to be helpful. There may be a token pressure to function, but even greater pressure to stay home and help out. One widowed mother had fussed at her unemployed, alcoholic son for years about his failure to work. He finally got a job. On the second day of the job, she insisted that he stay home, as the piano tuner was coming and she did not want to be in the house alone with him. The boy stayed home and was fired.

Crowded nests may become cozy nests when one parent leaves or gives up the struggle. Cozy nests may come to crisis when the working parent retires, so that both parents are at home, and it gets a bit crowded. Or the other children may begin to bring pressure to bear.

In cozy nests there may be intense resistance to family therapy, or even to seeing it as a problem. These situations are often incidentally uncovered as treatment is sought for something else. In one family the mother was manic-depressive, usually depressed and inactive for long periods. The father, detached and passive, had long ago lost any sense that he could influence the household. Their child, a woman in her mid-twenties, was plain, sad, silent, and utterly disinterested in the world. She had no friends and spent her days sitting by the TV. Her father saw her as being as much outside his influence as his wife was, and he enjoyed having her around. The mother was seen as the patient, at the same time that she was considered untreatable. While the mother pondered, as she had for 30 years, whether she should have married her husband, the husband cheerfully considered the mother genetically deficient. Both parents assumed the daughter suffered from the same deficiency and was therefore damaged, untreatable, and acceptable to the parents, but not to the world. The daughter gradually went to work, avoided any social life, and saw no defect in herself. Refusing the suggestion of therapy, she settled in at home. Only the therapist was uncomfortable.

In another cozy nest family, the mother, bored with the six children of her blended family, put all six children in institutions, not because they needed it but because the insurance would pay for their education that way, and then left her gentle, alcoholic but functional, physician husband. The kids were between 15 and 19 years old, had minor and expectable problems she was sick of handling alone, and she didn't trust her husband to handle them without her. She wanted to finish college in peace. She moved into a one-room shack in the woods. Her husband gradually got all the children home, but had no further expectations for their education or employment. He and his kids and her kids lived comfortably in a communal arrangement. Some of the kids eventually pursued lives of their own. Some did not. The father seemed to prefer having a couple of them around all the time and saw no need for treatment of them or the family.

Even when someone forces treatment on these families, they resist. These patterns may have gone on for many years before unusual circumstances dictate that something be done about them. One 85-year-old woman, pressured by a nephew, made an appointment to bring in her 50-year-old children, neither of whom had ever left home. She had waited on them, hand and foot, for a lifetime. They beat her up and refused to come. She said she had finally determined it was a problem when she recalculated and realized that, unless she lived to be 100, she would die before her children were old enough to go to the Old Folks' Home.

Crowded Nests

In these families the child is chronologically grown, but not leaving home, and that is the stress. The young person seems competent enough, but just stays home with restricted functioning while the parents rage ineffectually at the child or at one another. Both parents may make a show of pushing the child to leave, but, of course, if both parents really wanted it, it would happen. Overtly, or covertly, one or both parents are holding the child at home. Typically, the mother is reasonably competent but miserably married.

These mothers are depressed, anxious, and dependent with their kids, but critical, hostile, and stormy with their detached, perhaps workaholic husbands. They complain about their marriage, but don't leave or try to change it. The children who can't leave home side with the mother in the marital battle and may be encouraging divorce, as the trio goes through an unrelenting series of exacerbations of the same old battle about who will stay and who will go and who has the problem. This is a classic pattern, described by Haley in *Leaving Home*, and is both real and common.

Some of these families have earlier had a kid who couldn't leave home for a while but finally did so with therapy, only to be replaced in the crowded nest by another sibling. The kids may or may not be severly pathological. They may protest that they want to leave home, but either don't or make a mess of their efforts. Often there is a schizophrenic quality to their nonfunctioning, as well as a profound sensitivity to conflict and overstimulation. But there may also be a playful awareness that the refusal to function well enough to leave home is purposeful. They often seem like non-schizophrenics playing at being schizophrenic. They may use hallucinogens to exaggerate their symptoms. Their choice of outside relationships keeps other aspects of their lives in turmoil too. It is hard to see them as victims of anything—they actively choose their way of life and can become as crazy as they will to maintain it.

While this pseudoschizophrenic syndrome is common in these families, there are other clinical pictures that keep grown children in a crowded nest. Some of the young, and not so young, adults are alcoholic. Some of the pathology is less obvious, taking the form of work inhibition—the belief that work is the opposite of play and should be avoided if one does not feel motivated to do it. Perhaps a minor physical problem—backache or allergy are sufficiently vague to be popular—is used to justify the nonfunctioning. That justification may not be required if the protective parent is comfortable with the idea that the young man has "just not found himself" or the young woman "is not one of those liberated types." At the root of this is the belief, defended by one parent, that people should not have to do anything they don't want to do. One mother said of her son, "He wishes he wanted to work. He thinks about it all the time. But the spirit never moves him." Young women have found it easier than young men to avoid functioning, although that is changing. Increasingly, nonfunctioning males are considered acceptable marital prospects, while nonfunctioning females are less desirable than they were.

One method parents have found to keep their children from working or growing up in other ways is to set the goals unrealistically high. One young man—unsocial and dependent—supported himself as a truck driver, but his salesman father, at war with all authority, was determined that the young man would achieve self-fulfillment only as a self-employed salesman. He would fail at selling each time he tried it and then move back home. If any realistically possible job is considered degrading, and unemployment acceptable, there is little motivation for work. If, in addition, the other parent is degrading to the child and degraded by the protective parent, the syndrome is complete.

All of these kids have realistic expectations that their parents' marriage could not survive their emancipation. Their mothers need them at home to defuse the unresolvable dissatisfaction of their marriages. The process of making these kids more concerned with their mothers' unhappiness than with their own lives has been going on a long, long time. If the marriage improves, or ends, the pattern of nonfunctioning may well continue, but without the obligatory show of dissatisfaction with it. It is not uncommon for a widowed mother and her chronically alcoholic son to live cozily together for a lifetime after the less tolerant father dies and uncrowds the nest. These kids' primary relationship is with their mothers. I have not seen many such families in which the father's marital unhappiness was the magnet, but I've seen several over the years in which the father's alcoholism or physical illness has kept a child at home. The child has become the caretaker, to relieve the overburdened mother.

A memorable case involved a man whose late wife had protected their only daughter from his efforts to get her to grow up and leave home. When the wife died, he redoubled his efforts to no avail and finally moved out himself, leaving the 40-year-old nonfunctional daughter alone in the family home. Although he remarried, he slipped by the house daily to clean up for his daughter, since "she was sloppy and won't take good care of the antiques."

Fatal Flights

In other families, the kids do leave home — and promptly fall apart. Some even commit suicide soon after leaving home. Others end up in psychiatric hospitals or jails. It is as if they have a choice of either giving up on life or giving up on independence, and they would rather die than return home. These families are somewhat like those in which the kids are unable to leave home at all. One difference is that these mothers are more wildly disruptive and more unpleasant. The kids feel too responsible for their miserable mothers to grow up and leave them, but would rather die or go crazy than live with them.

These mothers are a demanding and disruptive group. Nothing pleases them, nothing is enough. Their husbands and children literally hide from them. The husbands who are still alive and around tend to be secretive, passive-aggressive, and cold. They are often adulterous. The kids are protective of the fathers and disdainful of the mothers — quite the opposite from the kids who cannot leave home. In these families the kids leave but make sure the leaving is unsuccessful, even dramatically so. These families, like those in which the kids stay at home, are dominated by the mother's marital or postmarital unhappiness. But the kids can't live with these women either, and the fathers offer no sanctuary.

The process by which these kids fall apart upon leaving home is somewhat uniform. Like the kids in crowded nests, they leave for a while, despite obvious problems. Some have had success in school, some have managed in relationships, but none of these kids has found life easy. They may have drug problems or more serious pathology. They may even be schizophrenic. Some have been hospitalized previously. They go off to college or wherever. When they can't make it, they don't return home for another pass through. In some cases the parents' marriage has ended upon their leaving; in others the parental battle has continued in their absence. They have no sanctuary to which they can return. They commit suicide or get themselves into an institution rather than return home.

In treating crowded nests (and cozy nests too for that matter), there must be concern about whether emancipation would result in a fatal flight. Obviously, there is greater danger when the parental home is gone or closed to the child. The child must be freed from centrality in the parent's unhappiness and learn to base his or her comings and goings on his or her own needs, not those of the parents. It is not the home to which the child should be denied access, but the marriage and unhappiness of the parents. Many kids need structure, assistance, and protection as they leave home; most need a safe haven or at least a waystation during transitions in their own lives. If the parents can't provide that, the grandparents or older siblings or other relatives may be able to provide it temporarily. Sending failing kids out on their own is not a solution. However, when the child does begin functioning, pressure to move back out can reassure the child that his or her presence is not required by the parents.

Empty Nests

I'm forced to conclude that Haley is correct in his observation that a major barrier to emancipation of children is the mothers' marital dissatisfaction. The unhappiness of the marriage is not made the business of the marriage, but the business of the mother-child relationship.

The kids afraid to leave home are often correct in fearing the impact of their leaving on the parent's marriage. Many marriages do end at this point. There are men who are in longstanding affairs who are planning on leaving home as soon as the children do. These men are probably correct in realizing that if they wait for their divorce until after the emancipation of the children, they will have a better chance of obtaining their children's acceptance of the divorce. They are quite dedicated to their children, but not to their marriage. Inadvertently though, they make it harder and more traumatic for their children to leave home.

The mothers are blamed when their children fail to emancipate, and that blame comes from fathers, children, and therapists. The contribution of the fathers is a bit more subtle, but still important to the syndromes. The cozy nest fathers tend to be soft and sometimes pitiful, perhaps too agreeable for their wives' taste, at least while sober. Many of these fathers I have seen through the years have been alcoholic. The crowded nest and fatal flight fathers have consistently been demanding, critical, even explosive when not depressed. They don't like their wives, and usually don't like their kids, and it shows. The most pleasant of them have been the ones invested in long-term affairs, which may drive their wives crazy but help them maintain their equanimity. Despite their unpleasantness, they don't seem to have much control over what goes on in their families. Often they are right about how to handle the unemancipating kids, but disqualify their opinions by their general nastiness or deviousness.

TREATMENT OF LEAVING HOME CRISES

Step 1: Emergency Response

The hallmark of cozy nests is the lack of sense of crisis. In crowded nests, by contrast, there may be a sense of impending disaster, and an appointment may seem urgent. In fatal flights, the disaster is real and intense. The fleeing youth may have just made a successful or unsuccessful suicide attempt, gotten into a hospital or jail, or run away. Some emergency intervention may be required. Often there is resistance to a family appointment, and an individual one is being requested.

Step 2: Involving the Family

In cozy nests the family sees no problem. In crowded nests the family may attempt to keep treatment of the child and the marriage separate. After a fatal flight, the survivors may be seen together, back in their crowded nest. After a catastrophic effort at emancipation, the family usually feels sufficient emergency to be involved. Once the kid is out of the home, separate therapy for the parents and the kid may prevent the kid's reinvolvement in the marital or postmarital unhappiness.

Step 3: Defining the Crisis

These three syndromes should be accurately diagnosed, and differentiated from one another. The basis for differentiation is the comfort with the situation. If all are comfortable with the child's failure to emancipate, it is a cozy nest, so go slowly and set modest goals—change will be slow or not at all. If the child seems comfortable at home and the couple is battling over it, it is a crowded nest, and the child must leave before the marriage can be dealt with. If the child resists being at home amidst the marital chaos, but keeps failing in his or her flights from the home, it is a potentially dangerous situation.

In any of the syndromes in which a young adult does not leave home successfully, there must be definition of his or her disability, which is generally seen as schizophrenia whether it is or not. Getting the family to see the connection between the youth's failure to emancipate successfully and the mother's marital unhappiness is a tricky therapeutic task. Since this task may be difficult to perform quickly, the definition may unfold gradually. It is not necessary for the family to totally accept a definition that connects the child's problems and the parents' marriage — this connection has been debated between the marital partners for some time and may not be resolvable prior to being solved. In these cases, the solution may be offered prior to general agreement about the definition of the problem.

Step 4 and 5: Prescriptions

The expectation of eventual functioning is soothing — desperate efforts at separation are not. Focus should be on functioning rather than emancipation. The kid who is not yet functioning should not be kicked out. In these syndromes, especially fatal flights, the emancipating child may be schizophrenic and may benefit from phenothiazines, or he may be depressed enough for antidepressants. If this is a fatal flight situation, in which the young adult is panicky about being at home, a neutral sanctuary short of hospitalization is nearly always available, especially if the youth is medicated. Even then, the young person should not be sent out on his or her own.

The task in all three syndromes is to get the youth launched and the parents involved with one another. Getting the young person functional may have to come first. The pace is different in each syndrome: very slow in cozy nests; challenging and conflictual in crowded nests; and desperate in fatal flights. The therapist takes over from the children the role of marriage counselor. The second part of the therapeutic task involves the marriage. The father takes over from the children the position of emotional partner to the mother. If the mother (or father) is single, putting her into group therapy is an effective stopgap as she begins a life without the children. The format of couples or group therapy is in itself the major specific prescription, as it is the involvement with relationships other than mothering which resolves the crisis immediately for the depressed mother and eventually for the child who can't leave home.

Step 6: Negotiating Resistance

The resistances come fast and furious to the tasks of getting the kid out of the marriage, immediately into some sort of functioning, and eventually out of the home. First the kid and one of the parents will try to prove the child is incapable of functioning, while the other parent tries to kick the kid out before he or she has any chance of making it in the world. The therapist may have to find schools or jobs or programs to get the kid out of the house. The couple may continue to battle about the kid or in cozy nests, deny any problem at all, thus resisting the therapist's effort to deal with the marriage at all.

The usual resistance is for the family to treat the problem as an individual one on the kid's part. Sometimes, individual treatment of the child, temporarily, is helpful in separating the child's plans for functioning from the parents' interference. Likewise, the couple may be seen separately, especially as the child is leaving. But it is dangerous to see one of the marital pair, either with the child or alone — that sidetracks both issues and just reinforces the sense of helplessness. In crowded nest and fatal flight families, I've usually been able to work with both parents, even when the child is resistant to continuing the therapy and prefers to function and leave. One danger is for the child to enter a protective individual therapy arrangement with a therapist who will not communicate with the parents while the child is still at home.

Step 7: Termination

The child, if necessary, may be seen separately or referred to a separate therapist upon emancipation, but as long as the child is at home family therapy is by far the treatment of choice. The crisis tends to be recurrent, especially in crowded nests, and the family may pass through therapy several times before the child leaves home permanently and the mother settles into the marriage or fills the empty spaces in her life.

Growing old isn't so bad when you consider the alternative.

— Maurice Chevalier

Youth was not the pleasurable time you may think it was. Our
memories are treacherous, eliminating the unpleasant and
painting the pleasant in unrealistically bright colors. Take my
advice and be as you are, old and decrepit though you may be.

— Isaac Asimov, *New York Times*, October 5, 1986

CHAPTER 12

Aging

THE BRIGHTER ALTERNATIVE

FOR MOST HAPPY PEOPLE, the happiest time of all is the penultimate period, the time after the achievement of full maturity, with the children grown
or growing and the careers settled and the ambitions reduced to a manageable level so that they don't interfere with the pleasure of one's day. In the
turmoil of adolescence or under the burden of youth or in the stubborn
refusal of midlife, the comfort of old age is hard to anticipate.

Some, those who fear they've missed some of the excitement or success
of youth, may fight aging and go through the anachronistic craziness of
trying to stay young—not youthful or vital or active, but *young*, as if the
structure of their life were still open. Seventy-year-olds who climb mountains or take up painting are alive; 70-year-olds who chase after 30-year-olds
are silly. Those who fight growing older are missing the best part of life. As
William Holden told Gloria Swanson in *Sunset Boulevard*, "Norma, you're
a woman of 50. Now, grow up! There's nothing tragic about being 50—not
unless you try to be 25."

Eventually, almost everyone relaxes into the autumnal comfort of late middle age and discovers its liberation from pretense and struggle. Then, into this happy time, old age intrudes. It may actually hit in the fifties, but it may not appear until the eighties or even the nineties. It may be more attitudinal than physiological. Old age can be a way of life. It can have some similarities to depression. It can be a giving up, an awaiting of death, with the hope that death will come before disability, before the money runs out, before the children lose interest, before the nursing home, before the partner dies.

CRISES OF OLD AGE

The crises of old age are manifold, covering the full range from bolts from the blue to caretaker crises, yet old people are not as likely to come to therapy as young people are. They seem more likely to go to hospitals, less likely to seek outpatient solutions. There are exceptions. The elderly may still be struggling with manic-depression, with alcoholism, with extramarital affairs, with phobias, with psychosomatic disorders, and even with anorexia, and it is no different at 80 than at 20. They can still struggle with the misinformation they got from their parents 70 or 80 years ago, and with the disappointments of their childhood. Old people may also use therapy to interrupt loneliness rather than to bring about change. Some come to therapy at 75 because they've never tried it and they don't want to miss anything in life, but such people are not old at whatever age.

Developmental Crises

They say the legs go first, then the mind. That's not quite true — it is eyes, the teeth, and the spirit of adventure that go first. But going over the hill follows no uniform pattern. Physical strength lessens, stamina fades. Older men just can't keep up with the younger ones — it's not the muscles as much as the joints. You begin to creak and stiffen, and things that made you feel good begin to make you feel bad. You go past the point where you do things well for your age, toward the point where doing them at all is cause for pride. Sex need not shrivel up and fall off, but it often does. Certainly age detracts from one's sense of sexual attractiveness. Despite Benjamin Franklin's advice about choosing an older mistress, most women and many men face aging with more bitterness over their lost youthfulness than over their lost youth. The equation of youthfulness with sexuality leaves older people feeling shy and apologetic about their appearance and reluctant to pursue sex. Maggie Smith, in Neil Simon's *California Suite*, says "I've aged, Sidney. There are new lines in my face. I look like a brand-new, steel belted radial tire."

But there are decades between the loss of youth and the onset of old age. The loss of youthful vigor and beauty, the passing of those batons, is tragic only to the narcissistic. To those who've successfully weathered those little narcissistic crises, it is faintly whimsical. The onset of old age is quite different. It signals the loss of real powers, and it is far more real than the first pair of bifocals, or being assigned "elder statesman" status, or the decision to let the gray hair go natural, or the realization that a bikini no longer shows you at your best.

The first signs are frightening, as you notice how old your friends look — or your husband or wife — and you realize that they see it in you too. Illnesses take their toll. Sometimes the process is sudden, rather than the process being gradual and the awareness being sudden. People begin to talk about how it used to be rather than how it is going to be. Patterns get set, and it is disorienting to change them. Change of any sort is resented. People begin to prefer the comfort of the familiar to the stimulation of the novel. The little details of living give the most pleasure and the most security. That security takes top priority. All resources — emotional, physical, economic — must be conserved. There is so little time, and so little to do.

There are definite turning points in this process of deterioration. Retirement is the most dramatic. Suddenly, someone who had been producing, active, competitive, and even ambitious, who certainly had been useful and involved with other people, is now at leisure, unscheduled, at loose ends. With retirement there is a loss of structure, a loss of purpose, a loss of context. In exchange, there is a freedom which may or may not be welcome. If there is a good marriage to stay home for, retirement may be the most glorious time of life. Many, even those who have dreaded it, find they not only tolerate it, but actually savor it. Retirement is life's greatest opportunity for the playful, the imaginative, the adventurous, and the loving.

Retirement is a danger for those who don't know how to play or learn or love. Retired people are at risk for becoming inactive, conservative, bored, and depressed. They had anticipated having time to play, but play doesn't make for a life, and play alone takes on the desperation of a vacation that lasts too long. And there may be no one to play with. If the retiree is male and his wife is not employed outside the home, her life has changed less than his. Her work has been expanded rather than contracted by his retirement. They have more time together, which may or may not be wonderful. Even if they get along well, he intrudes. He intrudes into her life, interrupts her schedule and activities, restricts her freedom of movement, and disrupts her pace of doing things. He's underfoot at home and has no headquarters of his own. A relationship that worked part-time may be stifling fulltime. They begin to get on each other's nerves.

If the man retires while the woman keeps working, he may find enough to do at home to make a life. A retired man with a working wife may belatedly learn domestic skills, take over at home, and be useful, occupied and appreciated. It can be the best time in the marriage. It is often recommended that the first thing a woman should do when her husband retires is go get a job. Yet the husband, unable to take care of himself or tolerate being alone, may push her to retire also and take on the fulltime task of his care and feeding and entertainment. She may be younger than he and just hitting the crest of her own career success; indeed, she may resent his pressure so much that she may, understandably, choose her career over her marriage.

As William Powers (1981) points out, research has shown that "women are as work oriented as men, and more likely than men to take a long time in adjusting to retirement." This may be because of work-based friendships. It also may be because, whether or not she works outside the home, a woman is expected to work at home. There is no such thing as retirement for a woman; there is just a change in the workplace. I find myself regularly urging a woman not to quit work until her husband can learn to get along without her at home. Such an arrangement can bring a belated balance to gender relationships and make for a far more equal marriage after both are retired.

Once they are both retired, they may have too little to do. The couple may try to move to a retirement home. Florida beckons. They may live in cramped quarters among strangers, become far more interdependent than their marriage can tolerate, and devote themselves to making crises to get their children's attention. This is the age of least mental and physical flexibility. Unless the retirement and the move occur early in the aging process, it can be a disaster.

Old people need one another more, but they begin to bore one another and themselves. They begin to realize that their children and grandchildren visit them only out of duty, and the youngsters make excuses to avoid them. That's not as painful as it might be, because the oldsters may not want the interruptions as much as they want the security of knowing that someone cares. They may enjoy the grandchildren's pictures more than they enjoy the grandchildren's visits. The grandchildren may know that too.

In every marriage that lasts into this stage, one partner begins to age before the other. The couple goes out less. They talk to one another less and fuss at one another more. They don't seem to enjoy one another anymore, or maybe they never did, but they become inseparable. A caretaker crisis ensues. Can Mom and Dad, who never liked being together much anyway, survive being tied together so tightly and dependently? Will Dad's failing physical health tolerate the manifold demands of senile Mom? Sometimes, one can't take it and leaves, but that is rare. It is too late to leave—dignity and integrity become more important than survival.

It may happen that the couple cannot continue living together. One 80-year-old is still vital and eager for life; the other is slipping into crotchety dependency and even senility. How does one escape a marriage in which he or she is the necessary caretaker? Few things, short of running off with another woman while your wife is in the delivery room giving birth to your baby, seem so ignoble. Leaving a senile spouse is beyond the pale. It is done, but lining up support for such a move is difficult. The children, who will have to take over the caretaking functions, are not likely to be sympathetic. The friends and relatives, who might like to run from their responsibilities too but are prevented by honor and duty, are indignant.

The death of a spouse at 90 is more expectable, but little easier, than at 30. It may be harder, as the chances of remarriage are minimal and the loneliness is more intense. Also, after the first half century or so, even the most cantankerous of us begins to settle into our marriage and accept the interdependency. The end of that intimacy is cruel and bitter. Even after marriages in which the battle against submission to intimacy consumed a lifetime, the surviving partner seems able to remember only the initial hope and the final warmth.

Women, unless they have married younger men, expect to spend their last decade or so as widows. Women usually marry older men. Men usually die younger. Men, knowing that, may work themselves to death in order to achieve the honorable distinction of having left a widow who is "well taken care of." When a woman loses her aged husband to death, it is not really unexpected, rarely unplanned for, and certainly never unconsidered. It may give her a financial power and an independence she's never had before, and while she may miss him for many things, her life may proceed very nicely, perhaps even more actively than before. If her husband's last illness was a long one, her life resumes at his death. The likelihood of remarrying is not great, and those who do may not be pleased with the result — widowhood has been planned for and produces few unexpected changes, but remarriage brings a multitude of new factors. Since she is likely to be in control of whatever new marriage she enters, her children may be delighted and give full support.

If the wife should die first, and that happens more than we realize, the husband may not have planned for it and may be helpless and overwhelmed with unexpected changes. He is likely to remarry, often abruptly, to find someone to relieve the loneliness and to take care of him. Old men don't seem to do well alone. If he chooses someone familiar, an old friend or someone with similar interests and profession, it may be wonderful. But this is not the age for adventure and risk-taking, particularly in choosing marriage partners. The new couple may not blend well and may even have to maintain two households. The children may find it all disconcerting. However grateful they may be to have a nurse for Dad, they don't need a stepmother for themselves. They lose access to Dad and may launch into rivalries and feuds, while the poor old man doesn't quite know what hit him. Some of the most interesting work a family therapist does is with families in this situation, unraveling custody battles over an old man who is trying to hold his own family together while starting a new one, when he's past the point of maximum flexibility or sensitivity, and when he may be sitting on an estate all the vultures are eyeing. The poor new wife can't seem to win, especially if she too is expecting financial security from the deal. Her children may bitterly resent the way his children are treating their mother.

This difference in the way grown children view their aged father's remarriage and their aged mother's remarriage is not absolute, but it is characteristic. It seems based on the expectation that women control the family and men control the money. The family continues when Mom remarries—she sees to that. But the money isn't secure when Dad remarries and Dad's new marriage puts a buffer between him and his children. He joins the new wife's family. These concerns may bring the family much pain and may bring them to therapy, particularly when there is money in the family. One of the advantages of being poor is that your children are usually delighted when you marry again in your dotage.

The children don't find it much easier when the aged parent is living alone. The earlier stages of the aging process seem like irritating character flaws. The family accuses the aging member of becoming irritable over minor changes, of trying to control things too rigidly, of never wanting to do things, of being hypochondriacal, of only talking about the past, of being stingy and conservative, of demanding attention. It is only after that person begins to get confused and to forget things that the family realizes that the brain isn't hitting on all cylinders and the irritating habits were efforts at holding on. Then the old person begins to ignore personal hygiene, to lose things, and to hide things. He or she may talk about people who are long dead, wander off during a conversation and leave the phone off the hook, forget that you just called them and fuss about your not doing so. He or she may fail to cash checks, may put the bills in the refrigerator, and save old newspapers because they might contain something important but they can't remember what. He or she may try to make a show of holding on, like the old lady in the movie *The Private Function*, who so feared being sent to a nursing home that every time the doctor came to visit she recited the multiplication tables for him to prove her mind was still working. These habits are understood and may irritate or worry the family only a little. Mostly, they're sad.

Caretaker Crises

In time, the aging process develops to the point that the old person becomes dependent. The grown children may become caretakers. When the child becomes parent to the parent there is some friction. Either may be offended. Either may overplay the role—the child may be autocratic, the old person may collapse dependently and demandingly. The children may have to force the parent to make a will, to make decisions about funeral arrangements or division of property. These dreaded subjects may detonate explosions and may have to be negotiated by a therapist. One of the most awkward is the encounter during which the aging autocrat must be asked by his children to turn over the helm of the family business he had created and developed, when he knows very well that none of his children is what he was, even though he can't face that he's not what he was either.

Neurological assessment is not within the province of family therapy, nor really of psychiatry, but the therapist must see the elderly family member in order to be on firm footing in helping the family react to the aged member. And, in dealing with an older person, there must be attention, informally, to the mental status. It seems dumb to have to mention that, but therapists often spend session after session with a family stewing over decisions about what to do with "Grandpa who is old and feeble and driving us all crazy" without ever seeing Grandpa. Families have been known to panic over rather subtle signs of intellectual decline.

The most painful developmental crisis of aging comes when an old person can no longer live alone. When the old person leaves the stove on all night, smokes in bed and sets fire to the mattress, falls and can't get up, can't get out of the bathtub, wanders off in pajamas — the situation is dangerous, and someone must be there all the time. And that may not be convenient or possible. Something has to be done, and therapy may be sought to determine what the family is to do. These are some of the most painful decisions a family must make, and most families have to make them. The old person hopes for a little more time at home, or at least for a home with the children. The children can't bear the thought of sending a parent into a nursing home while the parent is still able to recognize anybody, even intermittently. The expense and the bother all have to be considered. It is so much easier when the old person has been living usefully and enjoyably with family before senility sets in.

The changes come about more gracefully when the older person has been part of the household all along. But for the children to rearrange their lives to make room for a marginally functional parent, especially one who is now an invalid who cannot be left alone in this unfamiliar and perhaps makeshift and somewhat hostile environment, imposes a new structure that is laden with crises. One of the grandchildren may have to give up a bedroom, one of the adults may have to give up a study, or the whole house may have to be rebuilt or rearranged. The family may even have to move. It is a tossup whether the old person's presence is more resented by the son or daughter, or by the son- or daughter-in-law. Both may welcome it, both may resent it, or one may be delighted and the other enraged. Whether the old person's arrival is seen as a blessing or a curse, it is a crisis which arouses all manner of feelings on the part of all concerned. It is always hardest on the old person, who must make the most adjustments and give up the most of a familiar life.

The matter of what to do with Mom or Dad who is now old and feeble can also produce conflict between siblings. Either all the oldster's children want custody or none do, and they fight about who gets the pleasure or the pain of Mom's or Dad's presence in their household. The brothers and sisters may set up split custody, whereby the aged parent summers with one and winters with another, and then they can squabble over who is doing too much or not enough. They may sound like two dogs fighting over a bone or two kids fighting over whose turn it is to wash and whose turn it is to dry. One of the children may try to get a medical or psychiatric excuse; another may plead poverty. If one sibling wants the aged parent, the other children may resent that just as much, and the sibling who wants the old person may distrust the sincerity of the others who want to do their "duty." Meanwhile the poor oldster is shipped back and forth from coast to coast without getting much voice or any place he or she can call home. If the siblings really want to fight, they can set up battles between one another's doctors, who are either overlooking the oldster's serious medical problems or overprescribing sedation.

The overuse of sedation for old people is a real and significant problem. A withered brain does not tolerate mind altering drugs well, yet they are prescribed in abundance and usually taken regularly by the health conscious older person. Sleeping pills and minor tranquilizers at night can mimic senility in the morning and produce periods of agitation later in the day. Quaaludes were first used for nighttime sedation for old folks, who would then go beserk if awakened during the night. The most common crisis I see in older people is the confusion caused by the overuse of drugs and alcohol. A little exercise is a far more effective tranquilizer. Low doses of antidepressants work far better than tranquilizers for the totally inactive elderly. Old people deserve physicians who respect their remaining facilities enough to encourage them to tolerate a little discomfort or restlessness if necessary to keep them alert and functional.

Structural Crises

As people age, their bad marriages and strained relationships with their children may begin to soften. As their powers decline, they become more accessible, less frightening, and easier to forgive. The issues that have kept them at war begin to fade into insignificance. An elderly person may carry the glory of past deeds, but not the inglory of past misdeeds. It is hard to bear malice against one who is merely a relic of his or her past. As the elderly become more dependent, their guilt production loses little of its obnoxiousness but much of its sting. The old battles just don't mean as much.

Unless the old person controls money. When an estate is in question, the power remains and so does the danger of conflict. The elderly rich must be appeased or the will could be changed. I used to keep a collection of disinheritance letters, powerful weapons to keep one's children from ever getting comfortable. Most were written by people entering their dotage. Even as they face death, some people cannot stop the battle that has kept them powerful and miserable, but unforgotten, for a lifetime.

In understanding the intergenerational battles, the source of the parents' power must be understood. Do the older people control money that the younger people want? Do they want it now or later? Do the older people represent a financial burden? Do the oldsters control through guilt? Do the older people perform some useful emotional or instrumental function for the family? Often the older people want to make themselves more useful than the younger people will permit. The youngsters, who may be 60 or older themselves, may still fear being dependent upon the parents. People don't really become parents to their parents; they are always children around their parents. But they may be at risk for becoming parentified and overcontrolled by guilt, obligation, and the drive to be a good little boy or girl, which is a fulltime job.

Family sessions with the older generation, always fascinating and productive, are usually the ones the family remembers years later. I push for inclusion of the oldsters, but I probably should insist upon it. Grownups remain their parents' children, and just as adolescents tend to fear the parents want to take their puberty away, grownups continue to fear their parents want to infantilize them. So the family may try to keep their guilty secrets from the old folks and resist including them regularly, even if they permit one or two visits.

Ivan Boszormenyi-Nagy and Geraldine Spark (1984) include grandparents routinely, to relieve the "blame syndrome" and to examine the divided loyalties between the generations. I share their optimism about involving the older generation and cannot recall an unproductive session of this sort, although I have had some uncomfortable episodes in which grown children have reverted to the most alarming early adolescent stage of blaming the most amazing things on their parents. The parents would then respond parentally. Nagy and Spark comment:

Often, it is incorrectly assumed that a person who is in the aged or grandparental phase of life cannot change or modify his familial relationships. However, in some instances the grandparents may be less rigid and fixated than a younger member. Moreover, most aged parents remain committed to their offspring and grandchildren, which helps the three generations to face the nature of the current relationship and obligations rather than the internalized, early distortions regarding one's parents.

Some people remain frightened by their parents even into the grave. The parents maneuver to keep that aspect of their influence intact. Most people, though, have wonderful relationships with the elderly members of the family and mourn fully and genuinely when the older members die. The old problems just seem to fade away with time — and faulty memory.

Bolts From the Blue

The elderly expect to grow old and die, preferably in the care of their children. The death of a child is, in our society, the most tragic of occurrences. When an old person loses a child, it is not only a loss of the invested hopes and dreams, but also a real loss of security. The elderly can experience the expected depression, with the added factor of guilt for living so long when their child has died. "Why was he taken in the prime of life, while I sit here waiting to die? Why wasn't I the one to die?"

Another unique situation the elderly face is violence. Old people are easy targets for street crime, easy to knock down and rob or break in on and tyrannize. They may be defenseless and made to feel even more so after being victimized by strangers. It is hard enough to be old and weak, but it is intolerable to be old and weak in a hostile world. Old people can be brutalized by their own family too, in the same way and for the same reasons that small children are beaten — because they require more than they can give. We don't seem to know how to use old people; like old cars and old clothes, they arouse anger when they no longer get us where we're going and make us look our best.

In a time of economic inflation, the elderly's resources lose value. They may become unexpectedly poor. Poverty is hard on the elderly, as there can be no hope of escaping it. Their primary resource, their only security, is their children — and they are at risk for depleting that resource too. Illnesses are dreaded, financially as well as physically and emotionally. Death isn't cheap either, and the old may pay their only available dollars for a burial policy that won't cover the cost of the funeral. The elderly are dependent in so many ways and powerless to escape their powerlessness. And even if they have nothing else to hope for, they can still hope for dignity.

TREATING THE CRISES OF OLD AGE

The most important principle to keep in mind when doing therapy with the elderly is that no one ever grows up. There is no such thing as an adult — at any age we still doubt ourselves and long for our idealized loving parents. Younger therapists may be awed by the presumed wisdom of age, may misinterpret dignity as power, and may not reach the scared child inside the old person. At my father's bedside, just before he died at 73, my 93-year-old grandmother cried on his hand and looked up to me, saying "It is times like this that I most miss my mother." Her mother had been dead for 85 years.

Another guiding principle for dealing with the elderly is that they are perfectly capable of change, even if they were not willing to change to suit their adolescent children a generation before. Old people must change, and probably do so more rapidly and wrenchingly than at any time since their own adolescence. But they do try to keep an unchanging organizing structure around themselves to buffer against the terrifying changes taking place inside them and the people to whom they are closest.

Thirdly, it must be realized how frightening this period is for people. They fear their death, their disability, loss of their faculties, loss of bladder control, loss of memory, loss of money, loss of love. They fear losing their power, wherever it comes from. And they want to retain their influence and pass it on to their descendants.

Fourth, they still scare their children, and sometimes this fear is passed on to their grandchildren. The therapist must be careful not to get caught up in that, which is not likely to happen if the old people are included in the therapy.

Fifth, they face the same crises as everyone else. The obstacle course of life does not stop on a certain birthday, but it speeds up toward the end just when people are slowing down. The elderly, who do so well in family therapy, may need it most.

CASE ILLUSTRATIONS

CASE 17   *Playing the Palace*

I had seen both the children and their families separately, as they struggled through painful marriages to people who were safely weak and beautiful and unthreatening, reminding them of their sweet, passive mother rather than their stormy, intrusive, controlling, and incredibly wealthy father. The family had long ago decreed that the daughter was too strong and the son was too weak and both their spouses agreed. But the daughter continued to throw her endless energy into controlling everything, succeeding with everything except her husband's anxiety and her daughter's weight or grades or table manners or whatever else was her latest project for improvement. The son managed to bumble along, clumsily asking everyone (except his wife) for advice and trying to follow everyone's advice at the same time, producing about what one would expect to come from a warring committee. The point of their lives seemed to be to fulfill the parental definition that he would always be too weak and she would always be too strong: That was their destiny and that would be their downfall. His marriage failed and hers was failing, and I had the sense that my therapeutic effect had been to turn both of their spouses into extremely healthy people who were fed up and wouldn't take it anymore.

All somehow blamed their lives on the tyrannical tycoon of a father. So I saw the brother and sister with their parents, who were in their seventies, in love, and happy with everything except their sense that they had failed with their children. The father was large, loud, and effusively Italian. The mother was tiny, round, and dark, so quiet she barely seemed present.

In the family interviews, the children naturally attacked their father obnoxiously for giving her a mansion that was bigger than his, for being too close to the grandchildren, for always coming over and being helpful. The father blustered, then cried and offered to give larger mansions, to stop seeing his grandchildren, to stop being helpful, and they attacked him for that. Whatever he offered, they attacked. He became frantic. The children loved it. Their mother remained out of the fray; when the dust cleared she would look up from her knitting and softly say something very wise and very practical. Her remark would make the salient point and move her husband and us back onto the subject. I gradually came to see that this phenomenally successful man was no different from his son — he had to please everyone, without regard to whether it would help them or him. His power, of which his children and their spouses were in such awe, was a myth created by his wife. He made the show, while she made the decisions. The son, in trying to emulate the father, had incorporated all of the old man's weakness, but hadn't found a wife who could direct this desperate people-pleasing. The daughter had overlooked the mother's power too and tried to use force, bluster, loud noises, and threats, turning every night into Halloween in an effort to work up some semblance of what she saw as her father's power. They had each married people who seemed soft like their mother but lacked her calm, quiet wisdom behind the stage.

I blew the old couple's cover, pointing out that the mother was making all the decisions while the old man merely blustered and ingratiated (one of the few I've ever known who could do both at the same time — it seems a skill that takes money to work effectively). The parents said, "Of course, we thought you knew," but it still took weeks of explanations and examples for the brother and sister to catch on.

After that, the children permitted the father to please them (he'd become a great cook and a good carpenter), consulted the mother about all decisions (particularly about child-raising — I wanted to hire her myself), and began to change. The son remarried far more satisfactorily to a strong, silent type who felt comfortable with his sweetness. The daughter finally divorced and permitted herself to experience doubt and generosity and calm.

Years later, they dropped by the office. It's one big, happy family again, and the old folks feel completely successful now, although they can't understand how their children failed to see who the real power was all those years.

CASE 18   *When the Opportunity Arises*

Though both were near 80, Gerri had left Tom and was job hunting. She had told him at 70, when he'd had his last affair, that she would leave him if he did it again. He did. She'd put up with his infidelities for over 50 years, she had her pride, and she wasn't going to spend the rest of her life with this sort of indignity. Tom, though retired, was still a schoolteacher, so he explained, as he did each time, how illogical Gerri was being and how many important thinkers had kept mistresses on the side. Unimpressed, Gerri stormed more loudly. Tom just looked proud, which enfuriated her more. She told him she was not coming home until either he agreed to give up his philandering or she had an affair herself. He refused to agree to fidelity.

The next week Gerri told him she had had an affair. Tom congratulated her and invited her home. She agreed to come. He and I were careful not to question her too closely in the matter. Instead, we looked at the difficulties of two strong-willed people facing retirement together.

The third session, Tom came alone. Gerri had moved back home, but an emergency had come up with one of the great-grandchildren so she was out of town. He confessed that he hadn't actually consummated his affair, but wanted to keep his options open in case the opportunity should ever arise again. I never saw them again, but expect an exacerbation as they approach 90. There are marital patterns that age cannot wither nor custom stale.

In this pure structural crisis, a 50-year marriage was kept at just the desired level of intimacy through intermittent crises of infidelity. This time around the couple needed a little distance during their retirement, so they faked a pair of affairs. The crisis with the great-grandchild, which may have been fabricated, permitted the same distance without having to go further into the infidelity debate.

CASE 19   *The Eternal Dinner Party*

Pearl, an 80-year-old woman, widowed for many years and living carefully on her investments, had two children — a daughter who was a psychiatrist and a son who was a schizophrenic. She was a well-known hostess and raconteur. Despite her lifelong efforts to be scandalous, a dinner party without her would have been unthinkable. Then she developed cancer of the esophagus. Although she survived the surgery, she knew she would not live as long as she might like, and certainly not as well, since her dearest pleasure, good food, was now both a messy nuisance and a source of pain. She decided to starve herself to death before she could die from the cancer. She had heard that anorexics became energetic and frantically happy. Having spent her life frustratingly overweight, she thought she'd like to go out thin and giddy.

When Pearl announced her intention, tube-feeding was attempted and a psychiatric consult requested. I was honored to see her and found her of utterly sound mind and in full control of her ability to make such a decision. Her doctor agreed that the only alternative was unacceptable — to commit her to a hospital where she would be tied down and forcefed. Her children concurred that no one had ever had success in telling her what to do, say, or eat. She wanted psychotherapy, a procedure she had purchased for everyone in her family, but an experience she had regretfully missed. So I saw her weekly with her nurse and, off and on, with her children. She entertained us with tales of her life and travels and the way in which she had maintained control of every life or dinner party she encountered. Both her children understood this ceremony and supported it.

Pearl continued to entertain and to feed her guests, if not herself. When there were no guests, she had a formal dinner with her nurse, though she wouldn't actually eat. It was hard on her friends, and even harder on her nurse, who learned much about control and dignity, even if she didn't like learning it. It was not easy for me either, but the family reassurance helped. Much of the effort was directed toward helping the son prepare for the death. He began to date, and considered working, but thought better of it. It was clear that she was not going to leave her son to her daughter, which was a relief for both.

In this case, a bolt from the blue, the cancer and its mutilating surgery, left an old woman in the position of choosing whether to live out her remaining life in a caretaker situation or to go out with her life's familiar structure. She chose what was familiar. The task was simple — let life proceed as usual. There was no resistance, except from the nurse, who had to rethink her belief that life should be extended whatever changes that entailed.

Her death took months. I'd never seen anyone die so happily and so shockingly in control.

SECTION V

Families in Perpetual Crisis

While it is noble to assist a stricken elephant in rising, it is
foolhardy to catch one that is falling down.

— Ancient Vietnamese proverb

CHAPTER 13

Crisis Prone Families

THE STRUGGLE TO STAY THE SAME

ALL FAMILIES EXPECT to face unexpected crises arriving from unpredictable directions at unpredictable times. All families also should expect crises
at predictable points in the course of the family's development. However,
there are some families who live from crisis to crisis, going through a predictable pattern of crisis behavior at irregular intervals, whatever the stage
of the family's development, whether or not there is some external stress.
These families contain a structural defect, much like an earthquake fault,
which can become exacerbated because some outside force exerts pressure —
or just because the time is "right" for crisis.

What are we to make of those people who center their lives around a
pathological pattern, demanding that everyone respect it and even share it,
no matter how much pain and disability it produces? Anybody can screw
up, and everybody does so, but some people do it habitually and enlist their

233

families in protecting the pattern over and over again. There are alcoholic families, violent families, psychosomatic families, families in which people continually threaten suicide or divorce, have affairs, get into trouble with the law, fear the normal experiences of life, or just carry on a lot. To therapists and perhaps to any other outside observer, this seems insane. Such families, with their repetitive patterns of exacerbated crises, are structurally "defective."

Structurally defective families may experience essentially the same crisis over and over again, and go through therapy over and over again, while successfully protecting themselves from change. People, of course, come into therapy in order to *not* change; in fact, therapy which seems unsuccessful to the therapist may be completely successful to the patients because it succeeds in relieving symptoms while still protecting the family from change. Most people do not want to be made "normal" and have all their unique idiosyncrasies bleached out so they will be just like everyone else. Many of us see our faults as our virtues, and certainly as our identity.

Indeed, faults are merely virtues in excess. The idea of being made normal does not seem merely dehumanizing—it seems downright dangerous. Normality would seem to be disarmament while under attack from a hostile world. People who do destructive things may do them in order to protect against an imagined or exaggerated danger that they believe to be far more destructive. We all grow up with the sense that the world is somehow dangerous, but we each have a different view of where the dangers lie. As we go through our maneuvers and rituals to protect ourselves from the dangers we imagine, we may seem odd indeed to others, who fail to appreciate the dangers we imagine and instead see dangers in just the rituals we use to guard against our dangers.

Natives who coat their hair with yak shit see themselves as providing protection from evil spirits (and perhaps from rape or kidnapping) and feel more secure. To us, they are interfering with their social acceptability; we don't want to be on a crowded elevator with them, much less have them over for dinner. As they sense the world's rejection, they may become uncomfortable and coat their hair with thicker and fresher yak shit, feeling rather baffled when the invitations don't arrive.

We imagine the evil spirits as existing in the world at large, or in those of a different gender or race or social class or ethnic background or generation—whoever has more power or at least power different from our own. Or we imagine the danger as residing within ourselves, in our impulses or our characteristics. We all know people who overcome their sense of being short by becoming loud or aggressive, or their sense of being poor by wearing extravagant jewelry or designer clothes, or their sense of being ugly by painting their faces and glamorizing their costumes.

We all spend a lifetime overcompensating for the deficiencies we think we have and overprotecting ourselves from the dangers we think the world

presents. Even the most destructive behavior is, on some level, a well intentioned effort to provide security and ensure survival and well-being.

Some families center life around a certain set of defenses, a shared view
of where the dangers in life are coming from. Since their view may differ
from that of the therapist, the therapy may seem dangerous indeed. We all,
therapists and patients alike, come into the world with different and invariably faulty instruction books. The harder we try to follow the rules as we
understand them, the less successful we become and the more frustrated and
threatened we feel, so the harder we cling to what we think we know about
how to make our lives work. To the therapist and the world, who watch
people mess up in the same old ways over and over again, this seems like an
oddly perverse dance. We want to relieve the pain by stopping the pattern.
And we're baffled when our efforts to stop this painful perversity are defended against. But it is this painfully perverse dance that is protecting
people from the evil spirits they have been taught to fear. People hold their
yak shit dear. It is their security in a dangerous world. The clumsy therapist
who fails to appreciate this (each of us, at least some of the time) may seem
to be the evil spirit.

It has been postulated by observers of the human comedy that people
choose spouses who share their fears of the world, who believe in the same
evil spirits. Their individual superstitions become their family religion. The
new couple, with shared fears and shared defenses, can then together erect
emotional and behavioral barriers against the assault from the evil spirits in
the world. What looks like yak shit to others looks like shining armor to
them. They then attempt to raise their children with the same fears and
defenses, frantically stifling any counterphobic behavior in the growing children.

Each family is unique in its shared view of what is danger and what is
security. Still, there are some syndromes, some familiar patterns of family
values which are intended to provide protection for the family. And while
they do tighten the family relationships, they are sufficiently at odds with
the rest of the world to make the family crisis prone. The stresses may come
from encounters with a world with differing values or from forces within the
family as turning points are reached—the children differentiate, the marital
partners experience the slings and arrows of life, or expected rewards do not
materialize and disillusionment sets in. There are forces that prompt the
family to reconsider its most cherished and organizing values, and forces
within the family that resist as if the family itself were at stake.

There are certain common family syndromes that value patterns of behavior that the rest of the world might consider pathological or at best
unhelpful. Perhaps every family has some cherished but unworkable patterns. Some give up these patterns when they must. Others just hold more
dearly to the very patterns that seem to work least well. The result is that at
each of life's turning points the same destructive behavior emerges. Its

protection becomes the center of the family's being. Whatever the reality, whether there is a problem, or a holiday, or a lull in which people are getting comfortable, the family response is the same — mother will get drunk, daddy will have an affair, son will threaten suicide, or daughter will throw a fit, and all will pull together. Neurosis is God and must be defended with one's life. It is ritual, an expression of faith in the family.

Nothing is terrible except fear itself.

— Francis Bacon, 1623

Where love is great, the littlest doubts are fear;
When little fears grow great, great love grows there.

— William Shakespeare, *Hamlet*

CHAPTER 14

Phobic Families

HIDING TOGETHER

Some years ago our family was hiking together in the Tetons. Well, not quite together — Ginger, the youngest, had stayed back at the inn hoping to meet some other children around the pool. Betsy and I and the older two hiked up to a wonderful waterfall surrounded by wildflowers. Betsy decided to stay there to read and watch the moose and the mountains while we went ahead. Frank, the runner, decided to run on up the next mountain. Tina and I made it to the top and were on our way down when she met up with some boys who were backpacking and joined them.

So I was trudging along by myself, feeling all alone in that vast country under the big dark blue sky. I don't recall noticing the serene quietness until it was subtly ruffled by an unnatural tinkling sound. Over the next few miles, the disturbance went from a ruffle to a rattle as the tinkling became a clinking and finally a clanging. Over the next hill I saw a small band of people clinging together and realized they were the source of this disturbing noise. When I finally reached them, I saw they were rattling soda cans filled with pebbles, which wasn't easy for them to do since they were also clinging to one another, holding hands and locking arms. There were a mother, a father, grandmother and several children, all of them looking very much alike.

When I reached them, I fear I burst out, "Why the hell are y'all ruining the mountains with that ungodly racket?" They seemed startled and told me they were afraid of bears and were scaring them away with these homemade alarm bells. Surprised at my lack of gratitude to them for protecting me from bears, they insisted that they would not cease in their efforts to protect us all from danger. I threatened to throttle them, but I, being visible, could not frighten them, while the unseen bears could. I mumbled a few obscenities and hurried on down the mountain, away from the clanging.

As the family gathered at Betsy's waterfall, I realized that the timorous family may have experienced more togetherness than our intrepid one — they were together because of their fears, while we, with our adventurous spirits, had spent the day apart.

I see families who can hardly wait for a thunderstorm so they can all snuggle together in the closet to protect themselves from the danger of lightning striking the living room. There are families in which the children must share the parents' bed because the parents are afraid of the child's fear of the dark or the child is afraid the parents will have sex. There are wives who can't leave the house to go to the grocery store, much less to work, and sometimes can't even drive a car. Their husbands must transport and accompany them through life. There are men with a fear that their wives and daughters will be raped or perhaps hear dirty words if they go out at night, so the women go into domestic lockup at sundown. There are women with a fear that their husbands will be seduced by predatory females, so the husbands must never be out of their sights. They find their anxiety to be an effective chastity belt. There are parents who fear their children will learn things contrary to their religion, so they keep the children out of school and teach them at home or in small private schools with the children of similarly minded parents. There are old people, living alone, who must have some friendly relative check under their bed each night for Jack the Ripper. There are children who must have their parents search their rooms each night for Jason, the homicidal hero of *Friday the 13th*.

The impracticality and illogic of our fears were pointed out by a veterinarian who explained that in our country 100,000 people die each year of lung cancer, 50,000 die of automobile accidents, and two of shark bite. Yet when people on the beach think they see a shark, they run to their cars and light a cigarette. Phobias don't protect — they bring people together.

Every phobia has a name. There are names for unusual fears — the fear of needles (alchmophobia), of thread (linonophobia), of the number 13 (triskadekaphobia). And there are names for more common and destructive fears — the fear of closed spaces (claustrophobia), of open spaces (agoraphobia), of foreigners (xenophobia), of misshapen people (dysmorphophobia), of men (androphobia), of women (gynophobia), of homosexuals (homophobia), of heterosexuals (heterophobia), of work (ergasiophobia), of sex (erotophobia). There is even a word for the fear of phobias (phobophobia). There are probably names for the fears we most often deal with—the fear of honesty, the fear of dishonesty, the fear of intimacy, the fear of lack of intimacy, the fear of emotion, the fear of lack of emotion, the fear of therapy, the fear of lack of therapy.

In an individual these phobias may go on for years without creating much of a problem, since the other family members will bow to the phobia and permit the phobic to control their distance and activities. Then, when someone in the family begins to break away, the phobia will be exacerbated and a crisis will ensue. Even the most insignificant of phobias can control the life of an individual and a family.

For instance, a middle-aged woman complained that she couldn't remarry because of her 30-year-old daughter's fear of balloons. The younger woman's balloon phobia began when as a child she refused to go to birthday parties for fear that someone would burst a balloon and frighten her and she would wet her pants and be publicly humiliated. Her parents protected her from social occasions, and she grew up without going to parties. As an adult, this woman couldn't date for fear a man would take her to a festive place filled with revellers bursting balloons. And she couldn't work for fear of office parties. (She had had so little social exposure that she saw the outside world as a five-year old's birthday party.)

She grew up nonetheless, living at home with her widowed mother until the mother decided to remarry. Then the young woman panicked, ostensibly at the thought of going to a wedding reception where there might be balloons, despite the mother's reassurance that it wasn't going to be that kind of party. The mother postponed the marriage until the daughter was more comfortable, but the phobia just intensified. I instructed the mother to reschedule the wedding, arranged for the daughter to live with her sister and work for her brother-in-law, and put her in a group. In the group, after some preparation, the other members blew up balloons and burst them. The young woman screamed but did not wet her pants. Her mother came to the group to see her daughter not wetting her pants at the sound of balloons popping and even popping a balloon herself (rather skittishly). As the daughter moved into a more active life, she explained her more reasonable fears about the remarriage and the mother again postponed the wedding.

Freud treated, indirectly, Little Hans' fear of horses (hippophobia). All the symbolism of horses and father are explored in the famous case, but there is only the briefest mention of the parents' estrangement and planned divorce. Phobias have roots in some actual experience or some symbolic connection, but phobias also have effects. As with all pieces of recurrent behavior, it must be assumed that the predictable outcome of the behavior is indeed the purpose of the behavior. A phobia, even one so seemingly circumscribed as a fear of horses or bears or balloons, can be disabling, can prevent independence, can require the family to hover protectively, and can therefore hold a family together against the forces of wilderness, revelry, or change.

A phobia is a way of telling one's loved ones, "The world scares me. Don't desert me." Treating that interpersonal meaning of phobic behavior seems more productive than exploring the symbolic meaning of the specific phobia. However phobias start, they do not continue unless they work. Usually they are actively encouraged and rewarded by forces in the family. The phobic's purposes can be achieved by having the family actively involved in overcoming the phobia, accompanying the phobic person into the phobic situation. However, it is typical to find more than one person in the family with the same phobia. If all the family members fear the same thing, there may be no one in the family to accompany people into the feared arena. Often it is the smallest child who can bring the other family members out of the closet. As children in immigrant families introduce the family to their new land, the children in phobic families may lead the others into the strange world outside the home.

TREATING PHOBIC FAMILIES

Therapists, rather nonspecifically, expose people to the unfamiliar and, through their own lack of alarm, reduce the fear of the emotions and experiences revealed. With phobic families the therapist may have to be more active than that. I may have to hold the collective hand of an entire family on an elevator ride. Or I may have to find a friend to accompany them on an airplane or onto a rollercoaster. It seems important to help the family discover that they do not need their fears to keep them together.

Contrary to the warnings about symptom substitution, my experience has been that overcoming one phobia liberates people to overcome their other fears—but, of course, only if giving up the phobia does not mean giving up the attention and involvement the phobia brings. Once the family members begin to loosen the family boundaries, to venture out of reach of one another, someone may get phobic of something and pull them all back in. It is safe to assume that members of phobic families don't want much distance from one another. Issues of distance and emancipation must be considered at the same time that the phobic is made to face the phobic situation, with the family hovering over the process of desensitization to the phobia proper.

Peggy Papp (1983) describes the basic assumptions the therapist must make about the reciprocal relationship between the symptom and the system. While Papp's assumptions may not apply to all symptoms, they certainly apply well to phobias. As Papp sees it:

1. The occurrence of a symptom usually coincides with some change or anticipated change in the family that threatens to upset the equilibrium (such as a family member leaving home, getting married, changing jobs, starting school, getting divorced, reaching adolescence, approaching middle age, becoming ill, or dying).
2. The anxiety about this change activates conflicts that have been lying dormant, and these conflicts, rather than being resolved, are expressed through a symptom.
3. The symptom can be a means for either preventing this threatened change or providing a way for it to take place.

In other words, whatever the symbolism of a phobia, whatever its historical roots, the basic definition of the crisis continues to rest with those two essential questions: "Why now?" and "What, above all, do you not want to change?"

Perhaps the most common fear is the fear of demonstrating fear—the fear that one will blush or appear awkward and anxious in public, thereby calling attention to one's weaknesses. This fear of becoming phobic, phobophobia, is also called metanxiety, anxiety about becoming anxious. It may be particularly problematic in those situations where any rational person is at least a little bit anxious—anticipating a public speech, entering a room full of unfamiliar people, or boarding an airplane. The fear is that the anxiety will show, bringing ridicule or even public humiliation. People strapped into their seats in an airplane may fear they will go berserk and begin screaming into the carefully arranged oxygen mask or vomit bag. Both the MRI group (Watzlawick, Weakland, & Fisch, 1974) and Haley (1984) have described treating such cases using an approach originated by Milton Erickson. Their treatment is to prescribe the symptom, enabling the patient to make an obvious display of the anxiety and thereby seeing that the world will not fall apart. Speakers who announce their stage fright, guests who proudly proclaim their shyness, and airplane passengers who tell the flight attendants and the surrounding passengers to expect them to scream and kick and vomit on takeoff and landing will find sympathetic support. This approach is intended for metanxiety, phobophobia, rather than for phobias themselves.

I've often told the story of the woman whose husband, a transsexual, was disinterested in sex with her. She feared that she would become adulterous, as her mother had been in conceiving her, and bring disgrace upon the family. She was encouraged to go to work in anticipation of emancipating herself from the situation. She found a job in the medical school as a research assistant—to a urologist doing research on congenital anomalies of the penis. She spent her day going through library stacks and hospital chart files looking at pictures of misshapen penises. She became increasingly anxious and could no longer enter the stacks. Finally, she could not comfortably enter similar situations, such as the grocery aisles at the supermarket. She feared she would scream in the grocery store. I sent her to the supermarket, instructing her to scream. She went to the soup section and did so. The assistant manager came and helped her gather her groceries and leave the store. Subsequently, she was less frightened in the grocery store and found they always let her go first through the checkout line.

This therapeutic approach reduced the symptom, but some work with the couple was required to deal with the question of "Why now?" (the husband's revelation of his transsexualism), and some work with the family of origin was needed to resolve the matters of "What, above all, do you want not to change?" (the feared loss of her respectability, related to her illegitimacy, if she were free again to seek sexual partners).

Agoraphobia

Agoraphobia is a common, troublesome, and instructive symptom. It is considered to occur almost exclusively in women. It is the fear of the marketplace, of open spaces, and ultimately of leaving home. The inability to leave home can be rather limiting and enormously controlling. If a woman cannot leave home, she cannot work, or socialize, or shop. I've seen several women who could not leave home for any purpose except to go to the beauty parlor, others who could only visit their mothers. Some could go out during the day, but not at night. Almost all could go out if they were accompanied by their husbands. Often the husband had done all the shopping, car pooling, and manifold household errands, while being rather pleased that his wife was keeping the home fires burning. While she was housebound, he got to be more involved with the children and with her. Her agoraphobia was actually being encouraged.

Psychoanalytic theories have related agoraphobia to the fear of breaking free sexually. Feminist theories see it slightly differently (Eichenbaum & Orbach, 1982). They see the home as a substitute for psychological boundaries. "Agoraphobia and claustrophobia are representations of the psychic prison the woman is in — she has not been allowed to be dependent." The phobia represents "her wish to be connected." Agoraphobia is not so much a fear of breaking loose and raping the male population as a way of connecting the home and family to herself.

Obviously, a full-scale agoraphobia is not likely to develop unless there is someone, usually a husband, sometimes a parent or a child, who will reward the agoraphobia with hovering care. It is as if the need for connectedness cannot be expressed legitimately and must become "help" with a "condition" that neither the phobic nor the hoverer explicitly acknowledges wishing it. Agoraphobia is one popular route into a Doll's House marriage, a relationship of intense inequality.

There are times, of course, when the expected hoverer fails to hover and the symptom intensifies without response, or with the wrong response, or with a response from the wrong person, perhaps from a child when it is the husband who is being called for. In such situations the crisis can escalate rapidly and help will be called for quickly. If the desired hoverer does indeed hover on cue, the condition can continue indefinitely, until the husband's health fails or his job is threatened, or until a child enters therapy. Then the working agoraphobic relationship must change.

Agoraphobia may exacerbate at crisis points in a marriage. A woman may become agoraphobic when her husband begins an affair, or when he starts a new job or business, or when she begins to feel unattractive, or perhaps after a child leaves home or starts school. The mothers of school phobic children are often agoraphobic. Or, as if to partially confirm the psychoanalytic theories of agoraphobia, it may develop in response to a sexual attraction the woman has been struggling with, successfully or unsuccessfully. In my experience, agoraphobia is less often a response to the phobic's sexual brinksmanship than to her fear of her husband's sexual brinksmanship.

Agoraphobia is frequently accompanied by depression, and antidepressants are recommended—and are usually helpful. Antianxiety agents, frequently prescribed by the helpful family doctor, probably aggravate the situation by making the woman less active and more dependent. She may become rapidly addicted to minor tranquilizers, which produce panic several times a day as their effects begin to wear off.

The specific treatment for agoraphobia consists of having the hoverer hover in the marketplace rather than in the home. The degree of involvement between the phobic and the hoverer need not be reduced initially, but can instead be directed toward expanding the phobic's range of comfort. In negotiating the resistance to this treatment, it may be discovered that the hoverer is also rather phobic or desires the limitations of the phobic's activities.

Work Phobia

Work phobia (Pittman, Langsley, & DeYoung, 1968) is the adult form of school phobia. In work phobia, the phobic becomes panicky at the thought of going to work and so, instead of going to the job, hides at home. Work phobia overlaps with agoraphobia, and like agoraphobia is often found in adults who were school phobic children. Central is the separation anxiety. The patient is usually a man, perhaps because a woman with the same symptoms would be considered agoraphobic. It is all probably the same thing—the fear of leaving home to go out to whatever activities are expected, whether work, school, or market. The work phobic man typically has been a conscientious worker between periods of unemployment and has a wife or mother at home. He is depressed, worried about something going awry with his relationship with the woman at home, and afraid of leaving her. He may fear his wife will leave him or his mother will sicken and die. He may actually live alone but have a mother or ex-wife who will take care of him during the episode. He may be drinking heavily and deeply depressed, but he doesn't ordinarily have other phobic symptoms. He just wants to stay at home. He may use physical symptoms for a while or find some problematic relationship at work he wants to avoid, but it goes on too long for that to be the issue. Often this pattern has occurred before and is tolerated at the job and at home.

Work phobia can be differentiated from work inhibition and success neurosis. Work inhibition is diffuse, chronic, and characterological. It is the belief that work is the opposite of play, is imposed from outside, and should be resisted. Work-inhibited people want immediate rewards and react to responsibility like a country boy to shoes—it cramps and pinches and feels unnatural. Success neurosis is the fear of retaliation for assertion or achievement, with discomfort in competition and panic upon winning over one's competitors. This is a syndrome seen with increasing frequency among women with successful careers, but it still occurs primarily in men. It tends to occur abruptly in a highly specific situation of competitive success.

The work phobic's wife, like the agoraphobic's husband, may enjoy the hovering and hesitate to end the symptom and let the world and the usual distance come between them. Work phobic men are particularly sensitive to a woman's anxiety—it has become the most compelling of life's realities. They are still school phobic children staying home because "mother" might be upset. Some of these men never grew up and left home at all; they are still school phobic, just too old for school. Others do grow up and leave home, but relapse after a visit from the mother. A second pattern of work phobia occurs when the man leaves home, marries, and attempts to create a marital relationship similar to the mother-child symbiosis. The third pattern of work phobia involves a depressed man, who may not have been school phobic, and a wife who wants him at home, either because she is worried about him or because she is worried about herself. She may, like Caesar's wife on the Ides of March, have a dream that makes her fearful and beg him to stay at home.

The specific prescription for work phobia is the same as it is for school phobia or agoraphobia—the hoverer must get the phobic to work, rarely a difficult task. Negotiating the resistance requires dealing with the relationship and may require antidepressants and/or attention to alcoholism.

THE FAMILY TREATS THE PHOBIA TOGETHER

Usually phobias have been active for a long time, and emergencies are unusual, but the phobia may have to be faced and even overcome before the family can get to your office. Treating phobic families may require extensive preliminary telephone supervision. There is someone in the family from whom the phobic fears separation, and perhaps vice versa. That person can get the phobic out of the house and to your office. The other family members should come also, but frequently won't.

The phobia is easy enough to define, and even to trace historically, but the threat of separation that exacerbates the phobia right now may be trickier to determine. It is probably safe as a general rule to assume all phobias involve an element of separation anxiety, even though the phobia may have other meanings too.

Phobics frequently cannot be calmed until the phobia is faced. If medication is necessary, antidepressants work best, even if the dreaded symptom is panic rather than overt depression. The family is urged to hover as the phobic situation is faced, but not to hover if the phobic is panicking and failing to face the dreaded world. This is not the time to encourage intrafamilial independence—that will come later.

The family members must overcome their fear of the phobic's panic. Gradually, after the phobic situation becomes familiar, they are taught how to get close without going through the phobic process, as they permit alternating intimate activities and distance. Each specific phobia is cured quickly, but tends to recur, so therapeutic availability must be maintained—but intermittently. Phobics are dependent, so the therapeutic relationship should be episodic rather than continuous.

The important aspect of this approach is that the family is brought closer by overcoming the phobia, and freedom from the phobia does not, initially at least, mean independence from the family.

I think that, as life is action and passion, it is required of a man
that he should share the passion and action of his time at peril of
being judged not to have lived.

— Oliver Wendell Holmes, Jr., 1884

When the risk is taken out, there isn't much left.

— Sigmund Freud

CHAPTER 15

Psychosomatic Families

MAKING ONE ANOTHER SICK

THIS SEGMENT of an interview with the Lovely family is not a verbatim
transcript. The interview was recorded only in my memory of it.

MR. LOVELY Dr. Pittman, you remember my wife, Sugar Lovely, and our
daughter Rash, our older son Colic, and young Throb. I'd like for you to
meet my mother-in-law, Mrs. Sweet.

DR. PITTMAN I'm so delighted to see you all again, and how nice to meet
you, Mrs. Sweet. Your daughter has a lovely family. How long ago was it
that we met before?

MRS. LOVELY When we came last year it was right after we'd moved from
Philadelphia and Rash was upset. We thought she was unhappy about
leaving her boyfriend, but we found out she's just allergic to Georgia, so
she's getting shots for that every time she mentions Philadelphia, and
she's much better. She hasn't said a word in months. I do apologize for
not coming back for that second visit as we'd planned last year, but we

have been so busy. We had made an appointment once, but Colic here wasn't feeling well that day. We don't like to talk about problems during the school year—it interferes with the rhythms of Throb's studying. You know how important that is for a boy with a learning disability. Then with Rash's dance recitals, and my father's death, and the boys' soccer, and my husband's traveling, we just couldn't work it in.

DR. PITTMAN Your father's death?

MR. LOVELY We didn't want to talk about that in front of the children. I have a list here of . . .

DR. PITTMAN The children don't know their grandfather died?

THROB Colic found him, hanging in the garage, all purple. Colic threw up. Yuk.

DR. PITTMAN How awful! When was this, Colic?

MRS. LOVELY Dear, was that before or after our trip to Bermuda last month? Rash got the most awful sunburn, and Colic just couldn't eat that strange food. But we had a wonderful time, though the infirmary was not nearly as clean as it should have been. But that's where I heard about this new drug for anxiety. Dr. Quattlebaum wrote a book recommending this new drug, Valium, and it worked wonderfully to help me get through the plane flight. Though Colic was airsick despite the pill and . . .

DR. PITTMAN I am so sorry. Mrs. Sweet, your husband hanged himself last month?

MRS. SWEET Please call me Sweetthing, everybody does. That's what my father called me. Can you believe I'm 75 years old? I think the name was one of the reasons I married Mr. Sweet, may he rest in peace. So now I'm Sweething Sweet. Isn't that nice?

MRS. LOVELY You look cold, Mother. Can I get you a wrap?

DR. PITTMAN What did this mean?

MRS. SWEET No thank you, dear, I'm not cold at all. Are you cold?

DR. PITTMAN Tell me about Mr. Sweet.

MRS. LOVELY Actually, I'm a little warm. Dear, we should have checked the weather report more closely. I fear we've overdressed the children. Rash, you're looking a bit flushed. Are you menstruating? Colic, can you help your sister take off her coat?

DR. PITTMAN Please help me understand this. It must have been awful for all of you.

MR. LOVELY We really don't need to talk about that in front of the children. It is no problem. Everyone got through the funeral without a tear, real troopers. Of course, the children didn't go—they had homework—but the reason we're here is that Throb's grades dropped last month. He barely made the honor roll, and we think it may be because his grandmother has taken his room, so he's in the basement. We need to find a place for Sweetthing to go.

DR. PITTMAN Mrs. Sweet, what has this been like for you?

MRS. SWEET It was a lovely funeral. He had been vice president of the Rotary Club in 1957, and they sent beautiful flowers.

DR. PITTMAN He hanged himself?

MRS. SWEET Mostly gladiolas. I love gladiolas, don't you?

MRS. LOVELY I'm sure it was an accident. That note was just so vulgar. I won't think of that — we burned it. You look thirsty, Throb. I'm sure Dr. Pittman would let you have that Coca-Cola after all, but stir it and get all the gas out.

DR. PITTMAN What was this like for you, Colic?

MR. LOVELY I don't think we should ask him to talk about this . . . he's only 15 and he has soccer practice after we leave here.

MRS. LOVELY Are you comfortable now Rash, or would you like a sweater? Sit up straight, Colic.

THROB I like having Sweetthing staying with us. She lets me stay in the room with her sometimes, and tells me stories. It gets scary in the basement by the garage. I can still smell the . . .

MR. LOVELY Don't bother your grandmother now, Throb. We're here to talk about your grades. So just be quiet while Colic helps you stir your Coke.

MRS. LOVELY Could this be an early adolescent form of hyperactivity? Throb's starting his puberty now. His bowel movements have looked funny lately, and he spends too much time in the shower, and I read that that's a symptom of hyperactivity. Maybe it's the food coloring from the lunchroom at school.

DR. PITTMAN I think I'm beginning to understand Mr. Sweet.

There are people in the world who don't invest passion or action in their lives. They concern themselves with tending their physical survival and believe that survival is threatened by an awareness of their emotional life. They attempt to live without risk, without sensitivity to anything outside their own physical sensations and those of the people they're close to. They experience their bodies rather than their emotions. It isn't much of a life in the best of times, and during transitions and crises these psychosomatic personalities tend to develop physical symptoms that can be uncomfortable or even lethal. Such lives, intended to be lived without risk, are really quite risky.

These people seem to grow up in families which encourage this, and they often end up marrying similar people, so they can go through life quietly, monitoring one another's body functions. If a psychosomatic personality should marry someone of freer emotions, the pressures on both can be painful, even sickening.

Family therapists have described the psychosomatogenic family. Bowen (1966) emphasized the "undifferentiated ego mass" in these families and believed psychosomatic patients were caused by an immature helpless mother who in her job as family diagnostician can't differentiate her anxiety from the illnesses of other family members. Grolnick (1972) drew from Don Jackson's ideas about rigid family rules, deciding that "families with greater rigidity of stucture are associated with increased psychosomatic illness and perhaps chronicity of illness." Minuchin merged the Bowenian and the Jacksonian ideas. Minuchin (1977) and his co-workers (Liebman et al., 1976) have described the psychosomatogenic family as: (1) enmeshed, (2) overprotective, (3) rigid, (4) unable to resolve conflict, and therefore, likely to use a child's symptom to prevent change and to avoid conflict.

Members of these psychosomatogenic families think and feel for one another, so conflict between them can be avoided. The children are enmeshed and overprotected, unable to recognize, define and resolve conflict. They follow rules well. While ignoring one another's emotions, they can be quite attentive to one another's physical discomfort. In the more extreme psychosomatogenic families, a child who threatens suicide might be hushed as all rushed to the aid of the child who had missed her daily bowel movement.

The psychosomatic personality who emerges from such a family is someone who can't perceive and describe feelings, has a poverty of fantasy, can't symbolize linguistically, is conformist in attitude, and tries to strip relationships of depth, conflict, and acknowledged emotional dependency. These people may have a variety of temperaments but are likely to recognize and respect emotions only from their effects on their physical being. They may not even understand, respond to, or remember the emotions or relationships in movies or plays, but they notice the salt on the popcorn and the comfort of the seat.

The psychosomatic personality and the psychosomatogenic family aren't present in all situations in which the psyche affects the soma. Rigidity, enmeshment, and overprotectiveness do not seem to be universal, but conflict avoidance and preoccupation with physical symptoms are standard hallmarks of the syndrome. The variety of possible physical complaints, or full-blown physical illnesses, is at least as great as the number of available body organs capable of developing symptoms.

Minuchin, Rosman and Baker (1978) distinguish "primary" and "secondary" psychosomatic disorders. The primary disorders are those in which physiological dysfunction is already present and exacerbated by emotional reactions. They mention diabetes and asthma as primary disorders which are readily exacerbated. Angina, allergies, and multiple sclerosis are others in which the somatic disease is at the mercy of the buried and untapped psyche. The epinephrine released during anxiety may trigger unhealthy responses from the diseased organ or may merely exhaust a barely compensated organ system.

Minuchin, Rosman, and Baker's "secondary psychosomatic disorders" include those without a primary physiological dysfunction, from the simplest example, hyperventilation, to the most complex, anorexia nervosa, with ulcers, migraine, colitis, alopecia, and rashes somewhere in between. One organ is somehow more vulnerable to the physiological impact of psychological stress, and once that vulnerability develops, the psyche and soma and the family seem to direct all attention to that organ. The human body is set up in such a way that the organ one worries about is the one that attracts all the body's anxiety. A stomach, head, and a patch of skin are no different from an impotent penis or a stammering tongue in refusing to function properly when worried over.

RUNNING SCARED

Perhaps the simplest and most obvious expression of the psychosomatic personality and process is the hyperventilation syndrome, often considered a simple anxiety symptom. I used to see a large number of young men I call the Christian Athletes. They have been trained in their restrictive, concrete, conformist, antipsychological religion to ignore emotion, to have no fantasies, and to avoid symbolic language. (All men receive some training in emotion-free living, but these are A+ students.) Emotions have been handled with physical activity. In the structure of football or track, anger and fear can be acted out and expressed without reference to the individual's emotional state. Once these young men cease athletics and become desk bound by a demanding boss, there is no physical outlet for the emotional reactions and hyperventilation results. This is usually interpreted as a heart attack, which leads to further restriction of physical activity and fear of overt emotions, which of course worsens the condition, until the patient is a helpless invalid. Nowadays, when all good obsessive jocks run a few miles a day, hyperventilation and Christian Athletes are less common. But occasionally one can still be seen in a therapist's waiting room, sitting blandly and expressionlessly, not reading or talking, but taking his own pulse. If the young man is accompanied by his family, his parents and siblings will be calmly taking one another's pulse, while his wife, unnoticed, goes berserk.

Hyperventilation is physiologically simple. Anxiety triggers the primitive fight-flight response and prepares the organism for the violent physical activity of fighting or running away. Epinephrine is released. The heart beats faster and harder, pumping blood to all the muscles, while the lungs breath faster and harder to put oxygen into all that rapidly circulating blood. As the lungs fill with oxygen and the carbon dioxide is blown out, the pH of the blood changes, and respiratory alkalosis results. As the pH rises, calcium becomes less soluble. Calcium is deposited in the bones, and the nerves become more responsive and irritable. The hyperventilator feels a sense of impending doom, bewilderment and unreality. There may be a sensation of "smothering," a strange tightness in the chest, trembling, sweating, and a tingling sensation in the fingers and lips. The person may actually faint, but usually just feels fainting is imminent. It looks and feels like a heart attack, so the usual response is to remain very still.

If the anxiety is triggered by a rattlesnake or burglar, the anxious one is prepared to take action, does so, and then gradually cools down when the danger is gone. If the anxiety is the culturally produced fear of demonstrating a sexual, or fearful, or hostile emotion, things that would have been punished in the family of origin or which seem socially dangerous, the naive body responds to the anxiety in the only way an epinephrine-filled body can — preparation for fight or flight. (Human physiology cannot distinguish between a rattlesnake and an inappropriate erection, between a burglar and a critical boss.) The conscious mind tells the person to sit very still and not let the anxiety show, which of course makes it worse. If it is mistakenly diagnosed as a myocardial infarction, which happens often, subsequent episodes become even more severe, as death, rather than social disgrace, is anticipated.

The venerable treatment for hyperventilation was to have the person re-breath exhaled carbon dioxide. During my medical training, the emergency room had a special area where hyperventilators could sit in a row of chairs and breath into paper bags. Actually, exercise probably works faster and is more physiologically accurate, so having them run up and down stairs is an alternative approach. Either works faster than tranquilizers, and is infinitely more instructive and helpful for future management of episodes.

Most other psychosomatic illnesses are only a little bit more complex than hyperventilation. For instance, a 95-year-old woman lived alone, determined to maintain her semblance of independence. In reality, of course, she had been quite dependent on her daughter for a couple of years, since she lost her driver's license because of speeding when she was trying to get to church on time. Her daughter would call each morning to inquire after the older woman's health, only to be assured that she was fine and the call was quite unnecessary. Occasionally, her daughter would forget to call. The old lady could not call her — that would acknowledge the dependency. Instead she would have a palpitation of the heart, call an ambulance, go to the hospital, and have the hospital call her daughter while she protested that she didn't want to be a bother to the poor girl.

Or, consider the young man who had been raised by a grandmother who loved to dote on him. He was fine-looking, a good athlete, and an excellent mechanic, but he didn't know many words and he used them sparingly. He wasn't very bright, and he expected the same doting from his wife as he had received from his grandmother. When he didn't get it, he began to drink, chase women, and stay out late without calling. She left him. He didn't recall having any reaction to her leaving other than embarrassment, and he didn't want anyone to know she had gone, or why. He especially didn't want to tell his grandmother. However, at the July 4th barbecue, the old lady remarked that he looked feverish and sweaty, and something must be wrong. After that, he devoted his attention to the effort not to sweat, as he didn't want anyone to think there was something wrong and ask him about his wife. Each time he would think of sweating, water would appear over his whole body and run from his armpits. He tried instead to think very intently about not sweating, and the same thing happened. This had gone on for over a year before he came to therapy. The symptom gradually improved after he started telling people, including his grandmother, that his wife had left him.

CASE 20   *A Pain in the Back*

Lumbago came in alone, crying and cringing. His wife Leona had not only refused to come for the appointment, but had kicked him out. He was just about to lose his job at the store, and he didn't understand any of it. It was just that his back hurt. He said he would have to kill himself. He cried some more. I called his wife.

Leona told me that for weeks Lum had pretended to go to work each morning, but then he would sneak back in the house and stay in bed all day, refusing to answer the telephone. The blowup came when Leona came home unexpectedly and found Lum hiding in the closet where he had run when he heard the door open. She told him that she didn't want to be responsible for such a sniveling little wimp. He explained that his back hurt. She reminded him that she'd been through this with him about a dozen times already during their short marriage and that his doctor had told him to use exercise instead of rest. I relayed this all to Lum, who said sheepishly that his back hurt a lot.

I talked to his doctor, who assured me there was nothing wrong with his back except lack of exercise. I got the history. Lum's mother always rubbed his back when he got a backache, and he got a backache every time he feared he'd done something wrong. Leona wouldn't do that. He loved her totally and would really try to do everything right for her, but when he expected a pat on the back for his good works, she got mad. When he tried to have sex with her, it just made her mad. It scared him when she got mad, and made his back hurt. And now she wanted them to get a house and think about having babies. He'd have to take a better job that was being offered him, and that scared him and made his back hurt.

Leona wouldn't come with him to therapy. When she had tried that before, the therapist had blamed her for his wimpiness. She was too busy working as a high school basketball coach to put up with this anymore. But she would let him come home if I'd see him individually for a while, if he'd shut up about his back, and if he'd go back to work.

I agreed to her terms and sent Lum to a masseur, which cleared up his back for a while. I saw him alone, trying to teach him to talk about emotions rather than physical sensations, to get some exercise for his anxiety, to experiment with doing things for fun, and to confront Leona about her detachment from him and from therapy. He did change jobs, he did buy the house, and he did start functioning competently. He even had notable successes. And he felt strong enough after a few years to push for sex. Leona saw that he was changing, but thought it was for the worse. She finally came in to tell me what a bad job I had done. She was right. In my delight over his functional and attitudinal successes, I'd overlooked that he was good at following instructions but had no concept of relationships.

Leona explained what it was like for her to live with Lum. Even with his successes in the world and his relative freedom from his lifelong symptoms, he was still no different with her. She described an evening with Lum. Lum would spend the evening avoiding her, busying himself with his solitary hobbies and the details of living. He would then arrange a ceremony around her favorite TV show, Championship Wrestling. He would fluff up her pillow, put out a flower beside her chair, and grow increasingly frantic in his efforts to please her. While she watched the wrestling matches, he would start telling her what a good boy he'd been for not mentioning his aches and pains. He would try to convince her that he had earned sex, that he had been good and had done what she'd asked, and that he now deserved her therapeutic attention. Leona could see that he was trying, but thought his efforts were all wrong. She saw how little he understood about what she wanted, and she did not want to have to spell out her expectations. She did not want to instruct him on how to make love to her. She then opened up about her own insecurities.

Leona confessed that no man had ever lusted after her, including Lum, and she thought she might like sex better if he did. He came up with the idea that one thing they could do together would be to take a walk. They tried walking together (the most exercise he had ever risked) and actually got rather friendly. They even had sex from time to time, if he hadn't acted pitiful lately and asked for it directly and in some emotional context that included her. Lum finally learned that an organ recital was a poor seduction technique. This surprised him. His mother had always loved to hear about his pains.

There are few more tedious jobs than treating psychosomatic personalities. A particular symptom may miraculously disappear when the conflicts are openly faced, but the basic pattern persists. Bringing psychosomatic personalities to life is a slow and incomplete endeavor—it is hard to keep in mind how little these people have experienced and understood in their lifelong effort to live safely and free of disturbing interaction. There is no way for therapy to make life seem sufficiently free from risk.

EATING DISORDERS

Eating disorders form a special group of psychosomatic illnesses, special in part because of their difficulty, in part because of their voluntary nature, but also because they have attracted the interest of so many family therapy researchers. Generally, there are three specific eating disorders, though they are related and alternate with one another. They are conditions that primarily affect females and are most common in adolescence and early adulthood. All three have been considered outgrowths of society's obsession with thinness in women. They are obesity, anorexia, and bulimia.

Obesity is the result of eating more calories than one burns. The treatment for it is to eat less and exercise more. But that is simplistic. Diets abound, yet the population remains overweight. Society's standards of female beauty involve weights and measures that are absurdly and cripplingly low. Women can spend a lifetime feeling overweight, trying to diet excessively and uncomfortably, hating it, giving up, and settling in to the depressing position of going through life fat. Ambitious parents can turn an adolescent's diet into such a power struggle that the poor little girl gets the only love she knows from the furtive bag of Milanos under her bed. Little boys aren't so severely penalized for their obesity—it can even be considered an advantage for adolescent football players.

In adulthood, obesity is a greater health hazard for men, though it is dreaded as a social disadvantage for women. Successful men don't often want fat wives—it is not a status symbol. And whatever the sexual advantages of a soft pillow versus a bag of bones, fat is not considered sexy unless it is in the breasts, which may not be how nature distributes it. So men, of whatever weight, may humiliate and even reject a wife of healthy size and shape and start a power struggle which destroys the relationship, the self-esteem of both, and any diet that might be attempted. Preoccupation with diet just produces the usual psychosomatic syndrome of worsening a situation by focusing one's anxiety on it. Families can get into ego-destroying, marriage-threatening or even life-threatening crises in their efforts to control one another's eating and weight. Such struggles don't work, and that becomes obvious long before family members are at one another's throats about what is being stuffed down them.

It has been estimated that 50% of female college students rely occasionally on vomiting to keep weight down without having to diet. Female flight attendants often vomit before their monthly weight checks. The recurrent cycle of bingeing and purging is terribly unhealthy, burns the esophagus, rots the teeth, and lowers the potassium level in the blood. It is also expensive and repulsive. Weight can be kept quite stable by this method, while hunger never has to be faced. Bulimia, as it is called, has recently been considered an illness, though it is more properly a bad habit with features of addiction. The real problem underlying bulimia is the familiar struggle with ideals of weight and their implications for dependence and independence, perfection and imperfection (Root, Fallon, & Friedrich, 1986). Those who binge and purge have some things in common with those who suffer from the less voluntary forms of psychosomatic illness. They too overvalue and are at the mercy of physical sensations. Their families are much like those of other psychosomatic patients. In fact, bulimia regularly alternates and coexists with anorexia. The bulimics are healthier perhaps, or at least at a healthier stage of the illness, but the dynamics seem the same—up to a point.

Anorectics are nearly always female. These girls have a bizarre body image—they do not see their skinniness. They find any body fat disgusting—perhaps because it would make them look as if they were growing up and becoming sexual (Bruch, 1978). They experience no hunger (if they do, they gorge themselves and vomit). Their energy does not seem to wind down. They are in a dance of death. They can be bribed, coaxed, seduced, cajoled, or forced to eat, but they cheerfully keep dancing around the food and refuse to eat it. Such a girl can devote a full day to preparing a meal of one lettuce leaf, and feel sated after the first bite, nauseated after the second, and berserk if anyone is foolhardy enough to force a third.

This is unlike anything else, and has no counterpart in other psychosomatic conditions. People with ulcers or asthma or rashes know they hurt and gasp and itch—they may not know what their mind feels, but they know what their body feels. In anorexia, rather than the usual psychosomatic overawareness of the body, there is a refusal to consider it and even an effort to make it go away. Selvini Palazzoli, in *Self Starvation* (1978), saw the pathology as just this—the anorectic treats her body as if it were not her own and refuses to pay attention to its signals. Her self may enter adolescence, but her body still belongs to her parents.

Anorexia, like compulsive jogging, might be seen as a treatment for depression. Anyone who has dieted strenuously or fasted has noticed the "high" that comes from burning one's own fat. Anorectics, who were often overweight before beginning the diet that proceeded on to anorexia, could become addicted to the habit of getting "high" on the combination of self starvation and exercise. Eating then causes a crashing down from that "high" into the underlying state of depression. Antidepressants are often amazingly effective for anorexia, and interestingly so for bulimia. Also, depression is common, if not universal, as anorectics begin to gain weight.

The families of anorectics are like other psychosomatic families, except more so. They are unique in their premorbid preoccupation with weight. In most cases, either the patient or the patient's mother was obese and concerned about matters of weight and dieting prior to the onset of the anorexia.

Treatment of anorexia, with its perverse, seemingly voluntary symptom, has ranged from the behavioral (which works well briefly, but tends toward relapses) to the psychoanalytic (which usually worked so slowly, if at all, that hospitalization and medical emergency treatment must be a regular adjunct to therapy). Family treatment has reported good results, yet the treatment techniques have been quite divergent. The Milan group (Sevini Palazzoli et al., 1978) reported good results after widely spaced interviews using circular questioning and the invariable paradoxical prescription to the family, "Don't change." Minuchin, Rosman, and Baker (1978) used a family meal with therapists, in which the therapists would encourage the parents to force the girl to eat, another paradoxical maneuver since the parents clearly could not force the child to eat. All hell would break loose while the parents demonstrated their good intentions, as well as their helplessness. Presumably they subsequently stopped the power struggle over food.

One might conclude that the therapeutic element in all of these approaches is not in the various invariable prescriptions or the forced feeding, by family or nurses or behavioral therapists, but in the demonstration that the anorectic alone must take control of her own body and learn awareness of her own physical sensations and emotions. In treating eating disorders in general and anorexics particularly, I believe the most important step in therapy is the therapist's expression of total bewilderment, frustration, and defeat, as well as encouragement of the family to express the same.

CASE 21   *Perfectly Beautiful*

Moonbeam, in her mid-twenties, was the next to the youngest of ten children. She had always been the focus of her mother's concern because of a disfiguring nose. As an adolescent she had four nose jobs. The family moved, and in the new community she became a beauty queen and later an exotic dancer. Moonbeam was her obese mother's pride. When the youngest child grew up, the mother kicked out her noncommunicative husband, started her own successful business and was quite happy. Moonbeam gained a few pounds, lost weight through bulimia and finally became anorectic. She came to the city so she could go to an outpatient eating disorders clinic. She gained a few pounds and became depressed, and the clinic had her involuntarily hospitalized. Her mother came and got her out and brought her to see me.

Moonbeam was bulimic, at a very low weight, and preoccupied with obesity. I saw her with her estranged parents. She demonstrated to us that when she did a strange sideways contortion there was a slight fold of fat visible at her waist. The interview centered around her parents' separation, which neither had any feelings about. The mother was in the habit of calling Moonbeam daily to get a report on what she ate and what she vomited and what the vomitus looked like. Her description of four partially digested Big Macs with pickles is emblazoned on my memory. I forbade her from discussing her bulimia or her weight with her mother, who began to call me regularly to check on her.

The mother, however, then decided to send the perfect younger son to live with his sister. He, a powerful athlete named Moose, threatened to get her eating under control. I saw him once with his sister, and explained that the problem was not one of discipline, but one of body image. She showed him her fold of waistline fat when she contorted to the side. Moose took off his shirt, revealing an almost perfect body, to show Moonbeam how his left nipple stuck out slightly, if viewed over his right shoulder as he leaned forward. He described the pain and embarrassment this had caused him.

Moonbeam laughed at the absurdity of both Moose and herself, and gained five pounds over the next week. The bulimia continued even as she gained weight and fretted about it. She soon found a man and got engaged and began to tell him about her vomitus. He was enthralled, but told her he wouldn't marry her until she stopped this nonsense. She did. Soon, her father developed cancer, and her mother took him back to nurse him and stopped calling her. Moonbeam has had no further eating problems, but I don't know which of these various factors was the one which worked.

I'm not convinced that we know the whole story with anorexia yet, but I agree that it is an addiction. I think we may overly pathologize the bad habit of bulimia. Certainly the societal revulsion at female fat is a factor, and bulimia may be best seen as a passive-aggressive rebellion against society's concern with diet and weight. Whatever other factors are involved, the treatment of eating disorders involves family therapy for the psychosomatic family. There are many techniques, planned or spontaneous, that will have the desired therapeutic effect of breaking up the psychosomatic family alliance and restoring everyone's body to its rightful owner. Only then can the owner begin to learn how to oversee its care — and feeding.

TREATING PSYCHOSOMATIC FAMILIES

The treatment for psychosomatic conditions should be simple enough, at least in concept. The psychosomatic person must learn to monitor his or her emotions before the sensitive organ does so. The mind must feel the emotion before the adrenalin hits the body. The trick is to get the patient's attention away from the body and onto the workings of the mind and the interaction with others. In practice, it is not easy to look past one's stomach or pulse to one's relationships. Biofeedback maneuvers have been helpful in teaching people how the emotions affect body functions. But learning how to feel emotionally rather than physically may seem dangerous.

The family therapy of psychosomatic disorders involves at least four areas of system concern: enmeshment, overprotectiveness, rigidity, and conflict avoidance. The enmeshment of the family may take the form of everyone's monitoring everyone else's physical functioning and reading everyone else's mind — perhaps so well that self-expression seems unnecessary and psychological awareness never develops. Psychosomatic children may never develop autonomy, even over their own bodies. They may become so sensitive to one another that they experience one another's anxiety, or hunger, or sadness, or pain, as if it were their own.

The overprotectiveness of psychosomatic families seems to encourage the one with the symptoms to experience danger and therefore become symptomatic at the point of impending conflict. The patient's symptoms then distract the family from the danger of actually fighting something out.

The rigidity of the psychosomatic family enlists everyone into maintaining the status quo. Change is abhorred and feared, growing up is discouraged, and negotiation for change impossible. Symptoms can be brought forth to prevent almost any threatened change.

The conflict avoidance of psychosomatic families makes therapy and change very difficult. They don't even acknowledge that there is conflict, much less that they don't like it. Yet, psychosomatic families are sufficiently involved with and concerned about one another, attentive to the rules, and determined not to fight about anything that they can be wonderfully cooperative patients in dealing with a therapist who doesn't scare them too badly by threatening to change them.

Step 1: Emergency Response

Serious medical emergencies may bring the psychosomatic patient into therapy. The situation may be seen as life-threatening. Yet the family may have little sense that psychotherapy of any sort is indicated, and certainly family therapy seems to them to be an odd choice, since they have no conflicts at all. If the therapist is gentle and unobtrusive and seems to know something about the condition, or if he is involved with or endorsed by the medical referrer, the family will cooperate and arrive with medical records.

Step 2: Involving the Family

The family, if available, is usually cooperative, however baffled. The treatment, however, is long and often dull, and the relatives may begin to fall away. They need to be encouraged to come—they respond dutifully to praise—as they have no motivation of their own. It is particularly important to keep up the involvement of the healthier siblings or spouse or daughter-in-law—or whoever has become less rigid and afraid of conflict, even if that relative is freer from the enmeshment and web of overprotectiveness. Alternate sessions without the most enmeshing forces of the family can be tried. Alternating family and group therapy can also be liberating.

When a psychosomatic personality has married someone with greater tolerance for conflict, the freer spouse may lose patience with the psychosomatic and with the therapy and try to speed it up, which just scares the psychosomatic one. No emotional tone can satisfy both spouses, which of course is at the root of the problem.

Step 3: Defining the Problem

This must be done gently. If the family sees their hovering defined as *the* problem, if there is a hint of *conflict* beneath the surface, if there is a threat to make anyone's marriage more communicative (i.e., more openly conflictual), the therapy may fall apart. Good definitions to use include things like: "He feels the pressures in his stomach rather than his head," or "She hasn't had enough experience on her own to face life without a lot of anxiety," or "He worries too much about the things you don't talk about." That works better than "You do his feeling for him," or "You're keeping her too close," or "He's become your marriage counselor." The one with the symptoms is seen as the one with the problems, and everyone else is just there to help. The problematic family problems will become apparent to all in good time. It must also be kept in mind that these psychosomatogenic dynamics are relative, may even be past, and may not even be present at all.

Step 4: General Prescription

Sex, exercise, joy and triumph are good for almost anything that ails you — except maybe anorexia and angina. So, generally, is following your doctor's advice — unless your doctor has prescribed tranquilizers to shut you up. Everyone in the family with an ill person also has certain remedies, most of which inhibit normal functioning. The patient needs to be given permission to do healthy things, and everyone who has been hovering, protecting, and stifling the patient can be enlisted in promoting health, which usually means breaking some family rules against doing healthy things.

Step 5: Specific Prescription

The specific prescription for psychosomatic illnesses cannot be given right off, but much of it is in the process of the therapy. The family members, in therapy, are encouraged to talk openly about things they don't ordinarily talk about, to comment openly about interactive issues, and to refuse to respond to feelings that are being felt physically rather than voiced. Just having the members explain their state of mind and their experience of life to one another is a step toward differentiation. Points of disagreement are gently noted, and rules are thrown open to negotiation. Families can be assigned tasks which move the members out of one another's reach, permit some independence, and soften the rigidity. Specifically, the marriage is shored up against the interdependency with the children or the in-laws. Most importantly, the patient's responsibility for his or her own symptom and its medical treatment must be encouraged. The symptom cannot be permitted to be a transaction with the family, or the distraction from the family's emotional life. The symptom must be dealt with by the symptom bearer alone.

Step 6: Negotiating the Resistance

The symptom bearer is likely to produce a medical crisis that will get all attention back on the symptom. This may be undercut by predicting it. The family can ally against the therapy by surreptitiously worrying about one another and huddling together in secret orgies of overprotectiveness. The details of the medical management of the symptom can distract, even as the symptom improves. Perhaps the most difficult resistance to overcome is that against conflict. The therapist must wait for the conflict to emerge, must sustain it and make it enjoyable, without letting it get intense enough to terrify the family or the therapist. There is no specific conflict that needs to be resolved; instead the point is to make the process of dealing with conflict seem safe, so the therapist may be choosy and even cautious about which conflicts are dealt with first.

Step 7: Termination

It must be made clear from the beginning that therapy will be long and may take an unfolding series of forms. The family must settle into therapy. The therapy may not last that long, but it should be approached as if it will, just to keep impatience and desperation from making it too intense.

The point of therapy with psychosomatic families is to take people who are preoccupied with their death and gently make them aware of life.

Alcoholism is a "profession."

—Malcolm Lowry, *Under the Volcano*

Alcoholism isn't a spectator sport. Eventually the whole family
gets to play.

—Joyce Rebeta-Burditt, *The Cracker Factory*, 1977

CHAPTER 16

Substance Abuse

A SPORT THE WHOLE FAMILY GETS TO PLAY

ETHYL ALCOHOL is a chemical much like ether. A little bit is tranquilizing, a little more is exciting and agitating, still more is anesthetic, and a heavy dose is fatal. It is both poisonous and addicting. If it were newly discovered, it would never have received approval from the FDA. It is amazingly popular and always has been.

There are people who have used alcohol throughout their adult lives to achieve daily tranquilization and intermittent agitation at socially prescribed times, and neither they nor their friends and relatives consider it a problem. They may be as elegant as the wine ads, as successful as the whiskey ads, and as gusto grabbing as the beer commercials. Other people, who achieve agitation less predictably, or who achieve anesthesia more often or tranquilization earlier in the day, are called "alcoholics" and are considered social outcasts.

The diagnosis of alcoholism is difficult because it is stigmatizing. It is not a diagnosis people apply to themselves first. It is an insult hurled at people. Just getting someone to acknowledge that he or she is an alcoholic may be the most difficult and powerful step in solving the problem.

The criteria for diagnosing alcoholism are vague. So many people have made alcohol a routine or even vital part of their lives that the diagnosis may be made rather subjectively—"an alcoholic is someone who drinks more than I do." The usual guideline is that someone is an alcoholic if his or her drinking interferes with functioning or relationships. By that guideline, the adolescent who drinks six beers and passes out at the school prom is an alcoholic, as is the occasional ceremonial wine sipper married to an anxious teetotaler. Of course, if the adolescent passes out a second time, or if the spouse of the teetotaler considers it important enough to sneak an occasional sip despite the predictable explosion, the drinking is certainly problematic.

Obviously, there are various patterns of alcoholism. The issue is not necessarily the amount or even the frequency of the drinking behavior. It may be the appropriateness. The medical, chemical realities of alcohol's effect on the body and brain get lost behind the social and moral concepts of what is right and proper.

We tend to think of alcoholics as being male, and male alcoholics are more obvious and more numerous. Two-fisted drinking has been considered "manly." Young boys go off to college or the service to learn to "hold their liquor," i.e., achieve a level of addiction that would permit them to drink a few drinks without throwing up or passing out. Traditionally, ladies are supposed to drink more moderately and ceremonially, if at all. It should be remembered, however, that social pressures against male abstinence and female indulgence are greater in some social classes.

Many female alcoholics remain "hidden," doing their drinking fairly quietly at home and restricting their lives, and their families' lives, around it. I recall a dry alcoholic whose liver and esophagus had been so damaged by her past drinking that she knew she would vomit blood and die if she drank alcohol at all. She did so, and her dying words were "Nobody can blame me for drinking champagne at a wedding. It would have been rude not to do so." Another woman assured me she had been raised to be a perfect lady and never drank anything except sherry in the evening. Further questioning revealed that she drank a quart of it at a time. A third woman told me she drank a quart of gin a day. I expressed shock. She recoiled, "You're just being moralistic about alcohol. You wouldn't react that way if I drank a quart of milk."

Per capita alcohol consumption is lower in our society than in many others, and is decreasing. It is higher among American Indians and the Irish, lower among Jews and Orientals. There seem to be genetic factors at work here, although cultural factors are most obvious. We tend to think of alcohol use as highest among males of the under classes, and blame it on society. Drink is considered the "curse of the working class," but it may be just as true that "work is the curse of the drinking class." Alcoholism is a profession and leaves little time and energy for second jobs. Except among the very rich, whose wealth is not their fault, heavy drinking causes people to be downwardly mobile — in every sense.

Alcoholism is a frustration for families and for therapists for several reasons. First, it is very difficult to stop people from doing something they are determined to do, particularly if they enjoy demonstrating that you can't stop them.

Second, alcoholism has been considered sinful, which makes it attractive, daring, defiant, and guilt-producing — a compelling combination for bad little boys and girls. Guilt does not stop people from drinking; rather, it seems to encourage self-destructive, escapist, hostile behavior.

Third, alcoholism has been considered a "disease," therefore beyond the diseased one's control. This concept has been horribly misunderstood. It was intended as a metaphor to help the alcoholic escape the moral burden of having a bad habit. It has rapidly become a justification for inaction and determined helplessness on the part of the alcoholic and the alcoholic's family.

Fourth, there has been the myth of "social drinking," the idea that some level of alcohol use is necessary for normal social functioning and that anyone who does not use it is joyless, rude, and weak. From this perspective a "true cure" requires regular, controlled drinking. It is sadistic to define health as the regular use of an addictive drug to which the person has already become addicted.

Fifth, alcoholics have been considered a homogenous group, as if all are doing essentially the same thing for the same reasons. Mansell Pattison (1979) makes a compelling argument for the multivariant nature of alcoholism, as well as for the corresponding need for a variety of treatment approaches according to the nature, severity, stage, and circumstances of the alcoholic problem.

PATTERNS OF ALCOHOL PROBLEMS

Developmental Crises

There are several rather distinct patterns of alcohol problems. First there is the developmental crisis of alcoholism. Children and adolescents who have had little experience with alcohol use may be naive in their judgments of what would be an appropriate dose. Children who get into the family liquor cabinet may poison themselves with it and become quite sick or even die from the overdose. Adolescents usually feel a need to learn to drink and nearly always start with a dose that is too high for a beginner. Having seen their parents chug down six beers or sip three scotch and sodas each evening, they may assume that is a safe dose, only to find themselves wildly intoxicated, or even comatose, a few hours later. Almost all teenagers go through one or more episodes of inadvertent drunkenness before finding a safe way to drink. During these exploratory episodes, they may wreck cars, vomit in the bed, pass out on the beach, end up in jail or at the emergency room of the hospital. They may go through this process over and over until they get it right. Parents may become frantic and punitive; they may even become sufficiently alarmed to hospitalize the child in an alcohol treatment center. These near universal experiences, frightening and infuriating as they are, have nothing to do with alcoholism.

There are, however, alcoholic children, those who drink a little each day before school or before going to sleep. They are treating their normal or abnormal adolescent anxiety with an addictive drug, perhaps to protect their family from having to share the fears of their age and the problems of their family. Children can become addicted to alcohol at an amazingly early age — eight is no longer shocking — and the percentage of alcoholics among those in their teens and early twenties is disturbing. These kids know they are in trouble and usually welcome intervention and treatment. Many do go on to be adult alcoholics and follow the usual pattern of those who seem to inherit the genetic tendency. Many drink during their stormy youth and have no adult problems with the drug. Quite obviously, the families of these childhood alcoholics are distracted elsewhere.

Another group that might be considered developmental are those older people who have been drinking at what they consider a moderate level daily for a lifetime, only to find that as their brain and arteries age the usual one or two drinks has become not a tranquilizing dose, but an agitating one. They might not implicate the familiar alcohol in their nocturnal organic confusion and may continue using it right into the nursing home.

Situational Crises

There are occasional cases that might be considered situational crises of alcoholism. People who have used alcohol only sparingly and intermittently, if at all, may abruptly begin using it daily or even hourly. This is usually a misguided effort to treat either physical pain or depression. Once the alcohol pattern becomes regular, the alcohol itself produces the daily depression for which the alcohol seems to be therapeutic. Alcohol seems to release endorphins, producing a brief sense of well-being, which permits surcease from the depression. But in doing so it depletes the brain levels of norepinephrine so that four hours later the person is actually clinically depressed and remains so the next day. Much insomnia is brought on by this mechanism: A few drinks will permit sleep but produce subsequent depression and awakening a few hours later in the typical depressive "dark night of the soul," complicated by a hangover. This cycle may be aggravated further by adding sleeping pills or minor tranquilizers to the already confusing brain chemistry. Perhaps even antidepressants are added, without discontinuing the alcohol; this proves disastrous, since alcohol reverses the effects of the antidepressants.

Such situational alcoholism may go on for months, with the alcohol seen by the alcoholic as the solution rather than the problem. The family may finally decide the drinker is suffering from the disease of alcoholism and try to remove the alcohol without addressing the already aggravated depression. This alienates everyone further. Once the depression is addressed and a more appropriate treatment for the depression found, the alcoholism magically disappears.

On the flip side, someone going into a manic episode may suddenly begin to use alcohol excessively in an effort to govern the mind's stuck accelerator. Many episodic alcoholics and binge drinkers are camouflaged manic-depressives. Consequently, lithium is dramatically therapeutic for some alcoholics.

STRUCTURAL CRISES

Structural alcoholism, by far the most common pattern, is the focus of most of the literature and the frustration of therapists and families. It occurs in two overlapping varieties—the *habit alcoholic* and the *compulsive alcoholic*. The habit alcoholic is someone who drinks daily, typically in the evening after work or while preparing dinner. Often the drinking involves an element of ceremony and sociability, celebrating the end of the workday. The drinking starts when "the sun drops below the yard arm." The drinking is done openly and with the spouse or coworkers or neighbors. Gradually, the drinkers become habituated to the usual dose and begin to raise it from one drink to two and then to three or more, achieving a level of intoxication that postpones the dinner under preparation or results in agitation and conflict or ends with one or more the the drinkers dozing off in a chair in front of the television. Some couples drink themselves into oblivion night after night, rarely seeing one another or their children while sober enough to conduct a relationship.

It is hard to convince someone who is drinking as he or she has always done that the proper term for this activity is alcoholism. These people are addicted to alcohol and may never have gone 48 hours without it, but they don't fit their own picture of alcoholism, which to them involves gutters and winos and people too drunk to hold a job. The habit may not even be a daily one. There are alcoholics who control their drinking all week and stay drunk all weekend. They may be more available during their days off from drinking, but they may be even more imperious, as they demand retribution for each moment of sobriety.

This pattern may go on for years, even decades, before reaching a crisis point. The crises in these situations occur when one member of the couple decides to stop the pattern, and the other one can't seem to do so. One may be hospitalized for something physical and may, to everyone's surprise, go into delirium tremens. Or one may develop an ulcer, or depression, or go on a diet, and give up the drinking for those health reasons. Or one may begin to notice that the other is drinking more and needs regular caretaking. Or the kids may begin to complain. One spouse stops the pattern. The other continues drinking, but it is now exposed and unsociable. The drinker feels deserted and picked on. There is conflict about the drinking, which usually escalates it and may drive it underground, or may cause the drinker at the point of agitation to fight rather than sing. If the couple enters therapy, the therapist may challenge the desirability of the drinking. The couple may have to choose between divorce and the continued alcohol habit.

An interesting variant on this habit pattern occurs in those marriages in which the spouse with the lowest tolerance, usually the wife, is considered an alcoholic, while the husband continues to drink daily too, but at a slightly more controlled rate. If the "alcoholic" spouse sobers up, leaves, or dies, the remaining spouse's alcoholism becomes exposed.

It helps to understand the nature of the drug. Habit alcoholism is an addiction, though often a carefully modulated one. The lives of habit alcoholics center around the effort to forestall withdrawal. (Those who drink only on weekends may spend the week in mild alcohol withdrawal, racing to reach Friday before DTs.) These people don't feel very good all day and may keep themselves going with intense activity and caffeine, just waiting until they can get relief with a drink. They may not crave more than the usual daily dose of alcohol, and they may be able to control their drinking precisely, although the drinking does control their lives. At the point at which they are called upon to change their drinking pattern, they may be shocked that anyone sees it as a problem. They have seen the alcohol as their source of pleasure, they don't consider themselves alcoholics in any sense, and they may even assume everyone drinks the way they do. Since they don't feel good during the times they are not drinking, they may assume the problem is their job or their marriage and family. They may well prefer to give up their work or their family rather than their alcohol. If they do give up their daily habit of drinking alcohol, they may evidence no pathology at all, no disturbance of family relations, and little craving for alcohol. They may not have any genetic tendency toward alcoholism, but may just have gotten into the habit of daily drinking, thinking it was normal, safe, and fun.

The classic alcoholic pattern is that of the compulsive drinker. These people cannot drink a little bit of alcohol. It is as if exposure to alcohol releases some biological devil that compels continuing drinking to the point of unconsciousness, to be resumed with equal frenzy when the drinker awakes. These people are clearly aware of the problem and try to control it. Some abstain for varying periods of time. Others measure or count carefully and try to keep the daily drinking at what they or someone else considers an appropriate amount. This may even work for a time.

This pattern seems to involve a genetic predisposition. Perhaps these people lack some natural toxic response that most people have to alcohol. They seem able to handle prodigious amounts without getting physically sick, and they seem to have had this ability since their first encounters with the drug. They may even get more pleasure from alcohol than most people do — it certainly seems to them to be worth throwing everything else away for another bout of drinking. Such people require caretakers, since they are in pitiful shape by the time they return from each binge. The alcoholic may come to consider the binges to be "vacations," although they are usually solo and rarely scheduled.

Alcoholics of the binge or compulsive variety may consume less alcohol per year than the habit alcoholics, but they are more disruptive, as they are unpredictable. The alcoholic may drink moderately and predictably — or not at all if the problem has previously been defined and treated — and then suddenly "fall off the wagon." During the periods of sobriety, the family scurries around trying not to upset the alcoholic with any reality, while pretending to serve cheerfully. The dry drunk commands even more attention and control than the wet one, since no one knows what will be the offense or disappointment that will trigger the next binge. All occasions or holidays or social events are to be dreaded. Every family member is required to behave perfectly at all times — no one must ever relax and be normal, as the alcoholic might just use that unguarded word or gesture as justification for the next binge. Other family members may sense that it is coming yet are helpless to prevent it.

Or the alcoholic may sadistically wait a bit longer between binges and permit the family to relax and commit the deadly error of not centering the family's whole existence around the alcoholic's commanding sobriety. Suddenly the fatal error is committed and the alcoholic begins the binge, perhaps with a bang, perhaps with a whimper. The alcoholic may disappear for a while or may retire with well hidden stash to a bedroom fortress. All efforts at functioning cease, and the family anxiously awaits the climax — violence or suicide or disappearance. This may go on for days or even weeks — the alcoholic may sleep for a while (but no one else can) and then awaken and terrorize the family some more. After the alcoholic's physical state has deteriorated sufficiently, the hospital may provide relief. Sometimes the binge ends as suddenly and unpredictably as it began, with everyone expected not to mention it.

Episodic binge drinkers drink compulsively. Whatever the nature of their genetic predisposition, it seems real and should be considered as such. These people may be able to subsitute other drugs for the alcohol; indeed, they seem easily addicted to minor tranquilizers — or for that matter to just about anything that either reduces pain and anxiety or produces euphoria. Unlike the habit alcoholics, compulsive alcoholics can never resume normal drinking safely.

The alcoholic family is tyrannized by the alcoholism. If the alcoholism is of the habit variety, it is predictable, however unpleasant. The family can expect the alcoholic or alcoholics to be anesthetized or agitated nightly, unavailable for relationships or problem-solving, in need of attentive care-taking, irritable or explosive or just inappropriate or irrelevant if stimulated, yet still demanding to be the center of power, of concern, and of attention. The alcohol habit may involve drinking away from home and stumbling in each evening too drunk to be helpful or enjoyable, sometimes alone, some-times with old drinking buddies or passing strangers, all expecting to be fed and put to bed. There may be no way to predict when the drunk will arrive home, but full court and ceremony are expected immediately. There is the dread of having the drunk stumble home to fight or keep everyone awake, but there is the greater fear of the drunk failing to come home, as the family awaits a call from the police, the hospital, or the morgue. (Alcoholics rarely call home, as they don't know their ultimate level of intoxication until they have reached it, and they don't want to be fussed at for something small or reasonable like running late.)

Families who live with either the binges or the habitual periods of intoxi-cation are under siege, whether the alcoholic is drunk or sober. The family is held captive. The normal ups and downs of life are not permitted. Crises cannot occur. Crisis resolution is impossible. There can be no change, no negotiation of anything. If the alcoholic's spouse is not sufficiently protec-tive and rescuing, if the spouse complains or attempts to control the drink-ing, other family members may come to the rescue. The alcoholic is so guilt-producing, so willing to destroy anyone in the effort to assign responsibility for the drinking to someone else's imperfection, that tyranny reigns. These are the most inflexible of families.

Children of alcoholics (Woititz, 1983) may be painfully guilt-ridden. They may strive for unprovocative perfection. Failing that, they may decide to grab their turn at tyrannizing the family and dramatically call attention to their own crises. They may threaten suicide or run away or throw temper tantrums. Since the alcoholic parent can outdisrupt them, they may give up and go underground, conforming on the surface and rebelling below, often abusing drugs and alcohol themselves, feeling a depressive entitlement to be as destructive as the parent. They receive little accurate social learning, and no training in openness and honesty, but careful instruction in manipulation and guilt.

Co-Alcoholism

The interaction between an alcoholic and his or her family is sufficiently startling to have been the subject of many theories and myths. Alcoholism has even been thought to be caused or required by families. Standing in contrast to the victim position taken by so many spouses, children, and parents of alcoholics is the concept of the "co-alcoholic." The co-alcoholic is the overfunctioning partner of an alcoholic. Even though this concept runs the risk of implying that the overfunctioning *causes* the alcoholism, rather than simply *permitting* it to continue, family therapy for alcoholism has increasingly focused on the family's overfunctioning as a factor which can and must be changed in solving the problem. Bepko and Krestan (1985) detail this in *The Responsibility Trap*.

Eric Berne's *Games People Play* (1964) popularized his description of the "game" of "Alcoholic" and the many roles taken by those who would later be considered "co-alcoholics." In Berne's description the game has as many as five players. First there is the Alcoholic, the one who does the drinking and wins the game by demonstrating that the other players not only can't stop him (or her), but also must take responsibility for the drinking behavior. The other players are Persecutor who "makes" Alcoholic drink by berating him for his behavior, Rescuer who protects him while pleading with him to change his ways, Patsy, who sympathizes and enables, and Connection who supplies. In real life, Persecutor, Rescuer, Patsy, and Connection may all be played by one or two players. Alcoholic's wife may take all four roles, supplying the alcohol, supporting him, rescuing him, and then berating him until she "drives him to drink." This exhausting game seems based on the idea that making the alcoholic feel guilty for the alcoholism is more rewarding to the loved ones than the alcoholic's sobriety would be. The spouses of alcoholics seem to bounce back and forth between being Rescuer and Persecutor, usually being careful to reward drinking behavior by rescuing, to punish sobriety by persecuting, and to end the sobriety by enabling.

Steinglass (1976) and Paolino and McCrady (1977) reviewed the hypotheses at that time about how marriage and alcoholism interact. Both reviews notice that everybody recommends a family approach to alcoholism, though there are few data, then or now, to support its effectiveness. Also, despite the enthusiasm with which family therapy is recommended, there is little enthusiasm among family therapists for actually doing it. Part of the problem is that there has not been any compelling explanation of how the marriage produces the alcoholism. There is certainly plentiful evidence that the alcoholism consumes the marriage. Paolino and McCrady's literature review dispels the notion that alcoholics' spouses have some sort of common pathology or even have more pathology of any sort than the average person. They also dispel the idea that an alcoholic's spouse needs the alcoholic behavior to prevent the spouse's decompensation. Steinglass looked at the literature supporting the notion that alcoholism is "paradigmatic of homeostatic behavior in a steady-state system"; however, neither he nor Paolino and McCrady found hard data to support this still popular notion. Instead they found that alcoholism is stressful to family members, rendering them helpless and frustrated, and that they feel better when it stops.

It has always been popular among therapists who can't solve a problem to blame the family for *causing* it rather than to align with the family in their joint helplessness with it. The usual generic family therapy may make alcoholism worse by spreading the blame and increasing the responsibility in the family. A more apt conclusion from these theories and reviews is that the efforts to stop the alcoholism may well have the paradoxical effect of keeping it going.

Alcoholics Anonymous has been sufficiently successful to warrant investigating its rather different premises for any light they may throw on the nature of the alcoholic family. Alcoholics Anonymous substitutes a semireligious fellowship group which permits dry alcoholics to play Rescuer (and often Persecutor) to other alcoholics. Al-Anon, the companion organization for families of alcoholics, teaches the families how to avoid playing the game by acknowledging and supporting their powerlessness over the alcoholic's drinking or sobriety. It takes a rather paradoxical stance about the responsibility for drinking behavior, assuming a "disease" model of alcoholism that is simplistic and unsophisticated, simply admitting that the alcoholic is "powerless over alcohol" and must become abstinent and turn him or herself over to "a Higher Power." The alcoholic thus gains the degrading stigma and helplessness without having to drink, becomes devoted to a lifetime of guilt and atonement for the past alcoholic sins, and remains beyond the control of anyone else. Meanwhile, Al-Anon is teaching the "coalcoholics" that they have the responsibility of not taking responsibility for the drinking or for the alcoholic. It is a set of paradoxes that works for many, though certainly not all, alcoholics.

With alcoholism, as with so many of the other problems faced by families and family therapists, it is dispiriting to hold people responsible for things they cannot control. The concept of the "co-alcoholic" may be a useful one, but only if it is not contaminated with blame. The only person who can make an alcoholic drink, or stop an alcoholic from drinking, is the alcoholic.

The Treatment of the Alcoholic Family

The treatment of alcoholism seems simple enough—stop drinking alcohol. The pattern or the episode can be interrupted by hospitalization, which is usually not necessary. In my youth in south Alabama in the '40s, hospitals were not used. Instead the binge was ended by having the family and friends take the drunk out in the woods and tie him to a tree for several days, with a skilled but untrained drunk-sitter. AA can provide a similar, though seemingly less brutal service, with a "sponsor" as the drunk-sitter. Family members can try to serve as drunk-sitters, but they are so easily controlled by the alcoholic that they usually do a lousy job. DTs requires hospitalization, as it can be fatal. The idea of a 30-day hospitalization for alcohol withdrawal seems to be dictated by insurance coverage, and while it permits the family to make a greater sacrifice, at least financially, it seems to add little after the first few days of withdrawal. Alcoholics seem to feel superior, for some reason, to the usual clientele of psychiatric hospitals, and have set up their own hospitals with resort amenities, dry alcoholic addictionologists, and even celebrity status. This is an extravagant vacation, but probably does less harm than most of the things alcoholics do.

To avoid long hospital stays, I prefer Antabuse, a drug which makes people allergic to alcohol. Those who are willing to render themselves allergic to alcohol lose their tyranny over their family—their constant threat of going on another binge; therefore many who insist they want to stop drinking refuse Antabuse. Those who take it can learn to live without alcohol while free of the constant temptation to drink and the interminable decision about whether they will do so or not. They may still crave alcohol, but they aren't often tempted to go through the allergic reaction, so they have no decision to make. Antabuse might be a temporary adjunct for habit alcoholics and might be needed indefinitely for the compulsive, binge alcoholics. Obviously, Antabuse should be taken deliberately by the alcoholic rather than forced or sneaked by the family.

Whether the alcoholic drinks or doesn't drink, the family has much to overcome and much to learn. First, family members must realize they don't cause the alcoholism or even the specific drinking episodes. Second, they must learn that they can't control the alcoholic's drinking or sobriety. Any attempt to control it seems to actually aggravate it and start another round of the game. Third, they must overcome their guilt and responsibility and their cringing, cautious subjugation to the will of the alcoholic. Fourth, they must learn to have, face, and deal with the crises of life, regardless of what the alcoholic is doing. Fifth, they must learn to reward sobriety by including the sober alcoholic in the life of the family and the world. Sixth, they must learn to permit the alcoholic to face whatever consequences the alcoholism warrants. They must not rescue or pamper. They don't have to make sure the alcoholic is being taken care of properly before they leave their caretaking post. Seventh, they need not take seriously anything a drunk person is saying or doing or demanding. There may be a loose tongue and some nasty insults or revelations, but there is no veritas in vino. All power should be alcohol soluble.

All of this centers on the family members' realizations that they are not responsible for the alcoholism but the alcoholic is, and that part of the fuel for the alcoholism is the family's guilt and the alcoholic's determination to be punished by his or her loved ones rather than by the forces of reality. As Bepko and Krestan (1985) describe, the real treatment of the alcoholic family does not end with sobriety, but is only then able to begin.

Steinglass et al. (1987) describe the "emotional desert" in a dry alcoholic family which has accommodated so totally to the alcoholic invasion that all its rituals have come to center around alcoholism. Once the alcoholic is dry, the family must face all those developmental transitions that have been bypassed while the family was frozen in time seeking "short-term stability of family life, to the detriment of all other issues."

The damage alcoholism does to every family member's sense of power and responsibility is astounding and must be corrected once the family is no longer under the tyranny of the drinking or of their sense of guilt and responsibility for it.

TREATMENT OF THE FAMILY CRISIS

The life of an alcoholic family is a chaotic succession of crises. Some of the crises involve the physical effects of the alcohol, the intoxication and accidents and embarrassments, the withdrawal, the physical deterioration, the mental deterioration, the vocational deterioration, the social deterioration. Other crises involve the alcoholic marriage and the decision of whether to continue it. The children of alcoholic parents have the usual crises of their age and no reliable parent available to help them through such crises. The children, hostile-dependent, hypermature caretakers to their infuriatingly dependent and demanding parents, go through stormy efforts to get permission to be children, depressive periods of guilt and concern and helplessness, and finally an underground life with lousy models of mature behavior or reciprocal relationships. These interminable crises can be seen as cries for help to stabilize the family, or they can be seen as efforts to break the damned thing apart. Whatever the crisis in an alcoholic family, the alcoholism is a major issue, but often a forbidden one. For the family to get the alcoholic to a therapist may be a major accomplishment, and even a turning point. The therapist must respond accordingly.

Step 1: Emergency Response

If the alcoholic is on a binge or in withdrawal, the family expects the therapist to take dramatic steps to get the alcoholic off their hands. They may have gone through this any number of times and may expect hospitalization. They may even arrive at the emergency room with suitcases packed and be horribly frustrated if the hospitalization does not take place. Whether to hospitalize is a crucial decision, one that has to be made fairly early in the evaluation. The family is furious with the alcoholic, but ever protective. They want something done that is drastic, punitive, and guilt-relieving. They usually have the situation backwards — they believe they have caused the alcoholism but do not need to be involved in the treatment. It may be difficult to persuade them to attempt an outpatient approach, although when they compare the cost of the hospital versus the Antabuse they may be convinced.

Step 2: Family Involvement

The families of alcoholics are wonderfully cooperative. They will make any sacrifice, especially when they know it won't work. Involving the alcoholic may be more difficult, especially if the family is reluctant to rattle the alcoholic's cage and insist. If the alcoholic is helplessly drunk or in withdrawal, there may be no problem. But the family may have a hard time getting the habit alcoholic to come to therapy for the habit he or she either hides or considers normal, so the family may have to produce another crisis — another family member's depression, a divorce or suicide threat, concern about one of the kids.

Step 3: Defining the Problem

The "Why Now?" may or may not be significant, even if it is a quite real crisis. Whatever the presenting problem, the alcoholism is probably more important — both the drinking behavior of the alcoholic or alcoholics and the secondary supporting, blaming, rescuing, enabling, stifling family patterns. With compulsive alcoholics, the nature of the alcoholism may not be in question, but the resultant tyranny may well be. A problem definition might be: "It seems clear that you are an alcoholic and so you can't drink. Now that that is settled, we have to figure out how your family can get comfortable with the idea that you won't drink, so they can love you instead of worrying about you."

With situational alcoholism, the underlying depression or mania may have been hidden by the rather obvious alcoholic behavior (these people are novice alcoholics and may not have yet bullied everyone into cringing submission). "This recent drinking of yours is not like you. It seems an effort to treat some other problem. Alcohol is the wrong drug for your problem. First we have to get you off the alcohol; then we'll approach the underlying problem."

In developmental alcohol crises, the family is trying to define as alcoholism something that is merely inexperience with the drug. "It looks as if he doesn't know how to drink. Seems like he needs lessons in it rather than messing around with it on his own. This is not alcoholism. Everybody goes through this. Didn't you? I sure did."

Habit alcoholics tend to reject, even ridicule, the idea that their drinking is a problem. Not uncommonly they will refuse to return if the therapist insists on the alcoholic label. The therapist may have to stop at defining the problem with less stigma, perhaps saying, "Your family sees your drinking as a problem. They are concerned about your health and functioning, and they can't make contact with you because the alcohol makes you unavailable. They think you'd all feel better if you gave it up. If, as you say, you are not addicted to it, then you should have no difficulty stopping it, for their sake. If you find you are addicted to it, and many people become addicted to it just by drinking it daily for a long time, even without any genetic predisposition, then you can break the habit and probably find yourself feeling better than you have for years. Meanwhile they need you for these other problems, and they need you as clear-headed as possible."

The problem is also defined to the family: "You didn't cause it. You can't control it. You don't have to put up with it. But meanwhile, it has controlled your lives, so you have to learn to live normally without all this guilt and protectiveness and caution."

Step 4: General Prescription

Perhaps the most important thing that happens in treating an alcoholic family is the opportunity for everyone in the family to actually talk about the alcoholism, as well as about the process of living and the crises of life. Family therapy rather offhandedly repeals the rules against noticing and talking about the drinking or about talking about things that might cause the drinking or upset the drinker. Therapy for alcoholic families has sometimes been successful when it consisted of nothing more than that.

Step 5: Specific Prescription

The alcoholic is told not to drink. If withdrawal or immediate intoxication is a problem, then hospitalization, a drunk-sitter, or Antabuse can be offered. (Someone must be off alcohol for only 12 hours before starting Antabuse.) The control of the drinking is left up to the alcoholic, the only one who can control it. All others in the family are instructed that they can't control the drinking. Of course they know that already, but they don't know that this is a truth about alcoholism in general rather than a deficiency specific to them. They are also told that they must not rescue the alcoholic from the drinking or cater to an intoxicated person. They are urged not to try to make the alcoholic feel guilty for drinking, only for what happens when the drinking is going on. They are urged to avoid, ignore and, if necessary, leave the drunk. But they are urged to be loving and involving with the alcoholic when he or she is sober. It is also suggested that the other family members discontinue alcohol use at home or on a routine basis. If the spouse insists that alcohol is necessary for normal functioning, another alcohol problem is thereby uncovered.

The family is then encouraged to plan life around sobriety, with meals, activities and emotional interaction appropriate to a group of normal people rather than to a group huddled around someone whose brain is poisoned. The idea is to plan on the alcoholic's sobriety and to proceed without him or her if that is necessitated by intoxication.

The family may want to talk about drinking to a habit alcoholic who distrusts the definition. But there is no point in talking about drinking to someone who is already doing it. There is no point in attempting to stop the drinking in mid-drink or to prove to a drunk that he or she is drunk. Drunks should be avoided; they don't fight fair. When someone drinks, that person is off duty as an authority figure and need not be honored, respected, or obeyed. No one can control an alcoholic, but the alcoholic can only control those who permit it. Conversations about it are best reserved for the very cold light of dawn.

Step 6: Negotiating Resistance

Situational alcoholics and those with developmental alcohol crises don't put up any resistance to drinking differently. If they do, it probably means that they were structural alcoholics all along.

Binge drinkers usually accept abstinence, monitored by Antabuse or not, if the family insists, and they keep it up for a while. Then there is another binge. The family, however, has been given a period in which to become open, healthy and communicative, rather than guilt-ridden and on guard. Since some spouses of binge drinkers resist sober intimacy, a variety of previously drowned problems may surface. I recall seeing the bottom of a pond that had just been drained — you can't imagine what all is lurking beneath the water until the pond is drained and dry. The therapist may have to give the dry alcoholic a great deal of support as the family flounders around with the flotsam and jetsam of their own issues.

Habit alcoholics sometimes stop the drinking, feel better than ever, and live happily ever after. More often they resist like hell. They try to sabotage the therapy and often succeed. They may defend their drinking; they may take it underground. They may become compulsive alcoholics. But their failure to stop the drinking for the family's sake defines the problem to all and releases the family from the tyranny. Consideration must be given to whether the family wants to live with someone who drinks in a tyrannical manner. The spouse may not have to leave the alcoholic and may not want to do so, but he or she certainly must *be able* to do so. Separation may force the change that permits the marriage to continue. I do not recall anyone I have seen over the last 25 years who regretted divorcing an alcoholic, despite the well-known tendency to marry one after another of them. Living with an alcoholic must be more appealing in theory than in practice.

Habit alcoholics may offer to cut back on their drinking. This doesn't work. They are addicted and should discontinue all alcohol use, at least for six months or so. Some may be able to drink a little intermittently after that, although any drinking by the previously addicted has that "controlled drinking" aura of obsessively measuring each dose and determining when, how, why and where a drink is allowed. Measured drinking can become a tyranny too and seems both a deprivation and a punishment. Nonetheless, many are determined to try it; a few succeed, but more become binge drinkers, releasing the compulsion as soon as they are exposed to the drug. Of course, habit alcoholics cannot resume daily drinking even if the dose is very low.

Family therapy can proceed whether the alcoholic stops drinking or not. In fact, it may be needed even more if the drinking continues. And it can proceed even without the alcoholic. The family is trying to learn to live without being tyrannized by the alcoholic; that may be beneficial to the alcoholic or not, but it is certainly beneficial to the family.

Step 7: Termination

An alcoholic family never terminates therapy. They slip back into the old patterns and try out new therapists sometimes, but they never get well. This is one of the Alcoholics Anonymous principles that must be taken literally — the fight against alcoholism is a lifelong one. It may not take much therapy, just the reminder not to relax in the lifelong battle against temptation. My father-in-law, James N. Brawner, Jr., M.D., a psychiatrist specializing somewhat in treating addicts, has one patient who has called him each year on the date of his last indulgence — for 28 years. Alcoholics, even if they become alcohol counselors and addictionologists, will never again wield as much power as they did when drinking or threatening to. They may continue to struggle with that loss, and they want someone to know it. AA or ongoing group therapy may provide this need, since the family may find it oppressive.

CASE ILLUSTRATIONS

CASE 22   A Drinking Man

A lawyer in his mid thirties was in the habit of drinking each night. The dose gradually rose from three carefully measured martinis to an amount beyond reckoning. He continued to work well, but gained weight and underwent a coarsening of his appearance and of his personality. His wife drank too. She too gained weight. She decided to put both of them on diets. She tried to get him to stop drinking. He responded by drinking more, and they began to fight about it each night. He started going to bars before he came home. She went to an attorney and filed for divorce. He was shocked and came with her to see me. I told him he was an alcoholic and that he should stop drinking. He protested that he had always been a drinking man and that everyone drank the way he did and that his drinking would protect him from heart attacks and that his wife must be crazy and having an affair with the divorce attorney. She said she didn't care, she would leave him if he didn't stop drinking. He stopped. That was an unusual case.

CASE 23   Closeted

This is a more typical case. Nona was a wealthy widow with two brilliant, handsome, charming sons. The older one, Nipper, was married and living in Colorado. (I'd briefly seen Nip and his wife a decade before, in Colorado, and was concerned about his daily drinking then.) The younger one, Neissler, was in post-collegiate inertia. All three drank. The mother had been considered an alcoholic by her late husband, a belief he whispered to his sons. No one had actually seen her drink more than her daily two glasses of sherry, but she had a toxic closet from which she would emerge reeling and overperfumed.

The family had money, and Neissler didn't work but stayed depressed as he pondered his career and commiserated with his mother in her frantic concerns about Nip, which had become a fulltime job. Neissler had an apartment, but was usually at home with his mother. Gradually Nip had begun spending his life and fortune in bars, had an affair, failed in business, and finally was sent to an alcoholic hospital for 30 days and $30,000. He got drunk on the way home and stayed so. His wife left him and remarried. Nip and his new girlfriend did well until she told him she would leave him if he drank again. He did. She did. He began making tearful, drunk, suicide telephone calls to his mother and brother, describing the gun or the knife or the poison, but not letting them know where he could be found.

They consulted me. They were falling apart over Nip. I encouraged them not to respond to his pleas. The cries for help got worse. I gave in and told them to go get Nip and bring him home, but to discontinue their own drinking. In a fascinating series of adventures, which brought Neissler to life as an adult, they found Nip up in the mountains and brought him to me. He was in awful shape. I hospitalized him for three days and put him on Antabuse. Nona stopped her own drinking, but would not let Nip live with her until he was employed and sober. He moved in with his now-employed and sober brother and floundered for a while, testing his mother, complaining to her of the inadequate amenities of his brother's little apartment, and accusing her of being a closet drinker. She stuck to our guidelines. He got a job and then moved in with her.

Nip soon quit his job, resumed drinking, stopped coming to the family sessions, moved a girlfriend into his mother's house with them, and told the neighbors his mother was a very crazy alcoholic. Nona would scream at him about it but take no action. His ability to displace responsibility and feel victimized was amazingly well developed, even for an alcoholic. He would get drunk and cry that all his prep school buddies were making half a million dollars a year, and he wasn't, and it was his mother's fault because of her drinking. She would actually try to reason with him about it or take Antabuse in front of him to prove she wasn't drinking! He would call me and tell me that if I cared anything about him I would have my rich friends give him money. I explained that there was a breatholyzer on my telephone which made it automatically hang up if it sensed that anyone was drinking. Ooops, click, there it went. He had temper tantrums, fought with his girlfriend using the neighbors as audience, and then insisted that his mother's stories about his behavior were drunk talk. Several times, Nona had to flee the house in the middle of the night and seek shelter with neighbors. She continued to assure everyone of her own sobriety. I couldn't get him to come in regularly, and I couldn't get her to kick him out. She'd try and he'd become pitiful, or threatening, or guilt-producing, or just embarrass her with the neighbors. This went on for several maddening months. Neissler and I thought he was trying to make her have a stroke so he could get her money, but we both thought Nip could be right about her closet drinking.

Neissler, trying to stay out of it, got his share of abuse from both his mother and his brother. Finally, things got so out of hand that he intervened. Neissler called the police, who came and took Nip away. When Nip called from jail threatening suicide, Nona refused to come get him. He went to Neissler's house, joined AA, got a job, and gradually moved back in with his mother. There was almost a year of sobriety and job successes. Then Nip began testing his mother. He'd drink a bit, or he'd demand money from her, or he'd go into rages and insist Nona was the one who was out of control. He refused treatment. She finally moved him out, paid up his past debts and his current rent, and told him she had now done all she was willing to do. He quit his job, went to jail, threatened suicide, and called from a gay bar saying she had forced him into prostitution. She wouldn't budge. He finally moved to another city. He called me, quite drunk, one night. My breatholyzer hung up, but I mailed him a prescription for Antabuse. I've heard nothing since.

How is Nip doing now? Reports are mixed. Sometimes he calls friends to tell them he is making a fortune. Sometimes he calls Nona or Neissler to tell them he is in the gutter and it is their fault. They hang up. He may be a millionaire or he may be a bum; he has the capacity to do either, or both. Nona feels little guilt now, and is socially active and happy again. Neissler is almost finished with social work school.

Was Nona drinking? Was Nip sacrificing himself to cure his mother's alcoholism as his father had wished on his death bed? Did Nip put everyone through all of this in order to replace Neissler as their mother's caretaker, so Neissler could get on with his life? Was it a mistake to let Nip come home? Was it a mistake to let Neissler move out? I don't know. It was a mistake, initially, to believe Nona might be drinking rather than taking a firm stand that it didn't matter. Nona and Neissler have emerged from this series of crises stronger than ever before. I can't worry about Nip. Whatever he is doing, it is his choice.

DRUG ADDICTION

Addiction to opiates, barbiturates, minor tranquilizers, and even stimulants and hallucinogens (psychologically addicting even if not physically so) is little different from addiction to alcohol. The family situation and the family treatment are essentially the same. There are a few differences. Alcohol is a legal, socially accepted drug which most people know and love. Alcoholics begin their careers by learning the social skill of "social" drinking. The fact that someone uses alcohol is not ordinarily considered a problem, while the fact that someone does not use alcohol might even be considered unusual and worthy of comment. Alcohol may be used openly, within the usual framework of one's life. The other drugs people abuse are either illegal (like hallucinogens, cocaine, and heroin) or supposedly reserved for sick people. The user and the family consider the use to be illegitimate, problematic, and unfamiliar. The use of illicit drugs involves some degree of break with mainstream society and family tradition. The result is that there are likely to be crises about the drugs at an earlier stage in the addiction, more like developmental crises than like habitual drug use. The drug use is more likely to be hidden from the family, and the family may be mystified by the resultant behavior. These developmental crises, like the comparable crises involving alcohol, are sometimes treated by getting the situation out in the open, educating everyone about the nature of the drug, and stopping the games of impotent control.

There are also situational crises of drug abuse, in which someone becomes addicted to a drug that was innocently used to treat some other problem. People become addicted quite inadvertently to legal narcotics, barbiturates, and minor tranquilizers. They may experience withdrawal and use the drug to stop the withdrawal, thinking they are treating the original condition. People can take sleeping pills indefinitely, thinking they suffer from insomnia when they can't sleep easily because they go into barbiturate withdrawal at bedtime each night. Barbiturate withdrawal is a nightmare and must be carefully monitored. Benzodiazepam (Valium) and the drugs of its class are both depressing and addicting, and they produce anxiety as they wear off, causing the user to think it is time for another pill for anxiety. These drugs produce so much muscle relaxation that the resumption of normal muscle tension becomes seen as a symptom for which the drug is indicated. The drug, as its blood level fluctuates during the day, may actually trigger panic attacks.

Withdrawal from minor tranquilizers is a very long process, with periods of discomfort that come and go for many months, producing a bizarre and confusing picture like a combination of manic-depression, anxiety, and schizophrenia. These drugs are addicting in very low doses, but the intensity of the withdrawal seems to depend on the dose. By contrast, narcotic withdrawal is a breeze. Even heroin withdrawal is easier and also has the advantage of being extremely quick. (When I was consultant to a shelter for female heroin addicts years ago, I was repeatedly told that heroin withdrawal is easy, methadone withdrawal far harder, and nicotine withdrawal hardest of all.) Those who are iatrogenically addicted to Valium and its siblings seem willing to go through withdrawal once they understand that what they are experiencing already is intermittent withdrawal symptoms. They seem to suffer few relapses—unless, of course, they were alcoholics and addicts before and were using the prescription drugs as a substitute.

The hallucinogens are not physically addicting and produce no withdrawal. Marijuana, for instance, seems harmless enough and probably produces only minor problems from occasional use. It contains THC, an hallucinogen similar to LSD, which is stored in fat cells and particularly in the brain. It has a half-life of 56 hours, and so users are somewhat stoned for days. If the drug is used more often than every 56 hours, THC builds up and is stored in the body, slowly releasing and producing a subtle amotivational syndrome, which interferes with learning and school work. The user has slow, inappropriate responses, little sensitivity to what other people might want, and minimal ability to set long-range goals at a higher priority than immediate gratification—in other words, a state comparable to the typical not very bright, not very well disciplined adolescent. At crisis points, the brain seems to squirt out THC and produce narcissistic crisis responses. The user who starts in adolescence may see no problem, since he or she hasn't really changed much since 14 and seems unconcerned that others might expect increasing maturity. After the marijuana is discontinued, it may take six months for the brain to clear.

The most typical chronic abuser of narcotics, barbiturates, amphetamines, and hallucinogens is an underground adolescent of whatever age, who never gets past the stage of underground adolescence and continues dependent on the family but separate from them, existing in the family just to keep it stirred up at irregular intervals (see Chapter 10 for more on underground adolescents). The form may be of the habit variety, with regular use at a level that does not seem a problem to the user, even though the user may keep it secret, knowing the family would disapprove but blaming the disapproval on the family's unfamiliarity with the drug in question. More often, the underground usage is episodic and compulsive, with the user resuming addictive behavior when reexposed to an addictive drug, such as heroin, barbs, ludes, cocaine or whatever. As long as the supply lasts, the user gives up on doing anything else, maybe even disappearing for a while. There's little effort made to keep up the appearance of leading a normal life.

The family situation for compulsive and habit addicts is essentially the same, whatever the drug, to the situation with alcoholism. The underground nature of the use, the adolescent status of the user of whatever age, and the unfamiliarity of the drug make it all a little more confusing, necessitating greater familial familiarity with both the drug and its user.

Stanton and Todd (1982) believe that drug abuse is related to issues within the family of origin (particularly the relationship with the mother) and that the parents' inclusion in therapy is more important than the spouse's involvement. It is as if the addict's mother must give permission for the addict to give up the drugs, grow up and leave home before he can be married. They report good results with an approach to young male heroin addicts with families, using extreme positive connotation ("noble ascriptions") of the behavior, home detoxification, weekly urine checks, cooperation on the part of the parents, and containment of crises within the family.

Another way of looking at the family dynamics of drug abuse is to assume that the addict is seeking a return to adolescent status, with its seductive combination of dependency, freedom from responsibility, tolerance of misbehavior, and parental protection from consequences. The addict may try to play adolescent to parents, to spouses, to friends, or to therapists; indeed he will collapse upon anyone who will accept that relationship. This perspective does not involve "noble ascription" and would consider such "noble ascription" to be a paradox, when paradoxes are not quite appropriate for crisis situations.

Whatever the original reason for exposing oneself to a dangerous drug (perhaps adolescent adventurism and social conformity) or for continuing the use of it (perhaps some current or past family dynamics), after one uses an addictive drug for a while one is addicted and the addiction produces its own energy. The brain produces its own craving quite aside from other forces in the body, the family, or the world. The addict can not control the craving, just the behavior, and perhaps the most the addict can do is to put him- or herself under the control of someone else.

If the addict is married, the spouse must be able to take charge of the situation before it gets out of control and must also be able to leave when control is impossible. Understanding the drug abuse, bringing it above ground, and monitoring it so there are few surprises may bring about a more intense involvement in the marriage, which some people don't want. The marriages of drug addicts are likely to be even sicker than the marriages of alcoholics, who at least are circumspect enough to develop their addiction more gradually, above ground, and in a socially and economically appropriate context. The wife of a male addict may stay in the marriage and become the enabling, protective mother who prevents the man from ever growing up. That can be consuming and is far from healthy for anyone, but it may fulfill the family destiny of the wife.

In contrast to intermittently nonfunctioning compulsive addicts, those with drug habits may remain fairly functional. The marriages may seem to the spouse to be worth saving, even if the addict continues the addiction. The addict is married to the drugs, not the spouse; he may be able to maintain a job but is not really available for a relationship. The habit addict may be a woman who smokes pot daily after work or a man who drinks all weekend and takes speed every weekday and Quaaludes every night, or one who drinks a six-pack every afternoon and looks for cocaine in his spare time, failing to come home if he finds it. Such marriages tend to be especially interdependent, though not very intimate and communicative, and they last until the spouse feels strong enough to leave.

The primary issue may be the maintenance of distance within the marriage. Increasing the independence of the spouse is crucial. As with alcohol, exposing the habit, understanding the drug, and recognizing the spouse's lack of control over it enable the pattern to be broken. While such marriages are often childless, there may be children who may be enlisted in the effort to stop the habit.

When the family members succeed in stopping the addict's habits, they may not like what they uncover. The addict may not have the wonderful characteristics they had assumed were beneath the drugs. They may then indirectly encourage a resumption of the habit.

Addicts may shift their drug of choice from time to time. They don't like to take the world head on, and they may have little experience with facing life with a clear brain. They will need enormous support, encouragement and structure to take on adult responsibility. This can be exhausting for everyone involved. Support groups for clean addicts and dry drunks seem essential.

It is difficult enough for people with clear heads, predictable patterns, and total honesty to maintain a marriage and a family. Those who run from adulthood and disorient anyone who gets close are a caretaker's nightmare.

That man is an aggressive creature will hardly be disputed. With the exception of certain rodents, no other vertebrate habitually destroys members of his own species. No other animal takes positive pleasure in the exercise of cruelty upon another of his kind—there is no parallel in nature to our savage treatment of each other. The somber fact is that we are the cruelest and most ruthless species that has ever walked the earth—we know in our hearts that each one of us harbors within himself those same savage impulses which lead to murder, to torture and to war.

—Anthony Storr, *Human Aggression*, 1968

CHAPTER 17

Violent Families

THE PAIN OF LOVE

"EVERY YEAR close to 2,000,000 children, 2,000,000 wives, and 2,000,000 husbands (yes, husbands) are punched, kicked, beaten up, or injured with a knife or gun by a member of their families" (Bassis, Gelles, and Levine, 1984, p. 404). These are low figures. The actual incidents of violence from Bassis, Gelles, and Levine's own figures, are several times that. Some degree of physical violence occurs in 30 percent of engaged couples. Sixteen percent of couples have experienced some form of marital violence in the past year. Fifty percent of high school seniors are hit by their parents, 8 percent of them actually injured. The data are all the more confusing because milder forms of violence are considered too normal to mention and major forms too embarrassing to report. It is somehow assumed that family violence is normal, but should be kept under some measure of control. Different families and different cultures have different ideas of what is too much or too little violence.

Americans are the most violent people in this violent world, the ones most likely to murder one another. The most nonviolent seem to be the Tarahumara tribe of Mexican Indians (West, 1980), a small, poor, isolated group with an infant mortality of 70-80 percent. The surviving children are so valued that they are never physically punished. On my office coffee table I have a large bronze statue of a Tarahumara mother, baby, and child. I once had to wrestle it from a woman who was trying to use it to bash her husband's head in.

CHILD ABUSE

Adult violence is rooted in childhood violence. Father's mother hits father, father hits mother, mother hits sister, sister hits little brother, and little brother sets fire to the cat, pulls wings off butterflies, and grows up to be a wife beater. It is family entertainment.

Ordinarily each parent checks and subtly restrains the other parent's violent impulses. In those unusual cases in which that doesn't happen, the results can be horrifying. Parents may not restrain one another when they are both drinking. Or they may intensify one another's violent behavior when it serves the function of uniting them against the children. Children are frustrating—don't stay under control all the time. Exhausted single mothers may encourage their new husbands or boyfriends to provide "masculine" strength to enforce their own ineffective efforts at controlling the children. The amateur new father figure, with no power except muscle in the family, may oblige by beating the child to death while the mother cheerleads for her macho hero. While women spend much more time with the children, the men in the household are as physically abusive to the children as the women are, perhaps because the women play the game of "Wait until your father comes home" and then assess Dad's or Newdad's strength and desirability by his effectiveness in silencing or stilling the frustrating child. If Dad were to take an approach that was not physical and did not rely on his muscle, his effectiveness would humiliate Mom, and though it would work better for the child, it would not please Mom. The child, by refusing to obey Mom and requiring that Dad beat him up, may be making a sacrifice for the sake of family stability, may be getting the only contact with Dad he can, or may just be slow at catching on.

Abused children, like initiates during college fraternity hazing, are just waiting until next year when they get to torture the presumptuous pledges.

Child abuse used to be considered perfectly appropriate. For many, it still is. It is seen as character building—after all, the abusing parents had their sterling characters built in this manner. Some religions, based on the concept of "original sin," assume that children are possessed by devils which must be exorcised out of them by torture. Failure to torture the children would be laxity of the parents' religious duty, almost sinful.

Children chosen for abuse may just have been born in the wrong family at the wrong time. Maybe not. It is callous to think that a small child, even a baby, is part of an interaction that is so disadvantageous. Yet abused children may well have an unattractive disposition that makes them unrewarding for the parent. As Dana Ackley (1980) points out, some children come into the world with a sunny disposition that makes them a delight for a parent. The child will coo and gurgle when the parent comes close, making the parent feel appreciated, honored, and loved. The child seems to be thanking the parent for loving and caring for him or her. Other babies are cranky and irritable from the beginning; they cringe and draw away and look mean and angry no matter how hard the parent tries. They seem to be accusing the parent of being unloving and uncaring. The parent has gone through pregnancy, childbirth, and truckloads of diapers in hopes of having a child to love; she has high expectations of love in return. When there is no love in return, the parent is hurt and may lash out in frustration at this one more person in life who is withholding love. Of course, once the parent has begun the pattern of hurting the child, the child becomes cranky and irritable, cringes and draws away from the abusing parent, and looks mean and angry no matter how the parent tries.

Abused children are in a particularly cruel bind. Abused children may react to cruel treatment from the parent upon whom they are totally dependent with anger, which feels unloving to the parent and brings abuse. Finally, the children may subordinate themselves passively; then they may be criticized or punished for their passivity.

In time the child may become clingingly protective of the abusing parent, developing into just the sort of guilt-ridden, hoveringly loving child the parent needs. And as an adult he or she may go right into a marriage in which the spouse's abuse is answered with the guilt-ridden hovering that was learned at home. While abused children often grow up to be abusing parents, they even more often grow up to be abused spouses. The experience of being battered as a child leads more often to the "victim" than the "villain" position.

It has long been known that therapists must perform a distasteful maneuver in dealing with child abuse. The therapist must identify the abusing parent as the "victim" of the unloving or imperfect child, must sympathize with the parent's hurt, and must then parent the abuser. Parenting the abused and compounding the abuser's sense of guilt and rejection only makes the abuse worse. If the abused child must be removed from the abusing parent, the guilt-ridden, neglected parent must be given enormous support.

Separating a parent and a child is sometimes necessary, however traumatic for the child and for the parent. Like divorce, it is a serious but potentially life-saving procedure. In evaluating these cases, the therapist may overreact to the physical aspects of the abuse and fail to make a distinction between spanking the child and shooting him. The emotional abuse may be at least as destructive. The child, taught to expect hostility and criticism from the world, will distrust new situations, including foster homes and the like. Physically separating the parent and the child may create more problems than it solves and should not be seen as an easy solution. Abused children who are separated from their abusing parents tend to isolate themselves even more fiercely — they've been hit with a double whammy, abused by their parents and orphaned by society. It works far better to teach violent families how to live nonviolently than for society to do violence to the family. That is not always possible; when it is not, the disruption of the family must be seen as a new and dangerous crisis rather than a solution.

As abused children grow older, their distrust of adults leads them to test and defy authority, and they may be disdainful of gentle structure. They may pay no attention to any adult who is too weak to beat them. They try to act tough, but underneath they are frightened. They find security in intense and often violent relationships like they knew growing up. They tolerate violence and lead lives that are filled with it. They have little capacity for tenderness, little sympathy for weakness or emotional vulnerability. They can seem paranoid and psychopathic, desperate for someone to love them yet unable to identify love when they encounter it. They even use violence in a desperate effort to get loved. Or they feel loved when they themselves are being abused. For them, love and violence have become so intertwined that they hardly know the difference.

Fortunately, many abused children eschew violence as they grow up. Many abused children grow up to be touchy, insecure, dependent adults, but most are not violent. Perhaps they were lucky enough to have someone who loved them gently, without either bringing or tolerating violence to the relationship. Some of the best people I know were brutally abused as children — each had a grandmother or an uncle or a teacher or a therapist or a sibling who provided some connection to human kindness, and each was able to identify the abusing parent as pathetically needy but stark raving mad.

MARITAL VIOLENCE

Man is violent, especially if he has been raised violently. Man is violent in the world, in sport, in wars, in bars, in crimes, and at home. Woman, though far less violent in the world, seems to be almost as violent at home: 12.1 percent of husbands beat their wives; 11.6 percent of wives beat their husbands (Strauss, 1978). Stump (1985) reports more statistics: 77 percent of murder victims are male, 10 percent of them murdered by their wives; 23 percent of murder victims are females, 40 percent of them murdered by their husbands. Thus, 7.7 percent of murders involve wives killing their husbands, 9.2 percent involve husbands killing their wives. Men are slightly more likely than women to murder their spouses, and husband-killing is most often considered self-defense. Men are far more likely to beat their wives to a degree that produces injury.

In 50% of the incidents of marital violence, it is the wife who strikes the first physical blow. Apparently, women are just as likely as men to escalate a fight to a physical level of combat, although they usually lose the fights and suffer injury, sometimes even death. There are a few women who physically win the fight, who spill blood, burn flesh, and break bones. Some women operate as if the winner of a domestic fight is the loser. The physical loser uses guilt to win the marriage. It is the same technique used so successfully by Gandhi and Martin Luther King.

Those who work in hospitals or shelters for battered women see the results of domestic violence but not the process. They see the impact of the man's greater physical strength. Those who see the couple together, whether the police arriving at the scene or the therapist overseeing the confrontation in the office, may be misled into believing the wife is the more violent spouse, because the wife, feeling some protection from her husband's brute strength when a protector is present, may feel safer in lashing out or striking back.

There are brutes in the world, King Kongish men who have a somewhat autistic inability to perceive their fellow humans as being alive. They cannot identify with anyone outside themselves, and women are members of another species altogether. Other people are objects or obstacles, to be used or gotten out of the way. These brutes squash their wives and children and passing strangers as they would bugs or members of an opposing football team. That's when they're sober — when they get drunk they turn mean. Most sane women do not marry brutes, at least not for long, unless they have come to believe brutish behavior to be quintessential masculinity.

Most violent men are not brutes. Some are psychotic, but most are not mentally ill. Strauss (1980) says: "To my knowledge there is no evidence that the rate of extreme aggressiveness or the rate of mental illness is any greater among wife-beaters and child abusers than it is among truck drivers, psychiatrists, or sociologists." Many wife beaters had parents who beat them or beat one another. Many did not. Actually, the battered wife is more likely than the battering husband to have been abused as a child. Battering men are often drunk; their battered wives are just as often drunk. However, the most consistent factor in the nature of men who are violent toward their wives is that they have an overdeveloped sense of gender. They believe they should be powerful, successful, adored, served, and desired — and they know they are not. They experience themselves as powerless, and they may be ashamed of that and want to deny it, or they may want to be reassured that it doesn't matter. Feeling like failures, they want to be seen as important so they can be loved.

Men who appear to be tyrants may be insensitive brutes, or they may be abused children showing love in the manner in which they themselves were loved, or they may merely be searching for a useful role. Their tyranny may express their sense of their own uselessness and dispensability.

Fundamentalist religion has recently been declaring the man "master of the household." This is an interesting paradox. The concept has some appeal for families who are trying to get an irresponsible, useless father back into the family he has turned over to his wife. Since he can do nothing useful, except maybe earn money, the only role he can be assigned is that of "boss," which doesn't require any useful skill. The man becomes titular Grand Duke, a ceremonial role, while the woman is Prime Minister—the sort of relationship fresh junior executives have with their seasoned secretaries.

Not so long ago and not too far away, it was expected that men would "physically chastise" their wives to "reduce them from their errors" (Freeman, 1979). Men were considered responsible for the behavior of their wives, and were expected to take whatever measures necessary to keep the wives under control. Domestic violence has gained attention because cultural norms are changing. As women have attained full legal equality, and men have been relieved of the legal burden of keeping them under control, wife battering has been frowned upon. It is increasingly considered unacceptable for a man to hit a woman. However, even if they have no legal responsibility to do it, many men have been taught that it is gentlemanly to protect women and keep them from going out of control, even if they have to break a few bones to do so. Men who do not control the behavior of their wives may be teased by their fellows and considered insufficiently manly. On the other hand, if macho men must resort to violence to control their wives, they are considered weak and are frowned upon even more severely. Many men still feel the old-fashioned pressure to provide such control, although they may not know how they are supposed to do it.

Some men take it upon themselves to physically punish their wives for displeasing them in some way. A man may whip his wife with a belt if she puts too much starch in his collar or smiles at the postman. He may beat his wife for being too servile, too competent, too pretty, too ugly, too happy, too sad. We are horrified, but these men and their wives have been raised to consider this quite appropriate.

Everstine and Everstine (1983) make a distinction between the domestic violence that occurs when the husband (rarely the wife) is a sadistic bully who administers punishment or just slaps his family around, and the violence that occurs when both spouses engage in escalating conflict which gradually becomes violent unilaterally or bilaterally. While the violent argument is by far the more common in our society, the bullying husband is the stereotype we usually think of in these cases. I only see such behavior among immigrants from Latin America and the Middle East, where it seems to be culturally condoned, but I understand that the people who work in shelters for battered women run across this frequently among the lower classes and occasionally among the better educated and acculturated people in our society. In my experience, domestic violence among the upper classes nearly always occurs in the context of an intense and escalating marital battle.

I do see cases of unilateral violence, sudden outbursts of temper, in which an anxiously obsessive or paranoid man will just hit his wife or children when he is having a bad day. It is an explosion of rage, which may startle him into sanity or just make him feel so ashamed that he keeps it going for a time while he thinks of someone or something to blame. It may be intensified if his wife tries to calm him by becoming servile and thereby guilt-producing. Alcohol is usually, but not always, involved. Afterwards, he may see the episode as temporary insanity and may undergo neurological workup. He may have a brain disorder. He may be paranoid, or manic, or he may just have been drunk. If he or his wife react to this behavior as if it were appropriate and sane, they have an even more serious problem.

Some men have what I call the "Billy Budd Syndrome," after the Herman Melville novel. Billy is the most perfect sailor and person on the ship, but has a speech impediment. When unjustly accused, he becomes tongue-tied and, unable to express his anger verbally, lashes out and inadvertently kills another man. Inarticulate men, frustrated and lacking verbal skills, may fall back on physical expressions of their emotions. It is a momentary paranoid rage, almost a seizure, very difficult to control except by distance and quick timing. If it occurs often, has no clear organic base, and continues even after discontinuing alcohol, the man may have to take low doses of Stelazine or live alone.

Violence occurs at least once in many, maybe even most marriages, but if either partner doesn't like it, it stops — or the marriage stops. Assuming, as is usual, that the man wins the first fight, the woman then must know that physical fighting is not her game. She can't play it to win. She can either stop playing or play to lose.

Battered wives, the ones who remain in marriages in which they regularly lose fights, are somewhat more distinctive in their psychopathology than their husbands. To say the least, they have low self-esteem. They expect to be mistreated, probably have been prior to this marriage, and were usually perfectly aware that the man they were marrying had a low tolerance for frustration and became violent when frustrated. The first violence usually occurred before the marriage. Perhaps she saw his bombastic temper tantrums as some sort of strength. She seems to believe she deserves this treatment, and she cringes along, acting pitiful and inept, accepting the violence and taking care of the man who beats her.

These women can frustrate their would-be rescuers. They are chronic victims, suffering and making everyone else feel guilty because they suffer. They determinedly refuse to acknowledge that they have any power, that they can positively or negatively influence what happens to them. Their lives are not their fault. They insist that they deserve the beatings, but that they can't help doing whatever it is they do that makes them so deserving of beatings, and they can't leave the situation or change it. But they beg for help.

Snell, Rosenwald, and Robey (1964), in a study of 12 women who had been repeatedly beaten by their husbands found that the beatings made the man feel less pitiful and more "masculine" and the women weaker and therefore more "feminine." These women were married to men whose only strength was physical. The women seemed uncomfortable with their own strength, preferring to see themselves in terms of "what that brute of a man did to poor little me." After being battered, they then nursed the batterers, who felt real bad about it. The man had had his chance to demonstrate his "masculine" strength, and the woman then got her chance to demonstrate her "feminine" nurturance. This pattern is graphically portrayed in *Oliver*, where Bill Sikes beats Nancy to a pulp, whereupon she sings, "As Long As He Needs Me."

The victim position is a strange one, and its popularity even stranger. Victims will fight tooth and toenail to prove how helpless they are, as if there is some reward for being powerless. Total victims seem to believe that they can get loved if they can first get mistreated. They may claim that they stay in the violent marriage only because they don't know how to support themselves. This may be true, but it may not. I've seen many financially independent women stay in violent marriages. It is more than an economic issue.

The violent marriage typically involves a man who believes someone will love him if he is powerful enough, and a woman who believes she will be loved if she is powerless and mistreated. They fight over her failure to show him love or his failure to show her love, and one hits the other (it hardly matters who strikes the first blow — the pattern is set and the outcome preordained). They fight. He wins. She collapses pitifully. His offense is no longer his weakness, but his excessive strength. He is now properly "masculine" and she properly "feminine." They can now love. Or perhaps not.

This pattern may continue for many years, until one of them, usually the woman, becomes ashamed for the children or the neighbors to see this extravagant courtship ritual and attempts to change the pattern. Yet this is a hard game to stop, as the refusal to play is seen as a rejection by the already desperately needy partner. Once the pattern of violence is established, an effort to change or end it almost inevitably leads to dangerous and rapid escalation. If a husband refuses to beat the wife, she may try to provoke him into victimizing her. More often, if the wife refuses to collapse pitifully, the husband may try ever more violent efforts to assert his "masculinity," to which she is supposed to submit. Somebody can get killed.

There are four turning points in violent marriages: when it begins, when someone tries to change it, when others get involved, and when someone tries to get out of it.

It Begins

The first episode of violence usually occurs in courtship and more often than not ends the relationship. Most people would not want to be in a relationship in which they find themselves hitting someone else or being hit. But the violence may bring a sense of intimacy, or security, or power, and may feel right to one or both of the participants. If the relationship continues, usually the violence continues and enters the couple's repertoire. These couples may come for prenuptial therapy, and although the therapist urges them to get as far from one another as possible, they usually go ahead and marry anyway. If they consider a violent relationship worth treating, they are insufficiently alarmed. As the romance fades, the violence may actually diminish, confirming the end of the honeymoon.

Sometimes the violence does not start until the couple marries. The first episode is generally early, perhaps soon after marriage. Many will just end the marriage at that point. Others will make a big enough protest and a serious enough effort at therapy to keep the violence out of the marital repertoire. If they do not react with alarm, the pattern may be set. There are many who consider divorce more devastating, embarrassing, and dangerous than violence, so they stick with the marriage, trying to control the violence with such ineffective and usually inflammatory techniques as guilt, submission, or counterviolence.

Violence that starts after the first year or so is usually thought of as an aberration, an indication that the more violent spouse is "sick." Therapy may be sought to prevent this change in a previously workable and nonviolent marriage. If either the man or the woman suddenly becomes violent, he or she may well be psychotic or alcoholic. Or, in a desperate attempt to gain some attention from a neglecting spouse, he or she may be using a technique that seemed to work in the family of origin or in some previous relationship. These marriages may be worth salvaging; if the non-violent spouse is sufficiently alarmed to seek therapy and sufficiently competent to separate for a time, the violent pattern may not develop. If both are alarmed by the violence, the problem may be nipped in the bud without drastic measures.

Someone Tries to Change It

Once the violent pattern is established, the marriage may go on for years or decades, seemingly satisfactory to both partners. Then, at some point, one will desire a change. The crisis that interrupts this cozy pattern may be internal. The violence may have gradually escalated to a point where it is no longer pleasant. The woman may have gotten hurt more than either intended, and the scars and bruises may have become embarrassing. The man may have become realistically competent enough not to need this psychodramatic display of mock masculinity. The woman may have become too strong or self-respecting for this degradation.

Therapists who fail to understand the pattern can be dangerous. The effort to overpower and humiliate the man and protect the woman misses the point. The "victim" may not be aware that she is also a partner to the marriage and to the violence — not an equal partner perhaps, but still retaining some power to influence the course of events. Reinforcing her sense of her powerlessness and seeing her as a helpless (i.e., "innocent") victim may be a seductive, somewhat paradoxical maneuver, which might irritate her and stop her from acting so helpless. She may, however, believe it. In her cringing effort to get loved for her pitifulness, she may escalate to produce even more of the abuse for which her therapist loves her. She needs to be empowered and to be loved for her competence, courage, and strength.

In therapy the "villain" may briefly delight in being seen as Godzilla. He is such a pathetic failure as a man, according to his concept of masculinity, that it is an unexpected compliment for someone to see him as a brute and a tyrant. So he may escalate the battle to get more such compliments.

In the "villain's" mind, he is the victim, the one who is being cringed at and avoided and criticized rather than loved and served and praised. However guilty he can be made to feel for his violence, he feels more guilty for his weakness.

The marital violence can be stopped when one partner is loving to the other before the violence starts, instead of postponing intimacy until the violence is over. If the "victim" is tired of playing, she can respond to her villainous partner's opening move by considering him upset and unhappy and in need of love. Of course, first she has to see herself as capable of giving something that would be worth receiving. This familiar move won't stop the pattern, but it will usually stop the episode.

Others Get Involved

The pattern may change when someone else becomes involved. The children may observe and object. Relatives or neighbors may react adversely, and embarrass the couple. A therapist may interrupt the pattern. Someone may call the police. I, squeamish for violence, used to call the police myself. When the police came, the couple would pull together and deny the violence happened or join forces and beat up the policeman. I rarely ended the violence by unilaterally calling the police — I just ended the therapy.

Someone Tries to Get Out

At the point at which one partner tries to stop the pattern by distancing the other partner, the violence will escalate. At that point the pacifist may try to leave. The violent partner may panic at this loss of love and threaten or even commit murder or suicide. Violent relationships are not easy to leave. Margaret Elbow (1980, p. 65) particularly appeals to therapists to avoid rescuing victims of family violence and points out how dangerous it is for longstanding victims to desert their pitiful violent husbands. There is no safety in leaving and no safety in staying. It is a hard pattern to stop, and there is no solution that is free of risk.

Women cannot afford to be ambivalent about leaving violent marriages. They must be all the way in or all the way out of the marriage. Violence is most likely when the wife makes a show of leaving (perhaps to please the therapist) but still tries to take care of the husband while she still responds to his "power." Such in and out teasing encourages the man to be ever more violent in hopes of getting her back. This is the pattern that leads to murder.

CASE ILLUSTRATIONS

CASE 24 *Under the Tent*

Omar, an Iranian, married Ophelia, a missionary's daughter and came to this country to live. Ophelia never had orgasms with him, as he thought she should. Omar went into a depression, for which he sought individual therapy. Ophelia became an apologetic caretaker. Later, he began to wake her from her sleep, insisting that she was orgiastically masturbating and demanding to know her fantasy. If she didn't respond at once, he would slap her until she told him some fantasy. Then he would cry over his failure to live up to the fantasy, and she would take care of him.

For several years, the episodes occurred about once a month. Ophelia finally began to pacify him with stories about affairs she had had during her split personality episodes. Omar sent her to therapy to solve her problem. The slappings stopped as long as she was in therapy and she could tell him fantastic stories about her therapy sessions. When the couple moved to Atlanta, I insisted upon seeing them together. I tried to see Omar as part of the problem. He took offense at my suggestion that it was taboo for a man to hit his wife. The slapping episodes resumed. I urged separation. She gave up the couples therapy instead and returned to the Scheherazade game, which must have pleased her as much as him. As long as she was in individual therapy, the violence stopped and the marriage continued.

CASE 25 *In the Dark*

Perhaps a more typical case involved a movie projectionist whose mother had run off with another man. He distrusted women and had never married. Most of his ideas about women came from his embittered father and from the movies. At 40, he met and married a secretary, who loved his romanticism. He sent flowers and insisted upon lighting her cigarette with his, as Paul Henried had done for Bette Davis in *Now, Voyager*. They had a wonderful romantic honeymoon and returned to work the next day. He surprised her by arriving at her office for lunch, bearing flowers. She was smoking a cigarette he hadn't lit, so he hit her in front of her amazed coworkers. They pulled him off. She ran, moved in with a couple she knew, and obtained a quick divorce. She would not consider coming in for therapy with him. I saw him alone for a while and then in a group. He finally gave up on her, but only after she consistently refused to respond to his pleas and presents. He returned to his lifelong misogyny, with the belief that women are inherently fickle. The women in the therapy group were pleased with his decision not to marry again.

CASE 26 *Poetic License*

I don't often get to see marital violence in action, so this case was instructive.

Petunia, a middle-aged housewife, became patroness to a burnt-out hippie poet who lived in a cardboard box behind J.C. Penney's and devoted his life to begging for drug money. Petunia chose him because he reminded her of her glorious younger brother, who had committed suicide. She took him food and clothes and pampered him. He read her poetry. She kept her relationship with this young man secret, but neglected her husband Penrod and wouldn't go out with him. Penrod began to suspect her of having an affair. He discovered the relationship and misinterpreted its nature. One night, he thought he heard a noise. He thought the poet was in the basement. He sat at the top of the basement stairs with a gun, hoping to catch him and kill him. After a few silent hours, he decided to kill himself instead and held the gun at his own head until dawn. He then called me, and I asked him to come with his wife to my office.

At the office, Penrod told Petunia what had happened and fell to his knees before her, begging her to give up her young lover. She laughed at him and leaped to her feet to shake her finger in his face and point out his various shortcomings. She then fled to the waiting room, where sat a young couple with a history of violence. Penrod and I soon followed. Petunia started hitting her husband. He tried to hold her, but she hit him 13 times, by my count, before he connected with a solid right to the jaw, which sent her reeling over a coffee table. Her wig flew off and landed on the lap of the young man of the waiting couple. He gallantly returned it. Petunia put her wig on and stormed out. I kept the tearful, cringing, apologetic Penrod with me until she got home, and they talked briefly on the phone. She got the gun out of the house. He called a cab and went home.

When Penrod got home, Petunia demanded that his punishment for his wife battering would be that he take her out to dinner. They reconciled quickly and I subsequently saw the two of them with the young poet, whose book of poetry they jointly published. Penrod never really felt comfortable with the young man and was glad when we got him cleaned up and employed. But Petunia, by finally producing a reaction, got what she wanted.

The young couple from the waiting room still talk about the scene and the wig and have had no further violence in their relationship. They didn't like what they saw, but, more importantly, the young wife could no longer find innocence for herself in the victim posture.

TREATMENT OF DOMESTIC VIOLENCE

Step 1: Emergency Response

Some of these cases require immediate intervention, separation of the combatants, and some stabilizing presence for both the husband and the wife. It works infinitely better for the therapist to get the couple to an office or some other neutral place, rather than going to the scene. I have done that a few times, but I have less authority in people's homes than in my own office, so I can't cool things down as quickly. If there has been some injury, the emergency room is convenient but emotionally cluttered. I prefer my office at whatever hour.

These crises may have to be handled over the telephone. There is much to be done, some of which is not strictly in the realm of therapy but must be done right away. Calling the police, taking legal action, establishing the medical reality of any injuries, and even filing for divorce are perfectly legitimate actions to emphasize the seriousness of the situation. Obviously, the battered woman must get herself outside the house to a telephone to call the police; she may be reluctant to leave the children in the house, so she may call someone else to get the police there. When the police arrive, there may be bilateral denial of the problem. Separating the combatants for a cooling off period works far better than bringing in seconds to enlarge the scope of the battle. It seems perfectly appropriate to cart the more violent of the two off to jail, though which is more violent is not always apparent. It may not matter. The point of taking someone off the premises is not to establish who is the good guy and who the bad, but to make sure the violence stops and no one gets killed. So usually the police take whoever is most injured to the hospital or whoever is drunkest to jail.

The posture of the therapist should be one of horror, always making clear that, whatever the provocation, the violence is shocking. At the same time, there must be concern for the emotional stress that led to the violence and sympathy for both parties. Neither "look what she made me do" nor "look what that big brute of a man did to poor helpless little me" is acceptable in the effort to understand the interaction. It is difficult, but necessary, to maintain neutrality about everything except the violence itself. As Bob Beavers points out (1985), "A systems perspective assures the therapist that there are no cops and robbers, just victims." While I don't like to see anyone as a victim, if there must be victims and villains, we're all both.

Step 2: Involving the Family

These situations should be seen while they are intense, even if it means having one partner in the office and the other on the telephone. It can be horribly misleading to hear one side of the story. Both combatants should be seen, even if they start out in different rooms. The presence of other family members is helpful and dampening. Important decisions must be made at once, including a decision about whether the couple must be separated for the night or, if they already have been, whether they could get back together. These decisions cannot be made with information from just one person.

Step 3: Defining the Crisis

Occasionally I see people, usually old or drunk, who believe they have been beaten in their sleep by their spouse. This may be imagined, but, like most imagined events, represents an emotional reality. Most family violence is real, though frequently exaggerated. The woman who was hit by her husband in my waiting room refused to believe that she had hit him repeatedly before he knocked her down. People remember receiving blows more clearly than they remember delivering them.

Domestic violence is embarrassing to both the participants and the observers. They typically try to keep it covert. Couples in therapy may even hide it from the therapist. Since domestic violence is so widespread, therapists might do well to routinely ask about it, not with the question, "Does it happen?" but with the assumption that it has happened and the question, "How has it been handled?" It can't be dealt with effectively unless it is overt.

The most relevant parameter is the degree to which violence is unique or habitual. The first physical battle is quite different from the 47th. Did the violence begin in courtship? (Did the spouses choose one another in anticipation of a violent relationship?) Did the violence begin soon after the marriage? (Did the couple accept violence as a way of ordering power alignments and gender relationships in marriage?) Or did the violence begin later in the course of the relationship? (Does violence represent an aberration in one or both spouses? Is the violence an effort to solve some other problem in the relationship?) If the violence is unique, and the couple comes for therapy, the relationship stands an excellent chance of continuing without violence. But if the violence is habitual, it has clearly been tolerated and likely encouraged. There must be ambivalence about whether it is bad for the marriage; violence may even seem necessary in some way for its continuation.

Is the domestic violence seen as natural or is it seen as peculiar to this family's structure? Do these people believe it is the nature of the beast to engage in these physical battles? Do they define one partner or one gender as categorically good and the other as categorically bad (a sure set up for throwing things out of control)? It is paralyzing to accept any definition of the problem that blames the violent nature of the human animal, the sexism of our society, some religion's notion of a male directive to control his family, or some sense of chivalry that permits women to hit men but does not tolerate men's being so ungentlemanly as to hit back. Domestic violence must be defined as structural, as arising from this specific relationship. However distasteful to the therapist, the problem must be defined in terms of the sequence of events and attitudes that leads to the violence. Virginia

Satir once told me, "It is when the issues are most personally and emotionally disturbing that we need our systems perspective most. We must all know
that we have the power to change our system by changing our own role in it."

Contained in a structural definition of family violence is the couple's
shared and conflictual attitudes toward violence, toward gender, toward
power and control, and toward the nature of marriage. One or both of the
pair very likely suffered child abuse or witnessed marital violence growing
up. But more specifically, there is a characteristic pattern in the relationship
that leads to the violence. It may occur only when the husband is drunk or
his team is losing, or when the wife is premenstrual or on a diet. It may
occur when he can't get her attention, when she is taunting him, when he
feels inadequate economically.

For instance, one couple experienced violence not when the alcoholic
husband was drinking, but when the wife was drunk and he was on the
telephone with his girlfriend. The wife at such times would shoot up the
house and break the furniture until she could get him off the phone, whereupon he would slap her. Another marriage involved a man who was chronically depressed, intolerant of conflict, and supported by his wife. She was
adept with words and loved to use them, as she berated him for not living up
to her fantasies after all she had done for him. He had learned to stop hitting
her when he felt overwhelmed by her barrage of words. He had learned to
leave the room when he couldn't get her to stop talking. When he had a
broken leg, he couldn't leave the room and attempted to stop her conversation with his crutch. It didn't work. She stayed out of crutch range and kept
talking.

Unless the "victim" knows what she did that led to the violence, she is
indeed helpless, because she doesn't know what she could do differently to
keep the violence from happening. Knowing what you did wrong is surely
the most liberating of knowledge. It may enable one to change the whole
game.

Step 4: General Prescription

First, the couple must be told clearly that violence is unacceptable and
must stop. The spouses are then helped to formulate a contingency plan
about where they will go and what they will do if the violence recurs. The
one most likely to get hurt must keep a bag packed and know where to go to
escape the battle. She may call on neighbors for help, if the neighbors are
sensible enough not to escalate the battle. She may hide at a friend's house,
if the violent man is likely to stalk her. Or she may move in with relatives, if
the relatives can avoid taking sides and increasing the humiliation of the
violent one.

Shelters for battered women seem to provide a needed societal service, although they tend to avoid seeing the conflict as a systems issue that is
fixable. (There are no shelters for battered husbands, which does not mean

that the battered husbands don't have to find somewhere else to go. It merely means that the battering wives are not likely to leave the home and stalk their prey.) A plan for handling subsequent episodes is a crucial part of the crisis management. Just having a therapist available to call during these episodes may be sufficient. I've never had the violence continue once I was on the telephone with the couple. And it is often the husband who makes the call to me, saying, "She won't leave me alone and let me stop hitting her."

Step 5: Specific Prescription

The couple is given alternative ways of handling the escalating conflict before the violence erupts. Most helpful is for the one who traditionally strikes the first blow (the wife as often as the husband) to learn to announce impending loss of control and call for a timeout. Then the other absolutely must respect that.

Since most domestic violence takes place under the influence of alcohol, there may have to be a change in the drinking pattern (see Chapter 16).

Guns should not be kept in the house with violent people. The danger to burglars is slight compared to the danger to family members. The presence of a gun in the home of someone willing to use it is tyrannical.

Ultimately, the treatment of marital violence is the treatment of the couple's gender stereotypes, their ideas about what is expected of men and women, of themselves and of their partner. Redefining masculinity and femininity, degenderizing the roles and rules, is threatening to both men and women. It concerns power, both real power and the appearance of power. Power alignments in marriage are not always based on gender, but couples traditionally have conspired to make it appear that the man has more power in the marriage. They may consider this appearance crucial, even if the reality is quite different. Equality must be made respectable for them, so there may have to be a show of empowering the woman.

Over time the couple is taught how to share power. As a first step, in the typical violent marriage, the wife is empowered and the husband is put on a kind of probation, in which he no longer has the responsibility of controlling everything. Since this can be carried too far for the man who uses violence because it provides his only power, the power reversal is set up only as an exercise along the road to true equality.

Step 6: Negotiating Resistance

If the woman is better with words and the man has more muscles, prohibiting violence leaves the man at a temporary disadvantage, which may be frustrating and eventually erupt into violence. Berating or belittling the man does not solve the problem, but he may benefit from sympathy with his awareness that he has less power than he thinks he's supposed to have. He must have a way to remain an equal in the relationship. The therapist may have to provide more support to the "villain" then to the "victim."

Unmuzzling the long restrained dissatisfactions of a recently liberated "victim" can be inflammatory. It has to be constantly kept in mind that the violence either occurred abruptly in a formerly good relationship, as an experiment that didn't work, or was part of a pattern these two people mutually protected for some time, tacitly agreeing to let it be part of their domestic repertoire. Resistance is most evident to the victim-villain dichotomy that declares the victor of the battle to be beyond the pale.

Therapy with violent couples must be kept at a low level of emotional intensity. Therapy cannot be stormy. The spouses are being taught that they can discuss anything in a soothing manner, without demonstrations of either verbal or physical pyrotechnics. They are given demonstrations of how disagreements can remain unresolved, how offenses can remain undefended, how hurts can be left unavenged.

There is also resistance from lifelong victims to seeing that their lives are in some way under their control. They may have difficulty accepting that their criticism or neglect of the brute has some effect on him. They may find it hard to accept responsibility for what goes on in the relationship. Victims may require some individual therapy before feeling equal enough to use couples therapy effectively. Villians may also benefit from some individual therapy, although group therapy may help them to see more clearly how their sense of gender and power and responsibility is different from that of the rest of the society. Couples groups may be best of all, after the phase of crisis resolution and clear definition of the systems patterns.

Step 7: Termination

A therapist may have to remain available to violent couples, as a little piece of security. In my experience, if the crisis therapy is handled with sufficient determination, if the definition of the pattern is clearly systemic, and if the negotiation of resistance considers the issues of power and responsibility for control on both sides, the violence does not continue. Or the marriage doesn't. I recall only a few cases in which both the violence and the marriage continued. These couples have made an alliance based on preferring their violence to my therapy.

CASE ILLUSTRATION

CASE 27   *Begetting Violence*

We were told over the telephone that the 15-year-old son of one of the nurses at the hospital had threatened to kill his stepfather or himself if the stepfather didn't stop beating his mother. Knowing such threats are not to be taken lightly, I saw the family right away.

Viola, an enormous middle-aged woman with bleached hair and a bandaged face, was led in on the arm of a frightened-looking boy in a cutoff football jersey. He had good manners but tried to look tough. They were soon followed by Vic, a cowed little man with tattoos and dirty fingernails. He didn't talk much but sweated and smiled a lot.

The history was sordid but not unusual. Viola was determined to tell me how mistreated she had been by men for a lifetime. Her father had been a violent alcoholic. She had married her first violent husband at 17. It didn't last long. He hit her for the first time on their honeymoon. She told her father, who threatened the boy with a gun and demanded she divorce him. She went back home. Soon afterwards, her father's heart attack brought a change in the old man's habits. Everyone blamed the father's heart attack on his anger at her hapless young bridegroom. Nobody could hit his children but him. She finished nursing school and married a violent but handsome alcoholic who was on her hospital floor after a motorcycle accident. She supported him for several years, visited him regularly while he was in prison for burglary, and let him beat her when he was drinking. She thought she was lucky that he didn't do as her father had done and beat the children. This second husband was finally killed in a knife fight over a woman at a bar. Viola was by now a 35-year-old widow with three children. She had a good job and money from her father's insurance.

She found her third husband, Vic, a mellow mechanic eight years younger, three inches shorter and 50 pounds lighter than she. He was from a gentle family in the country. He'd done little in life other than fish and smoke pot, and that was fine with all his family and friends. After the brutish second husband, Vic seemed safe to Viola. She was in love for the first time. It was not a very verbal relationship, but a very sexual one—at first. There was no violence. He was wonderful to the children. Soon, though, she was bored with him, ashamed of him, and embarrassed around her friends and family to be married to such a passive little wimp. She decided he needed to stop smoking pot and return to college. He did so reluctantly, but wouldn't study and began a firtatious friendship with another student. Viola was jealous and slapped him. An uncomfortable period followed. Viola kept him at a distance. He could find no way to make contact with her. He started drinking. One night, months after Viola's assault on him, he came home drunk and demanded sex. Viola pushed him out of bed and he actually hit her. She cried and then became nurturing and they had sex for the first time in months. The episodes became frequent, with wrestling followed by slapping followed by sex. Finally, things got a little out of hand and Viola's nose was bloodied. Her oldest son, now 15 and far larger than Vic, tried to beat up his stepfather. When his mother slapped him, the boy threatened to run away from home unless Viola kicked Vic out. At that point the family came to therapy—for the boy.

After getting the story, I congratulated the boy on his efforts to stop the fighting, but pointed out that the battle obviously upset him and me more than it did the couple. Vic protested that he never remembered the violence.

I expressed shock and alarm that he could hit the woman he loved, or anybody, and do it so unfeelingly that he wouldn't remember it. He then remembered it, but said it wasn't his fault because he'd been in Vietnam. Further questioning revealed that he'd been caught with drugs and booted out of the army his first week in Vietnam. He then remembered the violence, deplored it, and protested that he loved Viola but he could find no other way of reaching her.

I told Vic that if he couldn't find another approach he would have to leave the marriage. We focused on his sense of inadequacy to Viola, her failure to let him be the simple country boy he was, her determination to maintain control over everything he did and was. He felt inferior at college, unappreciated at home, and belittled in front of the children. Viola lit into him about his affair, about his passivity, his silence, and his unmacho seduction techniques. She insisted she only gave in sexually to the violence because she didn't want a scene in front of the kids.

The problem was defined as Vic's efforts to get close to Viola without violence, when Viola had never known a nonviolent relationship. Vic was defined as a potential brute, who must stop the violence now before he became a monster — he liked that. The hulking Viola was defined as a frightened little girl trying to find safety and security. We speculated on whether it was safe for the pitiful little 180-pound Viola to remain in the house with this 130-pound brute, and decided it would be safe to try, if the boy promised not to shoot but to call me if anyone got violent with anyone. Vic and Viola were given the task of figuring out how to make love without a physical battle first.

That night Vic actually asserted himself to Viola and asked directly, in words, for sex. It went well. The rest of the therapy maintained the same definition, that Viola was insecure because of her history of violence, so had to control things, and that Vic's strength was in his comfort with letting the world be. Violence was seen as an acknowledgment of powerlessness — a defeatist action. Viola was able to rethink her second marriage and see that handsome brute as a pathetic loser. She was even able to see her father's powerlessness. There was much attention paid to how Vic could make Viola feel less threatened and more confident. Everything they thought they knew about gender and power was redefined. Vic dropped out of college, got a job as a mechanic, and learned to talk a bit. There was no further violence. Each time I see Viola at the hospital, she looks happy and reassures me that all is well. I never saw the boy again. He's off at college now.

I don't blame myself (for the incest). See, Mr. Gittes, most people
never have to face the fact that at the right time and the right
place, they are capable of — anything!

— Robert Towne, *Chinatown*, 1974

CHAPTER 18

Incest

FAMILY AFFAIRS

I NCEST IS SUPPOSED to be taboo. So taboo, in fact, that when Freud had
encountered enough incest stories, he finally recoiled against what he heard.
He decided these were hysterical fantasies covering a universal wish, and he
based his psychoanalytic theories on the refusal to believe such a thing could
happen (see Masson, 1984).

The degree to which incest has been taboo has varied with time and place
(Serrano & Gunzburger, 1983). It was practiced by Greek gods, Egyp-
tian royalty, Roman emperors, and medieval popes. But it was so rigidly
prohibited in the early Christian era that even the two baptismal witnesses of
the same child could not marry. Incest makes family life very complicated, if
not impossible, so its prohibition is necessary in all societies. Apparently, it
is not innately repugnant or such prohibition would not be necessary. The
prohibition serves the purposes of stabilizing families and assuring out-

breeding, since inbreeding is bad for the genes. And, as Levi-Strauss points out (1969), an incest taboo assures exchange of females.

Our society has found incest jokes popular and considers incest funny, perhaps in recognition of the embarrassing universal incestuous longings. It has been assumed that incest has been widely practiced by isolated families. Parents and grandparents in some Western Indian tribes dutifully masturbate small children, and some have seriously suggested that this practice be adopted by the society as a whole. Sex play occurs normally among children of similar age, whatever their kinship, and elders wink at sex play among siblings and cousins. Even the marriage of first cousins is widespread, legal, and usually respectable (Ashley and Melanie in *Gone With the Wind*). In the last decade or so, there have been several popular movies that romanticized brother-sister incest (*Brotherly Love, The Hotel New Hampshire, Mandingo, Foot for Love, Scarface*). *The Savage is Loose, Luna*, and the original cut of *Where's Poppa?* pictured mother-son incest as a benign, even lifesaving act under emergency circumstances. Father-daughter incest, by marked contrast, has not usually been pictured favorably. It was seen as funny in the semipornographic *Candy*, but considered exploitive and destructive in *A View From the Bridge* and *Chinatown*. Our movies would almost have us believe that the act of incest is not taboo, but the exploitation of children by their fathers is horrifying.

The societal attitude seems to be that parent-child romance and flirtation are necessary for social and sexual development, but that the romance must not be genital. Children innocently play with the genitals of their siblings and cousins of similar prepubertal or early pubertal ages. If an adult intrudes genitality into this game, it is outrageous. Yet it occurs. Finkelhor (1978) reports that 20 percent of girls and 10 percent of boys have a childhood sexual involvement with some adult. There is every reason to assume that that figure is drastically, ridiculously low. We have not reached the point of assuming such experience is universal, but it may well be the norm. And a good percentage of childhood sexual experience is incestuous. Any estimate of its incidence is merely a guess. As reporting of incest is actively encouraged, the reports are astounding.

Incest may be part of a more general preoccupation with pedophilia. Child pornography and juvenile prostitution are big business. Little boys seem to be homosexual turn-ons. Pre-pubescent girls are encouraged to dress like hookers, emulating Jodie Foster's 12-year-old prostitute in *Taxi Driver*, an attraction so compelling that it triggered an assassination attempt on the president. *Lolita*, at a similar age, drove Humbert Humbert to murder in the Vladimir Nabokov novel. It is societally accepted, even encouraged, for pubertal and even prepubertal children to exploit their sexual appeal (Brooke Shields in *Pretty Baby*).

In general, the audience for the precocious sexual appeal of little boys and little girls is adult males. Child pornography is not an expression of the child's sexuality, but of the male search for a safe sex object. (Some crusaders want to segregate children from men. However, experts surmise that men become immunized against sexualizing children by changing enough dirty diapers.)

Do we have an incest taboo or not? We seem to need one. Our ambivalence about it is disturbing. Our attitudes range from amusement (Question, "What do you call a hillbilly girl who can outrun her brother?" Answer, "A virgin.") to blaming the child (A patient, who had just been arrested for exposing himself to a five-year-old girl: "She loved it, but she'd seen one before. The little whore.").

PATTERNS OF INCEST

Serrano and Gunzburger point out the obvious: if people were given completely free choice, a wholly biological choice, they would mate with those closest. Perhaps that explains why people have affairs with in-laws, spouses of close friends, and coworkers; it may in fact be surprising that incest is not even more common than it is.

Incest does occur from time to time between mothers and sons, though the only cases I've ever seen involved mothers trying to make contact with their schizophrenic sons. Stepfather-stepdaughter sex is common, and usually occurs when the child is adolescent or even grown. It is often reacted to simply as an infidelity and is not considered incest by many authorities. Stepmother-stepson incest is not at all rare, particularly with an adolescent stepson and a barely post-adolescent stepmother. It is rarely considered incest, but it can cause quite an uproar. I've known more than one man who had sex with his mother-in-law, one who had sex with his father-in-law, and any number who had sex with a sister-in-law—none of those is quite incest, however disrupting to the family.

Brother-sister incest is not unusual before and at puberty, and if the children are near the same age it may not be considered much of a problem. If one is near adult and the other a child, it is much like parent-child incest. Older brothers misuse their little sisters and brothers frequently, and the misuse of little boys by their older sisters is nowhere near as rare as mother-child incest. Brother-sister incest between adults implies rather extreme enmeshment.

The major crises of incest, the ones that get the most attention and produce the most societal revulsion, are between adult males and children. Older brothers, grandfathers, uncles, stepfathers, mothers' boyfriends, and fathers sexually use both boys and girls, from infancy to adulthood. Frequently, in the histories of homosexual and heterosexual men, there are stories of older brothers forcing fellatio or uncles purchasing sexual favors. When the activity is male to male, even father-son incest is reacted to as homosexuality rather than as incest. It is so embarrassing that it is rarely reported, yet it may be the determinant of the boy's subsequent sexuality (Langsley, Schwartz, & Fairbairn, 1968).

FATHER-DAUGHTER INCEST

We usually think of incest as involving a father and one or more of his daughters. A daughter, even if old enough to protest inappropriate sexual advances from her grandfather, her big brother, or even her stepfather, may have little ability to protect herself from the sexual advances of her own father. Susan Brownmiller (1973) makes little distinction between incest and rape. Although violence and physical harm to the child are not usual, it can occur. But the implicit power of the father over his daughter is so great that it need not be used explicitly.

Incest is surely bad for children. We have little reliable data because most cases are not reported and we see clinically only those girls or women who have been most obviously traumatized by it. Incest survivors tend to recall the incest as the most powerful influence on their sense of their own worth and on their ability to trust men subsequently. Many carry burdens of great guilt, are actively protective of their fathers, and direct most of their anger at their mothers! What are they guilty about? They rarely remember the sex as enjoyable, though some enjoyed the power and influence it brought them. Most found it terrifying at the time and feared each subsequent episode. Most did not tell, but found a way out of the family as quickly as possible, perhaps by running off with the first man who knew the exit. They may lead their lives seeing themselves as either innocent or guilty victims, but still trying not to let their mothers know it ever happened. They see themselves as having made a sacrifice of their own lives to save their parents' marriage, a sacrifice their mothers never appreciated or even acknowledged. It wasn't that the sex was so awful — it was more often a disgusting nuisance — but that the power of the secret was so terrifying.

The most important thing about parent-child incest is not that it is abuse (though it is certainly that) or even that it is harmful (there are forms of abuse even more harmful) but that it is an infidelity. It is an infidelity of a peculiar sort in that it provides a secret that threatens the parents' marriage, but at the same time serves as a stabilizer for the parents' marriage, in that it prevents, in the child's fantasy, the father from going out of the home in search of a sexier wife. The child becomes junior wife to the father, keeping him in the family.

Daughters

The girls who become the objects of their father's sexuality are typically hyperresponsible oldest daughters, and the incest increases the hyperresponsibility. Such a girl is both junior wife to her father and junior mother to her younger siblings and perhaps to her mother as well. The incest usually starts when she is prepubertal, although intercourse typically awaits puberty. It goes on for years, until the girl leaves home or reveals it (revealing it is not sufficient — someone must believe her and make a fuss about it). At first it is her own confusion and the father's threat of sending her off or being himself sent off that keep the girl from revealing it. Later it is her hyperresponsibility that maintains the secret. Typically the girl keeps it secret until she wants boys her own age, and the father will not permit her to date, preferring to keep her for himself. The girl knows that if she stops it, the father will turn to her younger sister, but if she reveals it the family may be broken up and the mother is not in a position to keep the family going without the father.

One 17-year-old finally revealed the eight-year affair with her stepfather, after pondering painfully over whether she should keep silent to protect the marriage or speak up to protect her little sister, whom she assumed would be next in line for her father's bed. She felt little guilt after the revelation, realizing she'd done what was best for everyone's protection. The nobility, however misplaced, of children caught in these situations is usually overlooked. These girls are given entirely too much responsibility and power in the family, and they recognize that they are sacrificing their own childhood for the greater good.

The situation is so repulsive and disgusting that it arouses strong emotions on the part of anyone who must deal with it. The quandary for the therapist, as well as for the legal system, is how to protect the child from the incest without destroying the family she is sacrificing herself to protect. The question must be raised: Is such a family worth saving? Actually, this question has three parts: (1) Will the father stop it once it is revealed? (2) Will the child reveal it if it recurs? (3) Can the mother put herself between the two to provide protection against recurrence?

Mothers

The mother is the hypotenuse in the incestuous triangle, theoretically capable of stabilizing the situation and maintaining appropriate distance between father and daughter. This is a heavy burden — God knows an unfair one — and at times an impossible one. To make matters worse, the idea that the mother has the responsibility of preventing recurrence has been perverted into the idea that the mother has caused the incest. It is often assumed that the mother "always" knows. This is not the case. Sometimes father and daughter go to great efforts to keep mother from knowing. Quite frequently, however, the mother has been told but does not believe it and certainly does not *want* to believe it. She may, in fact, punish the child for telling such a story. One mother even told her daughter, "Why do you want to hurt me by telling me this? You know I can't do anything about it. Handle it the best way you can, just don't tell anybody else."

The feminist literature is particularly and appropriately indignant at assigning such responsibility to the beleaguered mother. It has even been assumed that systems thinking characteristically blames the mother, an idea that Phyllis Chesler (1971) reproaches. It would be absurd to assume that a mother, even holding a gun to her husband's head, could make him have sex with his daughter against his will. Justina Pittman (1985) points out this absurdity in "Father-Daughter Incest and Power Hierarchies Within the Family": "Mothers are additionally berated for being frigid, which, of course, gives the father no choice but to seek sexual solace in his daughter."

The mothers in incestuous families are indeed often found to be quite pitiful creatures, unable to oppose their husbands or to protect their daughters. Judith Herman (1983) says, "Economically dependent, socially isolated, battered, ill, or encumbered with the care of many small children, mothers in incestuous families are generally not in a position to consider independent survival, and must therefore preserve their marriages at all costs, even if the cost includes the conscious or unconscious sacrifice of a daughter." This picture of the mothers as powerless and incompetent seems true much of the time; many are retarded, schizophrenic, alcoholic, or chronically depressed. But many are not.

The literature pictures these women, I think accurately, as feeling worthless as mothers, as wives, and as women. They are seen as reversing the mother-daughter roles with their daughters, thus assuming with the daughters the relationship they would have wished with their own rejecting mothers. A frequent dynamic in these families revolves around the father and the daughter huddling together with fierce anger at the woman who has deserted them to get her doctorate, get her business going, or care for her own mother. The mother is pictured as incompetent at home, however powerful in the world. These women give little love and suffer because they get little in return. They may have little sense of themselves as grownups, expect to be children to their children, and "exhibit lack of psychological investment in their children" (Zuelzer and Reposa, 1983, p. 98).

The significant powerlessness of the mother in an incestuous family may not be general ineptitude or economic helplessness or even domestic clumsiness and it may not be a lack of interest in what goes on in her family. It may, quite simply, be an inability to effectively supervise her husband. She may be unable to do this because he is too weak or because he is too strong; in either case he fails to supervise the appropriateness of his own behavior, leaves that monitoring process to others, and then defies the monitor he appoints.

Fathers

Incestuous fathers generally have a strong sense of gender, and it becomes relevant in at least four different areas:

(1) Incestuous fathers believe a man should be strong and should control his family. He may proceed then to tyrannize his family, as if his dignity or

his religion compelled it. Or he may recognize that he does not live up to his expected level of control and be passively surly because his family has failed to bring about this power in him. The feminist literature often pictures incestuous fathers as fire-breathing monsters, seeing the family as "a pathological exaggeration of generally accepted patriarchal norms" (Herman, 1983).

It seems true that the daughters who have survived the incestuous relationship consistently describe their fathers as "perfect patriarchs . . . without question, the heads of their households. Their authority was absolute" (Herman, 1981). I have no doubt that the incestuous father does appear that way to the daughter he has victimized. Incestuous fathers do not, however, appear tyrannical outside the family; in fact, they are generally mild-mannered, eager to please, hardworking, anxious, insecure, and frightened by their failure to live up to their sense of what a man should be. About two-thirds are alcoholic or abuse other substances. However these men appear to their daughters or to their wives, they appear quite pitiful to themselves. And, in my experience, many of their wives and daughters see them as pitiful as well.

(2) Incestuous fathers do not feel sexually adult. They frequently report that they have small penises or that they think their penis is too small (I never checked). They have difficulty with sex and would be uncomfortable having an affair. Usually they have had little sexual experience with grown women and see themselves as barely pubertal. Frequently they themselves have been victims of sexual abuse and incest. Fowler, Burns, and Roehl (1983, p. 92) report that 80 percent of the incestuous fathers in their sample had been sexually or physically maltreated as children. They are often baffled at the notion that anyone would see them as a sexual threat, since they experience themselves as sexually quite inadequate. During the incest, they do not see themselves as overpowering their child; they see it more like playing "doctor" with a peer.

(3) Incestuous fathers have a strong double standard. They believe that it is perfectly appropriate for a male to offer sex to a female, almost as if it were expected. Then it should be up to the female to set sexual limits, to refuse to catch the pass. Whether sex takes place should be up to the female, not the male, even if the female is three years old and the male is her grown father. Sexual restraint on the part of the male is not part of his value system. The reason he doesn't have affairs (and usually he does not) is not because it would be wrong, but because he's afraid to expose his sexual inadequacy to a real grown woman.

These men see themselves as having been invited by their children into sex, the invitation consisting of any effort to get close plus the subsequent refusal to resist effectively enough. Once the child has permitted some genital play, she is thenceforth a "little whore," not a derogatory evaluation, but one that relieves him of responsibility. These men do not experience much guilt during the years of incest, although they may be ashamed when the story comes out. Some are not even ashamed—they assume any man would do it if a child would permit it.

(4) The incestuous father believes that men need not concern themselves with the appropriateness of behavior in the family. That is the responsibility of females. It is up to his wife and daughter to make him do what is considered appropriate. He may feel a responsibility to prevent his family from having contact with the outside world, and the isolation of the family is most likely his idea, but boundaries within the family do not exist for him. He may not want them at all; however, if they are to be there, it is up to his wife to institute and maintain them. He may feel no impropriety in sleeping nude with his children, or wrestling nude with them, or bathing with them (though he might cover himself around his wife who is considered a grown woman and therefore a little frightening). He may be an exhibitionist or a voyeur and is often a casual nudist in the home. It is up to his wife to set limits on such behavior. And he can always excuse any impropriety by claiming to have been drunk at the time. I remember one incestuous father who vigorously denied the incest his daughter claimed, though he confessed, "It might have happened once or twice when I was drunk" (Machotka, Pittman, Flomenhaft, 1967).

THE INCESTUOUS FAMILY STRUCTURE

The feminist literature sees incest as a reflection of sexism and of excessive male power. Certainly a double standard, gender stereotypes, and the patriarchal system are part of the problem. However, there are other issues as well. Alexander (1985) reports on the isolation of these families, the degree to which they are "closed systems" and pathologically enmeshed. Incestuous families don't exchange information with the outside world, lack sufficient negentropy to permit generational differentiation, and are too homeostatic.

These families tend to maintain their disordered structure for years, the father sexually exploiting one child after another, with the mother apparently oblivious to the situation. The crisis in these families may come from the pathology of either parent, either of whom may develop severe symptoms. Or the child may become a bedwetter, a shoplifter, a runaway, or suicidal, psychotic, or sexually promiscuous. When outside intervention is required for these other problems, the family may close tightly and protect the incest secret.

THE CRISIS OF INCEST

The usual crisis occurs when the secret comes out. The girl may become pregnant and tell a friend, a boyfriend, or a teacher or counselor. The father may attempt to involve another child, who is less protective and reports it.

Rarely is it the mother who discovers and reports the incest. The father is never the reporter.

If the incest is between a stepdaughter and a stepfather, the girl may feel less protectiveness and responsibility and so report it earlier and more vigorously. One young girl was approached by her recently nudist stepfather, who was pointing an erection at her. She yelled, "Put that damned thing down!" and promptly called her mother. It seems that mothers are far more willing to divorce incestuous stepfathers than they are to divorce incestuous fathers. This may be because the mothers have already survived the loss of one husband, or because they see the incest as more of an infidelity, or because the daughter is less likely to intercede to keep the incestuous stepfather in the family. For whatever reason, the mother usually kicks the stepfather out of the house and proceeds with some sort of action.

Some mothers, reluctant to disrupt the natural family when incest occurs, may prefer to kick the child out(!) and try to think of her incestuous husband as "sick" rather than "evil." Even as she protects her husband, she may be quite punitive toward the daughter. In one unforgettable family, the five-year-old reported to neighbors that her father had her give him a blow job every morning before kindergarten. The mother railed at the little girl, insisting that "all these problems are because of you and your big mouth." I jumped in to point out the husband's horrifying behavior. She said, "You're supposed to be an expert and have compassion. How can you criticize this poor man — he's a victim of that little whore's incest." This case is extreme, but the trend in this direction is not rare.

When the incest is finally reported, the daughter feels some relief and begins to make contact with the outside world. It often surprises me how well these girls can adapt when they are given enormous amounts of extrafamilial support. They may not get much support at home. The mother is being called upon to take responsibility she may never have been good at or interested in. The father may go pitiful and deny everything, even as he reveals just enough of his inability to recognize boundaries to indirectly confess. The apparent weakness of these men seems startling to some of the feminist writers, who center their theory of incest around the father's excessive power in the family. He does of course have excessive power over his daughter, but his inadequacy is quite real and an integral part of the problem. Once the incest is exposed, his inadequacy is also exposed.

TREATMENT OF INCESTUOUS FAMILIES

Step 1: Emergency Response

The child, directly or indirectly, is the one who reveals the secret. The uproar produced by the revelation of the secret may be almost as damaging as the incest itself. In some states, the legal authorities must be involved, and in most cases they already are by the time the family gets to the therapist. The legal authorities seem to have a knack for either a full scale overreaction or no reaction at all, and their approach may vary from day to day. The therapeutic system is at their mercy.

Unless there is a threat of rape or violence, or the incestuous father is the only adult in the household, the situation is rarely an emergency requiring abrupt decisions about the future of the family. A temporary separation may be in order. If the mother divorces the father, or the legal authorities jail him, and the mother is and remains a detached, inept, distracted parent, the child victim may be deprived of both parents while taking the blame for destroying the family. Neither separation nor punishment is a suitable substitute for treatment, although all of these measures may be necessary in time.

Step 2: Involving the Family

All three corners of the incestuous triangle must be involved. Any other previous incest participants should be included. Other adult family members need to be included too, and the younger children should be alerted to "Daddy's problem" so that they can offer protection to one another. There should be no secrets permitted in this family which handles secrets so destructively. The mother's mother is often significant and can be included. If the mother is too inept or distracted to provide protection for the child, the legal authorities must become part of the treatment.

Step 3: Define the Problem

Is this the typical incest family? Or did the father make a unique inappropriate sexual gesture which was promptly reported and reacted to? If this family has the typical incestuous structure, why is the daughter reporting it now? Recognize that the father may not be completely honest about his sexual activities, and both the mother and the daughter may try to protect him further. The story is often metamorphic, expanding and contracting before the bewildered eyes of the therapist and the police. The details are not important, except to lawyers and judges; they have their job and you have yours. The dynamics of the family are rarely confusing.

As the crisis unfolds, the nature of the problem must be defined (Pittman, 1976, 1977). There should be determination of the degree to which the event is real or imagined, overt or covert, unique or habitual, structural or incidental.

Real-imagined. When a child reports incest or attempted incest by a parent or stepparent, it must be taken seriously. The incest may be imagined, but the misdirected sexual tensions, the sense of sexual threat, and perhaps a breach in generational boundaries are real. A report of incest may be seen as a request for protection from sexual threat or for maintenance of the protected child role in the family or as a demand that the informed parent act in a parental and sexually adult manner. The uninvolved parent who ignores or disbelieves the accusation may be trying to avoid a crisis in order to sustain a family pattern which is seriously pathological in its parental and sexual functioning. The reports of incest with biological fathers are usually true, but may not be. Reports of stepfather incest are frequently not literally true, and people make wild accusations in the wake of divorces and remarriages. All such reports must be taken very seriously, but they can't be automatically believed.

Overt-covert. For an incestuous relationship to be resolved, at least three people must be involved: the child, the accused parent, and the displaced parent, who is both "cuckold" and failed protector. When the child tries to keep the secret, fails to inform the displaced parent, informs and is ignored, the focus must be on this process of secrecy. Other family members may know about it too. It is particularly important to determine whether other children in the family have also been involved. Since the major fuel for the incest is the secret, revealing the secret is the core of the therapeutic effort.

Unique-habitual. An incestuous overture or event may be a unique happening which is then reported to the displaced parent, made overt, and handled as a family crisis. The pathology may be almost solely in the incestuous adult, who may be psychotic or alcoholic rather than pedophiliac. Recurrent incest is much more serious. If the child continues the incest without reporting it, something is amiss in the child's relationship with the displaced parent. If it is reported and permitted to continue, denied, or carefully overlooked, that is clearly a major part of the problem.

Structural-incidental. Real, covert, habitual incest occurs in a particular pathological family structure. The father is sexist, sexually insecure, dominating and weak, and is usually alcoholic as well. He may feel sexually estranged from his wife or sexually inadequate to her. In abusing his daughter he makes a hostile, inept sexual choice that protects him from venturing out of the home in search of adult women. The mother is infantile and dependent, at least at home, and has assumed with her daughter the relationship she wished she had with her own mother. The daughter is socially awkward, hyperresponsible, hostile toward the mother, and protective of the father. The family is isolated and enmeshed. It is unusual for families of other sorts to harbor incest, although isolated incidents may occur or be reported.

Step 4: General Prescription

The stress on all three participants is enormous, and all kinds of pathology may unfold. Each symptom needs careful attention. There is no way to cool the situation down quickly, and no resolution that will please everybody. Top priority must go to the comfort and security of the child and to honoring her nobility in revealing the secret and/or sacrificing for the family. Removing the father may be in order, but may not soothe the grieving child, who has chosen to sacrifice her father for the sake of some greater good.

Step 5: Specific Prescription

Family therapy is vital and may be bolstered by individual or specialized group therapy for one or more of the three. There are groups for incest victims and groups for incest offenders. I have not heard of groups for the mothers in incestuous families.

The uproar of it all is in itself therapeutic for the particularly isolated and enmeshed family. All manner of unfamiliar people begin to tromp through the family and tear apart its boundaries. The thrust of the family therapy should be toward restoring appropriate boundaries and role relationships in the family. The roles, rules and functions of parents and children must be clarified.

The immediate task is for the mother to take complete charge of the family and to monitor the relationship between her husband and her child. The father may have to leave the family for a time for that to happen. As quickly as possible, the mother-daughter relationship must be realigned so the mother can mother the child, provide protection, and open communication.

The father can't be in the home until the child can trust the mother to provide protection. While the timing seems particularly unfortunate, the sexual relationship between the mother and father should be quickly resumed. The mother, whether she wants to or not, must become both wife and mother if the family is to continue. At the same time the child is taught to be a child; this requires someone to be a parent, a task that may fall temporarily to a therapist.

The father's pathology may be more severe, and usually includes alcoholism. Antabuse and abstinence may be requisite to remaining in the home. The inappropriateness of his behavior should be made obvious, as well as the inappropriateness of his attitudes about sex, gender, power, secrets, adults/children, men/women, and who is responsible for what.

Step 6: Negotiating Resistance

The mother, instead of mothering the daughter, may instead use the incest as justification for further rejection of the girl and may attempt to push the child further into premature adulthood. Evaluating the financial advantages and disadvantages, she may kick the daughter out instead of the husband. Or she may dissolve into pitiful ineptitude and call upon her husband and daughter to join forces in mothering her. The mother may not want to resume sex with the father, using the incest for further sexual rejection. The father may go pitiful and throw himself on his daughter, or he may deny everything and sulk at the therapist's office and storm at home. Or he may acknowledge it all and then demand closure. The couple may desert the daughter and skip town together.

The legal authorities, the protective services, and the therapist may not be in agreement about what is best. The overzealous may want to crucify or castrate the father, while the mother may oppose having him leave the house at all. As the experts battle, the family chaos grows. Usually either nothing is done or entirely too much.

Much seems to depend upon the competence of the mother. Imprisoning the father seems a cruel punishment to the family which is financially dependent upon him. Still, it is often done. Getting the father out of the house temporarily may be necessary while the mother and daughter are restoring trust; this seems far less destructive to the family. A temporary separation may impress upon him the seriousness of the offense, although legally required separations always seem to come at the emotionally inappropriate moment and seem to turn the father into the societal victim, thereby defusing the whole point of the crisis.

There just doesn't seem to be a good alternative to providing a child with at least one competent parent.

Step 7: Termination

Therapy should be quite long-term. It usually isn't. Denial and avoidance set in as soon as the horror subsides. The girl may resume therapy later, as her distrust of men and her oversexualization of herself create problems in other relationships. If the family attempts to resolve the problem by divorce, that divorce usually doesn't take, and the couple gets back together. Since pedophilia is compulsive, almost addictive behavior, it is likely to recur, if not with this child, then with another, unless there is structural change in the family. All efforts should be made to keep the family in therapy.

We have little idea of what the long-range consequences of incest might be. The child may well have long-term emotional repercussions from it, and that seems most likely if the incest is not revealed and remains a guilty secret. Incestuous sex need not be crippling and probably is not crippling some of the time. Still, these girls have much to learn about boundaries, about trust, and about their own worth before they can lead normal lives, and they have no one in the family to teach them. Therapy seems crucial.

SECTION VI

Caretaking Families

The sick are the greatest danger for the healthy; it is not from the
strongest that harm comes to the strong, but from the weakest.

— Friedrich Wilhelm Nietzsche, *Genealogy of Morals*, 1889

CHAPTER 19

Caretakers and Chemistry

WHEN PEOPLE AREN'T QUITE RIGHT

T HE BRAIN CHEMISTRY of the family members is an especially important
part of the family system. No family can survive without one, or more,
brains and every brain is a delicate chemistry set, subject to malfunctioning.
Some of the most profound crises families face come about when the chemistry of one family member's brain goes kaflooey. The affected family member is helpless in the face of disordered brain chemistry, and other family
members are usually equally helpless caretakers. Some people bring about
this chemical state of uncontrollable helplessness by voluntarily taking drugs
that poison their brains. Others — manics, depressives, and schizophrenics —
experience this quite involuntarily. The family, unable to handle this effectively on their own, will seek outside help.

The family of someone with a chemical psychosis has had few choices in
the search for help. The pre-Freudian asylums offered a bucolic setting in
which psychotics could be protected from the pressures of reality while they

were being taught how to behave properly ("moral treatment"). It is not clear whether the asylums protected patients from their families or families from their patients. In the early Freudian era, there were psychiatric hospitals which provided years of psychoanalysis for psychotic patients. These programs shunned medication, kept the family out of therapy and out of the patients' life, and sought the cure in the chaotic unconscious. The family was considered to blame for these conditions, but the family was far too toxic to have contact with the patients. These programs were incredibly expensive, highly prestigious, and utterly ineffective. In the '50s, there were two developments. One of these was psychotropic medication, which worked so well the asylums were largely emptied. The other was family therapy, which tried to find ways to prevent either the psychoses or the inevitable relapses of patients who had received psychotropic medication and were well enough to leave the asylums and return home to their toxic families.

Family therapy has one of its roots planted in the effort during the '50s and '60s to find a way to treat psychotics with their families. The results were, in retrospect, less impressive than the theories, all of which blamed the families for producing the psychosis. The believers in chemical etiology were in direct competition with the believers in family etiology. The chemists had better data and better results, at least better results in getting patients out of their psychosis and out of the hospital. Neither the chemists nor the family therapists were doing such a great job of *keeping* patients out of the hospital.

In our work in Denver in the mid '60s (Pittman et al., 1966, Langsley et al., 1968), we could keep people out of hospitals, and we could keep people from being rehospitalized, but we couldn't do it without *both* family therapy and psychotropic medication. We were faulted at that time for using drugs. Actually, we should have been faulted for our primitive and insensitive style of family therapy. Like the other family therapists of that era, we misunderstood systems theory and sought explanations for why the family needed to drive its members crazy. Our therapy tried to bring family conflicts into sharp focus and thereby probably inadvertently exacerbated some situations. Fortunately, the medications dampened the destructiveness of our well-intentioned clumsiness. We could not, then or now, treat those psychotic people in or out of the hospital without psychotropic medication. But if we were to repeat the research, we would have better and more specific family therapy techniques.

The frustration of all of this has been the utterly unnecessary territorial conflict between neuropharmacology and family therapy. This conflict is still going on in the minds of some family theorists, some organic psychiatrists, and many families who have had the horrifying experience of seeking help in dealing with their chemically deficient loved ones, and then being blamed for causing the illness without being given any idea of how to cure it.

Disorders of brain chemistry must be treated both chemically and systemically. Family therapists who are also psychiatrists can provide both parts of the treatment. Psychiatrists who are not family therapists should share the treatment with a family therapist. Family therapists who are not also psychiatrists must involve a physician to handle the chemical aspect of the treatment. If the two therapists fail to respect one another's contributions, attempt to undercut one another, or compete for the patient, another level of caretaker crisis is produced. There are psychiatrists who see these disorders as only chemical or who offer individual therapy which ignores the family context, the family's need for psychoeducation, or the family's caretaker crisis in the face of alarming phenomena. There are family therapists who insist, against all evidence and experience, that these conditions can be treated without resort to chemical means. Both unitary positions fail to appreciate the marvelous results that can be obtained by coordinating the two approaches.

CASE 28   *In Orbit Around the Globe*

Quentin was a young graduate student when I first saw him. During the previous week, he had been running a write-in campaign for president. Although the presidential election had already been held, he had made speeches all over New York. To assist him in his campaign, he had attempted to commandeer the airplane on which he was flying to Louisiana for Thanksgiving. At that time, I had the ever-fascinating job of evaluating anyone who acted strangely on an airplane in the Southeast. Quentin hadn't slept for many days, as he monitored the television for the many veiled references he heard to his campaign. He was quite psychotic, had no family in Atlanta, and was hospitalized until they could arrive.

Quentin's parents arrived quickly. Exceedingly sensible people, they were shocked by this change in their quiet and studious son. He bore little resemblance to the son they had known. However, they did recall an uncle who had had a similar experience. Quentin was clearly manic. In a few days, on phenothiazines and lithium, he calmed enough to sleep. The parents tried to convince him that the election had been held and he had lost. After about a week, he began to mourn his political loss and assumed he had made such a mess of things that his life was effectively over. He just sat there.

He was discharged from the hospital and returned to Louisiana with his parents, who arranged further treatment for him. I urged him to stay on the lithium. I heard nothing more for a few years.

Then the family called. Quentin had gotten his M.B.A., had a good job in Boston, had married, and had discontinued his lithium at the recommendation of his new psychoanalyst. Within a few weeks, he was manic. He had left his bank job, had borrowed large sums of money to open a strip joint in

San Diego, and had taken up with a stripper. His psychiatrist refused to talk to his wife and told Quentin that he was leaving his wife for the stripper for reasons that were oedipal.

When the wife called me, I urged her to get him back on his lithium. (How she did it is a long and exasperating story, but one which endeared her to me forever.) Within a few days he was contrite and horrified by his behavior. His wife took him back, but his boss wouldn't. He went to work for a bank in rural Illinois. The impact on the marriage was such that I found a family therapist for him this time.

Quentin's next episode was only a few months later. The family therapist didn't believe in medication and had not followed through on it. Quentin was found prospecting for gold in Alaska. He got back on his lithium, stayed in family therapy, and found a psychiatrist to monitor the drug.

I heard nothing more for ten years. This time the father called. Quentin had gone crazy again, had invested everything he owned and could borrow in a scheme involving buried treasure in the Caribbean. He had left his wife and children for a skin diver from Martinique. This episode had begun when his psychiatrist had retired and the psychiatrist's partner had read something to the effect that manics should be given drug holidays from time to time. Quentin had taken his drug holiday in Martinique.

I got a supply of lithium to the father in Louisiana and one to the wife in Illinois, and they set out for the Caribbean to find and medicate Quentin. They finally got him to a motel in Miami, where they brought him back to normal on lithium.

Quentin called recently, to tell me he's still trying to get out of the financial disaster of the last episode. He assures me he won't get off the lithium again, though I have the sneaking suspicion that he enjoys these holidays from his usual sanity. I recommended that he could have fun more safely if he stayed on his lithium and took his wife with him when he goes on the travels he seems to enjoy. I realized as I got off the phone that I haven't seen Quentin in person for almost 20 years.

Family therapists willing to take on such messy cases should be willing to develop a working relationship with a medical therapist who can prescribe and oversee the chemical aspects of the case. Family therapists must understand these conditions and know when medical referral is indicated, what side effects the medicine produces, when the medicine should be raised or lowered. It is the family therapist who will be following the case and filtering the information. Psychiatrists, in general, rely too heavily on antipsychotic drugs, use doses that are far too high for far too long, and ignore the family totally. But exceptional psychiatrists can and should be found or educated to assist family therapists with these cases.

I often see, and appreciate, the bravado with which psychiatrophobic family therapists attempt to treat disordered brain chemistry without considering the chemistry. It may make the therapist feel independent, but it sure is a burden for the patient family. I cannot urge family therapists too strongly to consider the brain chemistry in the therapy. Please, try it!

Since I assume the reader of this is a family therapist who may not also be a psychiatrist, I will go into some detail about the presumed chemical nature of these disorders in the following chapters. My purpose is not neurochemical precision, but a simple working understanding of the conditions and how to combine the biological and systemic aspects of the treatment.

Don't look for happiness, Richie. It'll only make you miserable.

— Renee Taylor and Joseph Bologna, *Lovers and Other Strangers*, 1969

It doesn't matter what you do exactly, as long as you don't do it in the street and frighten the horses.

— attributed to Mrs. Patrick Campbell

CHAPTER 20

Mania

SO MUCH FUN IT HURTS

A MANIC MAN once launched a new scheme for controlling the universe by buying up all the used Coca-Cola trucks in Atlanta — on borrowed money. When he feared that the Coca-Cola company would respond by buying up used Pepsi-Cola trucks and repainting them, he began signing up unemployed truck painters to exclusive contracts. His wife didn't want to upset him by pointing out the absurdity of this. The bank wasn't so sensitive and had him arrested.

An older manic man was courtly with strange women he met on the psychiatric unit. He would make florid conversation and invite each to marry him. If she said "yes" he would order a wedding dress from Neiman-Marcus to be charged to the women's account and delivered to the psychiatric unit. If the hapless woman said "no," he would scream obscenities and bop her with his walking cane.

322

Manic depression, more recently called "bipolar depression," used to be among the more confusing and frustrating of psychiatric conditions. Untreated sufferers go through months of the deepest depression—withdrawn, inactive, feeling barely able to live through the day, certainly unable to respond to it or seize it. They reduce their activity and interest and passively hope for death. Then abruptly they spring to life, seizing not just the day but everything in their way. Their energy, activity, and imagination are boundless, literally, and anyone who attempts to bound them will be sorry. They burst through any restraint. They create and invent and initiate anything, except peace and order. As their elation mushrooms, grandiose schemes pile on top of one another, each incomplete. Impulsive, volatile, irritable, and even explosive when crossed, but euphoric throughout, they seem surprised and betrayed when anyone reacts less optimistically than they feel. But, no matter, they are distracted so easily and talking so much that they are not bothered long with anyone's reactions to them. This may go on for months, until suddenly they decide that everything is awful and sink back into total depression.

Classic psychoanalytic theory considered mania to be the denial of depression. Cohen et al. (1954) studied manics and their families and found the children who became manic adults to be hardworking, highly disciplined, and emotionally controlled—often the family "star" and destined to be the family "rescuer." Steirlin et al. (1986) confirm this, and note that the families make a sharp, strongly valued distinction between "positive" and "negative" emotions. In these families, normal depression is forbidden. These consistent observations don't mean that such a family pattern causes mania; it could mean that the family organizes around and idealizes the dauntless future manic, the undepressable ideal for the family.

It is now generally accepted that bipolar depression has a large organic component. Its occurrence follows genetic patterns, occurring in 1 percent of the general population and 80 percent of monozygotic twins. The blood and urine levels of the neurotransmitters norepinephrine and/or serotonin are decreased during depression and increased during mania (Schildkraut, 1970).

In Europe in the 1950s, lithium carbonate, a simple agricultural chemical that had previously been used as a salt substitute, was found to be dramatically effective in treating manic episodes and especially in preventing the manic cycles (Fieve, 1975; Schou, 1968). When lithium was finally approved by the FDA in 1968, it quickly became the treatment and prophylaxis of choice for mania, although it did not prove as dramatically useful for depression. Bipolar or manic depression was soon diagnosed more frequently, and many people who seemed to be alcoholics or paranoid schizophrenics proved to be suffering from this genetic, metabolic disorder. (When mania becomes sufficiently intense, the irritability and impatience take on a blatantly paranoid quality. Manics may attempt to stifle their moodswings with alcohol or other drugs and may go on intermittent binges that partially cover the underlying mania.)

Manic episodes can be triggered by the therapeutic use of steroids or by amphetamines, cocaine, or even antidepressants. Those situations may not indicate a genetic tendency toward manic depressive illness. Some episodes follow losses. I suppose, however, a retrospective search could reveal some sort of real or symbolic loss in anyone—manic, depressed, or not. Many manic episodes are preceded by depression, perhaps recurrent depression; many are not. Many manics have a family history of manic depression, or conditions diagnosed as alcoholism, agitated depression, or paranoid schizophrenia; many do not.

Mania is not hard to diagnose in its full flowering, but milder forms of hypomania may be considered almost desirable for overachievers. The hypomania may go on for years, with boundless energy and creativity and boldness and insensitivity and enthusiasm, interrupted perhaps by periodic depressions but never quite reaching psychotic levels and utter loss of control. Families may learn to live with this level of energy and just stand back in helpless awe as the hypomanic's irresistable force rolls over all the seemingly immovable objects in its path. Most people find it rather unsettling at close range, and spouses often take cover.

It is not easy for a family to bring a manic into therapy, as the manic is much too busy and sees no problem. If the manic is fired or arrested, or gets into an affair (each episode tends to culminate in a great romance, often a particularly bizarre one) and endangers the marriage, or spends fabulous enough to agree to seek help. The manic may be merely humoring everyone enough to agree to seek help. the manic may be merely humoring everyone else, may be impatient with the therapist, may show up early and demand to be seen instantly, or may have difficulty sitting through a session.

Usually, the diagnosis is not difficult to make. Hospitalization may be necessary, though protested. Actually, if the family can swing with the manic, medication will work nicely at home. Phenothiazines will bring a manic down more quickly than lithium, though not as gently, and injectable barbiturates may be quickest of all. Manics should be seen daily until under control, and may be kept under sufficient medication to maintain a few days of barely interrupted sleep. Manics are far easier to manage at home, if they are properly medicated and attended, and if guns and car keys are removed. The psychiatric hospital atmosphere may be confusing and stimulating.

Manics most often come in during the last act of the drama, as the curtain is falling, the lights coming on and the shock of reality glaring. At that time, there is no resistance to whatever a therapist or anyone else wants. The manic is tired and ready to go off duty. Each manic episode is followed by a depression of varying degree. Once the manic is safely on lithium and whatever else is needed to stop the episode, the depression may be terrifying and painful. Antidepressants may be used, but only while the manic depressive is on lithium, as antidepressants alone can bring the mania right back.

On lithium, manic depressives rarely go through mood swings, and their whole relationship with the world may change. A few don't like it; they may miss their customary highs and find normality rather drab, more like depression than like their cherished mania. Most find lithium liberating, connecting them more fully with the world than they have ever known. But they may not know what to do next. Some get off their lithium in hopes of experiencing another high, and they may do so. After a second or third manic episode, they will probably accept the lithium, if not to prevent the disastrous high, then to prevent the miserable low that inevitably follows.

Lithium is a reasonably safe drug, with few side effects, but can be toxic if it builds up in the body. If the kidneys are already diseased, the body may store lithium and it can be further damaging to the kidneys and other organs. The blood level must be monitored closely at first and from time to time afterwards. This procedure is a clumsy nuisance and may inhibit the use of the drug. In therapeutic doses, lithium is well tolerated; a fine hand tremor may be a reliable indicator of encroaching toxicity. The benefits of lithium are so astounding that the blood tests seem the most minor of inconveniences. While lithium does not always prevent the depressive phase of the bipolar swings, manic episodes on lithium are unusual.

Many authorities, including Maxmen (1986), recommend that the lithium be discontinued after six months, to see if another episode occurs. There is danger in doing this, and it should only be done under close supervision. You can't ask manics to call you if they go crazy; they go much too crazy to know they've gone crazy.

Once a manic depressive is on lithium, he or she may appear completely free of pathology. Other family members may experience such relief that they think no further treatment is required. Even on lithium, the manic depressive may be fairly well stabilized but with a thermostat set too high or too low. Some remain depressed on lithium and may require antidepressants in addition. A few seem to be mild paranoid schizophrenics and may require phenothiazines. Most are more normal than ever seemed possible, to them and to their family. However, getting the manic depressive on the lithium and bringing the cycles to an end is just the first step in the family therapy.

Manic depressives have a lifetime of being at the mercy of moods too overwhelming to resist. They were rarely hyperactive children (Weiss & Hechtman, 1986), instead being dutiful and on target to a fault. They were not problem children; they may never have expressed emotions at all. They may never have learned to modulate their moods the way other people have. They may have learned more drastic ways of defending against their moods, by controlling their behavior rigidly, their environment tightly, or their brain chemistry harshly. Manics, in their premorbid state, may be excruciatingly disciplined obsessive-compulsives who have forced themselves to buckle under clocks and calendars and rules. Or they may be autocratic managers, dominating all about them through their emotionless logic. Or they may be alcoholics or drug users, titrating their drugs to maintain the desired mood levels. Many have found no way to combat the force of their moods, drifting through life at whatever pace and in whatever direction the moods dictated, changing jobs, marriages, and homes with each shift in their brain chemistry and between episodes waiting helplessly for the next mood to come. These people are like motorless sailboats — with no power to set the speed or direction of their movement through life.

The family of a manic depressive has learned that it is usually pointless to try to exert influence, stimulation, or restraint. Interpersonal considerations can't compete with the ebb and flow of biogenic amines. The family has also learned not to provide anything to which an overreaction would be possible. The family members don't tell the manic-depressive either the good news or the bad, as the reaction will be unpredictable — either excessive or not at all. Strangely, these people live together and appear normal to the world and sometimes to themselves.

Once on lithium, there is an emotional stillness and flatness made more dramatic by contrast to what has preceded it, like an auditorium after the music has stopped and the audience gone home. The family must learn to be alive together, to have moods that don't terrify, to exchange emotions without fear of being ignored or overwhelmed. The family member who tyrannized everyone else with his or her manic excitement or clinging despair is now a stuffed teddy bear, mentally and physically come back to earth, but emotionally an amateur human being. To teach the normalized manic depressive to be normal may require intensive emotional training from a family which has learned the hard way to avoid and suppress emotional interaction.

For instance, a woman alternated profound clinging depressions in which she would lock herself in the back bedroom to sob just enough to keep the family frantic, with frenzied, sleepless redecorating schemes and blatant drunken affairs with whatever workmen came to the house. On lithium, she went to work, saved money, and made some modest investments. Her husband, unaccustomed to her normality, had private detectives monitoring her relationships with both the employer and the stockbroker; he was careful not to ask her what she was doing but didn't believe anything she said. Although he appeared to be paranoid, he was just continuing a now unnecessary set of protective maneuvers.

In the family therapy of stabilized manic depressives, there is much psychoeducation, always in the presence of the patient. Still the family assumes anything that goes on in front of the patient is a sham and the real story will be told only behind the patient's back, so they usually call to have the therapist tell them the real situation. In family interviews, it is useful to keep the emotional level high. A jaunty, joking, provocative atmosphere with rapid shifts of subject and mood can be a liberating role model for both patient and family. It is helpful to go over the history of the episodes and laugh together about the absurd horror of it all. These marriages are not very secure — awful things have happened during the manic episodes and the depressions have been hell for everyone. The family is not easily assured that the craziness is over.

Perhaps even more threatening to the family is the change in the patient. Instead of whatever pathology the family knew and loved, there is now health, albeit fumbling, embryonic health, which may be too threatening. More than one man has wanted his wife's mania brought back for another raucous vacation, and quite a few women have mourned their tractable, dependent, depressed husband. During manic episodes, many people abruptly divorce and marry unstable strangers, who are attracted to the mania and have little interest in being married to someone sane. There is no question that ex-manics have sacrificed some of their entertainment value.

If the marriage was sane prior to the latest episode and the initiation of lithium treatment, the return to sanity is welcomed and the temporary moodlessness understood. Still, even if the now predictable former patient is cherished, he or she may still be scrutinized for relapse. For instance, a man had been manic yearly for 30 years, had spent most of his adult life on disability, and had received uncounted electroshock treatments. Each episode had begun with impulsive spending sprees. On lithium, he remained stable for 14 years, returned to employment and dependability, and enjoyed his life and health. On the day of his retirement, he went to the grocery store, as he did every Thursday, and impulsively bought a candy bar. When he came home and showed his wife his little purchase, she panicked, locked him in the bathroom, and called me.

Another woman, a psychotherapist who understood manic depression well, was married to a man whose supercautious life was abruptly interrupted by a manic episode, in which he spent the family savings grandly. Once he was on lithium and the episode was over, he became distrustful of himself and bowed to her authority. She knew just how to treat him. She became unaccustomedly extravagant and helpless, coyly putting him back in the position of being the practical, rational member of the marriage. I assumed she knew just what she was doing, but she insisted for years that it just happened.

A REVIEW OF TREATMENT

Step 1: Emergency Response

Manic episodes are a true emergency and must be responded to with immediate availability and whatever force is necessary to contain the manic patient. Getting the patient to the office can be quite an adventure, sometimes requiring all the king's horses and all the king's men. Psychiatric hospitalization, voluntary or involuntary, may be required for containment, but need not go on long. The episode can often be treated at home, but it is a fulltime job for the family for several days.

Step 2: Family Involvement

Everybody in the family is already involved in getting the patient to you. And there may be some surprises that have surfaced too — manics never meet a stranger, and some of the stranger strangers may get incorporated into the episode and the beginning of therapy. Eventually, everyone will have to take part in the relearning of normality.

Steps 3 and 4: Definition and General Prescription

Mania, once diagnosed, must be explained to everyone. Then the manic must be contained and sedated. Family members must be supported and supervised as they go through the process (taking from one day to one week) of bringing the manic back to earth. They must be able to oversee him or her at all times. If they can't the hospital may have to. After a hefty shot of Thorazine, the manic may be quite tractable, even if not yet rational. It would be foolhardy and inhumane to try to bring down a manic without drugs or without constant supervision.

Step 5: Specific Prescription

The first and crucial treatment for manic depressive illness is lithium. While it may not be fast enough for outpatient reliability in ending a full-scale manic episode, it works smoothly for the milder episodes or while the patient is hospitalized and reasonably cooperative. Instituted right away though, it may blunt the post-manic depression. Lithium needs to be continued indefinitely with severe manic depressives. Lithium free trials must be closely supervised.

The other specific treatment can work only while the manic depressive is on the lithium. The manic must be taught how to be emotional, how to modify moods, how to be normal. The family must be taught how to both permit and teach emotional living. This can be a long process.

Step 6: Negotiating Resistance

Usually, the manic sees no problem and must be forced or coerced into therapy. In the festive atmosphere of the therapist's office, the manic, feeling invulnerable, is often surprisingly cooperative with anything that is quick and pays attention to him or her. A quick shot of Thorazine may be laughingly accepted. Once the manic is calmed, lithium is generally accepted, and compliance is high. If the family understands the drug, compliance is even higher. I often give out copies of Fieve's book *Moodswing*, which explains the situation convincingly to informed laypeople.

After a time of normality, the manic may miss the manic high and discontinue the lithium; few need more than one relapse to be convinced. Or the family may have difficulty permitting normality as the manic attempts to develop an emotional relationship with the world. Generally, family members benefit from teaching what they have learned about how to use thoughts, music, activity, exercise, hobbies, conversations, relationships, movies, and whatever else to bring about a desired mood. Still, they may need some adjustment time before they can let the former manic experience emotion without feeling panic.

Some of these marriages are shaky—and no wonder. Spouses may have spent so many years blaming themselves for the flat marriage or the crazy episodes that they distrust the value of the marriage. If they'll just hang in there long enough to experience some normality, they may like the marriage better—and they may not.

Step 7: Termination

Manic depressives disappear from therapy for long periods, but they never terminate. Therapy may consist of biannual brief social visits and lithium checks. There are no more grateful patients than stabilized manics and their families.

In a real dark night of the soul it is always three o'clock in the morning.

—F. Scott Fitzgerald, *The Crack Up*, 1936

Most of the work in the world is done by people who aren't feeling very well that day.

—Eleanor Roosevelt

CHAPTER 21

Depression

WRINGING THE HANKIE

Depression is no fun. So why is it so popular?

Everybody gets depressed sometimes. It is a normal part of the human emotional repertoire. We all have our bad days, even bad periods in our lives, and we would be callous not to react with sadness to much in life. Depression is one of the emotional exercises we put ourselves through routinely. Anyone of us who does not enjoy a good cry, or going into a brown study, or wrestling with our black beast, or hurling ourselves pathetically upon the ones we love, is missing the richness of life's experience. But depression can go far beyond those familiar emotional exercises and become all consuming, a devastating inability to anticipate pleasure or a successful outcome to any endeavor. People can get stuck in depression, like falling into a deep dark hole, from which they can see no light, no escape, no hope. Death can seem to be a blessing.

The classic idea about depression (Freud, *Mourning and Melancolia*) is that it is related to mourning and loss — or imagined loss, or anticipated loss, or symbolic loss, or fantasy loss, or even imagining a fantasy or an anticipated symbolic loss. Losses are painful, and adjustment to the loss of love or security or structure or hope can be terribly hard work, involving at least temporarily sinking into helpless sense of being overloaded and deprived at the same time. But most depressions do not follow real losses. And most people don't develop major depressions even after the gravest losses. The depression comes later, after the frustrating effort to keep going alone.

Another classic theory of depression is that it occurs when the self-image fails to approximate the ego ideal, when people can't seem to be what they think they should be. The problem may rest with their idea of what they are or with their idea of what they should be. That makes people feel ashamed of themselves and causes them to put up a show of trying, without bothering to do anything that would work, since the outcome is never in doubt — another in a lifetime series of failures.

Whatever its symbolic meaning or developmental roots, depression is quite real. Some are manic-depressives at the nadir of their roller coaster. Others have a real chemical deficiency in their brains, which can be episodic and recurrent, or chronic and continuous, or unique and dramatic. It can even be demonstrated and measured in the neuroendocrine systems of people with major depressive episodes. About half of people with major depressions fail to suppress serum cortisol after dexamethasone administration; another third or so have blunted thyroid stimulating hormone response to thyrotropin-releasing hormone (Targum, Sullivan, & Byrnes, 1982). The dexamethasone suppresson test has become almost standard in some hospitals, as it is diagnostic for certain types of severe depression and may help predict which antidepressant will be most effective. Even when it is not really that helpful, it is impressively scientific. Demonstrating that the depressed person does not suppress dexamethasone or has an excess of black bile or whatever does not prove that the biochemical situation preceded and caused the melancholia — the melancholia might well have come first. Still, some depressed people seem to have what amounts to a weak and easily run-down battery in the brain, generally thought to be a depletion of one of the neurotransmitters, norepinephrine.

While my description is not intended to be complete, this approximates what we think we know about the biochemistry of depression: There is a depletion of norepinephrine in the storage depots inside the brain cells. There is enough to keep the body going, but not enough to anticipate anything pleasurable. The brain is like a family's pocketbook at the end of the month — enough for necessities, nothing for luxuries. If the brain must do any work, it must borrow, and it may borrow epinephrine, the emergency stimulating hormone which can be called forth in times of anger and anxiety. The brain works on "nervous energy," but can feel no pleasure at rest. After a while, life consists only of pain, enough pain to keep going, but never of pleasure, and striving toward life and joy ceases. Appetite for food or sex or anything pleasurable is lost — there is nothing to transmit pleasure in the brain. Sleep becomes disturbed, in that the depressed person doesn't have enough norepinephrine left to permit the rest of sleep; the brain runs out and goes into red alert after about four hours' sleep, waking itself up to panic for a while in order to sustain life. Alcohol is appealing — it releases whatever norepinephrine is around and permits brief pleasure, but of course makes the depression deeper four hours later. Sleeping pills or tranquilizers may prevent the early a.m. waking for a while, but stifle the emergency repair system and gradually make the depression worse. If it gets bad enough, the emergency system gives up too and the patient just sits and waits for death.

This can go on for weeks, months, even for a lifetime. The patient could theoretically replenish norepinephrine through a steady diet of sex, exercise, joy, and triumph, but those aren't easy for people without hope or energy to achieve. Some people are so depressed they can only come to life when someone gets close enough to give offense and precipitate some stimulating fighting. The truly depressed are not laying illegitimate claim to an extra helping of love or attention. They may not know it but their brains are beyond love.

There are so many depressed people that we feel a need to classify them into smaller groups. This is a vague and inexact endeavor. The American Psychiatric Association, through *DSM-III*, tried once again to subdivide the continuum of depressions. Jerrold Maxmen (1986), in his authoritative guide to psychiatric diagnosis, explains this classification. There is "adjustment disorder with depressed mood," or reactive unhappiness, people who are unhappy about something. There is "dysthymia," or chronic neurotic unhappiness, people who are dissatisfied no matter what. There is "major depression," or abject misery, people who have lost interest in life. There is "cyclothymia," or alternating ups and downs. There are "bipolar depressions," the limp periods between manic episodes. There are depressions with psychosis, there are depressions with panic, and there are depressions secondary to drugs, alcohol, illness, or whatever. That's a lot of depression. As Maxmen points out, "during a lifetime, roughly 20% of women and 10% of men will suffer a major depressive episode." (The greater incidence in women might indicate a disadvantage to being female in our society, since the more clearly genetic bipolar depressions occur equally in men and women. However, it might merely mean that women have been taught, almost required, to face life's crises passively. Most serious mental illness occurs more commonly in men.)

Maxmen emphasizes the danger of blaming each depression on some event, since we all regularly experience potentially depressing blows to our self-esteem or security. He confirms what Paul and Paul (1975) and Freud (1917) have been telling us, that loss and mourning contribute to depression.

Over half of adult depressives lost a parent to death or separation in child-hood. The loss being mourned is not necessarily current; it may well be a long past loss. Depression is not just a mood; it is a way of relating to life, and it may have been learned and practiced since childhood.

I think it fair to assume from the data that depression is a chemical state which can be arrived at by a variety of paths, some situational, some psychological, some chemical, some genetic. Simply, the battery of the brain has run down.

The biochemical aspects of depression can be treated effectively with antidepressants. Milder depressions, those that come and go or haven't lasted very long or don't involve disturbances of sleeping or eating, don't respond well to antidepressants, but usually do respond to increased activity or almost anything that provides some emotional exercise. The protocol of "sex, exercise, joy, and triumph" can be seen as a formula for pumping norepinephrine to a mild to moderately depleted brain. Obviously, alcohol and minor tranquilizers should be avoided. But correcting the chemical disorder of depression is only the first phase of the treatment. Depression occurs in a context, when a susceptible person is in a conducive life situation. Attention must also be paid not only to the biochemistry of depression and the inadequate repertoire of the depressive, but also to the system that encourages it.

Most severe depressions come after a long period of the patient experiencing more pain than pleasure in life. It is as if the pleasure-producing hormones go out of business through lack of customer demand, leaving the pain-producing hormones with a monopoly. This pain-controlled life may be inadvertent. Circumstances just don't permit surcease from painful effort, from a life like Sisyphus', condemned to roll the heavy stone to the top of the hill, only to have it always roll back down, over and over, incessantly, forever — a life with all effort and no reward. But Sisyphus was condemned to his job; most people have a choice. Why would anyone choose to devote a life to incessantly doing something that is unpleasant to do and never works? Perhaps they were raised to believe that misery is virtue and pleasure vice, and there will be rewards for suffering and punishment for pleasure. Perhaps they were just misinformed about what their choices are or what will work. It is liberating for them to know.

So many people roll the rock up the hill because they don't have anyone else to do it for them, and their suffering dramatizes the world's failure to provide someone. Others lead Sisyphusean lives because they don't think they deserve to do anything else, and nothing else would work anyway. But I've always believed that Sisyphus had someone on the sidelines, a cheerleader chanting, "Roll, Sisyphus! Suffer for me, Baby!"

Some people tell one another loud and long and with obvious relish about their miserable state of mind. Perhaps they are proud of their sensitivity to psychic pain, or maybe they see depression as a free pass to impose their supposedly unique miseries on the world. If they can assure others that they are not enjoying their life, does the world then owe them something in return? If they find that they are victims of something, some past slight or disappointment, does this give them credit with everyone else?

Someone once said "No one ever becomes an adult until he realizes he never had a mother, just someone who stood in part-time." A depressed man explained to his wife why he could give no love to his son, whom he thought was being loved quite enough already, "How can you expect me to love anybody when no one has ever loved me. The only people who ever tried either gave up or pissed me off."

Depression is often a cry for attention and usually involves an element of blaming someone else for not caring enough or doing enough. Depression can be an illicit transaction, like breaking in line with the excuse that "I'll take your turn as well as mine because I can come up with more pain than you can." Depression may be aimed with a shotgun rather than rifle—it is broadcast nonspecifically to justify the failure to achieve something or other. Some people need to diagnose themselves as depressed before they can take a break from work, seeing rest as a "sick role." When someone announces that he or she is depressed, there is the implied statement of "Don't expect me to do anything for you" and the implied question of "What are you going to do to help?"

Feldman (1976) proposes a family systems theory of depression, describing a set of transactions that is all too familiar to family therapists: "Complementary cognitive structure in both spouses are triggered in the course of their interaction and lead to repetitive patterns of reciprocal stimulation and reinforcement." The up partner "innocently" undermines the down partner, the down one acts depressed and self-deprecating, the up one becomes oversolicitous, the down one feels more helpless and acts aggressive, passive-aggressive, or assertive, the up one then "innocently" undermines—and the cycle goes on indefinitely. One partner is always either pitiful or hostile, the other either the omnipotent rescuer or the undeserving object of the hostility—and may well decide that the other's depression is nicer than the anger. Depression can be induced by oversolicitousness just as surely as solicitousness can be induced by pitifulness.

Few families can afford, or require, more than one depressed person per generation. In most families there is one person who is seen as vulnerable to depression, a barometer to the pain of life, one who suffers and by suffering pulls everyone else back into a state of hypersolicitous hovering. The one who is vulnerable to depression, who has the weakest battery, keeps the others from getting too optimistic or comfortable. The depressed one may have a solicitous partner in control, a beseeching supplicant who constantly reminds the others not to take risks, not to go too far up or down or away, not to do anything foolish or feel anything strongly or be depressed themselves, as they might be a disappointment to their depressive mother/brother/wife/retarded child or might "break your mother's heart."

One potentially depressed family member can keep everyone else in a narrow emotional and functional range. A mother, who already has everyone feeling guilty because she has worked her fingers to the bone for them, can control a far-flung brood of grown children with just a sigh on the telephone and the unspoken threat of going into depression, especially if there is a father who beseeches the "children" that whatever they are doing or not doing in life might be a "disappointment" to their mother. Or the workaholic father who works himself to death to provide the best for his ungrateful family may have a wife who similarly beseeches the children. In *Death of a Salesman*, Linda Loman finds the tubing she thinks her depressed husband will use for his suicide, and she implores her sons to correct the errors of their ways—not of course because she is fed up with them or because the boys are making a pair of messes that couldn't be too nice to wallow in, but because, she says to each of them, "Attention must be paid. You're killing that man."

Depressed parents are murder. The children can hardly wait to get away from home and have their chance to be the depressed one who controls the world with a sigh. The hand that wrings the hankie rules the world.

Sometimes, after one family member has been the depressed dictator long enough, someone else will feel daring enough to attempt a coup. One of the children may try to usurp the omnipotent role of hankie wringer, the one who can lay claim to having the most breakable heart in the family, the one who must be obeyed to forestall depression. The candidates for the job line up with their respective boxes of Kleenex and they list their miseries. Unless the family has played this game before, the first one to hint at suicide wins. The child who will be heir to the power of depression may be chosen early in life. The price of this power is small—the depressive in training must learn to spurn obvious pleasure and to wrench each defeat from the jaws of victory. Every power grabbing move must be seen as a sacrifice.

Depression is seductive. A beautiful young woman in search of a champion to rescue her from parents who are abusive or neglectful or strict or tacky or boring is irresistible to young would-be champions. A woman's depression permits a man to feel powerful and good. Where would St. George be today without a damsel in distress? And imagined dragons are just as heroically slayable as real dragons (whether the dragon exists in the imagination of St. George or the damsel). When a depressed girl needs to get away from home, she needs a guy who'll drive fast, even if he doesn't know how to get anywhere. Such marriages last only until the next intersection. Depressed young men, who used to appeal only to nurses, have been in vogue in recent decades, as young women have wanted their equal right to flex some championship muscles and rescue a dumsel in distress.

Spouses of the depressed must get something out of it. They hang in there, fascinated perhaps by their power to alternately produce and relieve such intense suffering. They may not like living with a depressive as much as they fear the guilt of having a suicide on their hands. The fear of suicide is powerful glue.

Suicide is mean. It is the angriest possible act — total rejection and repudiation, with no opportunity to try again. Most suicide attempts are not successful and were never meant to be. A suicide attempt is generally considered a cry for help, an interpersonal message; if it is answered it almost ends the depression. It is aimed at someone and ordinarily works quite nicely to bring that someone under control, thereby relieving the depression for a time. But it corrects nothing in the relationship to the self, the world, or the "loved one" at whom it is aimed.

I've only worked with a handful of people who successfully committed suicide, and only one of those did so during the time I was actively involved. (His family had given up on him long before and could never understand why I kept trying to save an obviously wasted life — they called me to offer sympathy, knowing I was the only one who still felt anything like love for him.) In most of these cases, and in the cases I've known retrospectively by seeing the survivors, the family had given up and decided suicide was probably the best answer. Most of these were tortured people — schizophrenic, alcholic, drug-addicted, old and sick — or young male homosexuals whose families could not or did not have the opportunity to accept that choice. The suicide seemed to fulfill a perverse, almost Japanese, sense of honor.

But there were a few that were especially tragic because no one considered the life wasted, over, or pointless — young men (most suicides are male) who were much valued and who had shown little weakness before. Someone else in the family had always filled the depressive role and filled it quite fully. They had not been taught how to win through depression. They'd shown no weakness before, and didn't know its power. They jumped off buildings or shot themselves abruptly, without warning, in response to some quite temporary and easily solvable problem — a broken date, another separation of the parents, a failed test, a lost driver's license. Sometimes, there seemed to be no reason at all. But most of these people were not depressed in the classical manner, and never had been. Like the suicide attempters, these people were having fits of pique — but they also had a toxic level of pride. They couldn't just shed a few tears or take six Valium or a little Trac-II to the wrist. They couldn't accept themselves as the dumsel in distress; they'd only learned to play St. George. If they had called for help, someone would have come — everyone would have come — but they couldn't seem to face needing someone to help.

The most important thing I have learned about depression through the years is that it is very, very real. It may feel like moral weakness or it may feel like lack of love, but it isn't—it is lack of norepinephrine. It can't be cured by love and pampering. Attention of any sort, loving or not, can interrupt or postpone suicide, but love cannot cure any but the mildest and briefest depression. The depressive's activity, not someone else's solicitousness, is the solution.

TREATMENT OF DEPRESSION

Step 1: Emergency Response

Depressive emergencies come when the depressive overplays the role and frightens or infuriates someone else. Often they have made one suicide threat too many or have had their bluff called and have actually followed through and made the suicide attempt. The depressive is miserable, and so is everybody within sighing distance. Most often the depressive state has been going on for a few weeks, or even longer, and just keeps getting deeper despite all efforts. The usual efforts will, of course, make things worse. The depressive has ceased functioning, taken off from work, stopped sex and exercise, and increased the daily dose of alcohol or minor tranquilizers. The family doctor may have prescribed an overdose of Valium three times a day plus a homeopathic dose of an antidepressant to be washed down with alcohol. The family members hover, standing around looking miserable while protecting the depressive from any activity. A few weeks of that and the family is feeling desperate enough to call for outside help. The therapist's job is to move quickly but to keep everyone else from treating depression as an emergency.

If there is a real suicide threat, someone should stay with the depressive until there is time for a full-scale family evaluation. Do not panic and hospitalize. Hospitals aren't good for depression, may actually increase suicide danger, and make treatment far more difficult by interfering with activity and autonomy and by institutionalizing the "sick role." If the patient can't be seen right away, the therapist can speak to the depressed person briefly by telephone and be real nice, thereby seeming to reassure the depressive that therapy will respect the family tradition of being nice to whoever is being miserable.

Step 2: Family Involvement

When suicide has been attempted, threatened, or even hinted at, the suicide target must be involved immediately. The required confrontation will relieve the intensity of the episode. When the depressed one's biochemistry is flat on empty, the family's solicitous hovering may be almost irrelevant rather than actively destructive, and its destructive aspects are best approached after the biochemical situation has been stabilized. It can seem sadistic to call for an end to the hovering when the helpless family members can take their only permissible pleasure in demonstrating their guilt. So family members must be involved early and given precise instructions on what they can do to be more helpful rather than more c oncerned. If depression is only mild to moderate and does not involve vegetative symptoms, the family can be approached as a unit rather than as a concerned band of impotent, solicitous bystanders.

Step 3: Defining the Crisis

The question "Why now?" may open a floodgate of emotions but may not clarify as much as one might hope. This episode, even if worse than any others, may be no different. Or it may be unique, not part of the family's usual repertoire. What seems to be the precipitant is probably just the last straw on the already crushed camel. The factors that seem to family members to have caused it probably didn't. They will be focusing on losses and failures in ideal love, as well as on their own guilt for being bored with all this extractive, clinging depression. They would do better to look at destructive pain/pleasure ratios and aggravating feedback mechanisms.

The important definition must involve an explanation of the chemical, intrapsychic, and interpersonal nature of the illness. At all costs, depression must not be seen as an appropriate and inevitable response to being imperfectly loved.

Step 4: Biological Prescription

Antidepressants work for severe depression and are often necessary. If they are started right away, the depressive is more readily engaged in therapy and the family can reverse its approach. Tricyclic antidepressants take a few weeks to work, although the immediate effect may be to permit sleep, restore appetite, and stop the crying and agitation. Hope can be restored to the system even before the antidepressants have done their real job. Prescribing antidepressants also validates the reality of the depression, gives everyone a sense that something concrete is being done, and marks a point at which a change in interpersonal approach begins to make sense.

Antidepressants don't work for mild depressions. The side effects of the antidepressants may be worse than the biological symptoms of the depression. If people complain about the effects of the antidepressants, it may mean they were not very depressed initially. Antidepressants don't work in combination with alcohol — in fact, alcohol may abruptly reverse the effects of the antidepressant and throw the patient back into a state of more severe despair. Antidepressants do work in combination with phenothiazines for depressed schizophrenics and in combination with lithium for manic depressives who are stabilized with too low a thermostat. Low doses of antidepressants are effective sedation for anxious or insomniac patients with a tendency toward depression but insufficient biological signs of depression to warrant a full-scale course of antidepressants.

While the antidepressants are life-saving and dramatically effective, they solve only part of the problem. The depressive has an approach toward life and activity which encourages pain rather than pleasure. The depressive also is part of a system that induces and rewards the depression.

Step 5: Systemic Prescription

Anything that pumps norepinephrine is good for depression. Anything that gives the family something useful to do instead of hovering is going to be helpful to all concerned. After the depression has gone on for a while, and perhaps even before it began, other family members have been struggling with their own depressions; these must remain unspoken but lurk behind the sadistic solicitousness and the St. George posture that fuels the dragon and cues the distress. Now the family can be instructed to exercise the depressive, to force activity, interaction, and involvement in work and play, without regard to whether the depressive has begun to enjoy it yet. The family must address the depressive's activity level and biochemistry rather than her stated mood. The depressive may be playing "Ain't It Awful," but the family members must neither argue with that or cater to it; instead they must put the depressive through physical and emotional exercises running deliberately counter to the expressed mood. No one must respond to the depressive's mood—before such a fire breathing dragon can be safely slain, it must be unplugged. One way of unplugging it is to magnify the validity and relevance of the other family members' moods and experiences while ignoring the depressive's sighs and attributing them solely to low norepinephrine levels and the need to go for a walk. Thus, family members' loving concern and need to demonstrate noble championing can become biochemically accurate, can undercut the destructive power of the depression, and can serve as an outlet for their own angry impatience with the depressive's tyranny.

As the depression improves, there must be familial attention to the cognitive disorder in both the depressive's self-concept and the depressive's and perhaps the family's sense of who and what is "good enough." The correction of family standards of perfection and pickiness and self-esteem can be an enjoyable course of family therapy.

Finally, a depressive's ego deficiencies and perceived limitations can become indications for ego building adventures and undertakings, but only if the partner can respect the depressive's need for his or her own power, rather than subjugating the depressive to his supposedly stronger ego. If St. George can show the distressed damsel how to slay the dragon herself, rather than showing off for her, they may make quite a dragon-slaying team.

Simply, depression becomes an indication for exercise or activity rather than collapsing upon one's insufficiently loving loved ones. Taking a depressive for a walk or to a movie that offers a good cry is more therapeutic than bringing him or her breakfast in bed.

Step 6: Negotiating Resistance

It is hard to teach people how to get loved by loving or by making life fun, rather than by stumbling around begging with an emotional tin cup. But it is even harder to teach a family accustomed to responding only to one another's pain to ignore the pain and respond to an invitation to play. Depressive families must be taught lightness and humor, even when they identify joy as heartless and mean. After the distressed damsel or dumsel starts to slay his or her own dragons, St. George or Georgina may feel useless. At this point he may try to start the process over with excrutiating sensitivity to the former depressive's quite normal pain. It is not at all unusual for some other family member to become the focus of someone's rescuing heroics and for the depression to break out in another family member. Most families, after initial outrage, learn to like humor in their lives, to use it enthusiastically, and to lead lives that are far more pleasurable.

Step 7: Termination

People with major depressions may require antidepressants from time to time. Some with norepinephrine leaks in their brains may require antidepressants permanently. They do not usually require continued or even intermittent family therapy, though they may need a booster shot or two at times of crisis.

CASE ILLUSTRATION

CASE 29   *Canned*

Rebecca, a woman in her seventies, lived up in the mountains with her husband, Roy. She had never been a very adventurous person; she never went to school or had a job or drove a car or told a joke. But she raised ten children, went to church, tended her garden, and canned enough food for everyone to be fed through the winter. She had always been rather depressive, but no one had noticed much. Certainly Roy hadn't. He'd always blamed her moods on the weather or the season and told her not to worry about it.

Roy retired at 75 and went to bed. He'd never talked much so his company wasn't missed. One spring he told Rebecca that she was too old to tend her garden and he was too old to help with it (his job was to drive to town and buy the seeds — this year he didn't). They had never argued before so she didn't say anything.

By summertime Rebecca was depressed. Ruthie, one of her daughters, had been tending a husband who had been slowly dying of cancer, which at least was better than the alcoholism she'd tended him through for 25 years. He died, and Ruthie went to visit her mother, finding her in shocking condition. Ruthie notified everybody that the old lady was miserable, so all the other guilty children began to go by and see her, bringing the grandchildren to mess up her little house and wake her usually sleeping husband. They chattered away for a while to entertain her, brought her canned goods, and left. She felt more depressed. Finally Ruthie took up a collection and put a nurse in the house to do all the housework and cooking so Rebecca could rest. Her depression deepened. Ruthie then began spending each weekend at her parents' house, asking her mother how she felt every seven minutes and then calling the other children to report. Rebecca began talking about suicide.

Several of the children brought Rebecca to me, and I put her on antidepressants, dismissed the nurse, and told Ruthie to take her mother for a walk each day, but not to ask how she was feeling. The other children were instructed to do the same and urged to take fun trips and send their mother postcards. Ruthie was shocked and resisted, pointing out how depressed her mother was. The other siblings caught on quickly and explained it to her. The family did as prescribed. Rebecca began to feel better, went to church, and talked Roy into driving her to town once a week. A few months later Ruthie began to call me, frantically insisting that her mother was doing badly and needed the medicine changed. I would call Rebecca a few hours later and find she had felt bad for a while, but was now much better. The morning telephone calls between the mother and daughter had a toxic quality. I determined Rebecca's favorite television show, The Price Is Right, and had Ruthie call only during the time of the program. Rebecca would hurriedly get her daughter off the phone by reassuring her she was doing fine. She remained on a low dose of antidepressant.

The next year Ruthie helped her mother plant a garden. Then she joined a therapy group at the church and had less time to visit her parents. Rebecca sent me some canned okra. On her refrigerator she had postcards from her happy traveling children. She even urged Ruthie to take more trips. It was only after that last visit that I realized I had never seen Roy. He had not been part of the depressive cycle—he had never cared how his wife felt, he just had a healthy interest in how she functioned, which is probably why she had gotten along so well for most of her life.

Don't send me back to the deep end please,
I like it in the shallow where my body feels the breeze.
Talk about frivolity, Keep your mind at ease
No sense conjuring up some mental disease.
Give us a vodka and a good size splash
And a quick little smile and a Nikon flash.
But don't send me back to the deep end, Momma,
Where I kick and grasp to stay on top the water.
I like the shallow end best of all.
In the shallow end I can sure stand tall.

— David Murdock

Human kind cannot bear very much reality.

— T. S. Eliot, *Murder in the Cathedral*, 1935

CHAPTER 22

Schizophrenia

LIFE IN THE SHALLOW END

I NEVER UNDERSTOOD schizophrenia. It used to bother me that everyone else in the '60s seemed so willing to take sides in the nature/nurture wars about the etiology of schizophrenia, as the sides were drawn in Don Jackson's 1960 collection of papers from the experts of the day. Rereading that work, I don't find the lines drawn nearly as sharply as I remember them. Even then, it was not really as necessary as it seemed to utterly deny any data or theory that offered a genetic or biochemical explanation for schizophrenia. All family therapists did not reject the genetic data totally; great progress in treating schizophrenia has come since some family therapists have finally accepted it.

Schizophrenia occurs in about 1 percent of the population. It is familial, occurring in 50 percent of monozygotic twins and 15 percent of dizygotic twins and other siblings of schizophrenics. Schizophrenia is a matter of degree, with some people experiencing it for a lifetime, or at least from puberty on, in all situations, while others just show some symptoms of it when they are under particularly heavy stresses. Some shrink from all human contact and behave in a manner to assure that no one will get close enough to them to interrupt the lifelong love affair they are conducting inside their heads. Others function fairly well as long as the schedule is precise, even though they cannot quite complete a sentence or a thought without being distracted by some other stimulation. Some seem normal enough until they experience anger or anxiety, at which point they erupt with paranoia. Others become frantic and wild and suicidal when a relationship that exists primarily in their minds does not come to fruition in reality, as if the reality is faulty for not conforming to their perfectly clear fantasy. Many breeze through life until they make contact with hallucinogenic drugs, after which they view the drug experience as reality and the world as some sort of temporary play in which they are being forced to participate.

These people are having difficulty differentiating their thoughts from their perceptions, distinguishing what is going on outside their heads from what is going on inside.

We all have a little capacity for schizophrenia, some ability to daydream (to withdraw into our fanatasies), to read between the lines (to feel what others are feeling but not saying), and even to close out what is being said and done while we attune ourselves to a different level of reality. We also all have the ability to fall in love, to take a perfectly ordinary member of the opposite sex and project onto that person our fantasy ideals, and to then live out some dream-like romantic adventure, of which the other person may or may not be aware. We may fall in love just as totally with our children, projecting what is in our heads onto them with an intensity that may block out our awareness of what they are really like. When we were babies we did this with our parents too, and perhaps even knew that our parents were reciprocating and felt lost when they stopped seeing us as their fantasy ideals.

But these experiences are different from schizophrenia in that they can be turned off—there remains an awareness that the real world, if not more real than what is inside us, is at least the only world we can assuredly share with others. And the rest of us do want to share the world with others.

Like it or not, schizophrenics have a disorder of their brain chemistry, or at least a genetic tendency in that direction. Of course, it is not that simple. Schizophrenia occurs in a context that is almost a sine qua non for its emergence. Few seeds of any sort will grow without light, water, and fertilizer, but it is the seed itself that determines the nature of the foliage.

Schizophrenia is a genetic defect in the neuroendocrine chemistry of the brain. Some pieces of the mechanism have been demonstrated, but they are not fully worked out and the pieces have not been connected conclusively; thus, they remain hypotheses despite their general acceptance in psychiatry. We know that dopamine activity is increased, and that there are more dopamine sensitive receptors in the brains of schizophrenics. Dopamine receptors are stimulated by amphetamines and blocked by phenothiazines. The "dopamine hypothesis" is the most popular one at the moment (Maxmen, 1986), but there are other chemical explanations as well. Some researchers have found that schizophrenics produce a neurotoxin 6-hydroxydopamine, which inhibits goal-directed behavior and the pursuit of pleasure. The transmethylation hypothesis proposes that, in schizophrenia, dopamine and other cathecholamine precursors are broken down abnormally into psychotoxins like dimethyltryptamine, similar to the hallucinogen mescaline (Meltzer, 1979).

Even if the biochemical hypotheses are accurate, they don't explain everything. They do explain the probability that a schizophrenic brain, when stimulated strongly, will begin to produce strange chemicals, bringing on something like the hallucinatory experience, preoccupation with the internal world, loss of interest in the real world, lack of concern with goal-directed behavior, anhedonia, and loss of the ability to distinguish perceptions from thoughts.

The dramatic effectiveness of the phenothiazines, dopamine antagonists, in treating acute schizophrenic episodes and in preventing relapses certainly would seem to confirm all of this. The biochemical research on schizophrenia is tied in with the investigation of the actions of these drugs. Phenothiazines have side effects, some of them serious, but they enable many schizophrenics to lead normal or close to normal lives. Phenothiazines can keep schizophrenics out of hospitals, but they can't quite make them normal, and while the yearly relapse rates can be cut from 80 percent to half of that, there are clearly other factors at work too. Attention to those other factors can drop the relapse rate to something close to nil.

SCHIZOPHRENIC FAMILIES

The existence of a genetic, biochemical defect is hard to refute, even if the current hypotheses are faulty. Nonetheless, all people with the genetic tendency do not become clinically schizophrenic. Some psychological or environmental factors must be at work. And any of us who have worked with the families of schizophrenics know what a crazy-making experience that can be. It is sometimes impossible to know who's on first — or to get anyone to focus on the question.

Mothers used to be blamed for schizophrenia, as they were for everything else. The "schizophrenogenic mother" was christened by Frieda Fromm-Reichmann (1948), but as the concept was popularized it became unclear whether it referred to a rejecting mother (Fromm-Reichmann's original meaning) or a symbiotic one, one who holds the child close in order to meet the mother's needs without regard to the child's needs. It didn't matter whether she was close or distant, it still had to be her fault.

Murray Bowen (1960) noticed that schizophrenic families were symbiotic and undifferentiated, and characterized this illness as immaturity. These kids do not grow up and leave home. He concluded that it takes three generations to produce a schizophrenic, thus blaming it indirectly on grandmothers.

Our frustration was high; we could not believe in chemistry. It was during this period that Szasz (1961) decided that schizophrenia was a myth and Laing (1967) declared it sanity.

Optimistic theories arose which blamed schizophrenia on what the families were doing now, rather than what they had already done. The Golden Age of Theories About Schizophrenic Families began in 1956 when Bateson, Jackson, Haley, and Weakland presented the "double bind hypothesis." Their specific postulation involved mothers who withdrew from a child's love and simultaneously expressed overt loving, without a strong father to intervene with support. Singer and Wynne (1965) called this erratic closeness and distance "pseudomutuality" and could pick up such "communication deviance" on psychological testing. Lidz, Fleck, and Cornelison (1965) described families of schizophrenics as either "skewed" or "schismatic." In schismatic families the marital couple is in conflict and the child, usually female, is scapegoated or gets in the middle of the conflict. In skewed families, the battle is over; the eccentric, inappropriate, intrusive mother has defeated the passive father and is tightly bound to the son.

Mishler and Waxler (1968) tested these hypotheses. They found that normal families communicated in a more fragmentary and disorganized way than schizophrenic families. The striking finding was that schizophrenic families in which the schizophrenic had good premorbid adjustment consistently had rigidly organized and coherent patterns of speech, while those with poor premorbid adjustment came from families that were almost as incoherent as normals. They also found the same thing that Lidz and his group found, that male and female schizophrenics come from families with different structures. Schizophrenogenic mothers exist only for their sons, not for their daughters.

Mishler and Waxler understood that the peculiar nature of communication in schizophrenic families does not necessarily mean that the distorted communications caused the schizophrenia; rather, it could mean that living with a schizophrenic causes families to communicate strangely. I find it tempting to assume, whatever the data, that the child's schizophrenia causes the disordered communication in the parents. I think what it must be like to have a schizophrenic child, who has beauty or intelligence, or at least looks like you or speaks your language and shares your life, and who for some time seemed to fulfill your hopes and dreams. Perhaps the child was always a bit distant, and so you had to try harder to make contact. But then, perhaps at adolescence, the child becomes inaccessible, weird, embarrassing, and tortured; above all, he or she seems to shrink from you and your world.

I should think you would try any approach, however bizarre, in this interpersonal emergency of seeing the child you love possessed by the devils of schizophrenia and treating your love as if it were the most terrifying of those devils. And on top of that, to have therapists and the world blame *you* for it, the way you and your fellow parent have been blaming one another! I should think anyone would become incoherent under those circumstances. I'm impressed with how different schizophrenic parents are when their sick child is not psychotic or just not in the room. I'm also impressed with the eagerness and facility with which the families of schizophrenics change any aspects of their lives and behavior and speech to help solve the problem. Families of schizophrenics will try anything, from incest to suicide, to make contact with their child, and the harder they try, the worse it gets. Exacerbate it, yes. Cause it? I can't buy that, maybe just because I'd rather not.

I think of my grandmother, who was quite deaf. She had a hearing aid which would whistle and buzz wildly in response to loud noises. If people tried to speak loudly to her she couldn't hear a thing, so they would begin to shout. She would hear none of what they were shouting, but would get an awful buzzing in her head. She'd have to leave the room and retire to a place of silence for a while. She could only be reached by speaking very softly. Few people could catch on to that quickly, and some never could; even those of us closest to her slipped up sometimes.

Whatever the reasons for it, schizophrenic families are different. In one previous effort on the subject (Langsley, Pittman, & Swank 1969), we reported a confusing finding about the difference between schizophrenic and non-schizophrenic families. Both responded well to family crisis therapy outside the hospital. Non-schizophrenic families quickly learned to handle subsequent crises more efficiently without driving one another crazy. Schizophrenic families could avoid subsequent crises very well — they actually managed to reduce the number of things that happened to them, but once a crisis occurred and the whole family was required to interact around the crisis, the patient would relapse. Each crisis would be handled just as extravagantly and inefficiently as ever. Each psychotic episode was easy enough to treat pharmacologically, and that cooled the family down, but the process continued with noisy chaos at each intersection. In retrospect, what we were teaching other families about crisis management involved too much contact, communication, and emotional expression for schizophrenics. The families were trying to tell us that the interaction around transitions and crises was toxic.

Things started making more sense when Brown, Birley, and Wing (1972) realized that schizophrenics who live in families with a high level of "expressed emotion" are more likely to relapse. "Expressed emotion" consists of critical comments about the patient, hostility, and emotional overinvolvement. Low levels of EE lead to low rates of relapse. But limiting face-to-face contact with the relative with high EE can protect the patient from relapse. They showed that socially active families are best for schizophrenics. The more isolated the family is from outsiders, the higher the EE and the greater the emotional involvement with the patient, so extra social contacts on the part of the parents may be helpful.

Wynne (1980) has reviewed the current state of affairs in our understanding of schizophrenia. He accepts the genetic biochemical base for schizophrenia, considers "communication deviance" as a possible parental precursor of schizophrenia in an offspring, and believes that high "expressed emotion" on the part of another family member or members can predict later relapse of schizophrenia. In other words, schizophrenia occurs when (1) someone whose brain makes hallucinogens under pressure (2) is raised by parents who don't make sense and then (3) is exposed to emotionally noisy chaos.

TREATMENT OF SCHIZOPHRENIA

Treatment should be directed toward all of these three contributants. The schizophrenic can be (1) given phenothiazines to make the brain less vulnerable, (2) taught to make sense of the world in group or individual psychotherapy, and (3) put in a situation, at home or elsewhere, that is less stimulating.

The usual family therapy approaches, however effective in revealing the familial contributions to the problems of the past or present, has serious disadvantages for the schizophrenic patient. Beels and McFarlane (1982) point out some of these disadvantages, particularly the confirmation of "the parents' worst fear: that they had caused their child's schizophrenia." Also, the design of family therapy encourages the presentation of problems and negative experiences and emotions, which can amount to increasing "expressed emotionality." Anderson, Reiss, and Hogarty (1986) have outlined more of these disadvantages. Family therapy may encourage noncompliance with medication, may deny the reality of the illness, may imply the patient is a symptom of a family illness, and may imply that better communication will make the patient function better. Family therapy may also encourage premature emancipation, as if leaving home would cure the problem rather than just cool down the chaos.

Psychoeducational approaches, have been developed by Anderson et al. (1986), Bernheim and Lehman (1985), Falloon (1981), and Goldstein (1981). Psychoeducation, when combined with phenothiazines, reduces the relapse rates to a level well below 10 percent, from the annual expected relapse rate of 80 percent untreated and 40 percent with phenothiazines alone. Families are given empathy rather than blame, taught survival skills, joined into a network of families of schizophrenics, receive lectures about the biochemistry and subjective experience, learn how to use benign indifference rather than anxious overinvolvement, and are encouraged to set firm limits and low expectations. Only after the families master all of these skills do the therapists meet with the patient and family together. Falloon's approach involves similar techniques and similar outcomes, but with meeting in the patient's home. Goldstein used a short-term course in these matters, which worked extremely well temporarily, but the relapse rate eventually went up. Apparently, continuing availability for crisis management is a necessary part of maintaining schizophrenics outside the hospital.

To this regimen I would add one more crucial factor — the absolute avoidance of hallucinogens. Marijuana, whatever its subtle effects on non-schizophrenics, is a disaster for schizophrenics. It is popular with schizophrenics, perhaps because it provides euphoria along with social withdrawal, but it seems to add to the buildup of hallucinogen in the brain and encourages further passivity and withdrawal. Many acute schizophrenic episodes are triggered by hallucinogens.

Crisis Management

Each separate crises in a schizophrenic family is rather easy to manage, considering the enormity and complexity of the illness. I rarely hospitalize a schizophrenic, though those who have used the hospital frequently in the past may insist upon it. It used to make sense to me that schizophrenia, whose acute episodes were so easy to manage, was made chronic by psychiatric hospitalization. Hospitalization offers an excessive, drastic sanctuary for a schizophrenic who would like to take a "time-out" from life that has become too emotionally stimulating. Those who can take time-out at home don't need to be hospitalized. Home may be too demanding, but the hospital may be too protective.

While schizophrenics require a high dose of phenothiazines during an acute episode, most can be maintained on low doses subsequently. Most really can't function well on high doses; they are too unresponsive for life in the outside world. However, if they live in a mystifying, stormy family with high expressed emotion, their survival outside the hospital may require a high dose of phenothiazines. The combination of phenothiazines, psychoeducation for the family, social retraining and structuring for the patient, and availability for crisis management should enable almost all schizophrenics to function outside the hospital. First-break schizophrenics with clear, calm families and some experience with appropriate social functioning may regain lives of utter normality. Once they are stabilized in the world, they can even be given a trial without the phenothiazines, and they deserve this closely monitored chance.

Phenothiazines usually stop the acute episodes effectively, and if there is some functional role to return to, recovery can be rapid. If there is not a functional role waiting, this is more difficult. The tough job in treating schizophrenics is to maintain functioning. Schizophrenics just don't seem to consider functioning important enough to go through anxiety over it. They often lack the social skills to bring it about, and their families may be just as disjointed socially. There is a continuing struggle to prevent social deterioration even when everything is going fairly well otherwise. The emotional stimulation range in which a schizophrenic must live is extremely narrow; the tiniest crisis can throw the patient in one direction or another. Many give up and withdraw into a back room somewhere. Preventing that requires a lifetime therapeutic effort.

Being a schizophrenic male is different from being a schizophrenic female. The pressures on males for continuous instrumental functioning in the world, pressures that come from the world, from the family, and from the male's own shaky and concrete sense of sexual identity, may keep the young man in a quandary. He is being called upon to venture forth into a world that overwhelms him, to do so with respect for the family's social status and his own perceived potential, and to do so uninterruptedly. His alternative is to lower the level at which he enters the world, to mobilize downward to a socioeconomic level at which less is expected. But this brings him into contact with other unreliable, unstable, unpredictable people with whom stabilizing, gentle relationships do not come naturally. Hiding in his mother's back room may offer sanctuary, but is not respectable for a male. Not surprisingly, schizophrenic males become psychotic five years earlier than females (Loranger, 1984).

A female schizophrenic, on the other hand, loses less status by working intermittently at a low level or by continuing to live at home with her parents. She may be under less pressure from any direction to go forth and compete. A schizophrenic man may be lucky enough to find a strong, gentle wife who expects little either emotionally or functionally, but such men are not considered desirable marriage partners. By contrast, schizophrenic women can avoid functioning, chatter aimlessly, withdraw coyly, go through intermittent crises, and absolutely charm a man who is afraid of a normal woman but wants a doll for his doll house (Pittman & Flomenhaft, 1970). Flightly, incoherent, dependent women have a bizarre appeal for some men. Such marriages can work, often for a lifetime, but if the husband wants more, if a child overloads the woman, or if she in her insensitive pliability should drift into an affair and end her marriage, she may begin to slowly deteriorate (Sampson, Messenger, & Towne, 1964).

The world does not arrange itself steadily, tolerantly, and placidly enough for schizophrenics, and their lives are beset with crises, even when each specific crisis is handled well enough to avoid a full-blown psychotic episode. It seems cruelly pessimistic to say this, but the life of a schizophrenic goes best once everyone gives up on expecting normality and just helps the schizophrenic survive within the limitations of the defect.

The crises of schizophrenia are manifold and can be triggered by almost anything, yet the effect is essentially the same—the schizophrenic either takes a time-out and withdraws to save his or her sanity or goes ahead and becomes psychotic. Crises occur when the schizophrenic goes off the phenothiazines, feels better for two weeks, then goes quite crazy. Crises occur when the schizophrenic decides to smoke a little reefer. Crises occur when the family undergoes some transition and indulges in an orgy of emotional expressiveness. Crises occur when the world, the job, a friend, or a lover puts pressure on the schizophrenic and expects a normal response. An unexpected sexual overture, particularly a homosexual one, can trigger a crisis. The offer of a promotion at work can do it. A new therapist, a new boss, a new roommate, or the return of a relative to the family home can do it. Actual losses, such as the death of a parent, a divorce or the end of a romance, the loss of a job, or a physical illness, may be less of a problem, at least immediately. It may be easier for a schizophrenic to go to his mother's funeral than to his sister's graduation party. All new situations are difficult, especially those in which normal interpersonal behavior is expected. Schizophrenics must find ways to signal everyone not to expect normality.

AN OVERVIEW OF TREATMENT

Step 1: Emergency Response

Therapists must be available immediately. Every schizophrenic needs a therapist available for crisis intervention. Otherwise, the patient will go or be taken to a hospital, where the treatment is likely to be disruptive to whatever tenuous hold on functioning the patient has been able to painstakingly achieve. When a first break occurs, there is no therapist already involved and the tendency is to overreact and invest in far more intensive treatment than would be helpful. A frantic family may mortgage the house to provide a year in some fancy hospital when a shot of Thorazine would both solve the immediate problem and protect the functioning of the patient.

Step 2: Family Involvement

The family should be seen separately from the patient. They are all too willing to engage in stormy exercises in guilt and responsibility for the situation, which will intensify the overload on the patient rather than relieving it.

Step 3: Defining the Problem

Schizophrenia is not too difficult to diagnose, although it must be differentiated from acute mania, withdrawal from alcohol or sedatives, and intoxication with hallucinogens or stimulants. The history should clarify this. The illness should be diagnosed openly, named, and explained. It is vital to explain that the illness is genetic and biochemical, and that the family did not cause it but can assist in its management. The family may have gotten a quite different explanation previously, from previous therapists or from the grapevine. This must be corrected.

Step 4: Biological Prescription

Phenothiazines must be instituted right away, perhaps even by injection. The patient is to be sedated and really put to sleep with phenothiazines. Thorazine is most sedating and works most rapidly, though it has too many side effects to be used for maintenance. The family can be given a supply of Thorazine to feed the patient until he or she is asleep. Antiparkinsonian medication may accompany the patient in case there is an extrapyramidal reaction during the night, but antiparkinsonian medication need not be used routinely. A psychiatrist, of course, must be immediately available by telephone. The initial psychotic episode will clear gradually over the next few days, though stimulation may exacerbate it, and certain topics, particularly arguing with any paranoid delusions, may overload the circuits. The family is instructed to medicate, feed, and lightly structure the patient, but to give the patient distance. It is not helpful to keep someone in the room with the patient during the episode.

After the episode clears, the phenothiazine can be changed to something less sedating and more long-acting, such as Stelazine or Prolixin, which comes in an injectable, long-acting form. Reduction of phenothiazine dose must be modulated to the clinical picture and the tolerance of side effects. There is little advantage to keeping the dose high for some set period of time. High doses do discourage relapse but they also discourage functioning. The best dose may be found by trial and error. I find relapses easier to treat than apathetic withdrawal, and I may err on the side of lower doses, especially with patients with whom I'm in reliable contact.

If this is a first break, and especially if it was triggered by hallucinogens, the phenothiazines may be maintained for six months or thereabouts and then, if functioning has been satisfactorily resumed, cautiously discontinued. After a few psychotic episodes, it should be decided that the phenothiazines are permanent. The action, dangers, and possibility of tardive dyskinesia should be discussed with the patient and the family when someone is to be on phenothiazines long-term.

Step 5: Family Treatment

Family members must be educated about the illness. First their guilt and sense of responsibility for causing the schizophrenia must be assuaged. Then they must learn what we know of schizophrenia, its chemistry, its course, its subjective experience, and its prognosis. Family members are urged to protect themselves from the patient's disruptions and to protect the patient from theirs. Appropriate functioning at a low level, opportunities for withdrawal, and distance from the family must be arranged. Finally, the family must be taught to keep the level of emotional interaction with the patient low and encouraged to become more involved in an outside life.

Family therapy can then proceed with further training in all of these matters plus cautious effort to teach efficient calm crisis management. The patient may be seen alone alternately, or in group therapy, in order to better learn how the world works.

Step 6: Negotiation of Resistance

Some schizophrenics don't like taking phenothiazines, especially when they are very crazy. Injectable Prolixin may be required. Some schizophrenics don't like to function—they need slow and gentle pressure and structure. Stormy threats and ultimatums don't work well, which doesn't stop some parents from trying them. Some families of schizophrenics still want to feel that they have failed, and they are likely to push the schizophrenic to a higher level of functioning than possible in order to appear to the world to be successful parents.

There are a few families of schizophrenics who refuse to reduce their level of emotional expressiveness. Some of these are very crazy people themselves. They may need to be medicated too.

Compliance with this approach has been high. However, some families cannot stop overloading the schizophrenic. The schizophrenic may have to move out, perhaps into a roominghouse or with a relative. The myth of the overinvolved mother of schizophrenic boys is quite real, though certainly not universal or even characteristic. A few though seem to know no boundaries. One tried to give her son breathing lessons, so he would breath in rhythm with her. Although mother-son incest is quite rare, at least two mothers of schizophrenic sons have been actively incestuous, in well-intentioned efforts to assist the young men with their body-image and sexual identity, and many others have been terrifyingly intimate with their sons. If this can't be stopped quickly (and it is usually difficult to get the fathers much involved with their damaged sons), the boy may have to be removed from the home.

There is often a reluctance to let female schizophrenics go out on their own, and the families of female schizophrenics seem either less askew or just willing to make more of an effort to keep the girls at home. I have seen overinvolved and incestuous fathers of schizophrenic girls. It is a real danger. These parents seem willing to do anything to make contact with their schizophrenic children, even if their efforts make matters worse.

Step 7: Termination

Schizophrenic families do not terminate. They may become frustrated and seek out a different therapist or a different approach, or just something cheaper, but they don't go away forever, and they never "finish."

CASE ILLUSTRATIONS

CASE 30   *Nailed Down*

Xavier had his first schizophrenic episode at 14, a particularly nasty one in which he thought he was Jesus and nailed his hand to a two-by-four. He was hospitalized for many months and was kept on a very short rein after that, with his mother inspecting him daily for some surreptitious damage. There had been a schizophrenic uncle who had committed suicide. Xavier did well without medication, but rarely left home. At 16 he had another episode, and this time I saw him after a brief hospitalization and put him on phenothiazines. The nature of the illness was explained and the family encouraged, in a few visits, to reduce the intensity of their emotionality. They did. The father was actively alcoholic, was urged to stop drinking and go to AA. He did. The mother, urged to leave Xavier alone, decided to return to school for her master's degree.

The father was unemployed and they decided to save money by not seeing me, but they didn't tell me why they stopped. I lost contact with them for several years. The family did an excessively good job of keeping Xavier's stimulation low, discouraging any social life for him. However, his younger brother was coming of age and leading a joyously raunchy life. Xavier envied but feared his brother's good times. Xavier had been living at home and going to college in town. He had also been working and had saved enough money to go off to school at his own expense. Before he left for college, his mother read something about tardive dyskinesia and had him discontinue his medicine. He lasted about two weeks off at school, during which he had an unsuccessful effort at sex and a massive amount of marijuana—his first experience with either of these pleasures exulted in by his brother. He wound up hallucinating, writing strange religious poetry and wandering naked around the campus.

The family called. I had the college infirmary start the phenothiazines and I saw him as soon as he could be brought home. He recovered quickly on phenothiazines. I explained to the family the destructive action of marijuana (the father, still off alcohol, had been almost encouraging pot as an alternative to booze). We went through the psychoeducation lecture again, and I urged them to let Xavier experience more of life's adventures in preparation for a normal life. I emphasized that he could expand his experiential range more safely on the phenothiazines. I then saw them with Xavier and explained it all to him.

Xaiver sat out the quarter at home, working and dating and going out gingerly with his mother and his brother's friends. The dose of phenothiazine was reduced from the 400 mgm of Thorazine during the first few days to Stelazine 5 mgm each night. After he returned to college, he called to let me know he had been successful with sex, and was dating a girl.

He comes by when he is at home, knows he can call me if there is a problem, has joined a fraternity, but does not want to live in the fraternity house, and will soon graduate from college.

CASE 31   *All That Jazz*

Yolanda acknowledged that Yaz was the most exciting husband a woman could have. He was a jazz musician in New York, and he filled her life with the music of his drumming, and the excitement of stimulating friends all night and all day. Yaz composed songs to the poetry she tried to write in the back room. He worshipped her—he insisted upon taking her everywhere and introducing her to everybody. After about a year, she became pregnant. His excitement could not have been greater. He threw a large celebration. He panicked when she disappeared.

Yaz went looking for her. Weeks later, her found her in a bus station in California. She had had an abortion, apparently, though she didn't want to talk about it. She kept writing strange things about dead babies and acted frightened of Yaz. He brought her to Atlanta to her mother, and then to me. Yaz pushed her to explain herself. He was frantic and furious, desperately assuring her of his excruciatingly intense love. The widowed mother tried to shield Yolanda from him. I quickly put her to sleep on Thorazine—she barely left the bed for days while her mother quietly hovered. The mother told us that this had happened before, when Yolanda disappeared just before her wedding to another man.

I tried to calm Yaz. Over the next few months, the major effort was to calm Yaz, and Yaz was not easy to calm. He got a job and an apartment, and Yolanda gradually improved enough to leave her mother and join Yaz. He worked nights, and she stayed at her mother's during the day, so he could sleep. She still didn't want to talk about the pregnancy.

Yaz got busier and managed to keep his distance, though he didn't like distance. I tried a couples group, but Yaz dominated it and Yolanda just looked anxious. I finally started seeing them separately. Yolanda was limp, and I pushed her to go to work. She dragged her feet about it. I tried taking her off her medicine. She began smelling strange odors, insisting that Yaz' smell nauseated her. She believed Yaz was making her sick. I put her back on a maintenance level.

She finally did get a job in a lab and promptly got into an affair. She was surprised when Yaz went berserk over her infidelity. She moved back in with her mother, who told Yaz that his anger about the affair was "rude." Yaz began to drink and stay away. He could never get over his longing to be close to her. He could not adapt himself to the idea that beneath that beautiful exterior and that brilliant and creative mind there was nothing for him. At whatever level of sanity, she would rather be left alone than entertained or loved.

Yaz begged Yolanda to come back to him. Instead, she got the money from her mother to divorce him. Yaz went through years of crisis as he tried to adjust to the intense emotional loss. He talked to everyone about it, and wrote sad songs—for which he won awards.

Yolanda quickly found Boris, an accountant who rarely talked to her and had had a vasectomy. Yolanda married him and turned into a very tidy housekeeper. Boris was happy, too, we think. He never talked about such personal matters.

CODA

I F I CAN EMPHASIZE only one point in this book (other than the pleasure of working with families in crisis), that point would be that there is no magical way to treat families in the inevitable transitions and crises of life. People must change over time, and the process is specific for each person, each family, each transition, and each crisis. And it is hard work for everyone involved. Most frustrating is the realization that the therapist cannot immediately evaluate the effectiveness of the therapy.

I got this letter a few years ago:

Dear Dr. Pittman,

You probably don't remember me. My name was Zimbabwe in those days. I only saw you once, but I sat on the floor in the corner and covered my face and didn't say a word, so I'm sure you won't remember me. My parents were the ones who threw brussels sprouts at each other and then fought over who was going to clean them up.

I hadn't said anything for a few weeks, but I almost cheered when you told them to let my brother go to jail for stealing that car for his drug deal. They fought all the way home about it. Mom hated you for that, and Dad hated you for telling him to either break up with his girl friend or bring her

356

to the next session. Mom called the girl friend as soon as they got home, and Dad moved out a few days later. When I realized you couldn't help either, I moved out too. I'm living with my boyfriend in Montana and I'm real happy. I don't hear the voices out here — must be the natural food.

Anyway, Dad broke up with his girlfriend and wants to come back, but Mom's going to get her Ph.D. and doesn't want him. My brother's out of jail now and working and off drugs. He's great, and he tells me all this mess.

You weren't much help with me and my family, but you were a neat guy and have a neat wife. I just wanted to wish you both a happy holiday.

Zelda Zimmerman

REFERENCES

Ackerman, N. W. (1958). *The Psychodynamics of family life*. New York: Basic Books.

Ackley, D. (1980). A brief overview of child abuse. In M. Elbow (Ed.), *Patterns of family violence*. Family Service Association of America.

Ahrons, C. R. & Wallisch, L. S. (1986). The relationship between former spouses. In S. Duck & D. Perlman (Eds.), *Intimate relationships: Development, dynamics, and deterioration*. (pp. 269-296). Los Angeles: Sage Publications.

Alexander, P. G. (1985). A systems theory conceptualization of incest. *Family Process*, 24(1), 79-88.

Anderson, C. M., & Stewart, S. (1983). *Mastering resistance*. New York: Guilford.

Anderson, C. M., Reiss, D. J., & Hogarty, G. E. (1986). *Schizophrenia and the family: A practitioner's guide to psychoeducation and management*. New York: Guilford.

Bassis, M. S., Gelles, R. J., & Levine, A. (1984). *Sociology, an introduction*. New York: Random House.

Bateson, G., Jackson, D. D., Haley, J., & Weakland, J. H. (1956). Toward a theory of schizophrenia. *Behavioral Science, 1*(4).

Beal, E. W. (1980). Separation, divorce, and single parent families. In E. A. Carter & M. McGoldrick (Eds.), *The family life cycle* (pp. 241-264). New York: Gardner Press.

Beavers, W. R. (1985). *Successful marriage*. New York: Norton.

Beels, C. C., & McFarlane, W. R. (1982). Family treatments of schizophrenia: Background and state of the art. *Hospital and Community Psychiatry, 33*(7), 541-550.

Bepko. C., & Krestan, J. (1985). *The responsibility trap: A blueprint for treating the alcoholic family*. New York: Free Press.

Berne, E. (1964). *Games people play*. New York: Grove.

Bernheim, K. L., & Lehman, A. F. (1985). *Working with families of the mentally ill*. New York: Norton.

Boszormenyi-Nagy, I. & Spark, G. (1984). *Invisible loyalties*. New York: Brunner/Mazel.
Bowen, M. (1960). A family concept of schizophrenia. In D. D. Jackson (Ed.), *The etiology of schizophrenia*. New York: Basic Books.
Bowen, M. (1966). The use of family therapy in clinical practice. *Comprehensive Psychiatry, 7*, 345-374.
Brown, G. W., Birley, J. L., & Wing, J. K. (1972). Influence of family life on the course of schizophrenic disorders: A replication. *Brit. J. Psychiatry, 121*, 241-250.
Brownmiller, S. (1973). *Against our will*. New York: Simon and Schuster.
Bruch, H. (1978). *The golden cage: The enigma of anorexia nervosa*. Cambridge, MA: Harvard University Press.
Carter, E. A., & McGoldrick, M. (1980). *The family life cycle: A framework for family therapy*. New York: Gardner Press.
Chesler, P. (1972). *Women and madness*. Garden City, NJ: Doubleday.
Cohen, M. B., Baker, G., Cohen, R. A., Fromm-Reichmann, F., & Weigert, E. V. (1954). An intensive study of twelve cases of manic-depressive psychosis. *Psychiatry, 17*, 103.
Cohen, S. N., & Jones, F. N. (1983). Issues of divorce in family therapy. In B. B. Wolman & G. Stricker (Eds.), *Handbook of family and marital therapy*. New York: Plenum.
Eichenbaum, L., & Orbach, S. (1982). *Understanding women: A feminist psychoanalytic approach*. New York: Basic Books.
Erikson, E. (1980). *Identity and the life cycle*. New York: Norton.
Everstine, D. S., & Everstine, L. (1983). *People in crisis*. New York: Brunner/Mazel.
Falloon, I. R. H., & Liberman, R. P. (1983). Behavioral family interventions in the management of chronic schizophrenia. In W. R. McFarlane (Ed.), *Family therapy in schizophrenia* (pp. 117-140). New York: Guilford.
Falloon, I. R. H., Liberman, R. P., Lillie, F. J., & Vaughn, C. E. (1981). Family therapy of schizophrenics with high risk of relapse. *Family Process, 20*, 211-221.
Feldman, L. (1976). Depression and marital interaction. *Family Process, 15*(4), 389-396.
Fieve, R. R. (1975). *Moodswing*. New York: Morrow.
Finkelhor, D. (1978). Psychological, cultural, and family factors in incest and family abuse. *Journal of Marital and Family Therapy, 4*, 41-50.
Fisch, R., Weakland, J., & Segal, L. (1982). *The tactics of change: Doing therapy briefly*. San Francisco: Jossey-Bass.
Fowler, C., Burns, S. R., & Roehl, J. E. (1983). Counseling the incest offender, *Int. J. Fam. Ther., 5*(2), 92-98.
Framo, J. L. (1975). Husbands' reactions to wives' infidelity. Reprinted (1982) in *Explorations in marital and family therapy: Selected papers of James L. Framo*. New York: Springer.
Framo, J. L. (1965). Rationale and techniques of intensive family therapy. In I. Boszormenyi-Nagy & J. L. Framo (Eds.), *Intensive family therapy*. Hagerstown, MD: Hoeber Medical Division, Harper and Row, Inc.
Framo, J. L. (1980). Marital therapy and family therapy. In A. S. Gurman & D. Kniskern (Eds.), *Handbook of family therapy*. New York: Brunner/Mazel.
Freeman, H., & Simmons, O. (1963). *The mental patient comes home*. New York: Wiley.
Freeman, M. D. A. (1979). *Violence in the home*. Westmead, England: Saxon House.
Freud, S. (1909). Analysis of a phobia in a 5 year old boy (Little Hans). In *The complete psychological works: The standard edition, Volume X* (pp. 5-149) (Translated by J. Strachey). New York: Norton.
Freud, S. (1916). Some character types met with in psychoanalytic work: Those wrecked by success. In *The complete psychological works: The standard edition, Volume XIV* (pp. 311-333) (Translated by J. Strachey). New York: Norton.
Freud, S. (1917). Mourning and melancholia. In *The complete psychological works: The standard edition, Volume XIV* (pp. 243-258) (Translated by J. Strachey). New York: Norton.
Fromm-Reichmann, F. (1948). Notes on the development of treatment of schizophrenia by psychoanalytic psychotherapy. *Psychiatry, 11*, 263-273.
Goldstein, J., Freud, A., & Solnit, A. J. (1973). *Beyond the best interests of the child*. New York: Free Press.
Goldstein, M. J., Judd, L. L., Rodnick, E. J., Alkire, A., & Gould, E. (1968). A method for studying influence and coping patterns within families of disturbed adolescents. *Journal*

of Nervous and Mental Diseases, 147 (3), 233–251.

Goldstein, M. J. (Ed.) (1981). *New developments in interventions with families of schizophrenics*. San Francisco: Jossey-Bass.

Grolnick, L. (1972). A family perspective of psychosomatic factors in illness: A review of the literature. *Family Process, 11*(4), 457–486.

Haley, J. (1980). *Leaving home*. New York: McGraw-Hill.

Haley, J. (1984). *Ordeal therapy*. San Francisco: Jossey-Bass.

Haley, J., & Hoffman, L. (1967). *Techniques of family therapy*. New York: Basic Books.

Herman, J. (1981). Father and daughter incest. Cambridge, MA: Harvard University Press.

Herman, J. (1983). Recognition and treatment of incestuous families. *Int. J. Fam. Ther., 5*(2), 81–91.

Hetherington, E. M. (1979). Divorce: A child's perspective. *American Psychologist, 34*, 851–858.

Humphrey, F. G. (1983). *Marital therapy*. Englewood Cliffs, NJ: Prentice-Hall.

Jackson, D. D. (Ed.) (1960). *The etiology of schizophrenia*. New York: Basic Books.

Jacobsen, N. S., & Margolin, G. (1979). *Marital therapy: Strategies based on social learning and behavior exchange principles*. New York: Brunner/Mazel.

Kubie, L. (1956). Psychoanalysis and marriage: Practical and theoretical issues. In V. Eisenstein (Ed.), *Neurotic interaction in marriage*. New York: Basic Books.

Laing, R. D. (1967). *The politics of experience*. New York: Ballantine Books.

Langsley, D. G., Kaplan, D. M., Pittman, F. S., Machotka, P., Flomenhaft, K., DeYoung, C. D. (1968). *The treatment of families in crisis*. New York: Grune & Stratton.

Langsley, D. G., Pittman, F. S., Machotka, P., & Flomenhaft, K. (1968). Crisis family therapy: Results and implications. *Family Process, 7*(2), 145–168.

Langsley, D. G., Schwartz, M. N., & Fairbairn, R. H. (1968). Father-son incest. *Comp. Psych., 9*, 218–226.

Langsley, D. G., Pittman, F. S., & Swank, G. (1969). Family crises in schizophrenics and other mental patients. *J. Nerv. Ment. Dis., 149*(3), 270–276.

Leff, J. P. (1976). Schizophrenia and sensitivity to the family environment. *Schizophrenia Bulletin, 2*, 566–574.

Levi-Strauss, C.(1969). *The elementary structures of kinship*. Boston: Beacon.

Lidz, T., Fleck, S., & Cornelison, A. R. (1965). *Schizophrenia and the family*. New York: International Universities Press.

Liebman, R., Minuchin, S., Baker, L., & Rosman, B. L. (1976) The role of the family in the treatment of chronic asthma. In P. Guerin (Ed.), *Family Therapy* (pp. 309–324). New York: Gardner Press.

Loranger, A. W. (1984). Sex differences in age at onset of schizophrenia. *Arch. Gen. Psychiatry, 41*(2), 157–161.

MacGregor, R., Ritchie, A., Serrano, A., Schuster, F., McDonald, E., & Goolishian, H. (1964). *Multiple impact therapy with Families*. New York: McGraw-Hill.

Machotka, P., Pittman, F. S., & Flomenhaft, K. (1967). Incest as a family affair. *Family Process, 6*(1), 98–116.

Masson, J. (1984). *The Assault on Truth: Freud's Suppression of the Seduction Theory*. New York: Farrar, Straus, and Giroux.

Maxmen, J. S. (1986). *Essential psychopathology*. New York: Norton.

Meltzer, H. Y. (1979). Biochemical studies in schizophrenia. In L. Bellak (Ed.), *Disorders of the schizophrenic syndrome*. New York: Basic Books.

Minuchin, S. (1974). *Families and family therapy*. Cambridge, MA: Harvard University Press.

Minuchin, S. (1977). A conceptual model of psychosomatic illness in children: Family organization and family therapy. In E. D. Wittkower & H. Warnes (Eds.), *Psychosomatic medicine* (pp. 116–128). Hagerstown, MD: Harper and Row.

Minuchin, S., Rosman, B. L., & Baker, L. (1978). *Psychosomatic families: Anorexia nervosa in context*. Cambridge, MA: Harvard University Press.

Mishler, E. G., & Waxler, N. E. (1968). *Interaction in Families*. New York: John Wiley.

O'Neill, N., & O'Neill, G. (1972). *Open marriage*. New York: Avon.

Paolino, T. J., & McCrady, B. S. (1977). *The alcoholic marriage*. New York: Grune & Stratton.

Papp, P. (1983). *The process of change*. New York: Guilford.

Pattison, M. (1979). The selection of treatment modalities for the alcoholic patient. In J.

Mendelson & N. Mello (Eds.), *The diagnosis and treatment of alcoholism*. New York: McGraw-Hill.

Paul, N. H., & Paul, B. B. (1975). *A marital puzzle*. New York: Norton.

Pittman, F. S., Flomenhaft, K., DeYoung, C. D., Kaplan, D. M., & Langsley, D. G. (1966). Crisis family therapy. In J. Masserman (Ed.), *Current psychiatric therapies, Vol. VI* (pp. 187–196). New York: Grune & Stratton.

Pittman, F. S., Langsley, D. G., & DeYoung, C. D. (1968). Work and school phobias: A family approach to treatment. *Amer. J. Psychiatry, 124*(11), 93–99.

Pittman, F. S., & Flomenhaft, K. (1970). Treating the Doll's House marriage. *Family Process, 9*(2), 143–155.

Pittman, F. S., Langsley, D. G.., Flomenhaft, K., DeYoung, C. D., Machotka, P., & Kaplan, D. M. (1971). Therapy techniques of the family treatment unit. In J. Haley (Ed.), *Changing families: A family therapy reader* (pp. 259–271). New York: Grune & Stratton.

Pittman, F. S. (1973). Managing acute psychiatric emergencies: Defining the family crisis. In D. Bloch (Ed.), *Techniques of family psychotherapy. Seminars in Psychiatry, 5*(2), 219–227. New York: Grune & Stratton.

Pittman, F. S. (1976). Counseling incestuous families. *Medical Aspects of Human Sexuality*, April, 57–58.

Pittman, F. S. (1977). Incest. In J. Masserman (Ed.), *Current psychiatric therapies, Vol. XVII* (pp. 129–134). New York: Grune & Stratton.

Pittman, F. S. (1984). Wet cocker spaniel therapy: An essay on technique in family therapy. *Family Process, 23*(1), 1–9.

Pittman, F. S. (1985). Evaluating the family in crisis. In S. Henao & N. Grose (Eds.), *Principles of family systems in family medicine* (pp. 347–371). New York: Brunner/Mazel.

Pittman, J. B. (1985). Father-daughter incest and power hierarchies within the family. Unpublished manuscript.

Powers, W. (1981). Marital stress during the transition to retirement. In A. Gurman (Ed.), *Questions and answers in the practice of family therapy*. New York: Brunner/Mazel.

Root, M., Fallon, P., & Friedrich, W. (1986). *Bulimia: A systems approach to treatment*. New York: Norton.

Sager, C. J. (1976). *Marriage contracts and couple therapy*. New York: Brunner/Mazel.

Sager, C. J., Brown, H. S., Crohn, H., Engel, T., Rodstein, E., & Walker, L. (1983). *Treating the remarried family*. New York: Brunner/Mazel.

Sampson, H., Messenger, S. L., & Towne, R. D. (1964). *Schizophrenic women: Studies in marital crisis*. New York: Atherton.

Schildkraut, J. J. (1970). *Neuropsychopharmacology and the affective disorders*. Boston: Little, Brown.

Schou, M. (1968). Lithium in psychiatric therapy and prophylaxis. *J. Psychiatric Res., 6*, 67–95.

Selvini Palazzoli, M. (1978). *Self starvation*. New York: Aronson.

Selvini Palazzoli, M., Boscolo, L., Cecchin, G., & Prata, G. (1978). *Paradox and counterparadox*. New York: Aronson.

Serrano, A. C., & Gunzburger, D. W. (1983). An historical perspective of incest. *Int. J. Fam. Ther., 5*(2), 70–80.

Sheehy, G. (1976). *Passages: Predictable crises of adult life*. New York: Dutton.

Singer, M. T., & Wynne, L. C. (1965). Thought disorder and family relations of schizophrenics: III. *Arch. Gen. Psychiatry, 12*, 187–200.

Snell, J., Rosenwald, R., & Robey, A. (1964). The wifebeater's wife. *Arch. Gen. Psych., 11*, 107–113.

Stanton, M. D., & Todd, C. T., (1982). *The family therapy of drug abuse and addiction*. New York: Guilford.

Steinglass, P. (1976). Experimenting with family treatment approaches to alcoholism, 1950–1975: A review. *Family Process, 15*(1), 97–124.

Steinglass, P., Bennett, L., Wolin, S. J., & Reiss, D. (1987). *The alcoholic family*. New York: Basic Books.

Stierlin, H. (1973). A family perspective on adolescent runaways. *Arch. Gen. Psych., 29* (July), 46–62.

Stierlin, H., Weber, G., Schmidt, G., & Simon, F. (1986). Some features of families with major affective disorders. *Family Process, 25*(3), 325–336.

Storr, A. (1968). *Human Aggression*. New York: Atheneum.

Strauss, M. A. (1978). Wife beating: How common and why? *Victimology, 2*, 443–458.

Strauss, M. A. (1980). A sociological perspective on the causes of family violence. In Green, M. A. (Ed.), *Violence in the family*. Boulder, CO: Westview.

Stuart, R. B.(1980). *Helping couples change*. New York: Guilford.

Stump, J. B. (1985). *What's the difference?* New York: Morrow.

Szasz, T. (1961). *The myth of mental illness*. New York: Harper and Row.

Targum, S. D., Sullivan, A. C., & Byrnes, S. M. (1982). Neuroendocrine interrelationships in major depressive episodes. *Am. J. Psychiatry, 139*(3), 282–286.

Visher, E., & Visher, J. (1979). *Stepfamilies: A guide to working with stepparents and stepchildren*. New York: Brunner/Mazel.

Wallerstein, J. S., & Kelly, J. B. (1980). *Surviving the breakup: How children and parents cope with divorce*. New York: Basic Books.

Watzlawick, P., Weakland, J., & Fisch, R. (1974). *Change: Principles of problem formation and problem resolution*. New York: Norton.

Weiss, G., & Hechtman, L. T. (1986). *Hyperactive children grown up*. New York: Guilford.

West, L. J. (1980). Discussion: Violence and the family in perspective. In M. R. Green (Ed.), *Violence and the family*. Washington: American Association for the Advancement of Science.

Woititz, J. G. (1983). *Adult children of alcoholics*. Pompano Beach, FL: Health Communications.

Wynne, L. C. (1980). Current concepts about schizophrenics and family relationships. *J. Nerv. Men. Dis., 169*(2), 82–89.

Zuelzer, M. B., & Reposa, R. E. (1983). Mothers in incestuous families, *Int. J. Fam. Ther., 5*(2), 98–111.

INDEX

abortion, 155, 156
Ackley, Dana, 283
Adams, Lee, 175
adolescents, 175–204
  alcoholism in, 263–64
  diagnosis of, 180–81
  evaluating crises of, 195–99
  imperfect, 190–92
  marked for failure, 188–89
  parents and, 175–78
  rebellious, 180, 185–88
  rescuing, 192–95
  sociopathic, 183–85
  syndromes of, 180–95
  treating crises of, 199–204
  underground, 178–80, 181–82, 280
adultery, *see* infidelity
aging, 216–29
  as deterioration process, 217–18, 221
  marriage and, 62–64, 219–21
  retirement and, 218–19
  sexuality and, 217
aging crises, 217–29
  bolts from the blue and, 224–25
  caretaker, 221–23
  developmental, 217–21
  structural, 223–24
  treatment of, 225–29

agoraphobia, 238–39, 242–43
Ahrons, C. R., 136
Al-Anon, 270
alcohol:
  adolescents' use of, 178
  marital violence and, 287, 289
  per capita consumption of, 262–63
alcoholic families, 234, 268–78
  case studies of, 276–78
  treatment of, 272–78
Alcoholics Anonymous, 270
alcoholism, 261–78
  in adolescence, 263–64
  co-alcoholism and, 268–70
  compulsive, 265, 266–67
  developmental crises of, 263–64
  diagnosis of, 262
  families affected by, 268–70
  habit, 265–66
  male vs. female, 262
  marriage and, 269
  patterns of, 263–68
  situational crises of, 264–65
  structural crises of, 265–68
  treatment of, 270–78
Alexander, P. G., 309
Alzheimer's disease, 21
American Psychiatric Association, 332

Anderson, C. M., 28–29, 44, 347
Andolfi, Maurizio, 41, 46
anorexia, 180, 254, 255–56
Antabuse, 271, 274
antidepressants, 32, 120, 325, 338–39
Asimov, Isaac, 216
Auden, W. H., 49
Auerswald, Dick, 40

Bacon, Francis, 237
Baker, L., 249–50, 255–56
Barr, Donald, 175
Bassis, M. S., 283
Bateson, G., 345
Beal, E. W., 135
Beavers, W. R., 8, 295
Beels, C. C., 347
Bepko, C., 269, 271
Berne, Eric, 269
Bernheim, K. L., 74, 347
bipolar (manic) depression, 16, 32, 323–24,
    325
Birley, J. L., 346–47
birth defects, 158–59
blended families, 144–52
    authority over children in, 147–48
    case study of, 150–52
    children moving in and out of, 147
    financial issues in, 146–47, 148
    grandparental relationships in, 150
    intrusions from previous spouses in, 145–
        46
    parents' jealousy of children's allegiances
        in, 149
    sexual boundaries in, 149–50
    threats to continuation of marriage in,
        146, 148–49
    wranglings over finances in, 146–47
bolts from the blue, 7–9, 30, 33, 34, 36
    marital crises and, 66–68, 88
    old age crises and, 224–25
Boszormenyi-Nagy, Ivan, 224
Bowen, M., 248–49, 344–45
brain chemistry disorders, 317–21
    case study of, 319–20
Brawner, James N., Jr., 276
Brown, G. W., 346–47
Brownmiller, Susan, 305
Bruch, H., 255
bulimia, 180, 254–57
    case study of, 256–57
Burns, S. R., 308
Bye Bye Birdie (Adams), 175
Byrnes, S. M., 331

California Suite, 217
caretaker crises, 16–18, 28, 30, 34, 36

    in childhood, 163
    in marriage, 72–76, 88–89
    in old age, 221–23
caretaker families, 317–55
    brain chemistry disorders and, 317–21
    depression and, 330–41
    mania and, 322–29
    schizophrenia and, 342–55
Carter, E. A., 55
Carter, Hodding, 155
Chesler, Phyllis, 307
Chesterson, G. K., 27
Chevalier, Maurice, 216
child abuse, 158, 284–86
    marital violence linked to, 287, 288
childbirth, *see* parenting
childhood crises, 161–74
    caretaker, 163
    case studies of, 171–74
    inherent developmental crisis points and,
        164
    disabilities and, 163–64
    parental anxiety and, 162–63
    phobias, 164–65
    syndromes of, 166–67
    treatment of, 167–74
child pornography, 303–4
children:
    of alcoholics, 268
    anxious, 166
    in blended families, 144–45, 147–50
    death of, 224–25
    depression in, 165
    disabled, 163–64
    as family barometers, 161
    hyperactive in, 163
    leaving home by, 206–7
    neglected, 167
    parental or rescuing, 167
    rebellious, 167
    sneaky, 166–67
    unpopular, 163
    unsocialized, 166
    see also adolescents
Chinatown, 302
claustrophobia, 238
co-alcoholism, 268–70
cocaine, 180
Cohen, M. B., 323
Cohen, S. N., 135–36
communication, snag points about, 20–21
"communication deviance," 345, 347
Contributions to Analytical Psychology
    (Jung), 65
Cornelison, A. R., 345
Cosmopolitan, 102
counter-adultery, 100

courtship, *see* dating and courtship
cozy nest syndrome, 208–9
Cracker Factory, The (Rebeta-Burditt), 261
Crack Up, The (Fitzgerald), 330
crises, 3–4
   see also family crises; *specific crises and disorders*
"crises of generativity," 61
"crises of integrity," 63
crisis prone families, 233–36
   defenses of, 235
   structural defects in, 234
   superstition in, 234, 235
crisis proneness, 22, 23
   in marriage, 49–55
crowded nest syndrome, 209–11

dating and courtship:
   falling in love and, 55
   prenuptial panic in, 55–56
   violence in, 291
Dear Me (Ustinov), 155
death:
   of child, 224–25
   of spouse, 220
Death of a Salesman (Miller), 335
depression, 330–41
   agitated, 324
   bipolar, 16, 32, 323–24, 325
   case study of, 340–41
   in children, 165
   family systems theory of, 334
   maternal, 165
   post-abortion, 156
   postpartum, 157–58
   subdivisions of, 332
   suicide and, 335–36
   theories of, 330–31
   treatment of, 337–41
Desire Under the Elms (O'Neill), 149
development crises, 9–13, 30, 33, 34, 36, 155–229
   in adolescence, 9, 10, 175–204
   of alcoholism, 263–64
   case studies of, 11–13, 70–72
   diagnosis of, 88
   of drug abuse, 279
   empty nest syndrome as, 205–15
   of marriage, 69–72, 88
   in old age, 216–29
   parenting and, 155–74
DeYoung, Carol, 39–40, 243
disabilities, in children, 163–64
divorce, 129–42
   boundaries breached in, 136–37
   children affected by, 129–30, 134–35
   data on, 135–36

   empty nest syndrome and, 212
   extended family lost in, 134
   goals and values reexamined in, 137
   infidelity and, 130
   joint custody and, 136
   men's experiences in, 132–33
   in monogamous marriages, 131
   past conflicts revived in, 137–38
   reconciliation fantasies in, 132
   in second or subsequent marriages, 131
   tension in, 138
   treating crises of, 138–42
   as unpleasant experience, 129–36
   usual patterns disrupted in, 137
   women and, 133–35
"Doll's House Marriage, The" (Pittman & Flomenhaft), 115
dopamine, 344
double bind hypothesis, 345
drug abuse, 278–82
   by adolescents, 178, 179–80, 280
   developmental crises of, 279
   family situation and, 280–82
   situational crises of, 279
   withdrawal symptoms and, 279–80
DSM-III, 332

eating disorders, 253–57
Eichenbaum, L., 242
Elbow, Margaret, 292
Eliot, T. S., 342
emergency response, 28
empty nest syndrome, 10, 60, 205–15
   leaving home crises in, 208–15
   men's experience of, 206
   parent-child relationships and, 207
   treatment of, 213–15
   women's experience of, 205–6
ergasiophobia, 239, 243–44
Erickson, Milton, 41, 241
Erikson, Erik, 61, 63
Everstine, D. S., 288
Everstine, L., 288
"expressed emotion" (EE), 346–47
extended families, 53

"facts of life" stage, 60–61, 62
Fairbairn, R. H., 304–5
Fallon, P., 254
Falloon, I. R. H., 347–48
families:
   alcoholic, 234, 268–78
   blended, 144–52
   caretaker, 317–55
   crisis prone, 233–36
   of drug abusers, 280–82
   incest in, 149–50, 180, 302–14

families (*continued*)
  nuclear, 53–55
  phobic, 237–45
  psychosomatic, 234, 246–60
  schizophrenic, 344–47
  violent, 234, 283–301
family crises:
  bolts from the blue as, 7–9
  caretaker, 16–18
  categories of, 7–18
  defining of, 30–31
  developmental, 9–13
  inflexibilities in, 25–26
  loosening of boundaries in, 19, 20–22, 28
  snag points in, 18–26
  stress and, 4–6
  structural, 13–16
  tensions and, 4, 5, 19, 21–22
  theory of, 3–26
  unresolved conflict in, 23–24
  see also specific crises and disorders
family crisis therapy, 27–38
  crucial points in, 45–46
  defining crisis in, 30–31
  emergency response in, 28
  family focus in, 28–29
  general prescription in, 31–32
  illustration of, 37–38
  negotiating resistance in, 34–36
  nudges at snag points in, 42–44
  paradoxes in, 44
  specific prescriptions in, 33–34
  termination of, 36–37
  wet cocker spaniel techniques in, 39–46
  see also specific crises and disorders
family history, snag points about, 23–24
Family Life Cycle, The (Carter & McGoldrick), 55
fatal flight syndrome, 211–12
FDA (Food & Drug Administration), 261, 323
Fear of Flying (Jong), 108
Feldman, L., 334
Fieve, R. R., 323, 328
fight or flight response, 250, 251
financial issues, in blended families, 146–47, 148
Finkelhor, D., 303
Fisch, R., 31, 241
Fitzgerald, F. Scott, 330
Fleck, S., 345
Flomenhaft, K., 115, 309, 349
Fowler, C., 308
Framo, J. L., 54, 86, 97–98
Franklin, Benjamin, 217
Freeman, M. D. A., 288
Freud, Anna, 136

Freud, Sigmund, 30, 194, 239, 246, 302, 330, 332
Friday the 13th, 238
Friedrich, W., 254
friendships, marriage and, 57–58
Fromm-Reichmann, Frieda, 344
fundamentalist religion, 83, 288

Games People Play (Berne), 269
Gandhi, Mohandas K., 287
Gelles, R. J., 283
gender roles:
  and crisis proneness in marriage, 51–52
  incest and, 307–9
  marital violence and, 287
Genealogy of Morals (Nietzsche), 317
goals:
  reexamined in divorce crises, 137
  snag points in, 24–25
Goldstein, J., 136
Goldstein, M. J., 180, 347–48
"goodbye girls and guys," 56
grandparenting:
  aging and, 219
  blended families and, 150
Grolnick, L., 249
guilt, 35, 36
Gunzburger, D. W., 302, 304

Haley, Jay, 41, 210, 212, 241, 345
hallucinogens, 180, 278, 280
Hamlet (Shakespeare), 129, 132, 237
Hechtman, L. T., 325
Herman, Judith, 307, 308
Hetherington, E. M., 135
Hetrick, Emery, 40
Hogarty, G. E., 347
Holden, William, 216
Holmes, Oliver Wendell, Jr., 246
"homoclites," 79
"Human Aggression" (Storr), 283
Humphrey, F. G., 97
"Husbands' Reactions to Wives' Infidelity" (Framo), 97–98
hyperactivity, 163
hyperventilation, 250–51
hypomania, 324

incest, 180, 302–14
  in blended families, 149–50
  brother-sister, 303, 304
  crises of, 309–14
  family structure and, 309
  father-daughter, 303, 305–9
  mother-son, 303, 304
  patterns of, 304–5
  societal attitudes toward, 303–4

taboo on, 302–3
treatment of, 310–14
infants:
    abuse of, 158
    imperfect, 158–59
    see also childhood crises; children
        infidelity, 97–128
    cultural expectation of, 102
    data on, 98
    divorce and, 130
    empty nest syndrome and, 206
    habitual, 98, 109–13
    homosexual affairs and, 103
    "in love" affairs and, 116–20
    reasons for, 98–105
    revenge affairs and, 100–101
    structural, 113–16
    treating crises of, 120–28
    unique, 105–09
intimacy, snag points about, 21–22
isolation, and crisis proneness in marriage,
    53–55

Jackson, Don, 249, 342, 343
Jacobson, N. S., 78
Jones, F. N., 135–36
Jung, Carl G., 65
juvenile prostitution, 303–4

Kelly, J. B., 135
King, Martin Luther, 287
Krestan, J., 269, 271
Kubie, L., 53

Laing, R. D., 345
Langsley, D. G., 243, 304–5, 318, 346
learning disabled children, 163–64
Leaving Home (Haley), 210
leaving home crises, 206–15
    cozy nest syndrome in, 208–9
    crowded nest syndrome in, 209–11
    fatal flight syndrome in, 211–12
    treatment of, 213–15
Lehman, A. F., 74, 347
Levine, A., 283
Lévi-Strauss, Claude, 303
Lidz, T., 345
Liebman, R., 249
Lie Down in Darkness (Styron), 129
lithium carbonate, 323, 324–25, 326
"Lolita syndrome," 149
Loranger, A. W., 349
love:
    dating and, 55
    infidelity and, 116–20
Lowry, Malcolm, 261
Lutz, John, 80

McCrady, B. S., 269
McFarline, W. R., 347
McGoldrick, M., 55
Machotka, P., 309
Madanes, Cloé, 41
"male menopause," 61, 206
Man and Superman (Shaw), 61
mania, 322–29
    diagnosis of, 324
    lithium therapy for, 323, 324–25, 326
    treatment of, 327–29
manic (bipolar) depression, 16, 32, 323–24,
    325
Margolin, G., 78
marijuana, 179–80, 280
marital crises, 65–94
    bolts from the blue and, 66–68
    caretaker, 72–76, 88–89
    developmental, 69–72, 88
    structural, 77–82, 88–89
    treatment of, 83–94
marital violence, 286–301
    beginning of, 291
    case studies of, 293–94, 299–301
    changes attempted in, 291–92
    cultural norms and, 288
    distancing by partner in, 292–93
    escalating conflicts and, 288–89
    leaving spouse and, 292–93
    of men vs. women, 286–87
    outside involvement in, 292
    treatment of, 295–301
    unilateral, 288–89
    victim role assumed by wife in, 289–90,
        292
marriage, 49–94
    aging and, 62–64, 219–21
    crisis proneness in, 49–55
    death of spouse and, 220
    developmental crisis points of, 10, 55–64
    "disengaged," 77–78
    divorce and, 129–42
    drug abuse and, 281–82
    end of romance in, 56
    "enmeshed," 77–78
    equality in, 52, 54
    falling in love and, 55
    families of origin and, 57
    friendships and, 57–58
    infidelity in, 97–128
    midlife crises and, 60–61
    nature and transitions of, 49–64
    "one down" and "one up" positions in, 78
    open, 101
    parenting and, 57, 58, 160–61
    prenuptial panic and, 55–56
    second or subsequent, 142–52

marriage (*continued*)
  sex and, 58–60
Masson, J., 302
Maxmen, J. S., 325, 332, 344
Meltzer, H. Y., 344
menopause, 61
  "male," 61, 206
Messenger, S. L., 349
metanxiety, 241
midlife crises, 60–61
Minuchin, S., 42–43, 77, 249–50, 255–56
Mishler, E. G., 345
Mr. Mom, 160
Moodswing (Fieve), 328
Mourning and Melancholia (Freud), 330
Murder in the Cathedral (Eliot), 342
Murdock, David, 342

Nabokov, Vladimir, 149, 303
New York Times, 216
Nicholson, Harold, 65
Nietzsche, Friedrich, 317
nuclear families, 53–55

obesity, 254
old age crises, 217–25
  bolts from the blue in, 224–25
  caretaker, 221–23
  case studies of, 226–29
  developmental, 217–21
  structural, 223–24
  treatment of, 225–29
Oliver, 290
O'Neill, Eugene, 149
O'Neill, G., 101
O'Neill, N., 101
open marriage, 101
Orbach, S., 242
"outdoor therapists," 40

Paolino, T. J., 269
Papp, Peggy, 240–41
parenting, 155–74
  of adolescents, 175–78
  childrearing and, 161–67
  imperfect babies in, 158–59
  infant abuse in, 158
  marriage and, 57, 58, 160–61
  postpartum depression in, 157–58
  pregnancy as crisis in, 155–56
  and syndromes of childhood crises, 166–67
parents, single, 160–61
Passages (Sheehy), 55
Pattison, Mansell, 263
Paul, B. B., 332
Paul, N. H., 332
"Pepe le Peu syndrome," 77

phobias, 238–40
  agoraphobia, 238–39, 242–43
  in children, 164–65
  fear of, 239, 241
  symbolism of, 240–41
  symptom substitution in, 240
  work, 239, 243–44
phobic families, 237–45
  treatment of, 240–45
phobophobia, 239, 241
Pittman, F. S., 39, 115, 243, 246–48, 309, 311, 318, 346, 349
Pittman, J. B., 307
Playboy, 102
pornography, child, 303–4
postpartum depression, 157–58
Powers, William, 219
pregnancy, as crisis, 155–56
prenuptial panic, 55–56
Private Function, The, 221
Procrusteus, 19
Promise of Power, The (Stokes), 3
prostitution, juvenile, 303–4
"pseudomutuality," 345
psychosomatic families, 234, 246–60
  case studies of, 246–48, 252–53
  characteristics of, 248–49
  eating disorders in, 253–57
  enmeshed, 249
  hyperventilation syndrome in, 250–51
  overprotective, 249
  primary disorders in, 249
  rigidity of, 249
  secondary disorders in, 249–50
  symptoms in, 250–53
  treatment of, 257–60
  undifferentiated ego mass of, 248
psychotropic medication, 318

Rabkin, Richard, 40
"reaching of summit," 61
Rebeta-Burditt, Joyce, 261
Reiss, D. J., 347
remarriage, 142–52
  children and, 144–45, 147–50
  divorce and, 130, 131
  first marriages vs., 143
  in old age, 220–21
  wedding ceremonies in, 143–44
  see also blended families
Reposa, R. E., 307
Responsibility Trap, The (Bebko & Krestan), 269
retirement, 218–19
Robey, A., 290
Roehl, J. E., 308
roles, 19

gender, 51–52, 287, 307–9
  snag points about, 22–23
romance:
  and crisis proneness in marriage, 52–53
  end of, in marriage, 56
Roosevelt, Eleanor, 330
Root, M., 254
Rose Kennedy syndrome, 126
Rosenwald, R., 290
Rosman, B. L., 249–50, 255–56
rules, 19, 34
  snag points about, 23

Sager, C. J., 77, 144, 149
"St. Joseph syndrome," 80
Sampson, H., 349
Satir, Virginia, 296–97
Schildkraut, J. J., 323
schizophrenia, 16, 32, 180, 342–55
  "communication deviance" and, 345
  crises of, 348–50
  in dizygotic twins, 342
  double bind hypothesis of, 345
  "expressed emotion" in, 346–47
  as genetic defect, 343–44
  marijuana and, 180, 348
  in monozygotic twins, 342
  paranoid, 324
  phenothiazine therapy for, 344
  "pseudomutuality" in, 345
  treatment of, 347–55
schizophrenic families, 344–47
  communication in, 345
  mothers in, 344
  as schismatic, 345
  as symbiotic, 344–45
"schizophrenogenic mothers," 344
school phobia, 164–65, 167, 180
Schou, M., 323
Schwartz, M. N., 304–5
second marriages, *see* blended families;
    remarriage
Segal, L., 31
Self Starvation (Selvini Palazzoli), 255
Selvini Palazzoli, Mara, 41, 255
Serrano, A. C., 302, 304
sex:
  in adolescence, 178
  boundaries of, in blended families, 149–50
  marriage and, 58–60
  in old age, 217
  see also incest
Shakespeare, William, 129, 237
Shaw, George Bernard, 61
Sheehy, Gail, 55
Simon, Neil, 217
Singer, M. T., 345

single parents, 160–61
Smith, Maggie, 217
snag points, 18–26
  about communication, 20–21
  about family history, 23–24
  in goals, 24–25
  about intimacy, 21–22
  nudges at, in family crisis therapy, 42–44
  about roles, 22–23
  about rules, 23
  in values, 25–26
Snell, J., 290
sociopathic adolescents, 183–85
Solnit, A. J., 136
Spark, Geraldine, 224
Stanton, M. D., 280–81
Steinglass, P., 269, 271–72
stepfamilies, *see* blended families
Stewart, S., 28–29, 44
Stierlin, H., 180–81, 323
Stokes, Carl B., 3
Storr, Anthony, 283
Strauss, M. A., 286, 287
stress, 4–6
structural crises, 13–16, 30, 34
  of marriage, 77–82, 88–89
Stuart, R. B., 78
Stump, J. B., 286
Styron, William, 129
substance abuse, *see* alcoholism; drug abuse
Successful Marriage (Beavers), 8
success neurosis, 244
Sudden Infant Death Syndrome (SIDS), 159
suicide:
  depression and, 335–36
  divorce crises and, 138
Sullivan, A. C., 331
Sunset Boulevard, 216
Swank, G., 346
Swanson, Gloria, 216
Szasz, T., 345

Targum, S. D., 331
tension, in divorce crises, 138
therapists:
  allies of, 35
  cockiness of, 32
  conditions of, 29
  neutrality of, 92–93
  one-down position of, 31, 32
  patriarchal male, 83
  reality bases of, 27
  reductio ad absurdum technique of, 31
  respect shown by, 90–91
  symptoms bypassed by, 42
  therapeutic desperation and, 29
  see also family crisis therapy; *specific*

therapists (*continued*)
    crises and disorders
Thurber, J., 83
Time, 40
Todd, C. T., 280–81
Tolstoy, Leo, 30
Towne, R. D., 349
Towne, Robert, 302
tranquilizers, addiction to, 279
treatment, *see* family crisis therapy; *specific crises and disorders*

Under the Volcano (Lowry), 261
Ustinov, Peter, 155

Valium, addiction to, 279
values:
    reexamined in divorce crises, 137
    snag points in, 25–26
violent families, 234, 283–301
    child abuse in, 284–86
    statistics on, 283, 286–87
    structural crises and, 14
    see also marital violence

Visher, Emily, 145
Visher, John, 145

Wallerstein, J. S., 135
Wallisch, L. S., 136
Wall Street Journal, 108
Watzlawick, P., 241
Waxler, N. E., 345
Weakland, J., 31, 46, 241, 345
wedding ceremonies, in second or subsequent marriages, 143–44
Weiss, G., 325
West, L. J., 284
wet cocker spaniel therapy, 39–46
Whitaker, Carl, 41
Who Pushed Humpty Dumpty (Barr), 175
wife beating, *see* marital violence
Wink, J. K., 346–47
Woititz, J. G., 268
work phobia, 239, 243–44
Wynne, L. C., 345, 347

Zuelzer, M. B., 307